PSYCHOLOGY
A SOCIAL APPROACH

SECOND EDITION

PSYCHOLOGY
A SOCIAL APPROACH

DAVID F. WRENCH
CHRIS WRENCH

McGRAW-HILL BOOK COMPANY
New York   St. Louis   San Francisco   Düsseldorf   Johannesburg
Kuala Lumpur   London   Mexico   Montreal   New Delhi
Panama   Rio de Janeiro   Singapore   Sydney   Toronto

PSYCHOLOGY: A SOCIAL APPROACH

1234567890 KPKP 79876543

This book was set in Palatino by Textbook Services, Inc. The editors were Walter Maytham and John M. Morriss; the designer was J. E. O'Connor; and the production supervisor was John A. Sabella. Cover photograph by Cornell Capa/©Magnum Photos, Inc.
The printer and binder was Kingsport Press, Inc.

Library of Congress Cataloging in Publication Data

Wrench, David F
    Psychology: a social approach.

    Includes bibliographical references.
      1. Psychology. 2. Social psychology. I. Title.
[DNLM: 1. Psychology. 2. Psychology, Social.
BF 121 W945p 1973]
BF121.W7 1973   150   72-7336
ISBN 0-07-071917-9

CONTENTS

PREFACE

This book is very much a student's textbook. The authors have assumed that the reader has no familiarity with statistics and thus have avoided complex methodological discussions. The use of technical vocabulary has been kept to a minimum, and the technical terms which have been employed are defined in a glossary for the convenience of the reader. The book is intended to be used either as the sole textbook for a one-semester course in introductory psychology or in conjunction with other materials in a longer course. There are now many excellent supplementary materials available for use in introductory psychology courses, including a reader designed to accompany this text (*Readings in Psychology: Foundations and Applications*). It is the authors' belief that these materials have made the single, large introductory psychology textbook outdated. The present book is intended to provide a theoretical framework for the integration of supplementary materials when used in a longer course.

When the first edition of this book was published, it was the only introductory psychology textbook placing its main emphasis on man as he functions in his environment. Now there are several introductory texts with this emphasis. The way the field is developing necessitates such a change, and the first edition of this book attempted to organize and conceptualize the environmental approach. Since it was published, the field of psychology has accumulated new evidence important to this approach. The second edition incorporates some of this body of evidence and new understandings relevant to this growth.

When the scientific method first developed, the problems with which it could deal were quite limited. For a phenomenon to be investigated scientifically, it needed to be influenced by relatively few variables, and these variables had to be ones which could easily be controlled in simple experimental situations. Early science thus succeeded largely by isolating phenomena from their environments in order to achieve control of the relevant conditions. Its greatest achievements came in areas, such as Newtonian mechanics, where a broad range of events could be deduced from a few simple principles.

As more complex phenomena were analyzed, however, ideas about the nature of scientific theories changed also. Many phenomena are destroyed by removing them from their environments, and many cannot be accounted for in terms of simple theories. Complex phenomena are often better understood by studying them directly than by trying to deduce them from observations on simpler phenomena. Newtonian mechanics, for example, are not so much wrong as irrelevant to the understanding of most of the problems of modern physics.

Traditional psychological theories about man, such as Hull's learning theory, which for years served as the main theoretical framework for the field of psychology, have begun to stand in relation to contemporary psychology as Newtonian mechanics stood in relation to physics on the eve of the age of indeterminacy. They are not adequate to serve as a framework for the developing field, and are irrelevant to many areas of compelling attention. Such phenomena as Harlow's research on contact comfort, the work of the European ethologists, and Milgram's research on obedience simply cannot be dealt with within the old framework.

What is happening to the field of psychology may be understood from the perspective provided by Thomas Kuhn's *The Structure of Scientific Revolutions*.[1] Kuhn distinguishes between periods of chaos in a scientific discipline and quite distinct periods of more orderly investigation when there is a widely shared framework of explanation. In the more orderly periods, research is guided by generally accepted theory which suggests what problems are important to the field and predicts the results of experimental investigations of those areas. The research largely consists, in other words, of demonstrating that the theory's answers are indeed the correct ones. As the research inspired by a particular theoretical orientation accumulates, however, some of the results are not the ones the theory would have suggested. Eventually, large accumulations of research findings incompatible with the old orientation build up, causing people to perceive the inadequacy of the old theoretical framework. As some theorists go on defending the old framework, and others start proposing new (although often less inclusive) theoretical formulations, a period of confusion, conflict, and revolutionary change is ushered in. In the physical sciences, such periods of confusion have formed part of the Copernican, Newtonian, and Einsteinian revolutions. The field of psychology is at the present time undergoing such a scientific revolution. The present edition of this text is intended, as was the first, to be a small contribution to that revolution.

One final note: If psychology is to survive as a profession and as a field of study despite the very real apprehensions of many thoughtful people today regarding possible misuse of its techniques and power, then a growing orientation toward caring about peoples' actual individuality and needs may be timely. This orientation can indeed be discerned within its constantly exploding body of knowledge. This book is dedicated to the effort to communicate that new orientation.

David F. Wrench
Chris Wrench

Notes and Acknowledgments

1. Kuhn, Thomas S. *The Structure of Scientific Revolutions*. Chicago: The University of Chicago Press. Second edition, enlarged, volume II, number 2, of *International Encyclopedia of Unified Science*, 1970.

PSYCHOLOGY
A SOCIAL APPROACH

PART ONE

BASIC PROCESSES

ONE
INTRODUCTION

The Field of Psychology

Psychology is one of the fields concerned with understanding human experience and behavior. As such, it shares some interests, methods, and theories with each of the other fields concerned with the study of man. For example, it shares with biology an interest in man as an organism adapting to an environment; with anthropology, an interest in the ways that, and the extent to which, the individual may be influenced by his culture; and with sociology and anthropology, an interest in social structure.

Each field studying human beings, however, has concentrated its efforts on certain problems and methods which are central to that particular view of man. The nature of social disorganization is a major topic from a sociological perspective, whereas it is given only minor attention by the economist. The study of documents may be an important approach for the historian or political scientist, but would be of little use to an anthropologist who is concerned primarily with prehistory. Psychology similarly has limited itself to studying man from a particular point of view and through the use of certain methods. Some of the choices which psychologists have usually made in the past are as follows:

1. Psychology has concentrated on the study of human beings. While animals are often studied, this research is more often to obtain results which might be applicable to human beings than to satisfy curiosity about a particular nonhuman species.
2. Psychology has most frequently been interested in the single individual. Physiological psychologists sometimes study individual nerve cells, and social psychologists sometimes compare cultures, but the central concern of the field has been with the individual human being.
3. Psychology has made the experiment its preferred method. Experiments may be in error through their artificiality, and thus need to be supplemented by other types of data. They are also inappropriate for studying some of the things in which psychologists are interested. Nevertheless, where they can be appropriately used, they are a powerful tool and have been the favorite one in the field.
4. Psychology has studied both behavior and experience. Behavior is life viewed from the outside, and experience is life viewed from within. Although some theoretical approaches have excluded one or the other from the field of psychology, it has been more usual to consider the study of both of them essential to understanding human beings.
5. Psychology has been concerned both with the ways in which individuals are similar and with the ways in which they differ. There are some principles, called *nomothetic*, which apply to all relatively normal individuals. An example would be that the receptors for vision are found in the retina of the eye. Other principles, called *idiographic*, may describe the behavior of only one individual, such as, "John is always grumpy when he has to talk to Mr. Cartwright." Psychologists have been concerned with trying to discover both of these types of principles.

6. Finally, psychology has made use of statistical techniques. Human behavior is highly variable and only imperfectly understood. If a person limits himself to drawing generalizations that will precisely fit all the cases he has studied, there is relatively little he can say. Because of this, psychologists have also drawn generalizations which are only true on the average or in a probabilistic sense. Statistics, the study of distributions and probabilities, has thus been a major tool of the psychologist.

It can be seen that there is no simple way of defining the field of psychology which will clearly distinguish it from the other fields that study man. As with other psychological principles, we shall have to state our definition in probabilistic terms. Many, but not all, of the activities of psychologists fit the following definition: *Psychology is the science of individual experience and behavior, studied primarily through experimental and statistical means.*

If that is what psychology has been, what should it be in the future? Each psychologist will have his own answer to this question. The authors' view is embodied in this textbook. They would like to see the field of psychology composed of those generalizations about man which are relevant to understanding man's functioning on a social level. In line with this goal, they have attempted in this book, while covering the field of psychology as it now exists, to give greatest emphasis to those principles which can currently contribute most to our understanding of socially relevant human behavior.

The History of Psychology

THE BRITISH ASSOCIATIONISTS

Systematic speculation on man's nature is found in many sources stretching back into antiquity. Many individuals and traditions of thought can be regarded as contributing historically to the development of a field of study known as psychology. Nevertheless, a main stream of intellectual activity which merits particular attention developed among certain British philosophers of the eighteenth century who, because of similarities in their beliefs, are classified together. The two most important aspects of their beliefs are referred to in the two different names they are sometimes given. Sometimes they are called *empiricists* because they believed that ideas are not inherited but learned from experience, and sometimes *associationists* because of their interest in how ideas are associated with one another. (It is, of course, possible to be an empiricist without being an associationist, or to be an associationist without being an empiricist. John Locke and his followers, however, were generally both.) In being both empiricists and associationists, they raised the central problem of the future field of psychology and provided an answer to it.

The problem was where ideas come from. Their origin was not a problem if ideas came from God or the devil, as in popular belief of that time, or were assumed to be inherited as earlier philosophers had tended to believe. Plato, for instance, held the position that we had once known everything but that our memories were a bit bad and we needed to be reminded. This was, for him, a strong argument in favor of believing in reincarnation: if we had not lived before, how could we know so much? Similarly, Descartes held that there were some ideas which did not come from experience but which yet presented themselves to the mind with such certainty that they had to be believed. The rejection of innate ideas is the central theme of Locke's "An Essay Concerning Human Understanding," published in 1690, and it is the step which made a field of psychology necessary.[1] This point is made clear in the best-known quote from Locke's essay:

> All ideas come from sensation or reflection—*Let us then suppose the mind to be, as we say, white paper, void of all characters, without any ideas; how comes it to be furnished? Whence comes it by that vast store which the busy and boundless fancy of man has painted on it with an almost endless variety? Whence has it all the materials of reason and knowledge? To this I answer in one word, from experience. In that all our knowledge is founded, and from that it ultimately derives itself. Our observation, employed either about external and sensible objects, or about the internal operations of our minds, perceived and reflected on by ourselves, is that which supplies our understanding with all the material of thinking. These two are the fountains of knowledge, from whence all the ideas we have, or can naturally have, do spring.*[2]

It will be noticed in this quotation that Locke did not carry empiricism as far as some of the later members of the school. He believed that, while ideas are not inherited, the capacity for perceiving the world is, and that a person can learn by paying attention to the operations of his mind. Others, such as George Berkeley and David Hartley, developed the positions that we must learn to perceive and that all ideas are compounds of ideas of sensations. No longer was observing the operations of the mind a source of knowledge.

"Compounds of ideas" provides the clue to the other important role which associationism was to play in the history of psychology. Ideas were believed to be associated with one another, and, on the basis of this association, complex ideas built up out of simple ones. The answer to the question of where ideas came from was thus to look for the laws of association. Consciousness, like a chemical compound, could be analyzed into elements, and the laws of association were thought to govern how the elements combined to make the compounds. On the basis of introspection, the associationists suggested what the laws might be. For Hume, for example, there were three: resemblance, contiguity, and cause and effect. If automobile tires make you think of doughnuts, your thought is an example of associating ideas because of similarity of shape. Associating salt with pepper would follow a law of contiguity—associating things because they are frequently found together. If turtles make you think of turtle soup, it is perhaps association of cause and effect.

NINETEENTH-CENTURY PHYSIOLOGY

The associationists did not carry out experiments or carefully controlled observations, but based their conclusions on thinking about their everyday experiences. Thus, while they anticipated the subject matter and some of the principles of later psychological theories, they did not anticipate their experimental methods. These methods were more a legacy from a second major forerunner of the field of psychology, the investigation of the physical nature of man by anatomists and physiologists. A publication of Charles Bell in 1811 will serve as an example.

Although speculation about man is old, systematic study of him is not. Anthropologists are perhaps not fanciful to suggest that the reason animals are represented in considerable anatomical accuracy in cave paintings, while men are either very crudely sketched or not shown at all, is that early man often had strong religious taboos against any representation of human beings. (This type of belief can be seen in the more recent notion that the possession of an image of a person by a witch could give the witch a power over him.) In any case, man has been the last thing subject to scientific investigation. At the time Bell wrote, some people were just beginning to feel that perhaps man's anatomy might be amenable to scientific investigation. There still are many people who believe his thoughts, impulses, and emotions are outside the sphere of science. The novelty of studying even man's anatomy in the early nineteenth century is shown in this quote from Bell's "Idea of a New Anatomy of the Brain":

> *I have found some of my friends so mistaken in their conception of the object of the demonstrations which I have delivered in my lectures, that I wish to vindicate myself at all hazards. They would have it that I am in search of the seat of the soul; but I wish only to investigate the structure of the brain, as we examine the structure of the eye and ear. It is not more presumptuous to follow the tracts of nervous matter in the brain and to attempt to discover the course of sensation, than it is to trace the rays of light through the humours of the eye, and to say, that the retina is the seat of vision. Why are we to close the investigation with the discovery of the external organ?*[3]

Bell is more often remembered today for being one of the discoverers of the Bell-Magendie law than for his investigations of the brain. This law distinguishes between the sensory and motor nerves connecting with the spinal cord. The sensory nerves, which carry impulses toward the brain, connect with the cord through the dorsal roots (toward the back); the motor nerves which carry impulses away from the brain, emerge as the ventral roots from the cord. This implies that cutting the dorsal root will anesthetize the area served by the nerve, whereas injury to the ventral root will paralyze it. More important than this specific discovery, however, was the role which Bell and others like him played in introducing systematic observation and experimentation as methods of studying living organisms. In Magendie's rediscovery of Bell's law, for example, he utilized an experiment:

> *Magendie cut the posterior root, could get no movement by pricking or pressing the limb, and was about to conclude that the limb was paralyzed when the animal moved it spontaneously. Magendie concluded that the limb was not paralyzed but anesthetic. Then Magendie tried cutting the anterior root and found that he then had paralysis, whether the posterior root was cut or not, unless he stimulated the distal end of the anterior cut.*[4]

PSYCHOPHYSICS

A third forerunner of the field of psychology was a growing literature on the operation of the senses. Thomas Young had proposed a theory of color vision as early as 1802, and it was elaborated by the physicist von Helmholtz in 1860. More important, Weber and Fechner established the area of study known as *psychophysics*. The impact of their work on psychology was so great that E. G. Boring, in his standard history of experimental psychology, views Fechner as the founder of the field:

We come at last to the formal beginning of experimental psychology, and we start with Fechner: not with Wundt, thirty-one years Fechner's junior, who published his first important but youthful psychological study two years after Fechner's epoch-making work; not with Helmholtz, twenty years younger, who was primarily a physiologist and a physicist but whose great genius extended to include psychology; but with Fechner, who was not a great philosopher nor at all a physiologist, but who performed with scientific rigor those first experiments which laid the foundation for the new psychology and still lie at the basis of its methodology.[5]

The view that Fechner founded psychology is based on two things. He applied experimental methods such as those employed by physics and physiology, and he applied them to problems which were definitely psychological rather than physical or physiological. The problems dealt with the relationship between the physical stimulus a person was exposed to and the sensation he experienced. Weber had observed that the change in a stimulus which can be noticed is approximately a constant fraction of the value of the stimulus. In other words, if a 30-ounce weight must be changed in weight by an ounce for you to be able, on the average, to notice the difference, then a 30-pound weight would have to be changed by a pound for the change to be equally noticeable. This can be crudely observed in everyday life. If a room is illuminated only by moonlight coming through the windows, turning on even a 15-watt bulb will make a very noticeable difference in how bright the room seems. If sunlight is streaming through the windows, the change in illumination when the 15-watt light is turned on may not even be discernible.

Fechner considerably extended Weber's work both experimentally and theoretically. He expanded it to other senses than the ones Weber had worked with, and he conceived of using the just noticeable difference in stimulation as a unit in terms of which any sensation could be measured. Fechner thus did extensive work in psychology, yet the honor of founding the field is more commonly given to Wilhelm Wundt, who came later. This is partly because of disagreement on just how important Fechner's work was, and Boring quotes William James as having written of it:

. . . But it would be terrible if even such a dear old man as this could saddle our Science forever with his patient whimsies, and, in a world so full of more nutritious objects of attention, compel all future students to plough through the difficulties, not only of his own works, but of the still drier ones written in his refutation. Those who desire this dreadful literature can find it; it has a 'disciplinary value'; but I will not even enumerate it in a foot-note. The only amusing part of it is that Fechner's critics should always feel bound, after

smiting his theories hip and thigh and leaving not a stick of them standing, to wind up by saying that nevertheless to him belongs the imperishable glory *of first formulating them and thereby turning psychology into an* exact science.[6]

Probably a more important reason why Wundt is usually considered the founder of psychology, however, is that it was his students who became the leaders in the new field. Fechner may have created part of the field of psychology; Wundt created psychologists. Besides this, Wundt, unlike Fechner, set out intentionally to create a new field of study.

The field of psychology thus began imperceptibly. Some psychological research, such as that of Weber and Fechner, was done before Wundt founded his psychological laboratory in 1879. James even had a laboratory at Harvard for performing psychological experiments prior to Wundt's doing so. Wundt, however, defined psychology in a systematic way, and he had disciples. His work was no single piece of research, but the creation of a field. He adopted consistent positions on what the subject matter of the field should be, what methods should be used to study the subject matter, what assumptions needed to be made in order to utilize the methods, and what problems it was important to attack first in terms of the theoretical approach. His psychology is worthy of our attention, for even today's various approaches to the field are based on the answers given to the questions Wundt raised. The history of psychology is largely a history of accepting or rejecting various aspects of Wundt's psychology.

WUNDT'S PHYSIOLOGICAL PSYCHOLOGY

Wundt's psychology was just what one would expect it to be on the basis of its antecedents. From the associationistic philosophers came the tasks of the new field: the analysis of consciousness into elements, and the determination of the laws of connection of these elements. Also from the associationists came introspection as a method, but this was combined with the experimental method of the physiologists. The method adopted was thus experimental introspection! This method is not a contradiction in terms, and it was the method employed by Fechner. The experiment consists of creating various stimulus conditions, about which the subject introspects and reports his experiences.

Wundt was very clear about what psychology was and was not. In his view, it was the science of experience, and concerned only with the experiences of the normal, adult human mind. Other sciences were possible, but they would not be psychology. Similarly, he believed that the introspections of trained observers were the only source of acceptable data. Anything else would be unscientific. Finally, the basic task of the new science was to break down experience into elements. Wundt's system was a mental chemistry which hoped, like the science of chemistry, to find lawfulness by finding basic elements and seeing how they combined into compounds. Like chemical compounds, the mental compounds might show properties different from those of the elements making them up, an idea which had also been suggested by one of the later associationistic philosophers, John Stuart Mill. It was this search for a molecular structure of consciousness which led the systems descending from Wundt's system to be named *structuralism.*

THE IMPACT OF EVOLUTIONARY THEORY

In 1859 Charles Darwin published the book of the century, *The Origin of Species.*[7] That psychology today is not structuralism is probably due more to this remarkable work than to any other single cause. Later, Freud's writings were to have their effect, yet even today contemporary psychology probably shows the impact of evolutionary theory more clearly than that of psychoanalysis. What exactly was it that Darwin did? He was not the first to propose an evolutionary theory—his own grandfather Erasmus had been one of those who had formulated evolutionary theories before him. Instead, he was the first to propose a plausible mechanism by means of which evolution might have taken place, and he presented such a wide variety of evidence that his ideas had to be either accepted or disproved—they could not simply be ignored.

Before Darwin wrote, men were familiar with some of the evidence on which his theory was based. That some species which had previously been found on the earth were there no longer was evident from research in paleontology. Their disappearance was accounted for in terms of some great cataclysm rather than unsuccessful competition for survival. That new breeds of domestic animals, such as the Percheron horse, had been created by man was undeniable. These were merely breeds rather than species, however, and it was not considered possible that similar selective breeding might create new species. Species were held to have been divinely created, all at the same time and forever unchanging. Finally, similarities of embryological development of different species were noted and used as a basis of classification of the species. They were not, however, seen as indicating that the species had evolved from common ancestors.

Darwin brought all these sources of evidence into focus by showing their relationship to a mechanism of evolution; a mechanism of variation, differential survival, and resulting change of the population. His doing so created three new interests within the field of psychology. First, it led to an interest in the adaptive value of human thought and behavior. Instead of the contents of the mind, the basic question became the ways in which the mind helped man compete for survival. Second, evolutionary theory led to an interest in animal psychology. The mind of man and that of other organisms had been previously thought so different from one another that no comparison between them was possible. Evolution, in stating that man and primates had descended from common ancestors, stressed their similarity and made a comparison of their mental capacities desirable. Finally, evolutionary theory led to the study of individual differences. If man's intelligence had evolved through variation and differential survival, then the variations in intelligence found among individuals became vitally important, for they were the stuff of which evolution was made.

FUNCTIONALISM AND BEHAVIORISM

All three of these interests in psychology, primarily encouraged by evolutionary theory, soon came to characterize American psychology. The approach which embodied them was too loose and eclectic to be considered a system of psychology in the sense that structuralism was, but to distinguish it from structuralism it has been given the name of *functionalism*. From it developed *behaviorism* which was, like structuralism, a more rigidly defined theoretical system.

Because functionalism was more of a general point of view than a well-developed theoretical approach, it cannot be identified with one man the way structuralism can be associated with Wundt. It grew partly out of the work of William James at Harvard, and it was influenced by work on individual differences done by Galton in England and Binet in France. It developed into a distinctive approach at the University of Chicago under John Dewey and at Columbia University under James McKeen Cattell. Even these two schools differed somewhat in their emphases, with the theoretical developments at Chicago leading more directly to behaviorism, whereas the Columbia approach was more eclectic.

The central problem for functionalism, then, was how mental activity aided in adaptation to the environment. This included such subquestions as these: How do individuals differ in their adaptation? How do we develop the ability to adapt? What processes are common to the adaptation of animals and humans? How may our knowledge be applied to help people adapt? As is obvious from these questions, Wundt's nomethetic pure science of human experience was expanded into the study of experience and behavior, of animals and people, of individual differences and common characteristics, to be applied as well as understood. Even this list does not exhaust the ways in which functionalism differed from structuralism. It also opposed the analysis of experience into elements by stressing, as James had, that experience is a continuous process which can be broken down into elements only at the cost of distorting it. We not only cannot step into the same river twice, but we also cannot step into it once, for it changes while we are acting.

This opposition to analysis into elements was not shared by behaviorism, which grew out of functionalism. Behaviorism regarded functionalism as a compromise with an enemy which should have been slain. Behaviorism, as developed by John Watson and his followers, had as rigid rules about what psychology should be as structuralism did, even though the rules were almost diametrically opposed. For structuralism, psychology had been the study of experience; for Watson, only behavior was admissible data.

The study of behavior rather than of experience is a natural consequence of an interest in animal psychology, since animals are unable to report their experiences. Watson's primary interests were in animal and child psychology, and he carried functionalism to its logical extreme of excluding all but behavior from psychology. The new school was to lean so heavily on experiments with animals that there was something prophetic in the title of Watson's doctoral dissertation: "Animal Education: The Psychical Development of the White Rat."[8]

It was also from animal experiments that the elements of the new approach came. After winning the Nobel Prize for his research on digestion, the Russian physiologist Ivan Pavlov became interested in the role of higher mental processes in salivation. A dog would salivate not only when meat was placed in his mouth, a simple reflex action, but also when his food dish was rattled. This latter behavior was not an innate reflex but instead, Pavlov reasoned, a reflex which was conditional upon the training the animal had received. By pairing a neutral stimulus, such as a bell, with the stimulus of meat powder in the mouth, Pavlov "conditioned" his animals to salivate to the bell. His extensive research on these conditional or conditioned responses served as a major theoretical basis of behaviorism. Watson conceived of all learning as responses being conditioned to stimuli. The elements of the new psychology were not the sensations and images of structuralism, or the ideas of British associationism, but the stimuli and responses of physiology.

INDIVIDUAL DIFFERENCES AND PSYCHOANALYTIC THEORY

In tracing the evolution of functionalism, we have neglected other aspects of it which were not central to behaviorism: its concentration on individual differences and its applied nature. These two characteristics, which had their own historical origins, led to the development of clinical psychology.

The role which evolutionary theory played in making psychology an idiographic science as well as a nomethetic one may be seen by looking at the pioneer of the study of individual differences, who was Darwin's cousin. Sir Francis Galton was a man of science of a type not found today, for today's knowledge is so extensive and specialized that anyone other than a professional in a field rarely makes a basic contribution to it. Galton, on the other hand, was a dilettante who made basic contributions to anthropology, genetics, meteorology, psychology, physics, and statistics. He was a genius with an independent income who was productive without taking his work seriously. At one time he made a walking tour of the British Isles to determine where the girls were the prettiest. At another he established an anthropometric laboratory in London where he took physical and psychological measurements of thousands of people. Although almost all psychologists since Galton's time have had to pay their subjects to participate in experiments, Galton charged his an admission fee.

It was an interest in evolution which made Galton interested in individual differences. He saw in intelligence a major factor in adaptation and survival, and was convinced that it was inherited rather than acquired. In individual differences in intelligence, he saw evolution in progress. His major work in the area, *Inquiries into Human Faculty and Its Development*,[9] first published in 1883, was the beginning of individual psychology.

If testing of individual differences began because of Galton's interest in evolution, it continued for more practical reasons. Binet and Simon published in 1905 the first practical intelligence test for schoolchildren, prepared at the request of the Paris school authorities. Mental testing was transplanted to Columbia by Cattell, who had been Wundt's first assistant but was influenced more by Galton. As Edna Heidbreder put it in her excellent book *Seven Psychologies*:

> In the early days of psychology at Columbia, the dominating figure was, beyond question, James McKeen Cattell. Cattell, it will be remembered, was one of Wundt's first students at the Leipzig laboratory. It has almost passed into legend that, at his own suggestion, he became Wundt's first assistant, and that in Wundt's laboratory, where the object of study was the generalized human mind, and where Wundt regularly assigned students the problems for their doctoral dissertations, Cattell suggested his own problem and included in his plan a study of individual differences. Wundt pronounced the program gans Amerikanisch, and it is of great importance to psychology in the United States that Cattell remained ganz Amerikanisch and at the same time an active member of the Leipzig group.[10]

Clinical psychology would have had no place in the nomethetic structuralism of German experimental psychology and, at most, a questionable place in the theoretically pure behaviorism of Watson. It was soon to play a major role in an American functionalism which was oriented toward individual differences, mental testing, and the application of psychology to practical problems.

Although he was a medical doctor rather than a psychologist, Sigmund Freud changed psychological conceptions of man as a personality as much as Darwin had changed conceptions of man as an animal. Again, like Darwin, Freud was not completely original in his work, but he was original in developing a unified theory with supporting evidence which had to be seriously considered. The use of hypnosis in the treatment of mental disorder was an accepted technique before Freud, and William James was among those who used it to gather data on individuals with amnesia, publishing his observations in *The Principles of Psychology*[11] in 1890. Freud, however, made at least three major contributions. First, and perhaps most important in the long run, he expanded the scope of science to encompass new phenomena. Rather than dismiss the behavior of children, slips of the tongue of adults, the symptoms of psychotics, and the myths of various cultures as accidental and meaningless trivia, he viewed them as phenomena which a theory of man must explain. The second contribution was the theory he evolved to explain these data—a theory stressing the motivation of behavior, the unacceptability of many of the motives to the conscience of the individual, and the consequent importance of repression and unconscious conflict. This theory will be explored at length later in the book. Finally, Freud contributed a method of treatment of mental illness which differed significantly from the hypnosis from which it was evolved. While hypnosis sometimes produced dramatic cures, it sometimes seemed to cure only the surface symptoms without getting at the underlying problems. After one set of symptoms was cured, the patient soon developed different ones. The psychoanalytic technique of therapy was developed to lead people, while conscious, into discussing matters that they would usually reveal only under hypnosis.

Freud's theories served as a stimulus for the study of children, motivation, and individual differences. It was only through the testing movement, however, that clinical psychology evolved. Although some trained psychoanalysts were not medical doctors, soon the majority of analysts were, and eventually the precedent was established that only M.D.'s would receive psychoanalytic training. The main stream of psychoanalysis was obviously within medicine, and psychology was influenced only in the way it had been influenced by developments in philosophy, physiology, and biology. Psychologists, however, gradually developed two roles which were related to psychoanalysis. Through the development of mental testing, psychologists came to play a major role in psychiatric diagnosis, and through the development of research methodology, they became the people most concerned with the evaluation of the effects of psychoanalytic therapy. While the former of these two roles placed them in a role subordinate to psychiatrists, the latter gave them an expertise which placed them at least on a basis of equality with the medical specialists. From the combination of the two roles, and from the shortage of trained psychiatrists, clinical psychology developed into its present status of relatively independent, quasi-medical practice.

At the present time, approximately half of all psychologists in the United States are clinicians, and it is the clinical psychologist, rather than the industrial, child, comparative, social, or physiological psychologist, who is popularly thought of when the word "psychologist" is mentioned.

GESTALT THEORY

The final school of psychology which we shall consider is named *gestalt* theory, after a German word which may be roughly translated as "pattern." As its name implies, this school grew up as a protest against analysis and synthesis in psychology, and stressed that there are emergent properties when elements are combined. A triangle is more than three straight lines. Triangularity is an emergent property which appears when they are organized in a pattern.

Gestalt theory, arising as a theory of perception, was a reaction against the analysis of consciousness by German structuralism, but it became the chief alternative to the elementarism of behaviorism in the United States. In most ways, the two theoretical approaches were opposed. Gestalt psychologists, who had come to the United States to flee Hitler's Germany, were strong advocates of psychology's studying human values and social institutions, whereas behaviorism wanted to eliminate everything subjective from the field. Watson was a strong environmentalist who maintained that anyone could become anything with the proper training; the gestalt theorists were nativists in perception who stressed the innate organizing characteristics of the mind. Most important, however, the mind was, for behaviorism, a blank slate on which nothing but stimulus-response connections could be inscribed, while for the gestalt theorists it was something wondrously complex. Behaviorism was simple and optimistic, with a simple theory to account for everything. Gestalt theory concentrated on destroying the simple explanations.

Gestalt theory was the last of the great theoretical orientations in the field of psychology. Over the years the gathering of data led to the development of more specific and limited theories. Psychologists tended to stop thinking of themselves as adherents of one particular school of psychology and began to identify more with particular areas of specialization within the field.

Even though the period of conflicting schools of psychology is past, the differences in theoretical orientation which divided those schools are still important today. What a person assumes about the way in which heredity and environment interact or about the validity of analyzing wholes into elements will influence both what he studies and what explanations he will propose for his results. Let us look at some of the major theoretical issues which still lie behind more specific controversies in the field of psychology.

HEREDITY AND ENVIRONMENT

It is obvious that hereditary and environmental factors must interact to produce any particular human characteristic. If a fertilized ovum has the chromosomes of a rabbit, it cannot develop into a human being. Similarly, if it lacks those physiological conditions necessary to development which are normally provided in the uterus, it cannot develop at all. In what sense, then, is it possible to describe something as being "caused by heredity" or "caused by environment"?

In the case of one characteristic of one organism, it is not possible to cite either one of these causes exclusively. What can be ascribed to hereditary or environmental factors is a difference between organisms. The difference between a rat and a mouse is due to heredity even though both heredity and environment are necessary to produce either a rat or a mouse.

When a person talks about something being due more to heredity or more to environment, he is making an implicit comparison. He means that the way in which this organism differs from others (often a particular but unspecified group of others) is a result of hereditary or environmental influence. A man who lifts weights as a hobby is strong in comparison with other people because of environmental factors but weak in comparison with an elephant because of heredity.

Psychologists thus can agree that heredity and environment interact, but can disagree as to how significant each is in a particular case. The question is an important one, for the way in which something can be changed depends on how it was produced. For that reason we shall, at several points in this book, discuss the ways in which heredity and environment interact in producing a particular phenomenon.

SIMPLICITY AND COMPLEXITY

A second major difference between psychologists is their tendency to see phenomena as simple or complex. One theorist will be inclined to emphasize how much we know about human beings, and another to stress how much we do not know. Even more significantly, theorists will often differ on how we should go about learning more. The questions raised by the gestalt theorists on the extent to which complex phenomena may be understood by analysis are still very much alive today. Are studies of other animals relevant to understanding man? Can social phenomena be understood from a thorough knowledge of the individual? The answers one gives to these and similar questions are likely to depend on how simple or complex he views the world as being.

If the world is simple, then there are a few basic principles which will explain much of it. Similar principles will apply to rats and men, and to nonsocial and social situations. By studying simple situations where they are not disguised by apparent complexity, these principles may be discovered. Phenomena which seem on the surface to be more complex may then be understood through the application of the various basic principles.

This research strategy of seeking basic principles in simple situations and then applying them in more complex ones has often proved productive in scientific research. Gregor Mendel's experiments on heredity in garden peas, for example, revealed some basic principles of heredity which were then developed and modified to account for more complex hereditary phenomena.

In other cases, however, this strategy has led researchers astray. Theorists who stress the richness and complexity of human experience are likely to point out that researchers who simplify a real-life problem in order to study it more effectively often leave out many of the things which need studying. This omission may result in their building theories which are at best irrelevant to life, and at worst, misleading about it. Theorists (such as the authors of this book) who stress complexity are therefore inclined to make provisional statements about complex phenomena rather than build detailed models of simpler ones.

RATIONALITY AND IRRATIONALITY

A third major controversy concerns the extent to which man is rational. Some theorists see man as governed by his intellect, making choices on the basis of his values and knowing all the factors which influence his decisions. Others see him as greatly affected by factors of which he is unaware, whether these factors are innate instincts, early conditioning, or repressed motives. To the extent that he does not know what he wants or why he wants it, he is unable to make rational choices among ways of achieving his goals.

A theorist's view as to how rational man is influences the kind of experiment he is likely to design. Suppose, for example, that two theorists were both interested in psychological factors in international relations. If one of them assumed that man is rational, he might study bargaining behavior in a situation which had been simplified by the removal of many of the social and emotional factors present in the actual negotiation between nations. If man is rational, these factors would not have any effects anyway, so leaving them out would not be an important omission.

The investigator who believed that man is largely irrational would choose quite a different research strategy. He would assume that what an individual did in a real-life negotiation situation would be influenced by motives of which he had little awareness. He thus might study the effects of conformity pressure, guilt, authority, and similar factors on bargaining behavior. He would regard the research of the former investigator as unrealistic because it left these factors out, just as the other investigator would regard his research design as unrealistic because it gave them so much prominence.

Ultimately, the differences on this issue, like those on the other two we have considered, would be settled by the research results. Each theorist would need to account for the results which the other obtained, and eventually a useful theory of negotiation would be created. As long as there was room for doubt, however, each theorist would make assumptions in line with his overall theoretical orientation. Although schools of psychology are dead, psychologists often carry the approaches of behaviorism, psychoanalytic theory, and gestalt theory in new combinations to the problems they tackle. These unverbalized theoretical biases are part of the transmitted culture of psychology and make the field the accidental product of its history.

Theory and Data in Psychology

THEORY

Psychology differs from most other fields in that all people hold psychological theories. When a chainstore owner tries to decide in which shopping center to locate a branch store, or a boy calculates his chances of dropping in on a girl at a good time for seeing her alone, or a husband tries to understand why his spouse likes something he doesn't, each of these people is operating with a rich and complicated theory of human behavior and experience. Furthermore, each can point to concrete evidence to support his theories. The chainstore owner, for example, might argue that he should put his store where the greatest number of people had recently moved, and cite recent figures on business activity there to support this generalization. How, then, do the theories of psychologists differ from those gained through experience and commonsense reasoning? Some of the main ways are that they are more explicit and more internally consistent, and that they specify more clearly the relationships between the theories and the evidence they are based on. Let us look at each of these points in turn.

A person concerned with any area of human activity may develop a great deal of ability to predict events in that area without being able to communicate his expertise to anyone else. Thus, if we asked the store owner mentioned earlier to predict the fates of ten successive store locations in various suburbs, he might well predict accurately in most if not all cases. If he were asked how he made his predictions, he might predict success in one case on the basis of good parking access, failure in another case because of economic decline in the neighborhood even though it was growing, and borderline survival in a third because of a competing store going in nearby. The individual trying to learn from the expert how to predict such results himself would be as puzzled after learning these predictions as he was before. He would not know how to combine and weigh the various factors that seem to be involved, or what other factors the expert might invoke to aid in predicting a totally new situation. Suppose that people are flocking in droves to an area which has no access except on foot, and where a competitor store already has more business than it can handle? The method of prediction which has been communicated is not sufficiently explicit to use effectively. To develop theories which are explicit enough to state which variables should be looked at, how they should be measured, and how they should be put together in making predictions is the goal of theory building in the social sciences.

A second problem with commonsense theories is that they often seem to be self-contradictory. A self-made man who has risen from poverty to a position of wealth and power, for example, may ascribe his success to the obstacles he has had to overcome. In explaining his own career, he may attribute his success to the lessons learned in going hungry, fighting in the streets, and having to support himself from an early age. He may also give his children a home in the best residential neighborhood, enough money so that they do not have to work in childhood, and an education at the best preparatory schools. Will he predict that they will be unsuccessful because they will not have had the experiences upon which he said success depends when he "explained" his own career? In many areas of life, our commonsense theories may show similar apparent contradictions. Thus, we can simultaneously believe "Out of sight, out of mind" and "Absence makes the heart grow fonder."

Some of this internal inconsistency in commonsense theories may be more apparent than real, however. If a person believed that when two people did not know each other well, the maxim "Out of sight, out of mind" applied, but that after they developed strong bonds of affection, absence did make the heart grow fonder, there would be no contradiction. In this case, the commonsense theory would simply not be explicit enough through not stating when each principle is to be applied.

Perhaps the greatest difference between formal and informal theories, however, is that the formal theories specify what observations are relevant to them. In Mozart's opera *Cosi fan Tutte*, the two male protagonists debate whether women are "faithful" or not. They differ from others who have argued this matter in agreeing upon the evidence which they will use to settle the question. Each will appear in disguise and try to seduce his own fiancée. If he succeeds, it means she is not faithful, and with the question settled for the most perfect of womankind, the debate is over! In agreeing on just what evidence is and is not relevant to the question, they change it from one which cannot be answered to one which can. Thus, the two characters formulated the basis for a scientific theory, even if the evidence they chose to recognize turned it into whimsy. (The eighteenth-century librettist was in fact poking fun at the scientific method.)

Psychological theories, like Mozart's characters, specify how the concepts in them are to be related to operations or observations in the real world. To return to the case of the chainstore owner mentioned earlier, imagine that he has the simple theory that people buy his merchandise when they have money and can park near his store, and don't buy when they have no cash and can't park nearby. Each time that he hears about the success or failure of one of his branch stores, he will always be able to justify the results in terms of the theory, for he can always find evidence of either customer buying potential or details about the parking there which would fit the outcome. In order to make an adequate test of the theory, he would need to specify a general method of gathering evidence on customer buying and parking which is independent of his beliefs and prior to his knowledge of the actual success or failure of the store in question. He might, for example, specify the following procedure: All stores with the same ideal customer turnover as the store in question, in suburbs similar to that which it is in, should have their available and usable parking spaces counted. If those with fewer parking spaces than his all survive, and those with more parking space than he has actually boom, then his theory certainly predicts at least the survival of his store. If his store fails, then his theory of store survival has some basic flaw as an instrument of prediction. However, it may serve him as protection from the painful knowledge that his merchandise is terrible. Commonsense theories of psychology often fulfill other needs than the need for accurate prediction. Scientific theories, on the other hand, should be designed with the specific intention of avoiding this. They must be ultimately testable. Specifying the operations by which a particular concept may be measured, as we have done in this crude example, is a first step toward making a theory which will be acceptable to the science of psychology.

DATA

The ideal of data gathering in psychology goes something like this: In order to study the effects of a variable, called the *independent* variable, it is experimentally manipulated. (If we wanted to study the effects of a drug, for example, various groups of people would be given different amounts of the drug.) The effects of the independent variable are assessed by measuring other variables which might be influenced, called the *dependent* variables. (In the drug study, these might include both physical measures, such as pulse rate, and psychological measures, such as interpretation of ambiguous stimuli.) The various *experimental groups* would be the groups given different amounts of the drug, and the *control group* would be the one not given the drug at all. The effects of other variables would be controlled by making the conditions for the experimental and control groups identical except for the differences in the level of the independent variable. (In the drug study, for example, the members of the experimental and control groups should not differ in thinking they have—or have not—been given a drug. The control group should therefore be given some inert substance which will have no physical effect on them so that nobody will know whether he has received the real drug or not.) The results of the experiment should be based on enough observations so that they are reliable, and thus would be similar if the experiment were repeated. Conclusions drawn from the experiment should be applied only under conditions similar to the experimental conditions and to populations of people similar to the population of subjects.

These conditions are obviously impossible to create. If we want to study the effects of aspirin on people, we cannot start by getting a representative sample of the entire population of the world. Nevertheless, let us consider why the simple experiment has served as an ideal before we look at the ways in which actual research differs from the ideal.

The reason for varying only one thing at a time is easy to see. If more than one are varied, how is it possible to tell which one is responsible for the effects that are found? In the example of the drug study, if people who had taken the drug knew that they had done so, while individuals in the control group knew that they had not, this second difference between the two groups might be what was responsible for any effects that followed. Even if the drug had no physical effect, people might convince themselves that it was affecting them. Similarly, it is clear that the experiment should be performed on a population of people similar to the one to which the results were to be applied, for it might have different effects on people of different characteristics. The drug, for example, might have quite a different impact on diabetics and nondiabetics.

A somewhat more complicated point has to do with the levels of other variables during the experiment. All variables which influence the effect of the independent variable need to be kept at levels typical of the conditions to which the results are to be applied. As a simple example, suppose that you were studying the effects of large amounts of nitrogen fertilizer on corn. You tested the fertilizer on corn which was well watered and you obtained more rapid growth. Then you applied your result by fertilizing corn which was poorly watered, and you killed most of it. Amount of water is a variable which interacts with amount of nitrogen in influencing the growth of corn. In other words, the effect of the nitrogen will depend on the amount of water. (It is equally true to say that the effect of the water will depend on the amount of nitrogen.) Failure to keep variables which interact with the independent variable at levels typical of the population to which the result is being generalized would, in this and many other cases, lead to very great errors. This is perhaps the most common error of research strategy, and one which must constantly be kept in mind.

Finally, in our ideal experiment, it was specified that the results should be reliable and not due to chance. What is meant by this? Let us look at a very simple example. Imagine that half the population of Smogville lives on the east side of the river and half on the west side. A citizen of Smogville says that it is dangerous to go on the east side because more murders are committed there than on the west side. In support of this argument, he produces statistics showing that during the preceding year four murders were discovered on the east side of town and none on the west side. Is his theory supported? The question is, how many cases do you need before you conclude that there is a reliable difference and not just a chance one? First let us see what we mean by chance.

By chance we refer to all factors which have no relationship to the hypothesis we are testing. Each of the four citizens of Smogville was murdered, presumably, for reasons which seemed adequate to the murderers at the time. If these reasons had no relationship to whether the victim was on the east or west side of town, then we may speak of them as chance. This is the sense in which it is a matter of chance to let the toss of a coin decide a question. Physical laws determine whether the coin will come up heads or tails, but these laws have no relationship to the question being decided. We can decide whether the murders support the theory that the east side of town is dangerous by determining how often the observed frequencies would occur by chance, that is, if they were determined by factors unrelated to geography. If that were the case, any given murder would be equally likely to occur on the east or the west side of the river. The probability of any given murder's being on the east side would be one-half. Of the half of the first murders that occurred on the east side, on the average half of them would be followed by second murders that were committed on the east side. In more general terms, the probability that two independent events will both occur is the product of their individual probabilities. The probability that all four of the murders occurred on the east side simply through chance is $(1/2)$ $(1/2)$ $(1/2)$ $(1/2)$, or one chance in sixteen. This is illustrated in Figure 1-1. The evidence for the theory is weak, but some evidence does exist. If we regularly accept theories on evidence this weak, we shall be wrong about one-sixteenth of the time.

The example we have picked is a very simple one. In most psychological studies, the rules of probability which must be applied to decide whether results are statistically significant are considerably more complicated than those in this example. These statistical models are beyond the scope of this book and will not be discussed. Following the usual convention, unless specified otherwise, results described as "significant" are those which have a probability of less than one in twenty of being a result of chance.

The importance of the simple experiment as an ideal is not that it can be realized, but that deviations from it must be justified. Suppose that we were interested in the effects of extreme fear on individuals. We could not take a representative sample of the population of the world, divide it into experimental and control groups, and force the experimental group to undergo terrifying experiences. There are, however, a number of ways in which the problem can be approached. In each of them, the ways in which the study differs from the ideal reveal additional points which the researcher must establish to make the research valid. Let us first discuss the difficulty presented by having too many subjects to handle experimentally. Since we cannot sample all cultural groups in our research, for example, we shall have to make do with a less adequate sample. In adopting this strategy, we place the burden of proof on ourselves to establish that cultural differences are unlikely to influence our results. If we can show that several radically different cultural groups react similarly, then we are probably justified in generalizing from only a few cultural groups.

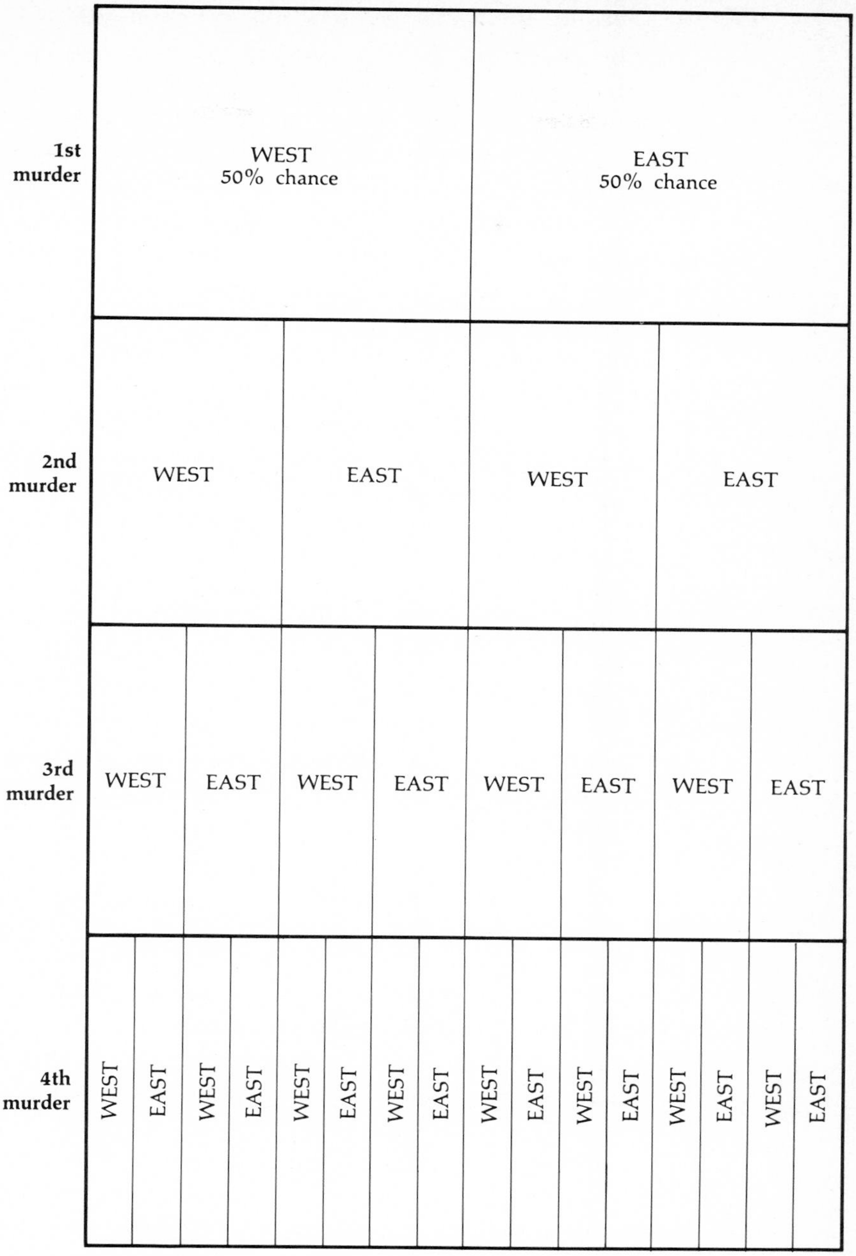

1st
murder

WEST	EAST
50% chance	50% chance

2nd
murder

| WEST | EAST | WEST | EAST |

3rd
murder

| WEST | EAST | WEST | EAST | WEST | EAST | WEST | EAST |

4th
murder

| WEST | EAST | WEST | EAST | WEST | EAST | WEST | EAST | WEST | EAST | WEST | EAST | WEST | EAST | WEST | EAST |

Figure 1–1 *All four murders occurring on the east side of the river is one of six-teen equally probable possibilities.*

Second, there are two basically different strategies we could adopt to cope with our ethical unwillingness to subject people to terrifying situations. One is to conduct an experiment using situations which are only slightly frightening. If we adopt this strategy, we must somehow manage to demonstrate that individuals do react to slightly and extremely frightening situations in basically the same way. The other strategy is to study individuals who are exposed to terrifying situations by circumstances beyond our or their control. Tornadoes, earthquakes, floods, fires, and all the age-old human disasters provide natural experiments which can be utilized. If this strategy is adopted, the researcher will find other ways in which his study deviates from the ideal, and he will need to demonstrate that differences of this type are unlikely to influence the results. It is unlikely, for example, that the research team will be ready and waiting at the time and place where disaster strikes. In what ways are the results liable to be influenced when the research is conducted after the fact rather than during the disaster?

By now it should be clear why there are few critical experiments in science which by themselves provide conclusive evidence supporting or refuting a theory. While the statistical test of one hypothesis in one experiment can be done objectively, the theoretical interpretation of a body of literature remains a subjective matter of interpreting each in the light of all the others. To each of us, readers and authors, falls the fascinating task of seeking general explanations of apparently contradictory research results.

Summary

Psychology, a science of individual experience and behavior studied primarily through experimental and statistical means, has a long history of development. This history includes most notably British associationist philosophers, nineteenth-century physiologists, psychophysicists, and biological evolutionists, and behaviorist, functionalist, psychoanalytic, and gestalt theorists of the early twentieth century. Early theoretical orientations, which attempted broad explanations of everything that psychology studies, have given way to specialized theories dealing with more limited areas of investigation, such as child development, brain chemistry, and the dynamics of group interaction.

Major enduring themes of controversy in psychology have been the relative contributions of heredity and environment to those phenomena studied by the science, the virtue of simple over complex models of explanation or vice versa, and the degree of man's rationality or irrationality.

The experimental approach in psychology is described in this chapter by an explanation of the usefulness of theory, the role of data, and the concept of statistical method. The ideal of experimental control is one in which one independent variable is actively manipulated, other relevant variables are controlled, and a dependent variable is accurately measured. Since this ideal is sometimes inappropriate to the study of variables in real-life situations, more complex statistical models for studying the interactions of multiple variables must frequently be employed.

Notes and Acknowledgments

1. Locke, John. "An essay concerning human understanding," in Edwin Burtt (Ed.), *The English Philosophers from Bacon to Mill*. New York: Random House, Inc., Modern Library, 1939, pp. 238–402.
2. Ibid., p. 248.
3. Bell, Charles. "Idea of a new anatomy of the brain," in Wayne Dennis (Ed.), *Readings in the History of Psychology*. New York: Appleton-Century-Crofts, Inc., 1948, p. 113. By permission of the publisher.
4. Boring, Edwin G. *A History of Experimental Psychology*. (2d ed.) New York: Appleton-Century-Crofts, Inc., 1957, pp. 32–33. By permission of the publisher.
5. Ibid., p. 275. By permission of the publisher.
6. Ibid., p. 294. By permission of the publisher.
7. Darwin, Charles R. *The Origin of Species by Means of Natural Selection*. New York: The Macmillan Company, 1927.
8. Watson, J. B. "Animal education: An experimental study on the psychical development of the white rat, correlated with the growth of its nervous system." Chicago: The University of Chicago Press, 1903.
9. Galton, Francis. *Inquiries into Human Faculty and Its Development*. New York: E. P. Dutton & Co., Inc., 1908.
10. Heidbreder, Edna. *Seven Psychologies*. New York: Appleton-Century-Crofts, Inc., 1933, p. 292. By permission of the publisher.
11. James, William. *The Principles of Psychology*. New York: Dover Publications, Inc., 1950.

Michael Mathers

TWO

PERCEPTION

Introduction

Let us begin our consideration of perception with a mystery. Fix your eyes on some point ahead of you, and have a friend hold up a photograph you have never seen before slightly to the left of your fixation point. Then ask him to hold it just to the right of the fixation point. You will be able to recognize it as the same photograph, and will probably not be surprised by your ability to do so. Yet this really is quite a surprising accomplishment and one which commonsense theories of perception cannot account for. The lens of your eye forms an image on light-sensitive cells in the *retina*, and these *receptor cells* fire when stimulated. The puzzle in your recognizing the photograph is that since it has been moved, none of the same receptor cells is stimulated the second time you look at it. If different cells fire, how do you recognize the photograph as the same?

The commonsense theory of form perception is that there are places in the brain which correspond to places on the retina, so that a triangular image on the retina, for example, would form a triangular image in the *visual cortex* of the brain. If this were the case, however, you would not recognize the photograph as being the same. At some point in the brain's analysis of vision, the same pattern must be represented in the same way regardless of the part of the retina on which the image falls. The brain is an information-processing system, and it may transform the information into different forms just as sound may be stored on recording tape in the form of magnetic charges. Location in space does not need to be represented by location in the brain but may be represented in quite a different way. The actual mechanisms by which we perceive form are just starting to be made clear by recent research.

The way in which the brain analyzes images can be studied in a number of ways, but probably the most direct is to study what makes nerve cells fire. Light falling on the retina of the eye stimulates the sensitive receptor cells there and makes them fire. The nerve impulse from these receptor cells is transmitted through half a dozen layers of the retina and a structure called the *lateral geniculate body* on its way to the many layers of the cerebral cortex of the brain. If the commonsense theory were correct, all these layers would do nothing but transmit the nerve impulse without changing it. At each level along the pathway, one given nerve cell would correspond to one of the receptor cells of the retina, and would fire when its own receptor cell was stimulated. If analysis of the image is already being carried out at these levels, however, this will not be the case. If, for example, we analyzed the image in terms of circular patches, then each nerve cell in the cortex would correspond to a particular circular patch on the retina. Stimulation of the receptor cells within that patch on the retina would make the cell in the cortex fire more rapidly. In a program of research lasting over five years, D. H. Hubel and T. N. Wiesel of Harvard Medical School have explored the relationships between retinal stimulation and the firing of nerve cells within the brain.[1] Let us look at their research.

The basic approach of Hubel and Wiesel was to isolate a given cell in the visual cortex, and then to try out various stimuli to see what increased its rate of firing. Their results indicate that the first analysis of the image which takes place in the cortex causes us to view the world as made up of straight lines oriented at different angles. For the typical cell in the cortex, its rate of firing is increased by stimulation of receptor cells lying in a straight line on the retina. Furthermore, stimulation of any of the cells surrounding this line of cells slows down the rate of firing. Or, to use slightly different terms, the cortical cell has a central line of cells on the retina which turn it on and surrounding cells which turn it off. There are variations on this pattern: Some cells are turned off by the central cells and on by the surrounding ones, and some correspond to edges with an "on" region on one side of the edge and an "off" region on the other side of the edge. On and off regions of typical cells are shown in Figure 2-1.

Besides these "simple" cells which respond to lines on the reti-

Figure 2–1 *Simple cortical cells have receptive fields of various types. In all of them, the on and off areas, represented by black and gray dots respectively, are separated by straight boundaries. Orientations vary, as indicated particularly at a and b. In the cat's visual system, such fields are generally 1 millimeter or less in diameter. (Hubel[2])*

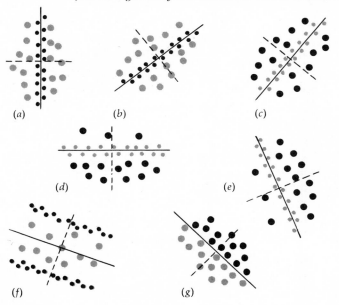

na, Hubel and Wiesel also found "complex" cells which were most stimulated by *moving* images on the retina. They were differentially responsive to movement in different directions, with some, for example, responding more to stimuli moving from left to right and others to stimuli moving from right to left. Even in the layer of the visual cortex which the nerve impulse enters first, considerable analysis of the image is already taking place. Response of a given nerve cell does not correspond to stimulation of one receptor of the retina, but instead corresponds to a line oriented at a particular angle or movement in a particular direction.

That some nerve cells seem to be specialized for the perception of movement should not surprise us, for the perception of movement is one of the basic functions of perception, and one which has a good deal of adaptive significance. An object which is either moving more than its background, such as an animal in a forest, or less than its background, such as a rock in a stream, stands out immediately in our attention. More surprising, however, is research which illustrates that movement of our eyes is necessary to perceiving anything continuously.

Normally, our eyes are in constant motion, making not only the large pursuit motions which are easy to see but also constant small tremor motions. Although these motions cannot be stopped without damage to the eye, investigators have recently found ways of making a visual image remain relatively motionless on the retina. If a tiny slide projector is mounted to a contact lens, the lens moves with the eyeball and the image remains at the same point on the retina as long as the lens does not slip. When this is done, the slide which is projected into the eye is first seen normally, and then fades and reappears, sometimes as a whole and sometimes by parts. The changes in stimulation which eye movements bring are necessary to normal perception.

In looking at evidence on how the brain begins to analyze visual images, we have seen that motion of the image on the retina is necessary to the perceptual process, and that the first steps of the analysis by the brain involve stationary and moving lines as the units of analysis. A question arising at this point is the extent to which the process of analysis is learned or innate. Is our brain somehow wired up at birth to analyze vision in terms of lines, or do we learn how to do so on the basis of visual experience? Again, Hubel and Wiesel's research provides some indications.[3] They fitted a baby kitten with translucent contact lenses just as its eyes were beginning to open. The lenses permitted diffuse light to reach the eyes but did not permit pattern vision. When the kitten was sixteen days old, the retinal on and off regions of some cortical cells were mapped. The results indicated that the analysis of sensations in terms of lines is largely inherited, for the on and off regions were quite similar to those in adult cats with visual experience. They were not exactly the same, however. Many of the regions were less clearly defined than they were in either adult cats or kittens of the same age with visual experience. Either the innate mechanism had started to deteriorate through lack of use, or it would normally have been improved through visual experience. The perception of lines may be both innate and learned.

Thus far, we have been looking at one of the interesting questions in the area of perception not only because the explanation of how we perceive form is important in its own right, but also because it illustrates several general characteristics of perception. *First*, we have noted that there is more to explain in perception than is apparent at first glance. Vision is not a simple matter of transmitting messages from the retina to the brain; it involves complex processes of recognizing objects when they are in different positions, turned at different angles, and located at differing distances from the eye. Although we take all these things for granted, they imply a complex system of analysis. *Second*, we have noted that perception is an active process. It involves not the mere passive recording of information, but the active seeking of stimulation through eye movements. Without activity on the part of the eye, the image fades. We shall see that this is only one of the ways in which perception is a dynamic process. *Third*, we have noted, in looking at Hubel and Wiesel's work, that information is transformed or coded by the nervous system. What we perceive as location is represented not by location in the brain but, instead, in some other way. We have already observed that straight edges are noted by the firing of individual cortical cells in the brain, and not by any straight edge of cells. As Gibson has stated:

> There is a naive theory of perception to the effect that the outer world somehow gets into the eye. Almost the first principle the beginning student learns is that nothing gets into the eye but light.[4]

Two of these three aspects of perception will be major topics in the remainder of this chapter. We will be concerned with perception as an active process through which some stimuli are attended to and others are ignored. We will also be interested in the organizing nature of perception through which stimuli are coded and transformed. In order to consider these topics, there are two others at which we shall also have to look. We will need to consider the sense organs with which the perceptual process starts, and the relative contributions of innate and learned factors to perceptual organization.

The Human Senses

Basic to an organism's adaptation is its acquisition of information about its environment. While some sensitivity to the environment is a general characteristic of all living organisms, the more complex organisms have developed highly specialized sense organs to process information about both external and internal stimulation. The human senses include the distance senses of vision and audition; the chemical senses of taste and olfaction; the skin senses of touch, pain, and temperature; and the position and movement senses of kinesthesis and the vestibular sense. (The kinesthetic sense conveys information about the position and movements of the joints and muscles. The vestibular sense, which works closely with it, conveys information about acceleration in space from the semicircular canals in the inner ear.)

RECEPTORS

While each of these senses is specialized to respond to particular types of energy, there are a number of characteristics which are shared by all of them. Let us look at how they are similar and how they differ.

The first step in perception is carried out by the receptor cells. They are specialized by their construction or location to react to a particular type of stimulation. Some are specialized in both ways. Receptor cells in the retina of the eye, for example, show specialization of construction. They are made so that they are sensitive to light, whereas other nerve cells, such as those in the skin, are not. The taste buds in the tongue show specialization of location. They are located so that material placed in the mouth will come in direct contact with them.

The receptor cells in the retina have some specialization of location as well as specialization of construction. They are located so that light will fall on them, although it must pass through a layer of blood vessels and nerve fibers to do so. On the other hand, they are quite well cushioned from mechanical shock. This is a good thing, for they are somewhat sensitive to mechanical stimulation, and will fire if jarred sufficiently. A severe blow to the head may jolt the retina sufficiently to stimulate the receptors there. When that happens, the individual interprets the stimulation as being visual and "sees stars."

CODING

The receptor cells can react to stimulation in only one way: by changing their rate of firing. This means that any information coming from the various sense organs must be transmitted in some form of code. Which nerve cells fire, and when they fire, are all that distinguish the pain of a toothache from the taste of a banana split.

Patterns of electrical activity originating at the receptor cells travel along sensory nerves into the central nervous system. Within the central nervous system, they carry impulses to two different locations. One of these is the *primary sensory area* for that particular sense in the cerebral cortex. This is the main location for processing that sense, and direct electrical stimulation of it will cause the individual to have an experience in that sensory modality. Impulses are also carried, however, to a structure, called the *reticular formation*, deep within the stem of the brain. This structure plays three important roles in the reception of sensory stimulation. First, it alerts the organism. Second, it causes it to orient its sense organism toward the source of the stimulation. Finally, it causes it to pay more attention to the sense which is being strongly stimulated than to other senses.

The reticular formation receives nerve impulses from higher brain centers as well as from the sense organs. This makes it possible for thoughts in these higher centers to alert the organism and direct its attention.

While there is a rough correspondence between the types of sensory receptor cells which exist and the sensory qualities which we experience, this correspondence is not perfect. We do not seem to be directly aware of the sensations from the vestibular apparatus, that part of the inner ear which helps us to orient ourselves in space. On the other hand, some sensations which seem to us to be discretely different apparently originate from the same receptor cells. Particularly puzzling in this regard is the sensitivity of the skin. Although most of our skin is provided with only two types of receptor cells, we experience such diverse sensations as warmth, pain, cold, touch, and tickle. Tickle seems to result from the slight stimulation of pain receptors, but the way in which the other sensory qualities are produced remains a mystery.

Despite these remaining ambiguities, we have a reasonably good idea of how most sensations are initially recorded at the level of the receptor cell. Sensations of touch from the hairy part of the skin, for example, come from "basket endings." These are endings of nerve cells which are specialized by being wound around the base of hairs. Very similar receptor cells are involved in hearing, but the ear involves a complex mechanical system which transforms the sound energy before the receptor cells are reached. The mechanical system changes the sound waves in the air into waves in the fluid filling a part of the ear called the *cochlear duct*. The hairs of the receptor cells stick out into this fluid, and are thus specialized by position to respond to auditory stimulation.

The coding of the sensory information in both audition and vision is quite complex. The frequency, or pitch, of a sound is coded in one of two ways, depending on whether it is a high or low frequency. If the sound is of low frequency, it is actually reflected in the frequency with which volleys of nerve impulses are transmitted to the brain. If it is of high frequency, the location of the receptor cells on the cochlear duct gives an indication of the pitch of the sound stimulating them. The former of these ways of coding pitch is called the *volley code*, and the latter is called the *place code*.

The receptor cells in the retina of the eye are called, from their shapes, rods and cones. The cones are color receptors and are of three types, which are maximally sensitive to blue, green, and yellow light, respectively. They are concentrated in the central portion of the retina, while the rods are distributed further toward the periphery. Although different rods are not differentially sensitive to light of various colors, they will respond to light of lower intensity than that necessary to stimulate the cones. It is for this reason that a faint star which can be seen out of the corner of your eye will disappear if you look directly at it.

We see, then, that, despite their differences, the various senses have much in common. Each is initially carried out by receptor cells.

Despite their specialization, these cells may be similar even when they serve diverse senses, such as touch and hearing. Each sense also serves to alert the organism when it is stimulated, and each must code its information so that it can be transmitted as a series of electrical impulses. On this foundation of sensory functioning our perceptual experiences are built.[5]

Perception as an Active Process

SLEEP AND WAKEFULNESS

The first step in perception is making the organism sufficiently alert to be able to perceive the stimulus. Although the regular alternation between sleep and wakefulness is one of the more striking things which happen to a person, it is only recently that sleep has been extensively studied.[6] Two methodological developments have been important in allowing it to become a major research topic. The first of these was the development, some years ago, of the *electroencephalograph*. This is a device making a record, an *EEG*, of the electrical activity of an area of the brain. With an EEG, it is possible objectively to identify various stages of alertness ranging from deep sleep to excited attention. The second important methodological development was the discovery that eye movements during sleep are an almost perfect indication of dreaming. By recording electrical potentials to a person's eye muscles and waking him during periods of rapid eye movements, it is possible to obtain a much more complete account of what he was dreaming than can be acquired if he is not awakened immediately. Because this technique makes possible the recording of many dreams under controlled conditions, it promises to provide objective data on hypotheses about the functions of dreaming which had previously seemed outside the realm of experimental testability.

As common sense would suggest, external stimulation (such as the ringing of an alarm clock) causes alertness. However, it does not do so because of the impulses transmitted to the sensory areas of the cerebral cortex Instead, it is the impulses which are carried from the sense organs to the *reticular activating system* which make the organism alert and capable of perceiving the stimulus. This was demonstrated in two experiments. One of them, carried out by Lindsley,

Bowden, and Magoun,[7] showed that cutting the nerve pathways to the reticular activating system led to an unending state of comatose unresponsiveness in an animal. The other, by Moruzzi and Magoun,[8] showed that stimulation of the system would make an animal alert.

The production of different states of sleep is not as simple as the production of alertness, and it is not yet completely understood. Deep, dreamless sleep seems to be caused by the action of a chemical called serotonin on a number of nerve centers, the Raphe nuclei, deep within the brain.[9] Surgical removal of these nuclei will produce experimental animals that never sleep, and temporary reduction of the amount of serotonin in the brain will lead to a temporary loss of sleep. The production of dreaming seems to involve the action of two other systems, each of which responds to a different chemical. Further research should help to make their complex interrelations more clear.

Various depths of sleep are identifiable from EEG patterns. Dreaming does not take place during the stage of deepest sleep, but instead, during what has been called *paradoxical sleep*. This is a stage which follows the stage of deepest sleep, and it is paradoxical in that in some ways it resembles deep sleep while in others it is similar to being awake. It is deep sleep in that the muscles are most relaxed and the person is more difficult to waken from this sleep than from any other type. It is similar to waking in the rapid eye movements which take place and in its pattern of electrical activity, which is barely distinguishable from that of the waking brain.

A survey of the rapidly growing literature on sleep and dreaming is beyond the scope of the present book. One study, however, carried out by William Dement and his coworkers, seems sufficiently important to consider at this point.[10] It implies that dreaming serves important psychological functions for the dreamer.

For several consecutive nights, each subject was awakened each time he or she started to dream, was kept awake a few minutes, and then was allowed to go back to sleep. The procedure allowed the subject to obtain an almost normal amount of sleep but prevented almost all dreaming. To make sure that any results which were found were due to not dreaming rather than to being awakened a number of times a night, a control condition was also run. Using the same subjects at a different time, they were awakened repeatedly when they were not dreaming, disturbing their sleep equally but not interfering with dreaming. How did the subjects react to the dream deprivation? First, it became more and more difficult to prevent them from dreaming as the experiment proceeded. After several nights of dream deprivation, they would go into rapid-eye-movement sleep soon after falling asleep. An even more significant finding was that all the subjects showed deterioration of psychological functioning when they were deprived of dreaming; they didn't show such deterioration when they were simply awakened while they were not dreaming. In general, they became tired, irritable, anxious, and unable to concentrate. It is this evidence of the psychological importance of dreaming, combined with the indication that dreams may now be studied in detail, which has led to the recognition that dreaming is an important new area of perceptual research.

SELECTIVE ATTENTION

After the question of whether the organism is generally alert, the next important question in understanding the effect of a stimulus upon it is the extent to which it is paying attention to that stimulus. The definitive experiment illustrating the existence of selective attention was done by Raúl Hernández-Peón, Harald Scherrer, and Michel Jouvet. Their results demonstrated that attention influences the sensations from a sense organ even before they reach the level of the brain. The experiment was an ingenious one done with cats. Recordings were made of electrical activity in each cat's *cochlear nucleus,* a neural center transmitting auditory stimuli to the brain. First, recordings were made while a click was sounded in the cat's ear. Each time the click sounded, there was a large change in electrical potential of the cochlear nucleus. Then the click was sounded while the cat's attention was attracted by a stimulus using some other sense modality —in one case, the sight of two mice in a jar. In each case, there was much less neural response to the sound of the click, as shown in Figure 2-2. In shifting its attention to a sight or a smell, the cat suppressed the neural activity resulting from the sound. As we have already noted, this selection of one sensory channel as the object of special attention is one of the functions of the reticular activating system.

Channel selection is only one of the mechanisms involved in attention. There is also evidence that individuals can select for a particular stimulus or message, even though different messages are being received over the same channel. To look at this evidence, we first

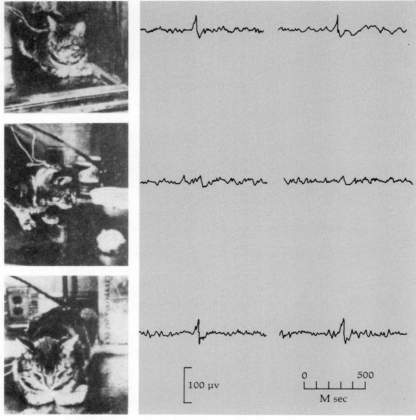

Figure 2–2 *Direct recording of click responses in the cochlear nucleus. (Her-nández-Peón, Scherrer, and Jouvet[11])*

need to raise the question of whether a person can think about two things at once.

If you have a radio handy, tune it to a station on which a person is talking. Now, try to listen to what he is saying while you simultaneously calculate the squares of the prime numbers. If you have any success at all, it will probably be by rapidly alternating your attention between the two tasks. Recent research suggests that the time required to shift attention is only a fraction of a second. Furthermore, we have a type of memory called *iconic*, or *sensory, memory* which will store sensory input for a very short time before we pay attention to it. By storing the voice in sensory memory while attending to the arithmetic, then rapidly switching back to the voice before the memory fades, you may make a little progress on the two tasks. You cannot actually think about both at the same time, however, so you need to use *serial processing* with them, noting first one and then the other.

Some things, however, can be handled simultaneously. They are said to be done by *parallel processing*, thought processes which can go on at the same time. A large object in your peripheral vision, if it suddenly moves while you are reading, can be noticed without taking your attention away from the reading. Generally, it is only the crudest aspects of stimulation which can be noticed without paying attention to the stimulus—for example, whether a person is talking or an object is moving, but not what the person says or what shape the moving object has.[12]

Perception thus seems to involve mechanisms of two kinds. The first, called *preattentive mechanisms*, carry out a crude analysis of stimulation. They go on all the time, whether you are particularly attending to that stimulation or not. On the basis of the information provided by these preattentive mechanisms, you can devote your *focal attention* to one channel or another. The focal attentive processes are the ones which make something occupy the center of your consciousness and permit you to perform a detailed analysis of it.

This combination of preattentive mechanisms with focal attention illustrates another general principle of human perceptual organization. The brain shows many examples of more highly developed neurological systems imposed upon less developed, often more evolutionarily primitive, systems. The working of the more complex system may mask the working of the simple one. This may make it difficult to study the latter's functioning, but does not necessarily mean that the old system is inoperative. In some cases the simpler system provides a useful mechanism which can take over when the more sophisticated one is lost.

The difference between preattentive mechanisms and focal attention is illustrated in an early finding of experimental psychology. Suppose that you are waiting to perform some act, such as starting to run a race. Will your reaction time be faster if you attend to the signal you are waiting for, or if you concentrate on the action you will perform when the signal is given? As was shown long ago by research on reaction time, your reaction will be faster if you attend to the response you are going to perform than if you attend to the stimulus. Attending to the response, however, has one disadvantage—it is more likely to lead to your making a false start. Attending to the stimulus means devoting focal attention to that stimulus and analyzing it to see whether it is the one you are waiting for. Because this analysis takes time, your reaction time is slower. Attending to the reaction, on the other hand, involves relying on preattentive mechanisms to tell you when to respond. This saves time, for you do not devote any time to analyzing the specific features of the stimulus. On the other hand, because preattentive mechanisms tell you little other than that the stimulation has changed, any change, whether it is the one you were waiting for or not, is likely to set off the response.

Now that we have distinguished between processes which a person can and cannot carry out in parallel, we can look at a study of whether a person can select one message rather than another when the two come in on the same channel. Treisman compared the efficiency with which subjects could attend to one desired verbal message and filter out an extraneous one under a variety of conditions.[13] In all cases, the messages were heard at the same time over the same channel. Sometimes one message was in a male voice and the other in a female voice. In other conditions, the voice did not provide strong cues, but either the subject matter or the language of the message differed.

The male and female voices resulted in almost perfect success in attending to one message rather than another, leading Treisman to conclude that the extraneous message was rejected at a stage before its content was analyzed. In other words, preattentive mechanisms seem to be adequate to sort out voices differing greatly in pitch. Much less success was experienced in separating the messages differing in content or language, particularly if the foreign language was known to the listener. Separating these irrelevant messages seemed to depend on analyzing their content and then rejecting it, a process requiring at least intermittent focal attention. The more similar the irrelevant message was to the relevant one, the more time needed to be devoted to understanding it before it could be rejected. When the messages were in the same language and had similar content, the listener got them quite mixed up with one another.

In summary, we see that selective attention operates at several different stages in the perceptual process. First, the individual may pay particular attention to one sensory modality, such as vision or hearing. While information coming in over different sensory channels will not be eliminated completely, it will be greatly reduced, as we saw in the study by Hernández-Peón et al. Next, the individual may use preattentive mechanisms to select only a portion of the incoming stimulation for further analysis. The success of this selective process will depend on whether the differences between the messages are of a type which preattentive mechanisms can recognize. Finally, when the content of the messages is being analyzed by focal attention, some messages may be discarded and others retained. This last process is least efficient, for some of the desired message will undoubtedly be lost while the one which is not desired is being analyzed.

Organization of Perception

INTRODUCTION

Not only is perception an active process in seeking out some stimuli and ignoring others, it is active in that the stimuli which are perceived are organized and transformed in the process. This is perhaps best illustrated in the perception of objects. We have already seen how the shape of an object does not get into the brain but is, instead, coded in other ways. In looking at Hubel and Wiesel's research, we have been able to observe the first stages of this coding. While later stages of coding cannot be observed so directly, they can to a great extent be inferred from what they accomplish. Particularly useful in this respect are visual illusions. The ways in which our perceptual processes can be tricked give some very good indications of what the processes are.

Let us consider an analogy. Suppose that a person was sorting potatoes into good ones and rotten ones, and we wanted to know how he was doing it. There are three ways he might do it. He might look at the potato and see if he saw a dark or moldy spot, smell it and see if it smelled good, or feel it and see whether it felt mushy. If we could not see him and wanted to find out which method he was using, we might disguise some rotten potatoes. Some would have had the moldy spots scrubbed off so they didn't show, but would still smell bad and feel mushy. Others would be treated with artificial essence of new potato, or injected with compounds to make them feel firm. By seeing how the person sorted these potatoes, we could tell what process he usually used to distinguish good and bad ones. If, for example, he rejected all the bad potatoes except the ones treated to make them smell good, it would be a good indication that he was using his nose to make the test.

Similarly, the study of perception has been to a great extent the study of illusions. Whenever we can find an experimental setup which will make a near object seem farther away than a distant object, or a small one seem larger than a big one, we obtain a clue as to how distance and size are usually perceived. In this section we shall therefore look at what visual organizing processes usually achieve and at the ways in which they can be tricked, as an indication of how they work.

THE PERCEPTION OF OBJECTS

When we open our eyes, we do not see the blooming, buzzing confusion which William James thought must characterize the visual experience of the newborn. Instead, we see a world of stable objects. Because of our focal attentive processes, some of these objects stand out clearly in our awareness while the rest recede into the background. This phenomenon, known as a *figure-ground relationship*, is illustrated by reversible figures, such as those in Figure 2-3. Are the knights marching to the right or to the left?

Even more important processes of organization are the ones which enable us to perceive the objects as remaining the same even though the stimulation we are receiving from them is changing. If you look at a plate lying on a table, you see it as round. Unless you are looking straight down on the table, the image on your retina is not round. Your ability to perceive an object as keeping the same shape even though the shape of the retinal image is constantly changing is known as *shape constancy*. Similarly, *size constancy* and *brightness constancy* are names for the perceptual processes which, respectively, make an object seem to remain the same size even when it is moving farther away and the same brightness even though more brightly or more dimly illuminated than when first seen. These types of organization are very important, for they enable us to perceive a world of stable objects rather than a wonderland in which everything is constantly changing its size, shape, and brightness. Our perception manages to go beyond changing aspects of reality and to infer stability behind them.

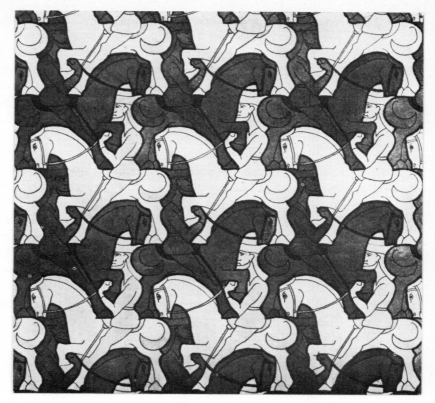

Figure 2–3 *Example of a figure-ground relationship. (Escher[14])*

One of the most basic questions of perception is how we perceive objects at all. I look up and see a lamp standing in front of a bookcase. What is it that makes me assign some stimuli to the lamp and others to the bookcase—to perceive objects rather than simply a complex pattern of various hues and brightnesses? Part of the bookcase is hidden behind the lamp, yet I do not see it as ending where the contours meet. How do I see the part that is behind the lamp? These questions were raised by Max Wertheimer, and they were basic for gestalt psychology.[15]

Some of the main factors which gestalt theorists found to cause stimuli to be grouped together are shown in Figure 2-4. In this figure, part *a* illustrates the principle of *proximity*. In the absence of any other factors of grouping, we will group together things which are close to one another. Part *a* of Figure 2-4 is thus seen as sets of two dots each rather than as just a row of dots. Part *b*, however, illustrates that other factors, such as *similarity*, can override proximity. Even though the figure has the same spacing as in part *a*, the small dots are seen as going together, as are the larger 0s. A second principle of how we organize our perceptions to see objects is therefore that we will perceive similar stimuli as going together. In part *c* of the figure, two intersecting lines are seen. In perceiving these lines, the observer assigns the dots near the intersection point to the pattern with which they are in line rather than to the one they are nearest. This illustrates the factor of *direction* in perceptual organization. Finally, part *d* of the figure shows our bias toward perceiving closed figures rather than open ones. Pairs of lines which are quite far from one another are seen as going together, thereby illustrating the principle of *closure*.

These principles of which stimuli go together usually have *ecological validity*. That is, the nature of the world is such that assigning stimuli to the same or different objects on the basis of these principles will usually lead to accurate, rather than inaccurate, perceptions of where one object stops and another starts. To return to the example of the bookcase and the lamp, the different parts of the

Figure 2–4 *Factors that cause stimuli to be grouped together, according to gestalt theorists.*

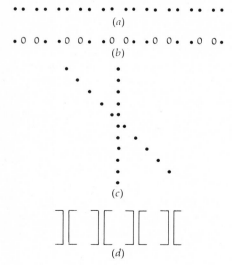

bookcase are similar to one another in color and are, on the average, closer to one another than they are to parts of the lamp. There are few sharp changes of direction of outline of either object, and of course the outline of each forms a closed curve. By using the types of cues which the gestalt theorists have pointed out, I will correctly perceive the bookcase as one object and the lamp as another.

Where unusual conditions make the cues inaccurate, an illusion or a misperception will occur. Each of the cues which we have been considering will be misleading if it causes us to class together sensations which are parts of different objects and not ones which are part of the same object. The principle of similarity, for example, lies behind much camouflage. By coloring things similarly which are part of different structures and coloring things differently which are part of the same structure, the true nature of the objects involved may be concealed.

Some of the most interesting perceptual illusions, developed by Adelbert Ames, Jr., are called the Ames demonstrations in perception. One of them, presented in an article by Ittelson and Kilpatrick, utilizes playing cards held on stands.[16] By cutting a corner off a card which is near the observer so that the cutout just fits the corner of a card that is farther away, the impression is created that the faraway card is obscuring the nearer one. This impression leads to an inaccurate perception on the part of the observer as to which card is closer. The illusion is an illustration of the misguided application of the gestalt principle of direction. The observer assumes that the outline of the card with the cutout does not change direction at the point where it intersects the outline of the whole card, and thus he incorrectly perceives it as a rectangular card obscured by another rectangular card, rather than an irregular card in front of a rectangular card. The observer "sees" the missing part of the card in the same way as I "see" the part of the bookcase which is behind the lamp. Under most circumstances, such an act of perceptual analysis, the outcome of which is called a *completion effect*, leads to accurate results. It is quite improbable that the bookcase is actually nearer to me than the lamp and that it has a cutout to enable me to see the lamp through it. If that really is the case, I will be in error in completing the bookcase.

The Ames demonstrations make another important point about perception. Many of our perceptual processes are unconscious. When we look at the cards in Ittelson and Kilpatrick's demonstration, we do not say to ourselves that one card must be farther from us because another card is interposed between ourselves and it. Instead, we simply *see* it as farthest away, and do not conceive of there being any other possibilities. This type of unconscious interpretation also characterizes social perceptions. Many qualities which we ascribe to other people are our own interpretations of ambiguous stimuli. When we meet someone who has a different interpretation of the same stimulus, we do not understand how this is possible because we incorrectly believe that our interpretation is part of the stimulus.

Besides illusions, there is another source of evidence which shows that visual images are analyzed in terms of the principles of proximity, similarity, direction, and closure. This is the evidence from stabilized images on the retina.

We have already noted that eye movement is necessary to perception, and that an image which is artificially maintained at the same point on the retina will fade and reappear, sometimes as a whole and sometimes by parts. A classic study by Pritchard, Heron, and Hebb indicated that the parts which fade and reappear together are those which would be classed together by the gestalt principles which we have been considering.[17] The effect of proximity was shown in a figure of a circle and a triangle next to each other, for the side of the triangle and the arc of the circle which were nearest together tended to appear and disappear together. Direction was also an important factor. Straight lines always acted as units, as we should expect from Hubel and Wiesel's work. Any smooth curve also tended to stay together as a unit, while parts of jagged lines often disappeared and reappeared independently. Closure was most strikingly shown in the case of one amoebalike figure, which sometimes behaved visually as if one of its pseudopods had been amputated. These visual changes would seem to consist of the activation and fatigue of higher-level visual analyzers than those studied by Hubel and Wiesel.

Innate and Learned Factors in Perception

THE EXTENT OF INNATE FACTORS

Ittelson and Kilpatrick explained the illusions they studied by reference to the past experience of the observer. In the illustration of the cards which we have been discussing, the observer has many times noted similar cases wherein the outline of one object is cut into by the outline of another. On all previous occasions, it has been because the latter object was between him and the former one. It is only the trickery of the experimenter which makes the observer's application of his past experience to the present case incorrect. One way to explain the illusion is to say that the observer unconsciously interprets the stimulation as being caused by what has most frequently caused that type of stimulation in the past, or that he makes use of an *assumptive context* based on past experience. Such an explanation considers the interpretations of the subject, and thus his misperceptions, to be based solely on the learning which he has carried out during his lifetime. This is the empiricist theory of perception.

Standing in opposition to the empiricist theory have been *nativist* theories, which hold that many of the organizational processes in perception are inherited rather than acquired. The gestalt theorists were in this tradition, and they believed that the perception of objects on the basis of cues such as proximity, similarity, direction, and closure was an innate ability of human beings. If this type of explanation is adopted, the validity of the cues we use in making accurate perceptions can be explained on the basis of evolution rather than individual learning. Organisms which based their perceptions on cues which were generally accurate would stand a better chance of surviving than those which based their perceptions on cues which were frequently inaccurate. Evolution would thus favor the use of valid cues if they were inherited rather than learned.

The question of how much of our perceptual ability is learned and how much is acquired is an old one, and many ingenious approaches to the problem have been devised. They include visual-deprivation studies, in which animals are denied normal visual experience and the effects studied; rearrangement studies, in which visual images are inverted, displaced, or distorted; and learning studies with very young children, in which visual experiences are inferred from such simple behaviors as eye fixations. We shall look primarily at this last class of study as providing the most direct evidence on the question. First, however, let us consider one natural experiment which may be the most revealing of all. This is the case of a man who first acquired vision at the age of fifty-two.

EVIDENCE FROM CORNEAL TRANSPLANTS

Some individuals are born with cataracts over their corneas and are able to perceive only the difference between light and dark. Before corneal transplants, the most that could be done for them was an operation which gave them some sight but left them with no lenses in their eyes. Observations on the visual experiences of those individuals when they first acquired sight have been reviewed by von Senden, but they obviously need to be interpreted with considerable caution, since the vision that the individuals acquired was far from normal.

Now that corneal transplants make it possible to give some congenitally blind individuals normal vision, the operation is not delayed until an age when the person can report his experiences on obtaining vision. One such case, however, has been described by Gregory and Wallace,[18] and a brief account of it is also included in Gregory's excellent book on vision, *Eye and Brain*.[19] Because of doubts as to whether the corneal transplants would be successful, the patient, S. B., was not given them until he was fifty-two years of age. He was therefore able to describe his experiences in detail when the operation was successful. Gregory describes the results as follows:

> When the bandages were first removed from his eyes, so that he was no longer blind, he heard the voice of the surgeon. He turned to the voice, and saw nothing but a blur. He realized that this must be a face, because of the voice, but he could not see it. He did not suddenly see the world of objects as we do when we open our eyes.

> But within a few days he could use his eyes to good effect. He could walk along the hospital corridors without recourse to touch; he could even tell the time from a large wall clock, having all his life carried a pocket watch having no glass, so that he could feel the time from its hands. . . .[20]

S. B.'s learning certainly was remarkably fast, suggesting that it was helped along considerably by innate mechanisms. We cannot draw definite conclusions from this case alone, however. His rapid learning may have been due to his using information acquired over the years with his other senses. On the other hand, some innate mechanisms may have deteriorated through long disuse.

While not conclusive, the case does suggest hypotheses similar to those stemming from Hubel and Wiesel's research with the young kittens. Both suggest an intimate interaction between innate factors and learning. In the case of Hubel and Wiesel's study, innate mechanisms for recognizing straight lines seem to be improved through learning experiences with actual lines.[21] In the case of S. B., he apparently did need to learn to perceive a world of objects. That learning, however, seems to have been aided by innate organizing mechanisms of the type suggested by the gestalt theorists. Let us see to what extent this view of the interaction of heredity and environment is supported by studies with young children.

STUDIES OF ATTENTION

One way of studying perception in young children is to see what they pay attention to. Fixations of the eyes and physiological changes such as heart deceleration are indicators of attention which are present right from birth, and many ingenious studies have used them to make inferences about the visual world of the infant. Studies of this type, by himself and others, have recently been reviewed by Jerome Kagan.[22]

Initially, the newborn infant's attention is held by edges contrasting with their background. These would activate the analyzers found by Hubel and Wiesel, with the edge receptors responding when the infant fixated his eyes and those activated by moving images responding when his fixation point moved across the edge. The size of the enclosed figure also seems to be a factor, perhaps corresponding to the activity of higher-level analyzers responding to closure. These attentive mechanisms are obviously adaptive, for they would cause the newborn to pay attention to objects, especially moving ones.

The infant apparently learns to prefer to look at human faces on the basis of these innate preferences. An infant below the age of two or three months does not seem to show any preference between a representation of a human face and a similar pattern with the features rearranged into a different spatial configuration.[23] By the age of a few months, he comes to prefer looking at the face, whereas, later in his development, this preference is reversed and he spends more time looking at the rearranged face. We shall return to this strange finding when we look at the nature of perceptual learning.

A TECHNIQUE UTILIZING LEARNED RESPONSES

If it takes the infant several months to come to prefer a face to a rearranged face, it might be thought that he has few perceptual abilities during this period of time. This, however, is not the case. Ingenious research by Bower indicates that infants have surprising perceptual skills even during this period.[24] His techniques make it possible to learn a great deal about the visual experiences of subjects between one and two months old. Let us look at his procedures and results.

Bower taught the infants to give a response in the presence of a particular stimulus and not to give a response when the stimulus was absent. He then presented stimuli which differed from the training stimulus in various ways. From the frequency with which the infant gave the learned response, the experimenter was able to infer how similar the new stimulus and the training stimulus looked from the infant's point of view.

The difficulty in doing this type of research with a young infant is in finding both a response which the baby can learn and some way of encouraging him to learn it. The response which Bower used was a turn of the head to the side. This is such a natural response for an infant that he can make it several hundred times without apparent fatigue. By placing a microswitch in the side of the baby's headrest, the responses which he gives can be automatically recorded.

To teach the infant the response, Bower also needed a *reinforcer*. This is a stimulus which will increase the probability of an event which it follows. The one which Bower used was the sudden appearance of a woman's smiling face in the infant's field of vision, as in the game of peekaboo. Infants as young as two weeks of age found the peekaboo highly reinforcing, and learned to repeat whatever behavior they were engaging in when it was presented. The basic plan of Bower's experiments was as follows: (1) A peekaboo was given each time the infant turned his head *when the training stimulus was present*. (2) The infant was taught to give the response to the stimulus with the peekaboo presented only one time in five on the average. (3) Various stimuli differing from the training stimulus were presented, and the frequency with which the infant responded to each of them was tabulated. The stimulus to which the infant responded most often was considered most similar to the training stimulus as the infant perceived the world.

One of Bower's experiments dealt with completion effects. A wire triangle, partially obscured by a metal bar passing in front of it, was used as a training stimulus. After training, the infant was tested on a complete triangle, a triangle with a gap where the bar had been, and a triangle above a trapezoid corresponding to the parts of the triangle which had been exposed. If the infant did not show completion effects, he should respond most to one of the incomplete triangles, since they corresponded to what he had actually been able to see of the triangle during training. Instead, the infant responded most frequently to the complete triangle. The infant "sees" the part of the triangle which is obscured by something passing in front of it, even though he is less than sixty days old and has never seen a triangle before. If this perceptual ability is not innate, it is certainly learned early—earlier, even, than his preference for human faces.

DEPTH PERCEPTION AND SIZE CONSTANCY

Bower also tested the infants to find out whether they had depth perception and size constancy. These two are closely related, for size constancy can be maintained only if depth is accurately perceived.

To test the two aspects of vision, Bower first trained an infant to respond to a stimulus of a given size at a given distance. Then he tested him with a stimulus which was farther away but larger, so that the retinal image was the same size; one that was farther away but the same size; and one that was the same distance away but larger. If the infant had size constancy and could perceive distance, he should respond most to both the stimulus that was the same size and the one which was the same distance away, and least to the stimulus which differed in both size and distance. If the infant had neither size constancy nor perception of depth, he should respond most to the stimulus which differed in both size and distance from the training stimulus, for that one projected a retinal image of the same size. Finally, if the infant perceived distance but did not have size constancy, he should respond to the object which was the same distance away as the training object. The fourth possibility, that of the infant's having size constancy without perceiving distance, was considered impossible on the basis that a perception of distance is necessary to size constancy.

How did the infants respond? They apparently had both size constancy and perception of distance, for they responded both to the stimulus which was the same real size as the training stimulus and to the stimulus which was the same distance away as the training stimulus. This is a striking result for an experiment with such young infants.

Finally, Bower tested the infants to find out what cues they used in judging depth. There are many cues which can be used by adults. Two of the most important ones are *binocular parallax* and *motion parallax*. The first is the differences in the images formed by the two eyes because of their being separated in space. It is the cue used in making pictures which appear three-dimensional when viewed through a stereoscope. Two photographs are taken by lenses which are separated just as the eyes are. When one is presented to each eye through the stereoscope, the differences in the two images give a clear impression of depth. Motion parallax, on the other hand, does not depend on having binocular vision. Move your head from side to side while looking at some scene. The objects closest to you are most displaced by the motion, while those farther away seem almost to be moving along with you as you move. This phenomenon also gives strong cues to depth.

Besides these two indicators of depth, however, there are many others. The artist trying to portray depth in a painting cannot use either binocular parallax or motion parallax in doing so. Yet he is able to make a striking portrayal of depth by using such cues as *linear perspective*, the convergence of contours with distance; *aerial perspective*, increased haziness of more distant objects; and *interposition*, the blocking of part of an object by something appearing in front of it. Perhaps the most complete discussion of these varied indicators of depth is that of Gibson in his comprehensive book *The Perception of the Visual World*.[25] He lists thirteen ways in which depth is indicated, eight of which he regards as clearly important!

Of the thirteen possible indicators of depth, which do we really use? There is no single answer to this question, for we use different ones depending on the circumstances. Size is a cue with known objects, for example, and we will see a ball as farther away if we are told that it is a billiard ball than if we are told that it is a ping-pong ball. Yet when size is overruled by a stronger cue, such as interposition, we will see even known objects as being of unusual size.

Knowing that different cues are used to infer depth under different circumstances, one next wonders which ones first signify depth as the organism develops. It seems quite likely that not all of them become effective at the same time, but that depth is first perceived on the basis of some cues and that others are then learned on the basis of being associated with them. By testing what cues the infants used, Bower was able to find out which cues are used first.[26]

He did this by repeating his experiment with various depth cues eliminated. When the cues the infant was using were eliminated, he would start responding most frequently to the object which gave the same size of retinal image as the training object. On this basis, Bower found that young infants made most use of motion parallax in perceiving depth, next most use of binocular parallax, and least use of the types of cues which can be used by an artist in painting a picture. Bower's result is fascinating, for it shows young infants making use of what would seem to be the most complex cues to depth. Despite the complexity of the mental processes which must be involved, the infant perceives depth on the basis of the differences between the views of the two eyes and the ways in which the perception is transformed when the head is moved in space.

Bower's results again suggest the importance of organizational processes of the type studied by the gestalt theorists. The existence of such processes would go a long way to explaining the paradox of how an infant can learn to judge depth by motion parallax before he can learn to recognize a human face. They would also explain the completion effect which his subjects showed. Until even more ingenious researchers find still better ways of investigating the visual world of the newborn infant, the best conclusions which we can draw about innate and learned factors would seem to be as follows:

1. Some visual analyzers are clearly innate.
2. These innate mechanisms are improved through learning.
3. Attention mechanisms based on these analyzers are also innate.
4. Organizational processes based on similarity, proximity, direction, and closure are probably innate. They are definitely present quite early.
5. The individual must learn to perceive objects. This learning, however, is made easy by the existence of the organizing processes.
6. Motion parallax and binocular parallax are the earliest cues to depth, and others are learned on the basis of them.

THE NATURE OF PERCEPTUAL LEARNING

What types of perceptual learning go on as the infant gains experience with the world? One of them we have already considered. Innate analysis involved in perceiving straight lines becomes more accurate. Another major type of learning, considered by Kagan,[27] is the learning of schemata.

A *schema* is a representation of what all members of a class have in common. (Schemata is the plural of schema.) It provides the context by which a new member of the class is interpreted. The nature of experience without this interpretive context is difficult for the adult to grasp, although presumably it is the normal state for the young infant. Sometimes, in states of extreme fatigue, an adult will see the world as a kaleidoscope of sensations without meaning or emotional importance. This is presumably what experience would be like before the development of schemata.

Normally, however, the adult interprets each experience by comparing it with similar experiences in the past, and this comparison process gives it meaning. A word printed on a page in a language known to the reader simply cannot be seen as the abstract, meaningless pattern which the infant must see. Instead, it activates memory processes which cause a partial reexperiencing of similar events in the past. Its meaning appears in experience as immediately as if it were a part of the physical stimulus.

A schema, then, is something more complex than a partial reexperiencing of one event in the past. The word on the page will be recognized whether it is printed or handwritten. The mental representation which it is referred to, like the nonexistent "generalized mammal" of the introductory biology course, abstracts something from each member of its class without being identical to any one of them.

The recognition of a three-dimensional object similarly involves more than equating two identical experiences. An object may be viewed from many different angles, and it will look different from each of them. The infant thus needs to develop a schema which is a mental representation of how the object is transformed as his viewpoint is changed.

A study by Super, Kagan, et al. illustrates the development of schemata and shows one of the consequences of developing them.[28] From a variety of studies, it appears that infants devote most attention to stimuli which are moderately different from their expectations. When the infant has developed a schema for an object, that object itself is no longer interesting. A radically different object, which is probably experienced as meaningless, is not very interesting either. What does interest the infant is an object that is somewhat different from the familiar one but still recognizably related to it. This principle, called the *discrepancy principle*, applies to adults also under some conditions. People seem, for example, to be equally bored by hearing an overly familiar musical recording and by hearing a selection in a completely alien musical tradition. A new selection in a familiar tradition, on the other hand, can capture a person's attention.

It represents a moderate, rather than a slight or an extreme, deviation from his expectations.

Super, Kagan, et al. used eye-fixation time as the main indication of attention. Their experiment involved first determining the visual responses of four-month-old infants to a three-dimensional stimulus. The stimulus was composed of four objects of different shapes and colors, arranged as a mobile. The length of time each infant fixed his eyes on this mobile in the laboratory was determined first so that changes in fixation time as a result of learning could be studied.

The infants were then divided into a number of groups, and the members of each group were given a different learning experience at home. One group, which served as a control, received no special learning experiences. Others were repeatedly exposed to mobiles more or less similar to the test stimulus in the laboratory.

The exposure to a mobile hung above his crib for 30 minutes a day for three weeks enabled each infant to develop a schema for it. The question was how the development of this schema would influence his attention to the mobile in the laboratory. The prediction from the discrepancy principle was that the effect of the learning would depend on how different the home mobile was from the laboratory one. If it was identical or nearly identical, the schema which was developed would correspond so closely to the laboratory mobile that the laboratory mobile would no longer be very interesting. Those infants who had viewed a mobile moderately different from the laboratory one, on the other hand, should find the laboratory mobile quite interesting, for it would be moderately different from their schema. Finally, those exposed at home to a very discrepant mobile should find the laboratory mobile less interesting.

These predictions were supported by the results. Moderate discrepancy between the schema which had been developed and the object which was viewed resulted in maximum attention to the object.

The discrepancy principle can also help us to make sense of the puzzling result mentioned earlier on preference for human faces. As you will remember, the infant first showed no preference between a representation of a face and one of a rearranged face. Next, he came to prefer the normal face, and finally, he began to spend the most time looking at the rearranged face. These three stages would correspond to the lack of a schema for faces, the beginning of such a

schema, and the thorough development of one. At first, without a relevant schema, the infant would have no preference. When he first
started developing one, it would still be quite inadequate to represent the variety which is found in faces, and the representation of a
face to which he was exposed would be discrepant enough from his
expectations to be interesting. Finally, when the schema was well
enough developed, normal faces would hold no surprises for him
and he would find the rearranged faces more fascinating.

The discrepancy principle may not be able to account for all the
results on looking at rearranged faces, however. The schema for faces
is probably reasonably complete by the age of a year, yet fixation
times to rearranged faces continue to increase until the age of three.
This increase probably corresponds, as suggested by Kagan, to the
development of hypothesis testing in the child.

ASSIMILATION AND CONTRAST EFFECTS

We have seen how the infant develops mental representations which
give meaning to his experiences, and how the amount of discrepancy
from his expectations is a major determinant of attention. If that were
the only result of the development of schemata, they would still be
important. They have, however, a more important effect. They influence the perception of new stimuli in ways which introduce systematic errors into our perceptions. It was the effect of schemata on the
perception of other stimuli, in fact, which first led to their discovery.

As we have seen, it is comparing new experiences with
previous ones which makes the new ones meaningful. This leads to
two basic types of error in interpreting the new experience. If it is
quite similar to the old one, differences are not noted and it is incorrectly perceived as virtually identical to the old experience. This is
known as *assimilation*. If, on the other hand, it differs from the old experience sufficiently for that difference to be noticeable, then the difference will be exaggerated in evaluating the new experience. This is
called *contrast*.

As Sherif and Hovland have amply documented in their book
Social Judgment, assimilation and contrast effects are found in a very
wide range of situations in which a person makes judgments about
a stimulus.[29] Even a blindfolded person trying to tell at what point
on his body he was touched shows this type of effect. He uses the
nearest joint as a reference point. If he was touched near that joint, he

will judge the point to have been nearer to the joint than it actually was, an assimilation effect. If the point where he was touched was quite far from any joint, he will show a contrast effect and perceive it as being even farther from the joint than it was.

If assimilation and contrast effects are caused by comparing the new stimulus or experience with one which is familiar, then the way the new stimulus is evaluated can be changed by changing the comparison points available to the person. This is illustrated in simple psychophysical experiments in which a person judges the weights of various objects.

Suppose that you give a person a large number of weights which differ in heaviness. You ask him to lift each weight once, to get an idea of the range of weight involved. Then you ask him to sort them into a given number of categories (seven, for example). You do not define the categories in any way except by telling him to arrange them so that each category differs from the two adjacent ones by approximately the same weight.

With these instructions, he will sort the weights so that the categories are reasonably equally spaced along the continuum from light to heavy. He may tend to put more weights into the categories of the lightest and of the heaviest weights than he puts into the other categories, however. There is some tendency to use the two end categories as *anchor points* or *reference points,* standards with which the weights are compared. This causes slight assimilation effects near the ends of the scale.

These effects can be made much stronger by changing the instructions. Suppose that you show the subject the heaviest weight in the group and tell him that it is the heaviest he will encounter. Furthermore, you tell him that he can lift that weight before lifting each of the others, so that he can compare them with it. By doing this, you make him develop a very strong schema for that weight or, in other words, make it his main reference point. He will now show very strong assimilation and contrast effects. Weights toward the heavy end of the scale will be sorted into heavier categories than they were under the other instructions, an assimilation effect. Those far from the reference point will be judged as lighter than they are. In other words, providing a stronger schema for a particular reference point will cause more assimilation and contrast around that reference point.

In our perception of attitude statements, just as strong assimilation and contrast effects are found as in our judgment of physical stimuli. Usually the individual's own attitude serves as his main reference point, and assimilation and contrast occur around it. In other words, he perceives attitude positions similar to his own as even more similar than they are, while he exaggerates how much his attitudes differ from those of people who do in fact disagree quite a bit with him. The stronger his own attitude is, the stronger schema he has and the more his perception of other positions is distorted. This distortion is not symmetrical, however. The stronger his attitude, the more positions he contrasts with his own and the fewer he assimilates to it.

The way in which contrast effects increase with strength of feeling about an issue can help us to understand the process of polarization of opinion which occurs when something becomes an important social issue. Before some particular question develops into a major issue, most people have not thought about it and do not have strong feelings about it. During this period they will assimilate more than they will contrast, and support for middle-of-the-road positions will be great since these will be assimilated by the majority who do not hold strong opinions. Political compromise seems, at such a time, to be a law of nature, or at least a law of the workings of the political system. Examples from history might include the middle-of-the-road position on the Catholic-Protestant issue adopted by Elizabeth I, the great compromises on the slavery issue in the United States Congress during the period of westward expansion, and the initial minor involvement in Vietnam from the time of Eisenhower through Johnson's first administration.

Elizabeth, however, was followed by James, and Henry Clay by Jefferson Davis. As the emerging issue was debated, each individual developed a strong schema for his own position. Not only did more individuals hold more extreme views on the issue, they held their beliefs with a fervor which caused them to assimilate less and contrast more of the range of opinion. Because both sides contrasted middle-of-the-road positions, compromise now seemed as impossible as it had earlier seemed inevitable. In the case of the slavery issue, this is perhaps best illustrated in the vehement attacks which strong abolitionists made on Lincoln. In the Vietnam issue, it is perhaps best exemplified by one member of congress who stated on television that he believed in either escalating the war or withdrawing, and he didn't care which.

These few examples may help to illustrate that the same perceptual processes which are studied in the laboratory can have important consequences in the real world. This is further illustrated in an example from de Rivera's book *The Psychological Dimension of Foreign Policy*.[30] Relating to Truman and MacArthur, it deals with judgments of complex stimuli which differ in many ways.

Stimuli in the real world do not just differ from one another in their values along a single dimension, as the weights in a psychophysical experiment do. Instead, they differ on many dimensions. The schemata which an individual brings to a real-life social judgment may cause him to emphasize some of these dimensions and neglect others. Assimilation to his schemata in these circumstances may cause great distortions of perception. This was the case in de Rivera's example. It deals with the perceptions which President Truman and General MacArthur had of American policy and of each other during the Korean war.

As de Rivera points out, Truman and MacArthur lived in different worlds. Truman was first and foremost a politician. The building of coalitions, the development of political power, and the taking of positions on complex issues were the stuff of which his working life was made. MacArthur, while a brilliant military strategist, did not perceive the subtleties of policy and politics with which Truman dealt. (In fact, he may have felt morally superior to them.)

Truman and the State Department tried, during the Korean war, to follow a complex policy: to defend South Korea, but to avoid intervening in the Chinese civil war; to defend Formosa, but to keep from becoming too closely tied to Chiang Kai-shek; to get the United Nations to support United States policy, but to go along with some deviations from U. S. policy to maintain United Nations support. This may or may not have been a good policy position. Its major goals were to maintain the status quo regarding territory in the Far East while making possible some reconciliation with the Chinese Communists. It was hoped that they could, in this way, be made more independent of the Soviet Union, as Yugoslavia had been, earlier.

MacArthur, on the other hand, saw the Korean war as almost a holy war against communism. When Truman made a decision, MacArthur asked himself what would have made him make that decision. Since he did not understand the political reasons for Truman's actions, he concluded that Truman had been misled by bad advisers and did not understand the Far Eastern situation. Another consequence of this perception was that he himself frequently made statements which did much to destroy the policy position that Truman was trying to create.

Truman, in turn, interpreted MacArthur's statements by assimilating them to his own strongest schema. Truman, the politician, saw MacArthur's speeches as carefully calculated political moves designed to undermine American policy and his authority as President. Ultimately, the two men came to view each other with contempt. MacArthur regarded Truman as a bungling fool, while Truman saw MacArthur as an insubordinate conniver. Governmental policies are made by human beings, and the perceptual processes by which they relate to one another may have important consequences for those policies. In the case of the interaction between Truman and MacArthur, the consequences were disastrous.

Summary

Receptor cells in the retina transmit nerve impulses through the lateral geniculate body to the cortex in the form of coded electrical impulses. An electrical impulse from a group of retinal cells indicates a specific event, such as that something in the visual field is moving left, has a straight edge, or is oriented at a particular angle away from the vertical. Research by Hubel and Wiesel revealed cortical cells which have their own arrangements of retinal cells which turn the cortical cells on or off by means of such electrical messages. Tiny motions of the eye occur constantly, and this activity is necessary for the perception of even stationary objects.

Perception by our other receptor organs and their analyzing systems in the brain is similar to visual perception in three important ways: the use of complex systems of analysis, the coding of information into electrical impulses, and the active seeking out of informatory stimulation from the environment. Preattentive mechanisms of perception carry on a crude analysis all the time, whereas focal attention allows concentration on one perception instead of on all uniformly at once.

Psychological analysis of perceptual processes is facilitated by analyzing how our perceptions can be tricked. The use of perceptual illusions helped reveal the visual phenomena of figure-ground relationship and the principles of shape, size, and brightness constancy. They enabled gestalt theorists to discover the principles of proximity, similarity, direction, and closure. Physiological studies and experimental research are beginning to show the physiological bases for these phenomena.

Our personal perception of our own visual reality is to a very large extent the result of interpreting rather ambiguous stimuli. Many qualities which we ascribe to the world and to other individuals are the result of our synthesizing and analyzing phenomena which can be given more than one type of interpretation. This can explain why various people can have very different perceptions of complex situations.

How a given person comes to perceive what he does has been explained historically by the empiricist theory of perception as the result of an assumptive context, and by the nativist theories as the result of inherited tendencies. Visual-deprivation studies and studies of infant vision show some basic innate systems for paying attention to and organizing raw stimuli. These systems make possible the experiential learning which seems to be necessary before we can perceive stable objects.

The recognition of an object as being familiar seems to involve the comparison of ongoing stimulation with a schema representing an earlier pattern of stimulation. When the new pattern of stimulation differs from the one with which it is being compared, assimilation and contrast effects may be found. These effects are important in the interpretation of social and historical events as well as of physical objects.

Notes and Acknowledgments

1. Hubel, David H., and Torsten N. Wiesel. "Receptive fields of single neurones in the cat's striate cortex." *Journal of Physiology*, 1959 (148), pp. 574–591.
   Wiesel, Torsten N., and David H. Hubel. "Effects of visual deprivation on morphology and physiology of cells in the cat's lateral geniculate body." *Journal of Neurophysiology*, 1963 (26), pp. 978–993.
   Hubel, David H., and Torsten N. Wiesel. "Receptive fields of cells in striate cortex of very young, visually inexperienced kittens." *Journal of Neurophysiology*, 1963 (26), pp. 994–1002.

Wiesel, Torsten N., and David H. Hubel. "Single-cell response in striate cortex of kittens deprived of vision in one eye." *Journal of Neurophysiology*, 1963 (26), pp. 1003-1017.

Hubel, David H. "The visual cortex of the brain." *Scientific American*, November 1963.

2. Hubel, David H. "The visual cortex of the brain." *Scientific American*, November 1963, bottom of p. 57. Copyright © 1963 by Scientific American, Inc. All rights reserved.

3. Hubel, David H., and Torsten N. Wiesel. "Receptive fields of cells in striate cortex of very young, visually inexperienced kittens." Op. cit.

4. Gibson, James L. *The Perception of the Visual World*. Boston: Houghton Mifflin Company, 1950, p. 9. By permission of the publisher.

5. More detailed information on the human senses may be found in Douglas K. Candland, *Psychology: The Experimental Approach*. New York: McGraw-Hill Book Company, 1968. An interesting discussion of perception as involving information processing may be found in Kent Dallett, *Problems of Psychology*. New York: John Wiley & Sons, Inc., 1969.

6. A useful introduction to the research on sleep is Ian Oswald, *Sleep*. Harmondsworth, Middlesex, England: Penguin Books, Inc., 1966. Research on dreaming is discussed in William C. Dement, "An essay on dreams: The role of physiology in understanding their nature," in Frank Barron et al., *New Directions in Psychology II*. New York: Holt, Rinehart and Winston, Inc., 1965, pp. 135-257.

7. Lindsley, D. B., J. Bowden, and H. W. Magoun. "Effect upon the EEG of acute injury to the brain stem activating system."*EEG and Clinical Neurophysiology*, 1949 (1), pp. 475-486.

8. Moruzzi, G., and H. W. Magoun. "Brain stem reticular formation and activation of the EEG." *EEG and Clinical Neurophysiology*, 1949 (1), pp. 455–473.

9. See Campbell, Louise. "Clues from a chemical." *Science News*, Oct. 3, 1970 (98), pp. 287–289.

10. Dement, W., and C. Fisher. "Experimental interference with the sleep cycle." *Canadian Psychiatric Association Journal*, 1963 (8), pp. 400–405.

11. Hernández-Peón, Raúl, Harald Scherrer, and Michel Jouvet. "Modification of electric activity in cochlear nucleus during 'attention' in unanesthetized cats." *Science*, February 1956 (123), pp. 331–332. Photograph, p. 331, reproduced by permission of The American Association for the Advancement of Science.

12. A more advanced treatment of parallel and serial processing in visual perception may be found in Ulric Neisser, *Cognitive Psychology*. New York: Appleton-Century-Crofts, Inc., 1966.

13. Treisman, Anne M. "Verbal cues, language, and meaning in selective attention." *American Journal of Psychology*, 1964 (77), pp. 215–216.

14. Escher, Maurits C. "Knights on Horseback." By kind permission of the artist.

15. Wertheimer, Max. "Laws of organization in perceptual forms," in Willis D. Ellis (Ed.), *A Source Book of Gestalt Psychology*. New York: Humanities Press, 1955, pp. 71–88.

16. Ittelson, William H., and F. P. Kilpatrick. "Experiments in perception." *Scientific American*, August 1951.
17. Pritchard, R. M., W. Heron, and D. O. Hebb. "Visual perception approached by the method of stabilized images." *Canadian Journal of Psychology*, 1960 (4), pp. 67–77.
18. Gregory, R. L., and J. G. Wallace. "Recovery from early blindness: A case study." *Experimental Psychology Society Monograph*, no. 2, Cambridge, England, 1963.
19. Gregory, R. L. *Eye and Brain: The Psychology of Seeing*. New York: McGraw-Hill Book Company, World University Library, 1966.
20. Ibid., p. 194. By permission of McGraw-Hill Book Company.
21. Hubel, David H., and Torsten N. Wiesel. "Receptive fields of cells in striate cortex in very young, visually inexperienced kittens." Op. cit.
22. Kagan, Jerome. "Attention and psychological change in the young child." *Science*, Nov. 20, 1970 (170), pp. 826–832.
23. Fantz, Robert L. "Visual perception and experience in early infancy: A look at the hidden side of behavior development," in H. W. Stevenson, E. H. Hess, and H. L. Rheingold (Eds.), *Early Behavior: Comparative and Developmental Approaches*. New York: John Wiley & Sons, Inc., 1967.
24. Bower, T. G. R. "The visual world of infants." *Scientific American*, December 1966.
25. Gibson, James J. *The Perception of the Visual World*. Boston: Houghton Mifflin Company, 1950.
26. Bower, T. G. R. Op. cit.
27. Kagan, Jerome. Op. cit.
28. Super, C., J. Kagan, F. Morrison, M. Haith, and J. Weiffenbach. Unpublished manuscript cited in Jerome Kagan, op. cit.
29. Sherif, Muzafer, and Carl I. Hovland. *Social Judgment*. New Haven: Yale University Press, 1961.
30. de Rivera, Joseph. *The Psychological Dimension of Foreign Policy*. Columbus, Ohio: Charles E. Merrill Books, Inc., 1968.

THREE

LEARNING

Introduction

Anyone who has experienced an organized classroom education will recognize the man in the photograph opposite as a teacher. The expression on his face, and his whole physical bearing, show confidence in his ability to teach, and in the ability of his students to learn. He is teaching the reading and writing of Spanish to children of the Peruvian jungle whose cultural heritage includes no written language at all.

The ability of children to absorb new cultural ways by learning, rather than by inheritance, was one of the great surprises for Europeans during their scientific explorations of the sixteenth through nine-teenth centuries. Education became a topic of absorbing interest to them. New religious orders were founded upon the vocation of teaching, and of course the discovery of the central role which learn-ing plays in shaping human behavior made it especially important in the field of psychology. Learning enters, in one way or another, into almost every chapter in this book. In this chapter, we shall focus on what it is and on what similarities in process underlie the diversity of its results.

At first, it seems obvious what learning is. An attempt to define it, however, demonstrates that it cannot be directly observed, but must instead be inferred from our observations. Let us consider an example. You observe a person shooting pool with relatively little success. As he plays longer and longer, his playing gets better and better. It seems that he is learning how to play pool, for generally we infer learning from a change in performance.

Learning is not the only thing which influences performance, however. Perhaps he was not trying to play well before, but instead deliberately doing badly in order to hustle the people with whom he was playing. Performance depends upon motivation as well as on learning. Similarly, drugs and fatigue lead to changes in performance which we would not ascribe to learning. We thus need to define learning not just as a change in performance, but as a change in per-formance which cannot be accounted for in terms of other factors such as motivation, fatigue, or chemical agents.

Innate Foundations of Learning

PERCEPTUAL SKILLS

Because learning is a change in the organism, it is important to con-sider what is built into the organism before learning takes place. First, as we learned in looking at perception, the organizm is innately endowed with some quite complex perceptual skills. Recent research suggests that, in cats, these innate perceptual skills may even include the ability to code numbers. Just as Hubel and Wiesel studied visual perception by placing electrodes in single neurons in the cat's visual cortex and studying what stimuli would make the cells fire, Thomp-son and his colleagues studied thought by recording the firing of single neurons in the association areas of the brain where ideas are related to each other.[1] In doing so, they found some cells which would fire when the cat was presented with a certain number of stimuli regardless of what the stimuli were. A "number 6" cell, for example, fires when the cat is presented with six stimuli in a row, whether the stimuli are sounds, flashes of light, or mild electric shocks. A "number 2" cell, similarly, responds when there are two stimuli in the series.

Not only do the cats have brain cells responding to numbers up through seven, but there are indications that the number analyzers may be innate rather than learned. When an eight-day-old kitten was tested, it was found to have a similar mechanism although, as in the case of the visual analyzers found by Hubel and Wiesel, the mechanism was somewhat less accurate in the younger animal than in the fully grown cats. Further research may reveal still other innate perceptual skills.

CONTROL OF MOVEMENT

A second important characteristic of the organism is the innate ability to produce certain coordinated muscular responses. It is obvious that the particular structure of bones and muscles in an organism enables it to make certain movements rather than others. Less obvious are the ways in which the central nervous system participates in the production of these movements. Two of these ways are quite important. First, the nervous system is involved in the control of *antagonistic muscles*, muscles which have opposite effects. In order to bend your arm at the elbow, you need to do two things—contract the muscles which flex your arm and relax those which extend it. Reflex connections between the two sets of muscles automatically relax one set when the other set is contracted.

Besides coordinating antagonistic muscles, the nervous system participates in creating certain specific movements. These innate movement patterns are called *fixed action patterns*, and are very important in instinctive behavior. If you give zoo animals toys and observe their activities, as Glickman and Sroges did, you will notice that different species do characteristically different things with them.[2] The cats, for example, will show such behaviors as stalking the object, pouncing on it, batting it with the paws, and biting it. These specific action patterns, which differ from those that a monkey or a rat would show, are innately built into the organism and serve as the building blocks for more complex learned behavior.

The role of the brain in organizing movement patterns has been demonstrated in a number of lower organisms. Take, for example, the undulating movements of the eel. It was once thought that this motion was organized in a very simple way by each segment activating the next either mechanically or through a very simple neural connection. As the work of E. v. Holst has shown, this is not the case.[3] Holst cut the sensory pathways in an eel so that its internal sensory organs became ineffective while the motor pathways from the brain to the muscles were left intact. The eel continued to show regular undulations, proving that the movement pattern was organized in the brain. Two additional points are worth making about this study. The possibility that mechanical stimulation transmits the wave of contraction was ruled out by mechanically restraining the middle one-third of the eel's body. The motion appeared at the tail end right on time, even though it could not be mechanically transmitted through the middle portion. Finally, this study, along with many others, illustrates that living organisms are spontaneously active, rather than that they respond only when externally stimulated.

Much less research has been done on fixed action patterns in man, partially because of the obvious impossibility of using surgical techniques to investigate them. An excellent review of some of the known innate patterns is given by Eibl-Eibesfeldt.[4] They include patterns involved in eating, affiliation, the acquisition of locomotion, and emotional expression. (The material on emotional expression includes some noteworthy photographs of facial expressions of children blind from birth.) Differences in fixed action patterns may be an important aspect of sexual difference also. If research on lower organisms is any indication, the hormones present early in a child's life may serve to organize the action patterns characteristic of each sex and to provide a basis for later sexual learning.

STIMULUS-RESPONSE CONNECTIONS

Besides perceptual skills and fixed action patterns, organisms are innately endowed with some stimulus-response connections. The simplest of these are reflexes, such as a flash of light causing the pupil of your eye to contract or a touch on the palm calling out a grasping reflex from an infant. Many of these reflexes are so simple that the response pattern does not need to be organized in the brain. More complex stimulus-response connections involve fairly complex fixed action patterns, and are called out not just by one stimulus but by any one of a class of stimuli. The stimuli which call out innate behavior patterns are called *releasers.* Let us look at some examples in the area of aggressive behavior.

Different motivational systems are in operation in the attack of predators on prey and in aggressive behavior between members of the same species.[5] The control of fighting between members of the same species generally involves not only releasers which will initiate fighting behavior, but also submissive behaviors which will terminate it. Even more striking, fighting between members of the same species is usually carried out without the animals' using their most dangerous weapons. A giraffe, for example, will use only its short horns to fight another giraffe, but it will kick a predator with its hoof, which is much more likely to be lethal.

One of the first releasers of intraspecies fighting behavior to be studied was the threat behavior of a small fish called the three-spined stickleback.[6] In the male stickleback, fighting behavior is called out by the red abdomen and vertical posture of a threatening male, whereas courting behavior is called out by the swollen abdomen of a gravid female. The vertical posture and red abdomen of the male are thus releasers for aggressive behavior, and the swollen abdomen of the female is a releaser for courtship. Since the research on the stickleback, many other species have been studied. Often the threat behaviors releasing aggression are displays which make the threatening animal look larger, as the cat or wolf looks bigger when its fur stands on end. Appeasement gestures, on the other hand, usually make the animal look small and defenseless. In a dog or wolf, cringing or rolling on the back indicates submission and will generally inhibit further attack by a member of the same species.

MOTIVATION

A final basis of learning which is built into the organism is motivation. Motives serve both to activate the organism, as when a hungry animal seeks food, and to strengthen learned responses when those responses lead to conditions satisfying the motive. A hungry animal which finds food in a certain place is more likely to go to that place again than it would be if it hadn't found food there. A stimulus which satisfies a motive, and thus increases the probability of a response which it follows, is called a *positive reinforcer.* A *negative rein-*

forcer is an aversive stimulus, such as an electric shock. A negative reinforcer may also serve to strengthen a response if the response leads to the termination of the negative reinforcer. Strengthening a response in either way is called *reinforcement*.

Punishment, on the other hand, consists of following the response either with a negative reinforcer or with the termination of a positive reinforcer. As we shall see in a later section, the effects of punishment are more complex than those of reinforcement.

Some Basic Types of Learning

BECOMING FAMILIAR WITH A STIMULUS

When psychologists first began the experimental study of learning, they concentrated their efforts on studies of giving a response to a stimulus, such as Pavlov's studies of a dog learning to salivate to the sound of a bell. A major reason for concentrating on this area of study was that it seemed to represent the simplest possible kind of learning. Today, however, even simpler forms of learning are known. The simplest of these forms is becoming familiar with a stimulus.

If you make a strange sound near a dog, such as by ringing a bell, the dog will usually prick up its ears and turn its head toward the source of the sound. As you could also learn by noting changes in the pattern of electrical activity in its brain, the dog is paying attention to the sound. If you repeat the sound at regular intervals, the dog will stop cocking its ears and paying attention. It is now familiar with the sound.

Quite early, a baby learns that certain faces presented to him all represent his mother, regardless of differences in lighting, and poses, and expressions; and that there are other faces which are not part of the schema he recognizes as "Mother's face." From that time, the process of becoming familiar with stimuli is an important part of much learning. If you look at Turkish writing, or listen to a person speaking Greek, you are impressed only by the uniform unfamiliarity of the stimuli. If you continue your exposure to the new language, however, you will begin to notice that some sounds or shapes are repeated. As you start to build up schemata for them, the familiar stimuli become pleasant, just as human faces come to be pleasing to the infant whose face-schema is just developing. Research by Zajonc, for example, shows that people prefer Turkish words to which they have most often been exposed to Turkish words to which they have had less exposure.[7] Even if you do not know what the words stand for, they now have meaning for you in that you recognize them as something you have been exposed to before. If a language uses different sounds or a different alphabet from any which you already know, a considerable amount of learning may need to take place just in becoming familiar with it. When familiarity with a stimulus is achieved, the stimulus functions as a perceptual unit, and exposure to part of it will remind you of the rest. You do not need to read every letter to recognize the word "rhinoceros."

HOW SOME STIMULI BECOME REINFORCING

A second simple type of learning occurs when a stimulus acquires reinforcing properties. The simplest example is found in *imprinting*, the type of learning by which young chicks, goslings, and ducklings acquire the tendency to follow their mothers. The young of these species are born with an innate tendency to follow. The stimulus which calls out this tendency, however, has to be learned. Shortly after hatching, the animal enters a critical period during which it will follow any moving object approximating a certain size, or even a flashing light. Using the terms introduced in the last section, we call the following behavior a fixed action pattern, and note that the moving or flashing stimulus is a releaser for this behavior.

As soon as the animal has become imprinted on a particular stimulus, it will follow that stimulus for months without any further learning experience. If, on the other hand, the animal is not imprinted early in its life, it seems to lose the ability to carry out this learning. It is easy to see that this is quite an adaptive mechanism for the young animal. Under most natural circumstances, the first moving object a chick, gosling, or duckling sees will be the mother bird, and the interaction of innate and learned factors will make it follow not just any chicken, goose, or duck but only its own parent.

It is obvious that, in imprinting, the animal has learned to connect up an innate behavior pattern to some stimulus, so that this stimulus will reliably call it out in the future. Because the behavior pattern is a rewarding one for the animal, the imprinted stimulus also becomes a positive reinforcer. After imprinting, the animal will not only follow the imprinted stimulus; it will perform tasks or learn new behaviors for the reward of being presented with the imprinted stimulus.

Imprinting is thus similar to the learning of a food preference. In both cases, the animal learns to use a particular object in the expression of a motive, and this makes the object into a positive reinforcer or reward. This learning to express motives toward certain objects has been given a number of names—*cathexis learning* or *object choice*, by personality theorists, and the *learning of preferences* or the *acquisition of secondary reinforcement properties*, by learning theorists. Whatever it is called, it is a type of learning which may have great significance for the future behavior of the organism, as two studies will show. Schutz imprinted mallard ducks on ducks of a different species.[8] When the ducks matured, they flocked with other ducks of their own species, but expressed their sexual instincts on the species they had been imprinted on. That similar processes may be involved in higher mammals is shown in research by Harlow.[9] Monkeys raised in the laboratory without contact with other monkeys failed to show normal sexual behavior toward other monkeys when they reached maturity. Those which did become mothers (through artificial insemination) also failed to show normal maternal behavior toward their offspring. These studies will be discussed at more length in later chapters.

The second simple type of learning may therefore be briefly summarized as follows: Certain behavior patterns are positively reinforcing when they are released. Stimulus objects which release these behavior patterns become strongly positively reinforcing themselves. They may be sought out when a relevant motive is activated, further strengthening the tendency to express the motive toward these particular objects.

COMBINING RESPONSE UNITS

Besides becoming familiar with a stimulus and making it a reinforcer, a third simple type of learning is the combination of response patterns. Tie a spool on a string and hang it on the rung of a kitchen chair. If you show this contrivance to a kitten that has never had such a toy, the kitten will spend a good deal of time batting the spool in various ways—lying on its back and juggling it from one paw to another, reaching around the leg of the chair and catching it with its claws, and so on. This type of activity, which characterizes much human and animal play, seems to involve the combination of fixed action patterns into new skills. In learning to play basketball, sign your name, play the piano, or fly an airplane, much of the process consists of building up new habitual response units out of simpler components.

Stimulus-Response Learning

CLASSICAL CONDITIONING

Many important phenomena of learning can be observed in the type of learning situation first studied by Ivan Pavlov at the beginning of the twentieth century. Pavlov, winner of a Nobel Prize for physiology, became interested in learning through his research on the digestive system. He noticed that a dog would not only salivate when meat powder was placed in its mouth, a simple reflex, but would also salivate when someone rattled its food pan. This second basis of salivation was obviously learned. Pavlov named it "psychic secretion," and undertook a program of research to discover how the learning took place.

After making arrangements to collect and measure the dog's saliva, Pavlov presented a stimulus, such as a bell, and followed it by putting meat powder into the dog's mouth. The first time he did this, the dog did not salivate until the meat was in its mouth. After the bell and the meat had been paired a few times, the dog started salivating a little as soon as it heard the bell. This response of salivating to the bell became stronger and stronger as the bell and meat were presented together again and again until eventually a limit was reached. A dog can only produce saliva at a certain rate, no matter how sure it is that it is about to receive a delicious dinner.

The first stage of training, in which the dog learns to salivate to the bell, is called the *acquisition phase*, since the dog is acquiring the learned response. Pavlov called the meat powder the *unconditional stimulus* because it always called out salivation regardless of what learning experiences the dog had had, and the salivation to it the *unconditional response* for the same reason. Because of the way the terms were first translated from the Russian, these terms in English have become *unconditioned stimulus* (abbreviated UCS) and *unconditioned response* (abbreviated UCR).

Similarly, the bell was called the *conditional stimulus* or *conditioned stimulus* (CS), because its effect was conditional upon what training the dog had received. Salivation to the bell was called the *conditional response* or *conditioned response* (CR).

The course of acquisition may now be reviewed, using these terms: Initially, before any training, the unconditioned stimulus of meat powder calls out the unconditioned response of salivation to meat powder, as in Figure 3-1, part *a*. The first acquisition trial is shown in Figure 3-1, part *b*. The conditioned stimulus is presented first, followed by the unconditioned stimulus. The conditioned stimulus does not call out any salivation at this point, but the unconditioned stimulus does, of course. Finally, after a number of training trials, we observe the situation portrayed in Figure 3-1, part *c*. Now the conditioned stimulus of the bell calls out salivation just as the unconditioned stimulus of meat powder does. Because saliva looks pretty much the same regardless of what calls it out, the conditioned response and the unconditioned response are indistinguishable in this learning situation.

Besides the attachment of the conditioned response to the conditioned stimulus, there are two other types of learning going on during the acquisition phase. First, the dog is becoming familiar with the bell. Second, through the bell's being paired with the reinforcing event of meat powder being put into the dog's mouth, the bell is acquiring reinforcing properties. If we present the dog with a new stimulus, such as a flash of light, and then follow it with the bell, the dog will learn to salivate to the flash of light even though it is never followed by meat powder. This use of a conditioned stimulus to reinforce new learning Pavlov called *higher-order conditioning*.

After the dog has acquired the conditioned response, other aspects of learning and performance may be demonstrated. Suppose that you repeatedly ring the bell without following it with the meat powder. The dog will come to salivate less and less to the bell, a process known as *extinction*. Extinction is not the same thing as forgetting, but seems to correspond more to the dog's learning not to respond. This may be shown in two ways.

First, a dog which has undergone training and then extinction

Figure 3–1   *The acquisition of a conditioned response.*

	CS	CS ⟶ CR
UCS ⟶ UCR	UCS ⟶ UCR	UCS ⟶ UCR
(*a*)	(*b*)	(*c*)

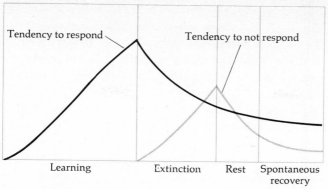

Figure 3–2 *The process of spontaneous recovery.*

can be given a vacation. After a few days without receiving the conditioned stimulus, the dog is tested again. Under these circumstances, the conditioned response reappears, a process known as *spontaneous recovery*. Its explanation is rather complex:

Learned material is forgotten most rapidly immediately after it is learned. In the case of the dog, acquisition took place before extinction. This means that by the end of extinction, the tendency to respond is not being forgotten as fast as the tendency not to respond is, since the tendency not to respond was acquired more recently and is still on the steepest part of the forgetting curve. During the rest period, the dog forgets more of its later tendency not to respond than it does of its earlier tendency to respond, so that at the end of the rest period its tendency to respond is relatively stronger.

This process is shown in Figure 3-2. The tendency to respond is shown by the black line. It becomes stronger during the initial period of learning, and weaker from then on as forgetting takes place. During the extinction training, the animal acquires a tendency to not respond, shown by the gray line. The extent to which the animal will salivate at any moment in time is shown by the relative heights of the black and gray lines. As can be seen in the figure, the gray line is higher at the start of the rest period and the black line is higher at its end. The two tendencies represented by the lines result in spontaneous recovery.

The other demonstration that the animal is actively learning not to respond during extinction is somewhat simpler. Recent learning is more disrupted by distraction than earlier learning is. If some extraneous stimulus, such as a flash of light, is presented during extinction, the dog will salivate more. In anthropomorphic terms, we might say that the dog was distracted and forgot that the bell would not be followed by meat. Because the extraneous stimulus results in the dog's no longer inhibiting his salivation, this phenomenon is called *disinhibition*.

Now let us return to an animal which has been trained but whose response has not been extinguished. If it is presented with a stimulus similar, but not identical, to the conditioned stimulus, such as a bell of a different pitch, it will give the conditioned response to that stimulus also. This process, called *generalization*, is what makes learning so significant. If we did not carry learned reactions over into new situations and give them in conditions different from those in which they were acquired, learning would have little significance for our behavior. As you might expect, the more similar the new bell is to the old one, the more strongly it will call out the learned response. If it is almost identical in pitch to the conditioned stimulus, the conditioned response will be given more rapidly, more saliva will be produced, and the response will be more resistant to extinction than if the bell differed quite a bit in pitch.

Although the dog will initially generalize its learning to a wide variety of different stimuli, it can be trained not to continue doing so. If the original bell is always followed by meat powder while the new bell never is, the animal will soon learn to respond to one stimulus and not to the other. This is known as *discrimination learning*, as the animal must learn to discriminate between the two stimuli. It may be analyzed in terms of the animal's building up a tendency to respond to one stimulus and a tendency not to respond to the other, much as we analyzed extinction in those terms.

THE SIGNIFICANCE OF CLASSICAL CONDITIONING

How applicable is classical conditioning to human learning? Because it can be used only to learn responses which are innately called out by some stimulus, it is not the way in which most human learning takes place. It probably is, however, the way in which we carry out most of the learning which influences those automatic functions of our bodies which are not usually under voluntary control. The regulation of heartbeat, blood pressure, gastric motility, and the secretions of the endocrine glands may be altered by classical conditioning, as a number of studies have shown. Especially interesting are learned stress reactions, for these play an important part in a number of psychological disorders.[10]

In a simple emotional-conditioning study, such as that of Hunt and Brady, a 5-minute-long auditory warning signal is terminated by a brief but painful shock to the animal's feet.[11] The emotional response to the tone which the animal learns is apparent in two ways: Other learned behavior, such as pressing a lever for food, is discontinued when the warning sound is heard; and stress by-products build up in the animal's bloodstream.

If the animal can learn a way to avoid the shock, the pattern of hormone activity that comes to be associated with the tone is different from that which results when the shock cannot be avoided. In a study by Mason, Brady, and Tolson, the sound of a truck horn preceded electric shock, but the animal was able to learn a response which would enable it to avoid the shock.[12] Before the avoidance response was learned, the sound of the horn caused the animal to secrete two hormones—epinephrine (adrenalin) and the closely related norepinephrine. After the animal had learned to avoid the shock, the sound of the horn led only to release of norepinephrine. This is a very interesting finding, for earlier research suggests that the secretion of norepinephrine usually accompanies the arousal of anger directed outward. Epinephrine secretion is more characteristic of states of fear and anxiety.[13]

As we shall see in a later chapter, the interrelationship between chemical states and emotions is a complex one, and any particular state of physiological arousal is susceptible to a variety of emotional interpretations. Nevertheless, current research is starting to make sense out of a complex picture. In the chapters on personality, we shall look at the effects of emotional learning in early childhood and at the role of psychological defense mechanisms in defending the individual against stress.

One final point about conditioning is worth noting. Even in conditioning, what is learned and how it is transferred to other situations will depend not just on the physical stimuli which are present but also on the meaning which the individual gives to them. This is illustrated in a phenomenon known as *semantic generalization*. An individual is conditioned to give an emotional response whenever a particular word is read. If other words are read, the emotional response will be given more to words that are similar in meaning to the conditioned stimulus than it will to words that have a similar sound.[14] The learned emotional responses which the individual gives in real-life situations will depend not just on the situations but also on how he interprets them. As we shall see when we look at psychotherapy, much of the treatment consists of changing the ways in which individuals interpret stimuli.

INSTRUMENTAL CONDITIONING

When Pavlov set out to study how dogs learn to salivate to a signal, he was in the fortunate position of knowing how to call out the response he wanted to train. All he needed to do was to put meat powder in the dog's mouth, and the dog would salivate. Suppose he had wanted, instead, to teach the dog to turn round and round in circles. That might not have been so easy, for we do not know any stimulus which will innately call out this response. Instead of merely attaching an old response to a new stimulus, Pavlov would have needed to create a new response. This may be done by a technique called *shaping*, which involves reinforcing successively closer approximations to the desired behavior, as in the following example.

Dogs are spontaneously active, and sometimes they just happen to be turning to the right. If you watch a dog and reward it as soon as it shows the slightest tendency to turn to the right, you will increase the probability of its making this movement. The next time it starts to turn to the right even a very little, you can reward it again. As the response becomes better established, you start requiring the dog to turn a little farther each time before you give it the meat or whatever you are using as the reward. Before long, you can get the dog to the point of circling quite strongly in the desired direction.

Let us introduce a few terms at this point. The salivation of Pavlov's dog is called *respondent* behavior because it will always be given in response to some particular stimulus. Behavior such as the circling of our dog, which cannot be called out by reflex but must instead be shaped by reinforcement, is called *operant* behavior. The training situation which Pavlov used to strengthen salivation in his dog is called a *classical conditioning* situation because it was studied first. A training situation in which the animal's behavior is instrumental in its obtaining the reinforcer, on the other hand, is called an *instrumental conditioning* situation. Most of the phenomena which we have discussed under classical conditioning may also be demonstrated with behavior learned through instrumental conditioning.

So far, we have shaped the operant behavior of circling. You probably do not want your dog turning in circles all the time, however, but only when you give some particular signal. We have delayed introducing the signal until this point because it is much easier to teach the animal when to give a response that has already been learned than it is to try to teach the animal both the response and the appropriate conditions at the same time. Now all we need to do is to start giving the signal from time to time, and to reinforce the circling movement only when the signal has been given. This will strengthen the response of turning when the signal is given, and will extinguish it in the absence of the signal. The response will become a *discriminated operant*, one which is only given under certain stimulus conditions.

In the example we have looked at, the circling response was established by reinforcing it every time it occurred. It is also possible to condition a response by reinforcing it only some of the time. This procedure, known as *partial reinforcement*, actually leads to learning which is much more resistant to extinction. If the response has only been erratically reinforced, a few trials without reinforcement will not decrease its probability, a principle which is put to practical application in slot machines and other games of chance.

A variety of different schedules of reinforcement have been employed in conditioning experiments, and each leads to a distinctive type of performance. A fixed-ratio schedule, in which, for example, every tenth or every fifteenth response is reinforced, will lead to a steady, fairly high rate of responding. A fixed-interval schedule, in which reinforcement is given for the first response after some specified time has elapsed since the last reinforcement, will cause little responding just after reinforcement and then an increasing rate of responding as the end of the interval approaches. Schedules in which the ratio or interval is varied introduce more uncertainty about the conditions of reinforcement, and they can lead to a very high rate of responding. The slot machine mentioned earlier employs a variable-ratio schedule.

EFFECTS OF PUNISHMENT

Thus far, we have seen how the tendency to give a response under certain stimulus conditions may be strengthened through the use of positive reinforcement. What effect does punishment have? If reinforcers, such as food, water, attention, comfort, or praise, will cause an organism to learn a response, will punishments, such as cold, pain, or electric shock, cause it to forget the response? The answer is not quite so simple as it seems. Punishment has a variety of diverse effects, so its impact will depend to a great extent on the learning situation.

First, punishment influences what the organism pays attention to. In a classic series of experiments, Muenzinger and his colleagues investigated the effects of punishment on maze learning. In a typical study, rats were run in a T-shaped maze.[15] On each trial, one arm of the maze was lighted and the other was dark. If the rat ran to the lighted side it found food. If it ran to the unlighted side, it reached a locked door instead. There were three groups of rats. One group received no electric shock; one group was shocked for the incorrect response of choosing the dark alley; and one group was shocked for the *correct* response of choosing the lighted alley. Although the group which was shocked for errors learned more quickly than the group which was not punished, so did the group which was punished for making correct responses. The no-shock group required 107 trials to learn the correct direction. The group which was shocked for errors required 35 trials, and the group which was shocked for correct responses required 45 trials. Muenzinger's explanation for these results was that the shock made the rats pay more attention to their choice of one arm of the maze. The rats which did not receive any shock ran through the maze very rapidly. Those which were shocked stopped at the choice point and looked first one way and then the other. Muenzinger called this behavior "vicarious trial and error," for the animals seemed to be considering what would happen to them if they went one way or the other.

A second effect of punishment is to call out negative emotional responses. They may then be attached to the stimulus situation by classical conditioning, as we have seen in the study by Hunt and Brady. They may also prevent the organism from paying attention and learning.

Consider, for example, an experiment by Maier.[16] Rats were given a discrimination-learning task on a Lashley jumping stand. In this type of problem, the animals are taught to jump through the air to one of two doors. If the correct door is chosen, it opens when the animal hits it and discloses food inside. If the incorrect door is chosen, it does not open and the animal falls into a net below. The stimuli to be discriminated are attached to the doors, but their position on the left or right is alternated in a random fashion so that the problem cannot be solved just by learning a position preference.

Maier's study differed from other such studies in that the problem was made insoluble. Not only was the position of the correct cue randomly alternated; the same cue might be either correct or incorrect. Half the time the rat found food, half the time it hit a locked door, and it had no way of knowing in advance which would happen. In this situation, the punishment involved in hitting the locked door caused the rat to pay not more attention, but less. The rat usually fixated on a position habit, always jumping at the door on the same side. If the problem was now made soluble by making one cue always correct, the rat still did not solve it. Suppose that the rat was jumping to the right. Even though it might always find the food when a black card was on that door, and might always hit a locked door when a white card was displayed, the rat still would not learn to jump to the left when the black card was there.

This example shows that we must modify the principle given in the study by Muenzinger. We now see that too great a degree of punishment can teach *in*attention. Mild punishment, sparingly used, may cause the learner to pay attention, but if the situation is made too frustrating, learned inattention will result.

A third effect of punishment is suppression of the punished response. This is illustrated in an experiment by Estes.[17] Estes first trained rats to press a lever in order to receive a pellet of food, and then started extinguishing the response by not reinforcing it with the food. At this point, the rats were divided into two groups. The members of one group were punished a number of times when they were near to, but not pressing, the lever. The other group was not punished. The main effect of the punishment was a temporary suppression of the lever pressing. The animals that had been shocked pressed the lever less often immediately afterward, but made up for lost time by pressing the lever more often later on. It took approximately the same number of responses for the response to extinguish, regardless of whether the animals had been punished or not. While some of Estes's other experiments indicated that responses may extinguish more rapidly if punished under some conditions, the main effect of punishment is to lead to a temporary suppression of behavior, yet not to eliminate it.

Finally, the suppression of one response through punishment

may lead to the learning of another response. If that happens, permanent change in behavior may result. Contrast two situations. In one, an animal can get food only by pressing a lever, which occasionally results also in electric shock. In the other, there are two levers which give food, and only one of them ever leads to shock. In the first case, the shock may temporarily inhibit lever pressing, but hunger will bring the animal back to the lever again. In the second situation, there is no reason why the animal should ever return to the lever which leads to shock, once it has learned that it can obtain food by pressing the other lever.

Punishment, then, has complex effects on learning. In small amounts, it may lead to an increase in attention, whereas strong punishment may call out emotional responses which interfere with learning. It will lead to a temporary suppression of the punished behavior, but whether permanent behavior change will result will depend on what else the organism learns during this suppression.

In talking about punishment, we have described how Muenzinger's animals behaved as if they were thinking about what would happen to them if they turned left or turned right. Thought processes such as these are obviously more important in human than in animal learning. Much human learning takes place through one person's observing another and vicariously experiencing the positive and negative reinforcements of the model. This type of vicarious operant conditioning may be illustrated in the laboratory by asking an audience to watch a subject undergoing the operant conditioning of a verbal response. Under some conditions, the members of the audience will show as much learning as the subject who is being reinforced.[18]

The existence of such vicarious processes makes it necessary for us to change somewhat our conceptions of learning, response, and reinforcement if we want to fit vicarious conditioning into an operant-conditioning framework. Learning obviously must be defined not as a change in performance, but as some sort of internal change which could potentially be shown through a change in performance. While the observer is learning by watching, this learning is not apparent in performance during the learning process. It can, however, be shown in performance if the observer is put into the situation which the model has occupied before.

Responses, similarly, must be broadened to include not just overt, observable, muscular responses but also implicit speech movements or even ideas. Finally, reinforcement in this situation does not consist of the administration of a positive or negative reinforcer by the experimenter. Instead, it consists of symbolic self-reinforcement by the learner. In order to apply reinforcement theory to man, then, we must take into account his symbolic processes. For example, even an extremely painful initiation ceremony may be a positive reinforcer if it symbolizes to the initiate that he is being accepted into adulthood in his culture. For that reason, we shall devote the rest of this chapter to the learning of ideas.

The Learning of Ideas

LEARNING ABOUT THE ENVIRONMENT

Another way of looking at vicarious conditioning is to say that what is learned may not be a response to a stimulus but, rather, an expectation of what will happen if a particular response is given. A study by Wickens illustrates that even in conditioning situations, what is learned may not always be a particular muscular response.[19] Wickens used what is called an avoidance-conditioning situation. The subject's wrist was fastened down, with his forefinger resting on an electrode. He was told not to try to control the movement of his finger, but just to let it take care of itself. He was then given a number of trials in which a signal was sounded, followed by shock through the electrode. Under these circumstances, the finger will make an involuntary extensor movement in response to the shock, and this movement will become conditioned to the signal so that, eventually, it will precede the shock and lead to the subject's avoiding the shock.

After this response had been learned, Wickens turned each subject's hand over so that the back of the finger was resting on the electrode. When the signal was given, the subject might either make the same muscular movement and press his finger against the electrode, or make a flexor movement removing the finger from the electrode. The majority of subjects did the latter.

A number of other studies show the importance of learning expectations rather than responses, even in animals without a symbolic language. In one early study, for example, Tinklepaugh looked at response learning in monkeys.[20] The monkey was restrained while an item of food was hidden under a tin cup. When the monkey was released, it looked under the cup, showing that it had some form of symbolic process which bridged the time gap. That this symbolic process involved an expectation of a particular reinforcer was demonstrated when the experimenter switched foods on the monkey. First he placed a banana, a highly preferred food, under the cup. Then he kept the monkey from watching while he removed the banana and substituted a head of lettuce. Although lettuce is usually an acceptable food to a monkey, it is not liked nearly so well as bananas. When the monkey was released and looked under the cup, it did not eat the lettuce which it found. Instead, it reacted with signs of surprise and frustration, engaging in such forms of behavior as continuing to search for the banana and shrieking at the experimenter. Clearly, the monkey expected to find a banana under the cup, and it evaluated the lettuce accordingly.

More elegant demonstrations of the learning of expectancies were given by Edward Tolman and his students in their studies of *place learning*. In these studies, an animal learned to reach food by running along a particular pathway. It was then given a chance to reach the food by a more direct route. If what it had learned was a response, it should continue to give the response for which it had been rewarded. If, on the other hand, it had formed what Tolman called a "cognitive map," a mental picture of the environment showing where food might be found, then it should take the more direct route. In many studies this is what it did, although in an environment which lacks cues for learning anything else, it will merely learn the simple response.

A study by Gleitman is especially instructive for illustrating place learning. It also demonstrated that overt, muscular practice of responses is not necessary for the learning of expectancies.[21] In this study, the animals did not run through the maze at all, but instead rode through the air in Plexiglas trolley cars. The journey was 10 feet long and took about 20 seconds, and the rats were given an electric shock all the way to the end. After a number of such trips, the trolley line was dismantled and a T-maze was set up in its place, with one end at the former starting point and the other at the former ending point of the trolley line. If the rats had learned anything from their previous experience, then in the maze they should run to the end where the electric shock had stopped rather than to the end where it had started. The vast majority of them did this, showing that they had learned the difference between a "good" place and a "bad" place without making any appropriate responses at all.

Although animals can learn expectations about the environment rather than muscular responses, they do not always do so. We have mentioned that an impoverished-stimulus environment leads to simple response rather than to learning through expectations of cues from the environment. Specifically, the more varied the routes which can be used to reach the goal, and the more distinctive the cues to location which are present in the maze, the more likely the animals are to learn about the environment. Overlearning of a single route under conditions of minimal cues, on the other hand, can lead to the learning of stereotyped muscular responses. John Watson, in an early study, experimented with a maze in which the alleys could be shortened or lengthened while the pattern was kept the same.[22] By using a walled maze in which few cues of location were present, and by having the rats learn it until their responses became "thoroughly automatic," he was able to demonstrate that they would run into the end wall when it was moved up to shorten an alley. However, studies later than Watson's have shown that rats which have learned one pattern of muscular responses (such as swimming motions) to get through a maze can get through it equally well by means of other motions (such as wading).[23] It therefore appears that specific muscular responses are not the only things which are usually learned in a maze, but probably represent stereotyped behavior resulting from too much routine drill. Theories of education stressing the learning of responses until they are "thoroughly automatic," following Watsonian precepts, caused one of the authors of this book to behave in first grade like the rats who ran into the wall. Despite knowing how to write her name before starting school, repeated daily drill made her write it "Barbarbara," which may explain a preference for her nickname "Chris."

Studies of human problem solving show analogous effects. Solving a great many problems of the same type can teach the learner to blindly follow a pattern and also interfere with his learning more general principles and approaches. Luchins, for example, gave his subjects problems in which they had to pour water in and out of several jugs to obtain a particular amount of water.[24] (If you had to obtain 2 quarts of water with a 3-quart container and a 5-quart container, for example, you might fill the 5-quart container, pour out 3 quarts into the other container, and have 2 quarts left.) Luchins's subjects first solved a number of problems which could only be solved by filling the B container and then removing one measure of the *A* container and two measures of the *C* container from it. They were then given problems which could be solved either by this complicated procedure or by the simpler expedient of filling the *A* container and removing a measure of the *C* container from it. Many of them continued to use the lengthy ritual. They said, for example, that the way to measure 20 quarts with a 23-quart container, a 49-quart container, and a 3-quart container was to fill the 49-quart container, pour out 23 quarts into the 23-quart container, and then twice remove 3 quarts with the 3-quart container.

What is learned, then, depends on the conditions of training. Solving twenty-five math problems that are all done exactly like the example at the top of the page may teach a student not how to solve problems of various kinds but only that he should always copy the example. Devising materials which will teach general principles and skills rather than stereotyped responses is one of the challenges of education.

LEARNING HOW TO LEARN

The type of learning which Luchins's subjects showed is called the formation of a learning set. *Set* implies readiness, and the formation of a learning set is the acquisition of readiness to approach problems of a given type in a particular way. While the set formed by Luchins's subjects was maladaptive because it was too narrow for the range of problems which might be encountered, learning sets are more frequently of help to us. Let us look at some examples of them.

Some of the earliest research on learning sets was carried out by Harry Harlow.[25] Reasoning that primate and human learning is characterized not just by the learning of individual solutions to individual problems but by the acquisition of strategies for dealing with repeated learning situations, he resolved to study how learning improves over a series of related learning tasks. He did this by presenting monkeys with a series of discrimination-learning problems.

The monkeys were run in a Wisconsin General Test Apparatus. This consists of a barred cage fitted with a shutter which can be raised or lowered over one side. On the same side as the shutter, there is a tray which can be moved up to the side of the cage within reach of the monkey inside. To use the apparatus, the experimenter first lowers the shutter so that the monkey cannot see what he is doing. He then places food in one of two holes in the stimulus tray and covers each of the holes with an object. The monkey's task is to learn which object has the food under it. The experimenter slides the tray up to the cage and opens the shutter. The monkey reaches out and displaces one of the objects. If the food is under that object, the monkey grabs it. If the food is under the other object, the experimenter pulls the tray away quickly before the monkey can look under that object too.

The problems can be made to vary in difficulty. To learn a position preference, such as always to choose the object on the right, or to choose one of two stimulus objects, is an exceptionally simple task for a monkey. More usual learning problems involve always choosing the object with a particular characteristic from among many objects differing in several ways. Objects might, for example, be small or large, light or dark, and smooth or pointed. A different pair of objects might be presented on each trial, and the learning task might be to learn always to choose the smooth object regardless of its position, size, or color. A still more complex task would be to learn a rule such as, "Choose the light object when all the objects are small and the dark object when they all are large." Even this task, however, is not too difficult for a cat, still less for a monkey.

Harlow used tasks in which the subject needed to consistently choose one sensory quality, such as largeness, while ignoring other qualities, such as color. With them, he was able to show that both monkeys and children show considerable improvement from one trial to the next. That it is a principle, or postulate, which is being learned, is perhaps most clearly demonstrated in *reversal learning*. On these tasks, the subject must first learn a fairly complex discrimination. Then, after it has been thoroughly learned, the correct answer is arbitrarily reversed. As might be expected, the first time this is done, the formerly correct solution is perseverated in for a considerable period before the other stimulus is tried. After solving a large number of problems such as this, a monkey can learn to consistently reverse his choice after only one trial of not being reinforced for the formerly correct choice. After reversing its selection, the animal persists in the newly correct discrimination and so makes no errors except on the one trial which tells it that the answer has been changed.

This last type of problem not only shows that animals can learn some simple rules, but also illustrates the goal-directed nature of much behavior. Behavior is hierarchically organized, with smaller learned units of behavior being used to help achieve longer-range objectives. Consequently, behavior is often more predictable when looked at on a macroscopic, rather than on a microscopic, level. A monkey in a Wisconsin General Test Apparatus may use a variety of different muscular movements to displace the stimulus object, yet it will always displace the correct one. Its behavior is more predictable in terms of the outcome of that behavior than it is in terms of the means used to achieve that outcome. Human behavior especially, being guided by symbolic analysis of varying situations, is more predictable in terms of the goals achieved than it is in terms of the means used to achieve them.

LANGUAGE LEARNING

Speech is perhaps the most distinctive of human abilities, and it differs from most animal languages in a number of ways. The animal languages are similar to human nonverbal communication in that the messages which are transmitted are an indication, and in fact a by-product, of some internal state of the organism. In nonverbal communications it is possible to express fear. It is not possible to talk about what it means to be afraid. Many other differences go along with this one.[26] In speech, a normal person can reproduce any message he hears, and can hear any message he reproduces. In nonverbal communication, he cannot communicate a state unless he happens to be in it, and he is often unaware of the messages which he is in fact transmitting. Nonverbal communications are thus *signs*, indications that particular states are present. Verbal communications make use of *symbols*, things which stand for other things but whose meanings depend on the verbal structures in which they are used. "Cats eat mice" has a very different meaning from "Mice eat cats."

The development of a symbolic language greatly increases man's ability to analyze situations and to give himself instructions. It is therefore fascinating to contemplate the possible effects of teaching a nonhuman a symbolic language. Although efforts to teach primates human speech have consistently failed, two approaches have recently succeeded. R. Allen Gardner and Beatrice T. Gardner have taught American Sign Language to a young female chimpanzee named Washoe,[27] and David Premack has taught a chimp named Sarah to manipulate word symbols on a magnetic board.[28] The performance of these and other animals on tasks involving learning and thinking should reveal much about the nature and usefulness of language.

The very importance of human language may perhaps be why it is so difficult to study. In studying simple learning tasks, the psychologist comes armed with all of man's linguistic ability. In studying language, he is attempting to use these same higher mental processes to study the very processes which he is employing as tools. In this situation, even though he may create metalanguages for the study of languages, his tools seem barely adequate to his task. Our understanding of human language must still be regarded as quite tentative at this time.[29]

Speech is easier to understand than language. It involves the combination of a small number of discrete elements into a large number of patterns. A vowel sound, for example, is made by simultaneously generating sounds of several different frequencies. The individual frequencies sounded are called *formants*, and most vowels can be understood from hearing the two formants lowest in pitch. While one speaker may have a higher voice than another, the "ɛ" sound (as in "head") of a bass will still be higher than the "ʊ" sound (as in "hood") of a soprano. Consonants are not separate sounds, but are modifications of the formants of the vowels. The way in which the vowel is modified, furthermore, depends on what sound preceded the one which is being produced.

The perception of *phonemes*, meaningful speech sounds, is obviously no simple matter. Different languages attach meaning to different aspects of the sounds which are produced. The child who is learning a language must therefore learn to attend to the distinctions which are given meaning in his language and to ignore those which are not. The distinction between "b" and "v" which exists in English does not carry any meaning in Spanish, for example. A Spanish speaker will assign the two sounds to the same category and will hear both of them as the same letter.

Learning to produce and recognize phonemes seems to involve two types of learning. One is a shaping process, by which the child learns to produce those sounds used by his language. This is done not by adding sounds but by eliminating them. The young child makes every sound that is used in any language, including clicks, gutturals, and trills. Adults reinforce some of the child's sounds by repeating those which most closely approximate meaningful units in the language of his culture, and the child eventually learns to produce the repeated sounds in preference to the others.

Along with appropriate sounds, the child learns a schema for each element he learns to recognize. In looking at perception, we have seen that stimuli are perceived as if the perceiver had compared his perceptions with his expectations, assimilating them to expectations if they were not too disparate but noting any large differences that existed. A similar process takes place in the recognition of speech. A given sound is compared with idealized memories of what each meaningful unit sounds like, and its differences from the most similar remembered sound are usually not attended to. Perceiving speech is thus a constructive process in which expectation and context are used to fill in gaps which are unintelligible. This is most apparent when a person says something so nearly inaudible that it seems necessary to ask him to repeat it. Sometimes, what he has said becomes clear before he has time to say it again. "I took the car to the garage" may come across as "I book the far. . .garbage," then "I look the car . . . ," finally, "I took the car to the garage." In cases of this sort, different possible messages are constructed by employing different schemata, and finally one is selected on the basis of internal consistency and appropriateness to the circumstances.

The processes of speech production and recognition thus serve to communicate a fixed number of recognizable sounds. The fact that a sound midway between "b" and "v" is not translated as some new unit but as either a "b" or a "v" is very important for human speech. Because there are a fixed number of recognizable speech elements, they may be combined into patterns without creating any ambiguity about what elements make up a given pattern. Each human language uses only a few of the potentially discriminable sounds which the human voice can generate. Each, however, combines the sounds into an almost limitless number of recognizable patterns.

Schemata are developed for words as well as for sounds, and they seem to have important implications for memory. The more precise name a given language provides for something, the easier that something is to remember. This was demonstrated in a classic experiment by Brown and Lenneberg.[30] Using colors as stimuli, they first looked at the ease of coding them into English. Some shades coincided well with English color names. These colors were named rapidly by the subjects, who all gave the same name for them. There are other colors, such as a brownish-grayish-green, which are difficult to describe in the English language. When presented with one of these colors, the subjects took longer to name it, needed more words to describe it, and often disagreed with one another in their descriptions.

The question was whether those things which were most easily named were best remembered. This was found to be true under some circumstances. If the subject needed to remember only one color, and that only for a very short time, ease of naming had little effect on accuracy of remembering. When the subject needed to remember four colors for several minutes, the most easily named colors were definitely the best remembered. Brown and Lenneberg further demonstrated the effects of codability on memory by showing that monolingual Hopi speakers, whose language does not distinguish between yellow and orange, often confused these two colors when remembering them. It is important to note that these effects are effects of memory and not of perception. A number of studies have shown that when the colors are actually present, a person's language will have no effect on his ability to discriminate one from another.

Moving from the recognition of sounds to the coding of experience into words takes us one step closer to the elusive problem of meaning. It is easy to say what speech is, but what is meaning? The anthropologist Kirk Endicott, in looking at the meaning of cultural elements while analyzing Malayan folk religion, found it useful to distinguish three kinds of meaning.[31] They are (1) inherent meaning, the basic, defining characteristics of a thing; (2) relational meaning, which the thing acquires from its relationships with other things; and (3) symbolic meaning, which the thing has through analogy with something occupying a similar position in a different set of relationships. As these three categories seem to provide a good, concise statement of meaning in human speech also, let us look at an example of each.

The inherent meaning of something is a partial reexperiencing of it. Immediately after viewing a single color, Brown and Lenneberg's subjects could often visualize it. As this ability to reexperience the color faded, they became more in need of using verbal coding to remember it, as we have seen. Their memory trace of the experience itself, whether or not it was verbally coded, was the inherent meaning that color had for them. If we ask the inherent meaning not just of one color experience but of the color-name "red," what we shall mean is the subjects' partial remembering of those experiences with the color they have labeled in that way. This will coincide with their schema for redness.

When we think of red, we also think of things which are usually of that color—fire engines, barns, and so on. These are relational meanings of redness—things which are associated with it in one way or another.

Finally, by symbolic meaning, we indicate that meaning which something acquires because we have drawn an analogy between it and something which has a similar relationship to some system of elements. If a person refers to a Clockmaker God, he does not mean to imply that this deity is a little old man who sits in a shop all day working with tools. Instead, he refers to the concept of a deity who has created a lawful and organized system which will proceed to run on according to a fixed order, just as the clock runs on without needing further intervention from the clockmaker. In this example, the speaker draws an analogy between the deity and the clockmaker because each stands in the same relationship to a relevant system—the clock or the universe. Human capacity for symbolic meaning is great, and it often seems to play an important part in creativity. Let us look at it in more detail.

We have already noted that "Cats eat mice" does not mean the same thing as "Mice eat cats." The meaning of each element of the sentence is transformed by the structure of which it is a part. The cat in the first statement is a mouse-eating-cat, while the cat in the second statement is a cat-eaten-by-mice. The meaning given to each term in the sentence is in a sense a symbolic meaning, for it is meaning which the term acquires by analogy between it and other elements occupying similar positions in other sentence structures. "Cat" in the first sentence becomes cat-the-actor by analogy with the subjects of other sentences having the same form. This is made more clear if we look at a sentence made up of nonsense syllables. In "Dax mibs jod," it is quite clear that it is "dax" which is doing the acting, that the acting is "mibing," and that it is being done to "jod." "Jod mibs dax" would have quite a different meaning.

If human languages indeed use structure to alter meaning, one interesting question is the extent to which this is a consequence of innate characteristics of the human brain. Pointing out that there are some grammatical principles which seem to characterize all human languages, and that present learning theories are inadequate to account for their acquisition, Chomsky has argued that more is built in at birth than psychologists have realized in the past.[32] Research has given considerable support to his position that there are cultural universals in the area of language, but their interpretation is still to a great extent a matter of opinion.

Let us look at an example. Greenberg analyzed thirty languages from a wide variety of cultural areas and found many features which characterized them all.[33] One of them is the order of subject (S), verb (V), and object (O) in simple declarative sentences. These three elements might conceivably be ordered in any of six different ways: SVO, SOV, VSO, VOS, OSV, OVS. Of these six possible orders, only three actually occur, for in each of the languages, object follows subject in a simple declarative sentence.

This is an interesting cultural universal. Is it innate or learned, or is it learned on the basis of something else which is innate? Earlier research on the perception of causation may provide a clue, though it has not been tested cross-culturally.[34] Films were made in which geometric figures moved on the screen, and subjects were asked to write descriptions of them. When one form approached another, and the second then changed its behavior, the first form was seen as acting on the second and causing the change in behavior. This is not surprising, for, in the physical world, a moving object coming in contact with a stationary one causes it to move (although the movement is not always great enough to see).

The tendency of human languages to have the actor come first and the thing acted on to come later could thus come about through analogy with the perception of causality. The grammatical structure would then be learned, but what about the perception of causality or the tendency to draw analogies? Obviously, the issues here are complex. The study of language acquisition by nonhumans may help to clarify them.

Even if we have not yet quite untangled the effects of heredity and environment in language acquisition, we have developed a much clearer idea of how language learning proceeds in childhood. Young children do not use all the grammatical structures which characterize adult language. An adult, for example, not only can note that cats eat mice but also can remark that, "Despite the existence of a variety of other predators, mice are, by and large, eaten by cats." In this sentence, the basic structure is still that of subject, verb, and object. This basic structure, however, has been amplified into a more complex structure in which the object now comes before the subject.[35] In simplest terms, a young child's sentences will be a more direct expression of the basic structure of the sentence. He will say, "Cats eat mice." He may also misunderstand complex constructions used by adults, although in general the child can comprehend more complex sentences than he produces. "Why don't you come over and play sometime when Sally is at home?" may be interpreted and repeated by the child as "Sally home." As the child grows older, more complex grammatical models are mastered.

We see, then, that for the child, human language involves not just the learning of responses but also the development of a set of grammatical structures which he has never heard, a property of language which is called *generativity*. It is perhaps most clearly demonstrated in those errors of childhood speech that apply a general principle instead of an irregular usage. The child who says "I goed" instead of "I went" makes clear that he is not just repeating statements, but is constructing them according to a set of principles. The open-ended and symbolic nature of human speech makes it a powerful tool indeed for analyzing the environment. In the next chapter, we shall look at how this tool may be used most effectively.

Summary

Learning is inferred from a change in the behavior of a living thing which is unaccounted for by any other factor, such as fatigue, motivation, or chemical stimulation. To recognize when a change has occurred, one must have an understanding of what the organism was like before, for example, what its innate capacities were. Examples of innate abilities would be the number-perceiver cells in the cat's visual cortex and the coordination patterns of the nervous system's control of body movements, including the complex fixed action patterns, which can be activated by stimuli called releasers. Living organisms also have a capacity, called motivation, which puts their various abilities into action. Studying these abilities and what motivates them has revealed some details about the learning process.

Classical conditioning experiments contributed an understanding of the unconditioned and conditioned response, of higher-order conditioning, and of extinction of the response. Instrumental learning experiments added details of respondent and operant behavior, partial reinforcement, and the effects of punishment. Psychologists were then able to use these understandings to study generalization of learning and discrimination learning. The study of learned hormonal response to stress, with its application to emotional learning in early childhood, has been a recent application.

The notable human capacity for semantic generalization connects our emotional state, through the mechanism of learning, with our verbal experience, and makes the learning process relevant to all aspects of feeling and consciousness and to psychotherapy.

Much of human learning is not amenable to the early type of study techniques because it can take place, in the absence of overt behavior, through symbolic self-reinforcement by the learner. Moreover, much learning, both animal and human, is not necessarily measurable by overt response. Thus, other studies have investigated vicarious conditioning, expectancies, and the learning of ideas. Such investigation has produced important facts; for example, concentration on learning a stereotyped response can interfere with further learning of more general principles and possibilities for action. Studies of the learning of concepts and general principles rather than of narrow responses have demonstrated that behavior is goal-oriented. It may be made up of simple building blocks, but the organism employs these blocks to reach a larger conceptual goal.

The recent success of teaching chimps a language expressed in a symbolic rather than a sign medium, as animal language had been understood necessarily to be, has illustrated how little we presently know about the learning of language. Speech itself is made up of analyzable segments of sound, and the perception of speech requires learning to recognize a certain set of sounds from among many ambiguous ones. Study of speech perception reveals similarities to the process of learning visual perception.

The learning of language involves the process of memory, of which coding is a crucial component. It is the meaning of sounds which determines how they will be coded, and they can have inherent, relational, and symbolic meanings. The order in which sounds are produced gives meaning also. Some similarity of structure exists among human languages, and the possibility that a basic aspect of brain function underlies this similarity is now a frontier of research. The most powerful tool of language—generativity—uses the process of learning concepts and principles.

Notes and Acknowledgments

1. Thompson, R. F., et al. "Number coding in association cortex of the cat." *Science*, 1970 (168), no. 3928, pp. 271–273.
2. Glickman, S. E., and R. W. Sroges. "Curiosity in zoo animals." *Behaviour*, 1966 (24), pp. 151–188.
3. A description of this work in English, with references to the original publications in German, may be found in I. Eibl-Eibesfeldt, *Ethology, the Biology of Behavior*. New York: Holt, Rinehart and Winston, Inc., 1970, pp. 32 ff.
4. Ibid., pp. 398–464.
5. Ibid., p. 315.
6. Tinbergen, N. *The Study of Instinct*. Fair Lawn, N. J.: Oxford University Press, 1958, p. 39.
7. Zajonc, R. B. "Attitudinal effects of mere exposure." *Journal of Personality and Social Psychology*, Monograph 8, pp. 1–29.
8. Schutz, F. "Objektfixierung geschlectlicher Reaktionen bei Anatiden und Hühnern," *Naturwissenschaft*, 1963 (19), pp. 624–625; and Schutz, F. "Die Bedeutung früher sozialer Eindrücke während der 'Kinder-und Jugendzeit' bei Enten," *Z. Exptl. Angew. Psychol.*, 1964 (11), no. 1, pp. 169–178.
9. Harlow, H. F. "The heterosexual affectional system in monkeys." *American Psychologist*, 1962 (17), pp. 1–10.
10. A good review of recent research in this area is J. V. Brady, "Emotion and sensitivity of psychoendocrine systems," in Glass, D. C. (Ed.), *Neurophysiology and Emotion*. New York: Rockefeller University Press and Russell Sage Foundation, 1967, pp. 70–95.
11. Hunt, H. F., and J. V. Brady. "Some effects of electro-convulsive shock on a conditioned emotional response ('anxiety')." *Journal of Comparative and Physiological Psychology*, 1951 (44), pp. 88–98.
12. Mason, J. W., J. V. Brady, and W. W. Tolson. "Behavioral adaptations and endocrine activity," in R. Levine (Ed.), *Endocrines and the Central Nervous System, Proceedings of the Assoc. for Res. Mental Diseases*, 1966 (43). Baltimore: The Williams and Wilkins Company, pp. 227–248.
13. Funkenstein, D. H. "The physiology of fear and anger." *Scientific American*, 1955 (192), pp. 74–80.
14. Riess, B. F. "Genetic changes in semantic conditioning." *Journal of Experimental Psychology*, 1946 (36), pp. 143–152.
15. Muenzinger, K. F., A. A. Bernstone, and L. Richards. "Motivation in learning: VIII." *Journal of Comparative Psychology*, 1938 (26), pp. 177–186.
16. Maier, N. R. F. *Frustration: The Study of Behavior without a Goal*. New York: McGraw-Hill Publishing Company, 1949.
17. Estes, W. K. "An experimental study of punishment." *Psychological Monographs*, no. 263, 1944 (57).
18. McBrearty, J. F., A. R. Marston, and F. H. Kanfer. "Conditioning a verbal operant in a group setting: Direct vs. vicarious reinforcement" (abstract). *American Psychologist*, 1961 (16), p. 425.

19. Wickens, D. D. "The transference of conditioned excitation and conditioned inhibition from one muscle group to the antagonistic muscle group." *Journal of Experimental Psychology*, 1938 (22), pp. 101–123; and Wickens, D. D. "The simultaneous transfer of conditioned excitation and conditioned inhibition." *Journal of Experimental Psychology*, 1939 (24), pp. 332–338.

20. Tinklepaugh, O. L. "An experimental study of representative factors in monkeys." *Journal of Comparative Psychology*, 1928 (8), pp. 197–236.

21. Gleitman, Henry. "Place learning." *Scientific American*, October 1963.

22. Carr, H., and J. B. Watson. "Orientation in the white rat." *Journal of Comparative Neurology and Psychology*, 1908 (18), pp. 27–44.

23. Macfarlane, D. A. "The role of kinesthesis in maze learning." Berkeley, Calif.: *University of California Publications in Psychology*, 1930 (4), pp. 277–305.

24. Luchins, A. S. "Mechanization in problem solving: The effect of 'Einstellung.'" *Psychological Monographs*, no. 248, 1942 (54).

25. Harlow, H. F. "The formation of learning sets." *Psychological Review*, 1949 (56), pp. 51–65.

26. See Charles Hockett's "The origin of speech." *Scientific American*, 1960 (203), pp. 88–96.

27. Gardner, R. Allen, and Beatrice T. Gardner. "Teaching sign language to a chimpanzee." *Science*, 1969 (165), pp. 664–672.

28. Premack, David. "Language in chimpanzee?" *Science*, 1971 (172), p. 808.

29. An excellent review of our knowledge at this time may be found in George A. Miller, and David McNeill, "Psycholinguistics," in Gardner Lindzey, and Elliot Aronson (Eds.), *The Handbook of Social Psychology*. Reading, Mass.: Addison-Wesley Publishing Company, Inc., 1969, pp. 666–794.

30. Brown, Roger, and E. H. Lenneberg. "A study in language and cognition." *Journal of Abnormal and Social Psychology*, 1954 (49), pp. 454–462.

31. Endicott, Kirk. *An Analysis of Malay Magic*. London: Oxford University Press, 1970.

32. Chomsky, N. "A review of Skinner's 'Verbal Behavior.'" *Language*, 1959 (35), pp. 26–58; and Chomsky, N. "Explanatory models in linguistics," in E. Nagel, P. Suppes, and A. Tarski (Eds.), *Logic, Methodology, and Philosophy of Science*. Stanford, Calif.: Stanford University Press, 1962, pp. 528–550.

33. Greenberg, J. H. "Some universals of language with particular reference to the order of meaningful elements," in J. H. Greenberg (Ed.), *Universals of Language*. Cambridge, Mass.: The M.I.T. Press, 1962, pp. 58–90.

34. Heider, F., and M. Simmel. "An experimental study of apparent behavior." *American Journal of Psychology*, 1944 (57), pp. 243–259.

35. Brown, R., and Ursula Bellugi. "Three processes in the child's acquisition of syntax." *Harvard Education Review*, 1964 (34), pp. 133–151.

FOUR

THINKING &
REMEMBERING

The Nature of Remembering

The way in which a human being functions depends not just on his past learning experiences but also on how he uses the results of those learning processes. In this chapter, we shall consider the thinking that goes on before and after learning. First, we shall look at the nature of remembering and forgetting, then we shall consider how memory may be used more effectively, and finally, we shall take up the nature of creative problem solving.

INTRODUCTION

Let us begin with some introspective evidence. There are two types of experience which everyone seems to have had. One is graphically described by Proust in his series of novels, *Remembrance of Things Past*. In the first of these books, he describes eating a tea cake, which brings his childhood vividly back to him. Although not everyone of us could write seven novels on what we remember when we have an experience of this type, each of us does occasionally reexperience the past. A smell of apple blossoms or of fresh hay, or even one of dusty blotting paper, may cause us to visualize people and places we have not visited or thought of for many years. The sensation which has reminded us of the past is reexperienced as part of the context in which it occurred, which explains why this type of memory is called *reintegration*.

The second type of common experience is one in which something cannot quite be remembered. It seems to be right on the tip of the tongue, its shape and sound are almost there, and then it fades without being remembered. This sort of experience seems to involve a search in memory on the basis of various features. In trying to remember the name "Ferguson," I may think, "It is similar to McPherson," and try out various Scottish names, particularly three-syllable ones and ones with an "f" sound. After much fruitless searching through the "Mc's" and "Mac's" in my memory, I may or may not come up with the right answer.

These two types of experience seem to give important clues as to how information is stored in memory. Some experiences seem to be recorded in perceptual terms. When they are remembered, they are reexperienced. Many of the things we can remember, however, are abstractions. These abstractions, often coded in verbal terms, are not so much reexperienced as reconstructed by a process of feature analysis. This is illustrated in an experiment by Brown and McNeill.[1]

VERBAL MEMORY

Brown and McNeill found a way to produce the tip-of-the-tongue phenomenon in the laboratory. They read dictionary definitions to their subjects and asked them to tell what word was being defined. In this way, they were able to produce hundreds of instances in which the subject was almost, but not quite, able to remember the word.

These cases provided clear evidence that people do, in fact, remember some characteristics of a word before remembering the word itself. The number of syllables in the word, its accent pattern, and its initial letter were among the most frequently recalled characteristics.

This result is what we would expect from material which we have already considered when dealing with the development of schemata. The individual classes together experiences which have some important characteristic in common and develops an expectation about further members of the class. New experiences are made meaningful by being related to these expectations, and assimilation and contrast effects result from the role of the schemata in perception. The tip-of-the-tongue phenomenon, from this point of view, consists of the assimilation of the word that is being sought to a number of schemata in which it participates.

VISUAL MEMORY

Some coding is, of course, involved even in storing visual images in memory, although not so much as would be used in assigning them verbal labels. This is perhaps best illustrated through research with individuals who have *eidetic imagery*, or, as it is sometimes called, *photographic memory*. While these individuals do have striking abilities, their memory images usually do not completely reproduce the appearance of the stimulus object. A classic study by Gordon Allport illustrates this phenomenon.[2]

Allport worked with eleven-year-olds, for eidetic imagery usually declines with age. He asked each subject to view a picture for 35 seconds and then asked him questions about it. Approximately half the subjects were able to recall a vivid and detailed image of the picture.

In order to answer Allport's questions, the subject with eidetic imagery seemed able to focus his attention on any particular part of the image, and to see it with more clarity than the rest of the image. Reading off the image in this way, the subject could count the number of buttons on a person's coat or the number of whiskers on a cat's lip. That the image was not perfect, however, was shown when the subject tried to reproduce a German word included in one picture. Only three of the thirty subjects who had strong imagery were able to spell the word correctly. Other distortions of memory, such as seeing things in which the subject was interested as larger than they really were, showed that even this type of memory is somewhat distorted by the way in which it is coded.

DEVELOPMENTAL CHANGES IN MEMORY

The decline of eidetic imagery with age is itself an interesting finding, for it would seem to show that schemata in remembering increase in importance as individuals acquire more experience with classes of stimulus objects. The relating of incoming stimulation to memories of previous experiences probably takes up much of focal attention, and it decreases the extent to which the individual can concentrate on the stimulation itself.

The increasing significance of conceptual analysis as the individual grows older is also shown in studies of problem solving by children. Consider, for example, a study by David Olson.[3] In it, children were shown two or three sample patterns. Each child then needed to discover which of the patterns was set up on a so-called bulb board.

The bulb board was made up of five rows of five bulbs each. Any given light bulb would light while it was pressed if it was part of the correct pattern, but not if it wasn't part of the correct pattern. Switches at the back of the board enabled the experimenter to set up different correct patterns on different experimental trials.

Children of various ages differed greatly in the strategies which they followed in solving the problems. Three- and four-year-olds tended to use a search strategy, pressing bulbs here and there to see whether they would light up without regard to the sample patterns they were trying to choose between. Slightly older children used a pattern-matching strategy. These children would choose one of the sample patterns and press bulbs participating in that pattern. Suppose, for example, that one of the patterns consisted of a horizontal row of turned-on bulbs at the bottom of the board, and the other consisted of a similar row, plus an illuminated vertical column. The child with a pattern-matching strategy might press all the bulbs in the horizontal row even though this row was part of both sample patterns and would be lit up regardless of which pattern was the correct answer.

Only the oldest children used an efficient strategy in solving the problems. They analyzed the sample patterns, noted the distinguishing features of each, and selected bulbs which would be informative in discriminating between the two patterns. The difference between this approach and the earlier one, where most of the pattern had to be lit up before it could be recognized, seems to correspond to the difference between remembering an image and analyzing stimulation in terms of concepts.

We see, then, that memory processes differ in the extent to which they reproduce an entire stimulus situation, or analyze it, abstract things from it, and code it in conceptual terms. The ability to carry out the latter type of process seems to be learned as the individual matures, but it is learned at a price. The ability to record stimulation relatively directly, completely, and impartially is correspondingly lost. Distortion seems in some ways to be the price of meaning.

THREE TYPES OF MEMORY

Thus far, in looking at memory, we have been considering only long-term memory. Memories, however, seem to be stored in two other ways before they become a part of the experiences we can recall after a period of years. Initially, they are a part of that sensory memory which we call *iconic memory*. The images in iconic memory are very similar to eidetic images except that they only last for about a second. Like eidetic images, they may be not only in the visual, but in any other, sensory modality. While they are present, the subject can pay attention to any part of them and read off material as if the stimulus were actually present.[4]

Of the vast amount of material which is stored momentarily in iconic memory, only a very small portion passes into short-term memory. This is the type of memory in which you hold an unfamiliar telephone number while you are dialing it. It requires focal attention to maintain it, and it will be permanently lost if your attention is distracted.

Finally, only a small portion of the material in short-term memory is permanently stored in long-term memory. Long-term memory is characterized by not being dependent on attention for its maintenance. If you know your own telephone number, you can recall it at any time. You do not continuously have to pay attention to it to remember it. This difference between long- and short-term memory suggests that information in short-term memory may be stored in the form of an ongoing process, whereas that in long-term memory may be stored as anatomical or chemical changes in the nervous system.

Two experiments will help to clarify the differences among these three types of memory process. The first, done by Sperling, illustrates the existence of iconic memory.[5] Using a tachistiscope, he projected three rows of three letters each on a screen for a period of half a second, and then asked his subjects to tell him what the letters were. Generally, the subjects were able to reproduce four, or at most five, of the nine letters.

Sperling then tried a different set of instructions. He told each subject that, immediately after the letters were presented, a tone would be sounded. If it was a high tone, the subject should tell him what letters had been present in the top row. Similarly, a medium or low tone indicated that the middle or bottom row should be recited. With these instructions, the subjects were able to recall any one of the three rows virtually without error.

At the instant the letters stopped being displayed, then, the subject had some form of memory for all of them, since he was able to read off any one of the three rows correctly. If he tried to read off all three rows, however, the iconic image faded before he could recite them all. The longer the tone was delayed, the more the image had faded and the less well the subject was able to read off the letters. When it was delayed for as much as a second, he did no better than if no signal was given. This is an indication of about how long the iconic image lasts, and thus of how long it is available for focal attention to take out information from it to put in short-term memory.

The other study, done by Posner, deals with differences between short-term and long-term memory.[6] He used quite a simple task, but the explanation of his results is a bit more complex.

The subject's task was that used in memory-span studies. A list of digits was read to him, and he was asked to recall them. The list was always eight digits long. Sometimes it was read rapidly and sometimes slowly. Also, the subject was sometimes required to remember the numbers in order and sometimes to give the last four digits before the first four. Let us see what difference this would make from the point of view of long- and short-term memory.

If numbers cannot be stored in long-term memory, the faster they are read the better they will be remembered. Short-term memory does not last very long, and the subject must give his answers quickly before he forgets them. If he must report the numbers in the order in which he heard them, this is what he finds—the faster rate leads to better recall.

If the subject can report the last four numbers before he reports the first four, this makes it possible for him to use long-term memory as well as short-term. Let us see how he does this. As the first numbers are being read, he tries to learn them really well—so well that he can remember them even after turning his attention to something else for a while. (The slower the numbers are being read, of course, the more time he will have to do this.) After learning the first few well, he will turn his attention away from them in order to get the last four digits into short-term memory. Because these have not been learned well, they must be repeated over and over to be remembered—that is, they will require focal attention.

The subject thus reaches the point where he must report his response with the first four numbers stored in long-term memory, and the last four repeated over and over again. If he can report the ones from short-term memory first (the ones seen last), all is well. He can then turn his focal attention to remembering the first four. If, however, he must report the numbers in order, the situation is quite different. When he turns his attention to retrieving the first four numbers from long-term memory, he will forget the last four, for they are in short-term memory and require continuous attention to be remembered.

The result of this is that long-term memory may be effectively used when the last four digits can be reported first. Under this condition, then, the fast presentation of the digits loses its advantage over the slow rate of presentation. The disadvantage to short-term memory of having them presented slowly is made up for by the advantage to long-term memory of the subject's having more time to store the first four digits.

This analysis in terms of short-term and long-term memory helps us to understand what Posner found, as well as a number of other puzzling results on the effect of rate of presentation on memory. When the digits need to be reported in the order in which they were presented, the subject will do best if the numbers are read rapidly. If he may report the last numbers first, on the other hand, he can do as well or better if the numbers are presented to him slowly.

We thus see that a memory is first recorded in iconic storage for a very brief period. If focal attention is then devoted to it continuously for sufficiently long, it may enter permanent storage as a perceptual memory. Time is short, however, and perceptions are many. Most memories are lost without receiving attention. Even the ones which have attention momentarily devoted to them may not be attended to long enough to be stored permanently.

Things which are attended only briefly, however, may be related to other things which have been learned in the past. Through active work by focal attention, they may be coded by being related to existing schemata. In this case, they may enter permanent storage in a more coded form. This process seems to be faster than that involved in learning novel perceptual material, with the result that much of what the adult learns is in abstract terms, frequently in verbal ones. What we remember is usually an interpretation of a little bit of what we experienced.

Forgetting

FAILURE OF CONSOLIDATION

The difference between short-term and long-term memory is important because failure to develop a permanent memory trace is one important source of forgetting. The process of making the memory trace permanent is called *consolidation*, and the idea that this process is not instantaneous but, instead, takes a period of time is called the *consolidation hypothesis*.

Failure of consolidation as a cause of forgetting was first suggested by cases of *retrograde amnesia*. An individual who has received a severe blow on the head may show an almost complete loss of memory immediately afterward. When his memories return, the earliest ones come back first, followed by progressively more recent ones. Memory for the events just before the blow never returns, a result which could be due to disruption of the short-term memory before it is stored in long-term memory.

It might seem at first glance that this loss of memory could be equally well accounted for by *repression*, the active forcing out of consciousness of anxiety-inducing material. Two aspects of amnesia cases, however, seem to fit a consolidation theory better. One is that the memories will not come back under drugs or hypnosis. These will often bring repressed material to the surface. Even more striking is the type of injury which will not cause amnesia. Gunshot wounds to the head, if the damage is quite localized, will often not result in amnesia. As such injuries must surely be as anxiety-inducing to remember as the events which do cause amnesia, repression would not seem to be the cause of the amnesia which follows accidents. As we shall see when we look at personality disorders, however, repression is the cause of some other types of amnesia.

The consolidation hypothesis has two important implications for forgetting. The first is that anything which disrupts the newly established memory before it has been consolidated will lead to permanent forgetting. The memory will not simply be repressed or unavailable—it will be gone completely. The second implication is especially exciting. It is that memory may be improved by improving consolidation.

DISRUPTION OF CONSOLIDATION

Many of the studies of disruption of consolidation have used electroconvulsive shock (ECS). Although it is now being largely replaced by tranquilizing drugs, shock treatment was once widely used in treating mental illness. Like a blow on the head, ECS leads to permanent forgetting of the events just before the shock. It is perhaps the completeness of this forgetting which keeps the patient from remembering the shock as a painful event, although repeated treatments may lead to his feeling an aversion to them.

The earliest consolidation studies used a conditioning situation. Animals were given positive reinforcement for making a simple response. They thus learned to make it more readily, except for those in the experimental group which received electroconvulsive shock immediately after the positive reinforcement. Those animals did not acquire any greater tendency to give the reinforced response, a result which could have been due to their failing to consolidate the memory of the learning experience.

Another explanation of the results was possible, however. Maybe the electroconvulsive shock served as punishment and inhibited the expression of the learned response. In that event, the experimental animals would fail to show the learned response not because they had forgotten it, but because they remembered that it would lead to punishment. How could this alternate explanation be ruled out?

One simple way is by using avoidance training in the original learning situation. Suppose that the animal was not learning to do something for positive reinforcement, but instead was learning not to do it in order avoid punishment. In that case, failure to carry out the learning could not be due to the impact of ECS serving as punishment, for additional punishment would cause the learning to be even more efficient.

One study of this type was done by Madsen and McGaugh.[7] A rat is placed on a platform above a metal floor. When the rat steps off the platform, a mild shock is delivered to its feet. After this happens only once, the rat, in a second test, is much less likely to step off the platform within 10 seconds of being placed on it. The rat has shown one-trial learning.

Now another rat is placed on the platform. It, too, receives a foot shock when it steps off. It is then removed from the apparatus and given an electroconvulsive shock. What behavior do we expect from it? If the effect of the ECS is seen as punishment, the second rat should be even less likely to step off the platform the next time than the first rat was, for it has received more punishment. If, on the other hand, the ECS interferes with consolidation of memory for immediately preceding events, the second rat should be more likely to step off the platform the next time than the first rat was, for it would have less memory of the foot shock. This latter effect is what Madsen and McGaugh found. Over half the rats in the first condition stayed on the platform in the second test, whereas less than one-fifth of the rats in the second condition did so. In this case, the ECS has interfered with consolidation rather than simply serving as a punishment.

IMPROVEMENT OF CONSOLIDATION

Studies in which consolidation is improved rather than disrupted have used stimulants rather than shock. That learning can be improved by giving a stimulant just before the learning takes place is not too surprising. That memory can be improved by giving a stimulant after the learning experience is much more unexpected. Yet this is what has been found. A representative study was done by McGaugh and his colleagues.[8] Animals were taught to run through a maze. Some of them were given strychnine sulfate (a stimulant when taken in very small, nonharmful doses) before the learning task, and some were given this compound after the learning task. The results are shown in Figure 4-1. When taken within 15 minutes after running the maze, the strychnine sulfate improved the animals' memory of what they had learned.

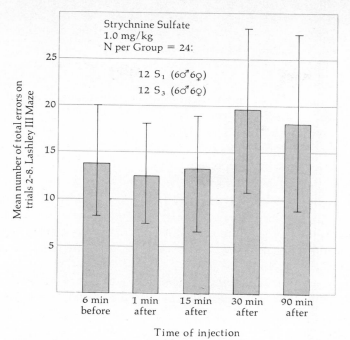

Figure 4–1 *Effect of strychnine sulfate on maze learning as a function of time of injection (either before or after each daily trial). Vertical lines indicate plus and minus one standard deviation from the mean of each group. (Kimble,[9] based on data from McGaugh, Thomson, Westbrook, and Hudspeth[8])*

We thus have convincing evidence that memories take time to be consolidated, and that some of them are lost through failing to be consolidated. Not only may the consolidation process be disrupted by physical or electrical shock; it may be improved through chemical stimulants. That the animals not treated with strychnine sulfate did not remember as much as those that received the stimulant was due to their failure, under normal conditions, to consolidate all they had learned.

INTERFERENCE

Besides repression and failure of consolidation, there are one or two other causes of forgetting. One clearly existing cause is *interference*, in which learning one thing interferes with learning or remembering something else. More ambiguous is the question of whether memories disappear simply from the passage of time, as proposed by the *passive decay* theory of forgetting.

There is no doubt that passive decay of memories takes place for things which are stored in iconic or short-term memory. We have already noted that iconic memory decays in about a second, and that material in short-term memory may decay before it has been consolidated. It is much more difficult to judge whether anything decays merely through the passage of time once it has been stored in long-term memory. In any period long enough to test whether decay has taken place, other things will be learned which may interfere with the memory to be tested. We therefore do not have any good way of testing whether passive decay of long-term memories takes place or not. It may be that memories, once put in permanent storage, will last for a lifetime unless a cerebrovascular accident destroys the nerve cells in which they are stored.

Interference, however, clearly exists, and is probably the most frequent cause of forgetting in real-life situations. New material which is learned may cause us to forget material which had been learned previously, a phenomenon known as *retroactive inhibition.* Furthermore, material which has already been learned may make it more difficult to learn some kinds of material in the future, a phenomenon which is called *proactive inhibition.* Let us look at an example of each.

Suppose that you are learning both French and Spanish. If you learn the French word for "chair" first, and doing so makes it harder for you to learn the Spanish word for it afterward, that would be a case of proactive inhibition. If you then study the Spanish word for "chair" until you forget the French word for it, that would be retroactive inhibition. As might be guessed from these examples, it is better not to try to learn French and Spanish at the same time.

The extent to which learning one thing will interfere with learning another or, conversely, will facilitate learning the other is a function of their similarity. Interference will be greatest when similar stimuli must call out greatly differing responses. Our example of words for "chair" in different languages falls in this category, for, to the English word "chair," you must associate the quite different responses of *"chaise"* and *"silla."*

Facilitation, on the other hand, will be the rule when similar stimuli must call out similar responses. Knowing the word for "one" in Latin makes it easier to learn the word for "one" in French or Spanish, as all three have the same root. Different stimuli calling out the same response may lead to some facilitation because no new response needs to be learned, whereas different stimuli calling out different responses should not have any effect on each other.

SUMMARY OF FORGETTING PROCESSES

Let us summarize what we have learned so far. Sensory impressions are first held in iconic memory in a relatively uncoded form. If enough attention is paid to them for a sufficient period of time, they may pass into long-term memory in this form. Because of the amount of time and effort that it takes to learn something new, however, most information is not learned in this way. Instead, it is further coded by being related to things which have already been learned in the past. This coding reduces the amount of learning which must be carried out, but it distorts the new information by assimilating it to existing concepts and schemata.

The ways in which forgetting takes place are largely implied in this model of how memory works. That interference is a major cause of forgetting would be expected from the role of schemata in remembering. If something new is remembered by relating it to something which has been learned before, it is not surprising that the two are sometimes confused with each other. Interference is merely a confusion of ideas which are coded in similar ways.

Failure of consolidation is another important cause of forgetting. Even beyond the time when conscious attention is being paid to new learning, active processing is necessary to put it into long-term memory. Until this is done, passive decay may take place, and even after the new learning has been stored away, it may be kept from consciousness by the active process of repression.

Efficient Learning and Remembering

Implicit in this discussion of memory are some suggestions on how material may be learned most efficiently. The two most obvious rules are that you must pay attention to something to learn it, and that you would be wise to reduce interference by not studying too many similar things at the same time. Less obvious is a suggestion on the role of self-testing.

We have noted that most learning involves relating something new to something already known. Since confusing the old material with the new is one of the major sources of error in remembering, it is important to recite the material which is already known so that the new material may be compared with it. Suppose, for example, that I was trying to remember the name of the English king who fought in the battle of Agincourt. If I merely repeated over and over again "Henry the Fifth," I might feel that I had learned it, only to give George the Fifth or Henry the Eighth when it came time to recite. By reciting early in the learning process, I could learn that I had a tendency to give these erroneous responses which needed to be suppressed. A classic study by Gates indicated that a person should spend as much as 80 percent of his time testing himself when learning new material and only 20 percent of his time looking at the material.[10]

ORGANIZATIONAL PROCESSES IN MEMORY

Relating new material to things already known is one way to make it meaningful. Another is by finding some internal pattern in the material to be learned. Pioneering research on the importance of such patterns was done by George Katona and discussed in his book *Organizing and Memorizing*.[11] Organizing was not, for Katona, a step in memorizing. Instead, he conceived of the two processes as being quite different; a matter of looking for patterns, in the case of organizing, and of simply repeating the material over and over again, in the case of memorizing. He did a series of experiments to compare the results of these two types of processes.

So that the two processes could be compared, it was necessary (1) that the same material be learned by each process, and (2) that it be learned equally well. If these conditions were met, how could the results of the processes differ at all? Katona considered two distinct ways. It was possible that the material learned in one way might be remembered longer than the material learned in the other, even though learning seemed to be equal in an immediate test. Also, it was possible that there might be differences in the extent to which the material learned could be applied in a new situation. Let us look at two of Katona's experiments demonstrating differences of these types.

The difference in retention of principles and memorized material is beautifully demonstrated in the first of these experiments, dealing with learning a table illustrating an economic tenet called the acceleration principle. It may be briefly stated as follows: Slight changes in demand for consumer goods will cause great changes in demand for the machinery to make these goods. The principle can be illustrated with a hypothetical example of demand for shoes and for machinery to make the shoes. Imagine that you had a stable demand for 1 million pairs of shoes each year, and that the shoes were made on machines that could make 2,000 pairs of shoes each per year. You would thus need to always have 500 shoemaking machines. Assume further that each machine lasted ten years. To replace the machines which became worn out, you would need to produce just 50 shoemaking machines each year.

Now imagine that the demand increased from 1 million pairs of shoes each year to 1.1 million pairs. This is an increase in demand of only 10 percent. Yet look at the effect that this would have on demand for the shoemaking machines. You would now need 550 machines instead of 500, so you would have to make not only 50 new machines to replace ones which had worn out, but also an additional 50 to meet the additional demand for shoes. An increase of only 10 percent in demand for shoes thus leads to an increase of 100 percent in demand for shoemaking machines.

In Katona's experiment, one group of subjects was given an explanation of the above principle and a table illustrating it. These subjects were not asked to learn the table, but merely to understand the economic principle. (The table is presented here as Table 4-1.) The other group of subjects was given the table but not the explanation. They were asked to memorize the table, and they repeated it until they could reproduce it without error.

Table 4–1   *Katona's example*

YEAR	NUMBER OF SHOES PRODUCED (PAIRS)	NUMBER OF MACHINES REQUIRED	PRODUCED
I	1,000,000	500	50
II	1,100,000	550	100*
III	1,150,000	575	80†

* 50 + 50.
† 55 + 25.
SOURCE: Katona [12]

After a month, subjects from both experimental treatments were asked to reproduce the table. Not one of the subjects who had memorized the table was able to reproduce it accurately enough for it to illustrate any principle. A typical reproduction, for example, showed the vertical columns of the table standing for the number of shoes produced and the number sold, and the horizontal rows standing for the quarters of the year. (This, incidentally, is a good example of assimilation. The table became more similar to a company's annual financial report.) On the other hand, half the subjects who had tried to understand the principle reproduced the table well enough to illustrate it, even though they had not been asked to learn the table and certainly did not expect to be tested on it a month later. This is an excellent demonstration of what may be the most important principle of effective learning, that material is most efficiently learned by understanding it.

Often, of course, finding general principles in material to be learned greatly reduces the amount of material that must be learned. An old spelling rule, for example, states that a word ending in a single consonant following a single vowel must double the consonant before adding a suffix beginning with a vowel. Learning the principle involves storing a great deal less information than learning the hundreds of thousands of words which follow the rule. Even where there is no apparent information reduction through organizing, however, it still seems to make material easier to learn. An especially interesting result in the preceding experiment is that the subjects who studied the general principle even remembered specific details better than the memorizers. Such words as "shoes" and "machines" were recalled much more frequently by those who had learned the material in an organized way.

Another of Katona's series of experiments dealt with the extent to which material learned in different ways could be transferred to a new situation. In these it was the memorizing of rules which was compared with the understanding of principles. For these experiments he used what he called "match tasks," which required moving match sticks to form various patterns. For example, how could you transform the five squares shown in Figure 4-2 into four squares by moving only three matches? (Note that each match must be used to form a side of a square, and that sides cannot be formed of two parallel matches lying close together.)

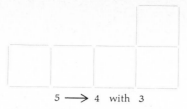

5 $\longrightarrow$ 4   with   3

Figure 4–2   *Match task. (Katona[13])*

Some of the subjects memorized rules for solving each task, while others were taught in various ways that emphasized general principles. These principles may be conceptualized in different ways. The same number of matches will make the most squares if the squares are bunched together so that one match can serve as one side of two squares at the same time, Or, to view it differently, a minimum number of squares constructed from a maximum number of matches will appear to be full of holes and to have a very long perimeter.

By now, you may have been able to solve the example. If not, try removing the two matches making up the lower right-hand corner square, and the match making up the bottom of the second square from the left. Use these three matches to form a square on top of what used to be the second square from the left. Can you see how this solution exemplifies the general principles? You have made four matches which formerly served double functions come to serve only single functions.

In a series of experiments using problems of this type, Katona reached two main conclusions: First, the subjects who learned with understanding retained their knowledge longer. Second, they were better able to transfer their knowledge to a new task.

MNEMONIC DEVICES

Besides using the general approaches to learning material of the types we have been considering, individuals have also devised various specific systems of memorizing. To what extent are these systems effective? Are there various tricks by means of which we can greatly improve our ability to learn? The evidence, so far, seems to be that memory systems, or *mnemonic devices*, do work but have only limited usefulness in most real-life situations. They do, however, illustrate how memory works.

The demonstrations of memory systems by performers are often very impressive. The man who can stand on a stage and learn, for example, the names of a large number of strangers seems to have a memory far superior to that of the rest of us. How many strangers can you meet at a party and not get their names mixed up? The memory expert, however, has at least one advantage. He is not expected to do anything else while he is learning the names. He stands on the stage, the center of attention. The names are presented to him, and he learns them. What do you do at a party? As your hostess takes you around the room introducing you to the strangers, you are careful not to trip over tables, dogs, loose rugs, other people, and so on. Your hostess addresses a stream of irrelevant comments to you, and the people to whom you are introduced say various things to which you are expected to respond. A number of interesting conversations continue throughout the process, and you probably do not hear a quarter of the names at all. In other words, the memory expert has the advantage of being able to give undivided attention to the material which he is learning, while much of your attention is focused on your own behavior and other irrelevant matters.

Attention is the first requirement for learning, and part of learning to have a better memory is probably a matter of learning to manipulate the situation so that you can pay attention to what you are supposed to be learning. Certain people, such as politicians who must meet many people and remember at least some of their names, probably learn to program their behavior to a great extent. By learning to run off the required social responses automatically, they free their attention for learning names.

The memory systems themselves, although they differ in details, usually seem to operate on two bases: through the use of visual imagery, and through learning a code which reduces the amount of information that must be learned. Of these systems, the one using visual imagery is the most puzzling. The more striking and bizarre the way in which the information is visualized, the more easily it is remembered. It may thus be that the process is effective for two reasons: Associating the material with the image may make it more meaningful and thus easier to learn, and the improbable nature of the image may make the material less subject to interference from similar material. This latter phenomenon has been observed in studies with nonsense syllables and is known as the *von Restorff effect*. If some syllables are made to stand out in the list, for example by printing them in red ink or a different type face, they will be better remembered than the rest of the list.

One of the simplest mnemonic systems, the *successive comparison system*, relies solely on the use of visual images. In learning a list of objects by means of images, each one is visualized in combination with the one following it. Suppose, for example, that you were to learn the list "tree, hat, barn, faucet." You would first try to form a visual image that combined tree and hat in a striking and unusual way. You would not want simply to visualize a hat in a tree, for that would be too commonplace. Instead, you would want to imagine something unusual, such as the hat inverted and used as a pot with the tree growing out of it, or a tree which had hats growing all over it as fruit. Next, you would form an image combining hat and barn, then one combining barn and faucet, and so on. Note that each item takes part in two images, one with the item before it and one with the item after it. If you merely learned an image combining tree and hat, and then another combining barn and faucet, you would have no way of knowing that "barn" followed "hat."

Even this very rudimentary system is apparently quite effective. Wallace, Turner, and Perkins asked subjects to employ it in learning not a list but paired associates.[14] The subjects were first instructed in the use of the system, then given a list of 500 pairs of words. In each case, they were to learn to give the second word in response to the first. After going through the list only once, they were able to remember 99 percent of the words. This performance is far superior to what is usually found in paired-associates learning.

More complex mnemonic systems involve learning and using a code either to reduce the amount of information which must be learned or at least to put it in a more meaningful form. In some ways, the most interesting of these systems is one devised by an English schoolmaster named Brayshaw and discussed in I. M. L. Hunter's stimulating paperback entitled *Memory*.[15] Brayshaw's system was used for translating dates and other numerical facts into words, and the students in the school of which Brayshaw was headmaster attempted to learn more than two thousand numbers by means of it. The code which needed to be learned is given in Table 4-2.

Table 4–2 *Brayshaw's code*

1	2	3	4	5	6	7	8	9	0	00
B	D	G	J	L	M	P	R	T	W	St.
C	F	H	K		N	Q		V	X	
			S			Z				

Once the student had learned the code, he learned a verse for each date. The word in which the date was coded was accented in the verse, and the content of the verse described what happened on that date. (In learning dates, the initial 1000 was not coded, so 1000 had to be added to each number.) Some examples are given below:

> 1066   By men, *near Hastings, William gains the crown:*
> 1087   A rap *in forest New brings Rufus down.*
> 1100   *Gaul's* coast *first Henry hates, whose son is drowned:*
> 1135   *Like* beagle, *Stephen fights with Maude renoun'd.*[16]

The code could work only because vowels, which appear very frequently in the English language, did not stand for any numbers. With long practice, the student could learn to translate the word back into the date quite easily. "Coast" stands for 1100, for example, because the "C" stands for 1 and the "St." for 00. This 100 is added to the already assumed base of 1000, making 1100. Because few people want to learn many dates these days, Brayshaw's system has fallen into disuse. It is, however, a well thought-out system, and uses rhyme and meter to make the material easier to learn.

For learning certain things, then, mnemonic systems do seem to work. Another study illustrating their value was done by S. Smith, and it is discussed by George Miller in a provocative article entitled "The magical number 7, plus or minus 2. . . ."[17] The study also revealed some effects of the limit on human information-processing capacity which we have already mentioned.

Smith's study involved the memorizing of binary digits. In our normal base ten number system, we have ten symbols to stand for numbers from zero through nine. After nine, we have run out of symbols, so we must use position combined with the various symbols to stand for larger numbers. Ten is the first number for which we must employ a new position, one place to the left of that symbolizing the single units. Every grade school child learns about the "ones column, the tens column, the hundreds column," and so on. Binary digits differ from base ten numbers in that only two symbols are employed, a symbol standing for zero and one standing for one. Position must thus be used to symbolize any number larger than one. Rather than a ones column and a tens column, binary notation has a ones column, a twos column, a fours column, an eights column, and so on by multiples of two. The following number in binary notation, "10011001," stands for: one times 128, plus no times 64, plus no times 32, plus one times 16, plus one times 8, plus no times 4, plus no times 2, plus one times 1. In base ten numbers, this is $128 + 16 + 8 + 1$, or 153. Awkward as binary notation seems at first glance, it is useful in working with computers because numbers may be symbolized simply by the presence or absence of electrical charges.

Smith's experiment involved transforming binary digits back into base ten digits to make them easier to learn. He first tried learning lists of binary digits, and found that he could remember twelve of them with a single repetition. He then tried grouping the digits by twos, so that instead of learning "11" he learned "3," and so on. This doubled the number of digits he could remember, for he still had to learn only twelve of the new digits to stand for twenty-four of the old ones. Next he tried coding the information by transforming the digits three at a time. That is, he translated "111" into "7," "110" into "6," and so on. Again he could remember twelve of the transformed digits, and now they enabled him to reconstruct thirty-six of the original binary digits. Is there no end to the process?

There is. When he coded the digits four at a time, he could only reproduce forty digits rather than the forty-eight which might be expected. When he coded them five at a time, he could still only recreate a list of forty. The reason is obvious if one imagines himself in Smith's position. Five digits must be kept in mind and translated. While this translation is going on, new digits are being read which must be stored in short-term memory until they are translated. A person can pay attention to only just so much at any one time. The improvement of Smith's digit span from twelve digits to forty, however, shows the effectiveness of the recoding of information which he did.

The studies which have been cited to show the effectiveness of mnemonic systems, however, also show their limitations. Most of them are only good for quite specialized purposes. How many people want to remember for a short time long lists of binary digits? Even systems which do have some generality, such as Brayshaw's, are only useful for rote memorization. As we have seen in looking at Katona's research, material is remembered most efficiently when it is organized in a meaningful way. It is only when no meaningful organization is possible, and when there is no alternative to rote memorization, that mnemonic systems are really useful.

A second limitation is related to the first. The material can be reproduced only in the exact form in which it is learned. Imagine, for example, that you devised some system to enable you to learn the names of all members of some organization in alphabetical order. The system would enable you to recite "Aitken, Allen, Anderson," etc. It would not enable you to remember that Aitken tended to drink too much at meetings, that Allen flirted with the secretary, and that Anderson was a karate champion.

Another interesting thing to note is that while mnemonic systems do work, they probably do not work quite so well as the research on them seems to indicate. Relevant experiments generally involve teaching new methods of memorizing to the subjects, who are then tested with these new methods before the subjects have used them to learn very much. This procedure minimizes the effects of proactive inhibition. The material learned by means of the memory system is unlike any previously learned material, so old learning does not get confused with the new material learned. If the subjects had regularly used the mnemonic system in their daily lives for a few years prior to the experiment, it perhaps would be found to be much less effective.

Creative Problem Solving

AN EXAMPLE

The type of thought engaged in when a person seeks general principles in material to be learned is quite similar to that which is involved in problem solving. Let us look at an example of a problem and consider the stages in its solution. Doing so may give us some insight into the creative process by which more complex problems are solved.

The example, an old one, concerns a king who was seeking a

chief adviser. He gathered together the three most brilliant people in the country—of which you are one—and gave them the following instructions: "I am going to mark the forehead of each of you with a spot. It will be either red or blue. After marking each of you, I will give a signal. If at that time you see a red spot, you should raise your right hand. When you can prove what color your own spot is, you should lower your hand and tell me what color the spot is and why." The king marked the three foreheads, and you noted that he marked each of the others with a red spot. When he gave the signal, each of you raised your right hand. After more than an hour, you figured out the color of your spot and lowered your hand. How had you reached your decision?

There are a number of simple solutions to the problem which are not correct. You were not able to rub any of the coloring off your forehead and look at it, or to look in a mirror, or anything like that. Nor is the answer that the king made all the spots red to give each person an equal chance. Spend a few minutes and see if you can work out the answer before reading on.

Have you been assuming that all the potential advisers were men? There is nothing in the problem to indicate that they were, so let us imagine that there was one man and one woman as well as yourself. This is irrelevant to the solution of the problem, but it does make an important point about problem solving in general. We often set limitations on our thought which are not implied in the problem we are trying to solve, and we fail to consider all the possibilities. It was "proved," on the basis of the properties of light, for example, that microscopes would never be able to produce images of objects below a certain size. Only later was it realized that microscopes do not need to use light, and that an electron microscope could extend the range of vision. It is often necessary to set aside commonsense ideas of what is possible in order to come up with a creative solution to a problem.

Have you managed to solve the problem of the three advisers? Let us return to it now. As in the case of the electron microscope, the first step in solving the problem often seems to be to prove that it can't be solved. For ease in talking about the other two advisers, let us call them Ann and Bill. Your reasoning is likely to have gone something like this: "Ann raised her hand, so she must see a red spot. However, she may not have seen it on me, as Bill has one too. If only one of the others had a blue spot, I would be able to solve this, for if the person looking at the one with a blue spot raised his hand, I would know that he saw the red one on me. As it is, however, it is impossible."

That is, it was impossible for you if you saw two people with red spots. It would not be impossible for you if you saw a person with a blue spot. What about Ann or Bill? According to the conditions of the problem, they were the two most brilliant people in the kingdom, with the exception of yourself. Surely either of them would be able to solve the problem if he saw a person with a blue spot. Yet they sat there for an hour without finding the answer. From this you deduced that neither of them saw a person with a blue spot, so your spot must be red. You solved the problem, and you certainly deserved to become the chief adviser to the king.

STAGES OF PROBLEM SOLVING

As indicated by early research, problem solving often seems to proceed in four relatively separate stages.[18] The first of these, *preparation*, involves becoming thoroughly familiar with the problem. This is sometimes followed by immediate solution, but more often by a period called *incubation,* during which the investigator thinks of the problem from time to time while also giving his attention to other things. If the problem is such that the essence of the solution can all be grasped at one time, it often comes as a sudden insight, causing the next step to be called *illumination*. Finally, the apparent solution must be thoroughly checked, a process of *verification*. The necessity of this last step is illustrated in a recent example. James Watson, who shared the Nobel Prize for discovering the structure of DNA, wrote a colleague about his discovery before he had verified the solution. After sending the letter, he found that his solution was wrong, but he managed to come up with the right one before the colleague had time to answer his letter. His book, *The Double Helix*, is one of the most interesting accounts of scientific discovery to date.[19]

PREPARATION

What is involved in becoming familiar with the problem? Besides assembling the available data, two other processes seem to be necessary. One is the abstracting of certain aspects of the problem and developing a language to talk about them. We did this in a very elementary form when we gave names to the king's other two potential advisers in order to simplify talking about them. James Watson performed the process in a much more complex form by spending hours playing with molecular models, as well as by using mathematical equations to represent the relationships of their components to one another. Let us consider one more example.

Suppose that you are interested in designing a house for yourself and your family. You start drawing various plans, and find that some of them are more successful than others. Some designs do not provide for enough windows, while others have enough windows but call for complex shapes which are expensive to build. Finally, it occurs to you that every shape has a certain amount of surface for its volume, and that there is an optimal surface/volume ratio for a house. You have invented a concept (although others have invented it before you without your knowledge), and you find that it is a great help to you in understanding some of the problems of design. From the ratio you can tell whether a given shape will provide enough windows without carrying the design through to completion. You also discover that you cannot make something the same shape but a different size without changing the ratio. Large buildings need to have more complex shapes to get the same ratio of surface area to volume. (The same thing is true of animals, which is one of the reasons why the giant ants of old science-fiction movies could never survive.)

While we have looked at the development of only one concept, entire symbolic languages may be invented to represent aspects of problems, as differential calculus was. The development of language makes possible the other important part of preparation, the formulation of hypotheses. Thus you may reason that making the building tall and skinny may give it enough surface area, or that arranging the atoms in a spiral will get them in the right relationship to one another.

INCUBATION

We have already noted that people often make unconscious assumptions which limit their ability to solve a problem The breakdown of these assumptions may be one of the major functions of the period of incubation. An experiment by Birch and Rabinowitz illustrates the operation of the type of set which needs to be broken.[20]

Basing their experiment on earlier research by Maier, Birch and

Rabinowitz gave their subjects the task of tying together two strings which were hanging from the ceiling a considerable distance apart. In doing this, the subjects were allowed to use only their hands and one of two objects sitting on a table—an electric switch or an electric relay. As the strings were too far apart to hold onto one and walk over and grab the other, only one way of solving the problem was left. Either the switch or the relay had to be tied to one string, which would then be set swinging like a pendulum. The subject then had to carry the end of the other string toward the pendulum, and catch the pendulum when it swung toward him.

What the experimenters were interested in was which object the subjects would use to weight the pendulum. Research by Duncker had indicated that familiarity with one use of an object made it more difficult to see a new use for it. He called this phenomenon *functional fixity*, for experience seemed to fix the function of the object in the familiar use.[21]

To test whether this effect would be obtained in their experiment, Birch and Rabinowitz gave their experimental subjects one of two experiences before confronting them with the two-string problem. (There was also a control group with no prior experience.) One experimental group had had the experience of using the switch to complete an electric circuit, while the other had had the experience of using the relay for this purpose.

The experimenters predicted that when the subjects confronted the new problem, they would solve it by using the object which they had not already utilized to make the electrical connection. This was strikingly confirmed. Of nine subjects who had used the switch to complete the connection, only two of them used it to make the pendulum. Of the ten subjects who had used the relay to make the connection, all ten of them used the switch to make the pendulum. When asked why they had made the choice they did, members of each group protested that any fool could see that the relay (or switch) made a better pendulum weight.

In approaching problems, then, we bring to them partial pictures of reality. When the aspects of reality which are represented are irrelevant to the problem which must be solved, they may set unnecessary constraints that will interfere with finding the solution without the problem solver's being aware of their effects. New experiences during the period of incubation may break the unproductive set and make a solution to the problem possible.

ILLUMINATION

When the solution does come, it often appears very suddenly without the investigator's being able to remember the steps which led up to it. When the intervening reasoning is remembered, it often seems to involve an analogy between the current problem and some other problem with which the investigator was familiar. Let us consider two examples.

The first example is well known. The chemist Kekulé discovered the structure of benzene, the first ring compound whose structure became known. He did so by means of a famous dream. After working all day on possible structures of the compound, he went to bed and dreamed of snakes chasing their tails. He awoke from his dream with the clear idea that the atoms of the compound were arranged in a ring, instead of in a chain like all other hydrocarbons whose structures were known at that time. In this case, the analogy between the configurations taken by the snakes and the atoms seems clear.

The role of analogy is also important in the second example, which concerns an amazing feat of historical research. Alex Haley, who is best known through his role in helping Malcolm X write his autobiography, has traced back his ancestry over a period of about two and a half centuries. This does not seem surprising until you consider that, for a century of this period, his ancestors were slaves, and that the historical records available on them were sparse, to say the least.

As Haley indicates in his fascinating book, tentatively entitled *Before This Anger*, he heard the story of his family as a child.[22] This story, which had been passed down orally from generation to generation, traced the history of an ancestor, simply called "The African," who had been captured while cutting wood in Africa and made a slave before the American Revolution. Through painstaking research, Haley managed to verify the oral history of the generations intervening between this ancestor and himself.

Haley's more striking achievement, however, was inspired by seeing the Rosetta Stone in London. This stone, bearing the same inscription in three languages, provided the first clues to the translation of ancient Egyptian hieroglyphics. After seeing it, Haley kept having the persistent feeling that somehow it was related to his research. Finally, the analogy came to him. The story of The African which he had learned contained some words in an African language.

If the Rosetta Stone, through matching a known with an unknown language, made possible the understanding of the unknown, then why could not the unknown African words be matched with known African languages, and the region of Africa from which The African came be determined?

This approach was successful. Haley not only discovered where his ancestor came from; he found a village historian in Africa who was still keeping alive the story of his ancestor's kidnapping two centuries earlier. As it is not possible to tell here even a small portion of what Haley found, the reader will have to get Haley's book if he wants to gain some understanding of the cultural heritage which has been denied to black Americans.

The one example we have looked at, however, is typical of many cases of creative discovery. A problem which seems impossible, and which in fact cannot be solved by a straightforward and direct approach, may suddenly yield to an indirect approach inspired by analysis and analogy.

VERIFICATION

Many people picture scientific research as the cautious and painstaking accumulation of facts. The investigator is seen as coldly impartial, rigorously defining his terms, assuming nothing he cannot prove, and remaining indifferent to whether his results support or disconfirm his hypotheses.

These orientations are, in fact, appropriate to the verification stage of problem solving. It is a mistake, however, to think that they apply to the making of the discovery itself. This, as we have seen, involves passionate involvement and partisanship, and thinking in terms which are no better defined than Kekulé's image of the snakes. It is *after* a creative solution has been achieved that it must be subjected to rigorous and impartial testing.

In research with human beings especially, the problems of obtaining objective data should not be minimized. Evidence in favor of almost anything can be obtained as long as the evidence which does not fit the hypothesis is ignored. The attitudes of the experimenter may influence his behavior in ways which he is not aware of but which affect the behavior of his subjects. This problem necessitates the experimenter himself to be ignorant of what is being tested, in some studies. As these problems are beyond the scope of the present work, the reader is referred to a good work on methodology, such as

Anderson's *The Psychology Experiment,* for further consideration of them.[23]

We see, then, that the thought processes which are involved in problem solving are similar to those used in remembering. Both often involve a feeling of search, of being close to an answer but not quite having it, and of directed thought. Neither is a cold and objective process, but, instead, each is accompanied by deep emotional involvement. It is not surprising that Barron finds that very creative individuals are self-dramatizing, rebellious, and moody, as well as deeply involved in intellectual matters.[24] Finally, problem solving and remembering both make great use of symbolic processes. It is the capacity for symbolic meaning which is most characteristic of human thought processes, and it is this capacity which is used in creative problem solving.

Summary

Thinking may consist of vivid reexperiencing of the past. A certain odor may invoke the entire perceptual and emotional context which it reminds us of. This is called reintegrative memory. By contrast, memory which consists of coded abstractions—for most people, these are most often verbal—are less reexperienced than reconstructed. Study of this reconstruction process reveals that when characteristics of a word or some other phenomenon are to be remembered, they are made memorable by being related to other, already known phenomena. Assimilation and contrast effects are shown by the rememberer as a result of relating a perception to a schema for coded storage. This kind of conceptual analysis becomes more important the more one needs to commit to memory. Age, which increases the experiences and facts to be stored, also increases the use of analysis into coded abstractions. Detail and perceptual and emotional context are necessarily sacrificed to facilitate this kind of memory storage.

Our flow of experience is retained for a moment in iconic memory (which can be in any or every sensory modality), lasts about a second, and can be attended to for that moment as if the stimuli were still present. Some of the material is then committed to short-term memory, which requires focal attention to be maintained. It will be permanently lost if attention is distracted from it. Some of this memory, in turn, is then committed to long-term memory, which may require anatomical or chemical changes in the nervous system. Developing a permanent memory trace is called consolidation. Failure of this process is an important cause of forgetting. According to the hypothesis explaining consolidation, the process takes a period of time, and anything that disrupts the newly established memory before consolidation is accomplished will cause that memory to be permanently lost. Anything that improves consolidation will improve memory.

Forgetting can be a result of consolidation failure, of proactive or retroactive inhibition, or, by means of repression, of actively keeping remembered material from reaching a certain level of consciousness. Memorizing has been facilitated experimentally in rats by chemical stimulation of their nervous systems during the consolidation period; and in people by deliberate organization of the material to be remembered. Organizing which enhances the meaning of the material is most effective for this purpose. Mnemonic systems facilitate memory also, but their real value is in enabling us to catch a glimpse of how material is coded and organized by the brain.

Creative problem solving utilizes the process of organizing facts into systems, but involves turning from one possible system to another when solutions do not result. Stages which have been demonstrated in creative problem solving are preparation, or seeing an initial way to conceptualize the problem; incubation, or testing the assumptions inherent in this conceptualization; illumination in the form of a discovery, often of a useful analogy with some known prior solution; and finally, verification, or demonstrating the solution to be a good one. The process of scientific proof adopted by Western science is representative of the verification stage. The process of creative problem solving is similar to remembering in its use of search, directed thought, the manipulation of symbols, the sense of almost capturing sought-after material, and the presence at times of deep emotion.

Notes and Acknowledgments

1. Brown, R., and D. McNeill. "The 'tip of the tongue' phenomenon." *Journal of Verbal Learning and Verbal Behavior,* 1966 (5), pp. 325–337.
2. Allport, Gordon W. "Eidetic imagery." *British Journal of Psychology,* 1924 (15), pp. 99–120.
3. Olson, David R. "On conceptual strategies," in Jerome S. Bruner et al., *Stud-*

    ies in Cognitive Growth. New York: John Wiley & Sons, Inc., 1966, pp. 135–153.

4. A good discussion of iconic memory may be found in Ulric Neisser, *Cognitive Psychology.* New York: Appleton Century Crofts Division of Meredith Publishing Company, 1966.

5. Sperling, G. "The information available in brief visual presentations." *Psychological Monographs,* no. 498, 1960.

6. Posner, M. I. "Rate of presentation and order of recall in immediate memory." *British Journal of Psychology,* 1964 (55), pp. 303–306.

7. Madsen, M. C., and J. L. McGaugh. "The effect of ECS on one-trial avoidance learning." *Journal of Comparative and Physiological Psychology,* 1961 (54), pp. 522–523.

8. McGaugh, J. L., C. W. Thomson, W. H. Westbrook, and W. J. Hudspeth. "A further study of learning facilitation with strychnine sulfate." *Psychopharmacologia,* 1962 (3), pp. 352–360.

9. Kimble, Daniel P. (Ed.) *The Anatomy of Memory.* Palo Alto, Calif.: Science and Behavior Books, 1965, p. 276 (based on data from McGaugh et al., op. cit.). By permission of the publisher.

10. Gates, I. A. "Recitation as a factor in memorizing." *Archives of Psychology,* no. 40, 1917.

11. Katona, George. *Organizing and Memorizing.* New York: Columbia University Press, 1940.

12. Ibid., p. 210. By permission of the publisher.

13. Ibid., p. 58. By permission of the publisher.

14. Wallace, Wallace H., Stanley H. Turner, and Cornelius C. Perkins. *Preliminary Studies of Human Information Storage.* Signal Corps Project 132c. University of Pennsylvania, Institute for Cooperative Research, 1957.

15. Hunter, I. M. L. *Memory.* Baltimore: Penguin Books, Inc., 1966.

16. Ibid., p. 299. By permission of the publisher.

17. Miller, George. "The magical number 7, plus or minus 2: Some limits on our capacity for processing information." *Psychological Review,* 1956 (60), pp. 81–97.

18. Wallas, G. *The Art of Thought.* New York: Harcourt, Brace, and Company, Inc., 1926, p. 839.

19. Watson, James D. *The Double Helix: A Personal Account of the Discovery of DNA.* New York: Atheneum Publishers, 1968.

20. Birch, H. G., and H. S. Rabinowitz. "The negative effect of previous experience on productive thinking." *Journal of Experimental Psychology,* 1951 (41), pp. 121–125.

21. Duncker, K. "On problem-solving," trans. L. S. Lees, *Psychological Monographs,* no. 270, 1945.

22. Haley, Alex. *Before This Anger.* To be published by Doubleday and Company, Inc.

23. Anderson, Barry F. *The Psychology Experiment.* (2d ed.) Belmont, Calif.: Brooks/Cole Publishing Company, 1971.

24. Baron, Frank. *New Directions in Psychology II.* New York: Holt, Rinehart and Winston, Inc., 1965, pp. 1–134.

Allan de Lay

FIVE

MOTIVATION & EMOTION

Introduction

The goal-oriented nature of human behavior has been apparent in many of the topics which we have already considered. From a very early age, the infant begins paying attention to some stimuli and ignoring others. As he develops the ability to organize the world in conceptual terms, he comes, to a great extent, to create the world in which he lives.

Similarly, in learning and thinking, the human being does much more than blindly repeat reinforced responses. Through his conceptual ability, he is able to create solutions to problems he has never before solved and to set goals that he has not yet achieved. These goals frequently have little apparent relationship to the biological needs which he must meet in order to sustain life, and it is this discrepancy between the physiological bases of human motivation and the actual motives on which human beings act from day to day which poses the greatest puzzle for the field of motivation. An understanding of human motivation would involve not only knowing the biological needs which form the earliest human motives, but also understanding the processes of personal and social development by which these motives are transformed. For this reason, this chapter forms only an introduction to the study of motivation. In this chapter we shall briefly consider the nature of motives and emotions. In the two chapters following, we shall consider how motives and emotions are transformed in the course of personality development.

Design Features of Motivational Systems

INTRODUCTION

Suppose that you were designing an organism so that it could survive in an environment. You might give it the information-processing capabilities discussed in the chapters on perception and learning, but these alone would not enable it to survive. To do that, the organism would also need systems which would make it engage in certain behaviors or strive for certain goals. In other words, it would have to be motivated. Viewed in this way, emotion and thought are not opposites, but necessary parts of the same process. Emotional motivation sets goals, and thought reveals ways in which they may be achieved. Either one without the other would be of little use in enabling our hypothetical organism to survive.

Given the need of the organism for some form of motivational system which would make it engage in some behaviors rather than others, there are still many different forms which that motivational system could take. Suppose, for example, that you wanted to build into the organism a motive for eating. First of all, you could build in a simple reflex, so that certain external stimuli would call out the response of eating. If the animal was a herbivore, and almost constant grazing would not lead to serious overeating given the available food supply, this simple mechanism might suffice. For most organisms, however, you would probably need some mechanism to stop eating behavior as well as one to start it. This could take one of several forms. The *on* mechanism which started eating could lead to brief eating behavior, which would then be inhibited for a period unless the *on* mechanism was activated again. Or the amount of food passing through the mouth could be monitored, and when this amount corresponded to what was needed, the eating could be stopped. Or any of the consequences of the eating behavior could be used to work the *off* mechanism, from a rise in blood sugar to uncomfortable fullness of the stomach.

All these mechanisms, however, would result in the animal's starving if its customary food supply was not available. There are other ways of building motivational systems which give more flexibility. Thus, the animal might be constructed so that it randomly placed objects in its mouth, but only swallowed those with a sweet taste. Or it could have a general motivational system which would result in its becoming attached to an older animal and imitating the behavior of that animal. Innate and learned factors could interact in other ways. If the animal was a predator, it might be given an innate mechanism which would cause it to attack and eat any small object which fled from it, and then, on the basis of this mechanism, learn to attack similar organisms in the future even if they were not fleeing.

All these mechanisms, and others, are used to control some behavioral systems in some organisms, and only very careful analysis can reveal how any particular motivational system works. Consider, for example, the song of various species of birds.[1] In some species it is innate. Oregon juncos will sing typical species-specific songs even if raised in isolation. In other species, the song is partly innate and partly learned. Chaffinches raised in isolation produce songs containing the elements of chaffinch song but lacking the usual patterning of these elements. When models of different songs are presented to them, they will imitate only those songs containing the elements which they produce innately. Finally, the male widow bird learns its song. This species is a breeding parasite which lays its eggs in the nest of the Estralid finch. The young widow bird learns to imitate the song of its foster parent so well that the two cannot be distinguished.

Even more complex interactions of innate and learned factors are apparent in some motivational systems. Sexual behavior in female ring doves is partly controlled by changes taking place in the ovaries, and these changes in turn are triggered by the male's courtship behavior. As D. S. Lehrman has shown, female ring doves separated from courting males by a glass partition will show the ovarian development, whereas females separated from castrated males who do not engage in courting behavior fail to do so.[2] It is thus not just the sight of a male, but the sight of a male engaging in certain behavior patterns, which triggers sexual development in the female ring dove.

FIVE FEATURES

Despite the variety in motivational mechanisms, they generally have a number of features in common. Two of them we have already referred to. They involve systems for both starting and stopping the motivated behavior, and they usually are adaptive for the organism in its native habitat. For some time, psychologists believed that these features were even more specific than this. They thought that all physiological motives were based on the needs of the organism to maintain physiological equilibrium, or *homeostasis*. Hunger, for example, serves to maintain nutrients in the blood stream within certain limits; thirst, to maintain the *osmotic pressure* of the internal environment; and so on. In assuming that all innate motives were similar to hunger and thirst, psychologists made assumptions about how the motivated behavior was started and stopped and why it was adaptive. It was assumed that the departure of a physiological index, such as the osmotic pressure of the blood, from some optimal value initiated the motivated behavior, that return of the value to the optimal range terminated the motivated behavior, and that failure of this mechanism to work would lead to the death of the organism.

Further research has shown that homeostatic motives are only one class of innate motives, and that the assumptions made about them were too restrictive. Although innate motives generally serve adaptive functions, failure to satisfy them does not always lead to the death of the organism through a failure of homeostasis. Even more important, motivated behavior is usually started and stopped by separate mechanisms. Consider the case of thirst. As an organism becomes dehydrated, its body fluids decline in volume. Since the quantity of salts dissolved in these fluids does not decrease, the osmotic pressure of the fluids is raised. Drinking behavior is initiated by an increase in the osmotic pressure of the body fluids acting on nerve cells within the brain. Because an organism takes some time to absorb water, however, this mechanism cannot be used to stop the drinking behavior. If it did govern intake, the thirsty person or animal would drink continuously for at least a quarter of an hour. A second control system, utilizing sensory receptors on the tongue, is therefore used to stop the drinking behavior.[3] Consequently, we must be careful not to assume that all innate motives are homeostatic, or that the homeostatic ones initiate and terminate the motivated behavior in the same way.

Besides the two design features of motivational systems which we have mentioned, there are two others which are shared by most innate motives and a fifth which is shared by quite a few. Innate motivational systems involve reinforcement mechanisms in a particular part of the brain, and they serve as a basis for learning. Finally, many of them are partially under the control of hormones secreted by ductless glands. Let us consider each of these characteristics in turn and then look at some specific motives.

THE ANATOMY OF REINFORCEMENT

Embryologically, the complex structures of the human brain develop out of a simple tube. In the process of this development, the tube grows more rapidly at some points than others, becomes folded upon itself, and brings different regions into proximity with one another. The parts of the brain most concerned with motivation and emotion develop out of the anterior portion (or head end) of the neural tube from that tissue lying at the base of the developing cerebral hemispheres. They are the *hypothalamus*, which is especially important in the functioning of homeostatic motives, and the *limbic system*, which serves the sense of smell in lower animals but is primarily concerned with emotional behavior in man. Although the hypothalamus and parts of the limbic system are spatially separated in the mature brain, they develop from adjacent areas in the embryo and remain connected by nerve fibers after moving apart.

The first clear indication that any of these structures plays a role in reinforcement came from a very clever experiment by James Olds.[4] At the time when he did his study, several methods were being used to discover the functions of various areas of the brain. Each of these methods, however, had important limitations. The oldest method was observation of the effect of brain injuries. The interpretation of them was somewhat ambiguous since a number of areas would typically be injured at once, and the method was obviously limited to the effects of injuries so slight that the patient survived them. Electrical stimulation of brain areas in experimental animals could reveal motor areas, but the animals of course could not report their experiences. Finally, electrical stimulation of the brains of human patients during brain surgery was an important source of information. This stimulation is a necessary part of the surgery, for only by stimulating areas and having the patient report what he experiences is the surgeon able to tell exactly where he is on the brain. This source of information, however, is limited to those portions of the brain which are relatively accessible from the surface.

Because the hypothalamus and the limbic system lie deep within the brain and are not motor areas, in Olds's time none of these methods had revealed their functions. Olds reasoned that the functions of some of the deep areas of the brain might be disclosed by giving experimental animals the chance to stimulate their own brains. Using rats as subjects, he permanently implanted electrodes in the septal region of the brain of each of them. (This region is a part of the limbic system, and the electrodes can be implanted by a minor operation from which the animal soon recovers.) He then wired up the electrodes so that the animal, by pressing a lever, could briefly stimulate its own brain. Through observation, Olds found that some regions seemed to have very pleasant effects when stimulated, and others to have very unpleasant effects. When electrodes were implanted in one of the former centers, the animal would press the lever again and again, stimulating its brain hundreds of thousands of times and almost never stopping even to eat or sleep. If the electrodes were in one of the latter locations, the animal would try the lever once or twice, and then avoid it in the future. Olds therefore argued that he had found centers of pleasure and lack of pleasure in the brain. This interpretation has since been supported by further research. Self-stimulation of *pleasure centers* has even been used as a treatment for some extremely painful disorders in human beings, who report strong pleasurable sensations when they are stimulated.

INTERACTION OF INNATE AND LEARNED FACTORS IN REINFORCEMENT

In the chapters on learning, we have seen the importance of positive and negative reinforcement in the learning process. The pleasure centers first discovered by Olds represent the system which carries out this positive and negative reinforcement. This still leaves unanswered, however, the question of what activates the reinforcement mechanisms. As we have already noted, the theory that all positive reinforcers are indications that the organism is restoring homeostasis has proved inadequate. A theory which may prove more satisfactory has been proposed by Glickman and Schiff.[5]

In approaching the field of motivation, Glickman and his colleagues were especially impressed by the differences in the behavior of different species of animals. Exhaustive observational studies of animals in their natural habitats by ethologists have revealed numerous behavior patterns which appear to be typical of particular species. Complex behavior patterns, such as courtship rituals and nest building, are made up of smaller, innate behavior patterns, the fixed action patterns to which we referred in Chapter 3. While crucial to the adaptation of the species to its environment, these species-specific behavior patterns do not reduce homeostatic needs.

Glickman used zoo animals to study the species-specific differences in behavior. Working with Richard Sroges, he observed the reactions of more than two hundred species of animals to each of five different objects (wooden blocks, steel chains, rubber tubes, etc.).[6] The species were found to differ both in their degree of reaction and in the particular actions which they performed with the objects. The way in which any particular species played with the objects, moreover, was related to how it normally adapts to its environment.

Animals which must seek out prey were considerably more reactive and less fearful, for example, than grazing animals which are preyed upon. The specific actions used in catching and killing prey were taken by animals such as the carnivores, which engaged in the swatting, chasing, and worrying of objects as well as a great deal of biting.

This result suggested a relationship between reinforcement mechanisms and an organism's adaptation to its environment. If, in the course of evolution, reinforcement mechanisms developed to facilitate adaptation, then the release of approach instincts should act as a positive reinforcer for the animals and the release of avoidance instincts should act as a negative reinforcer. Approach instincts, from this point of view, would include not only the actions involved in eating, drinking, mating, and approaching an imprinted stimulus, but also the attack on prey by a predator.

In support of this view, Glickman and Schiff have presented a good deal of evidence that the same neural mechanisms are involved in reinforcement and in releasing positive and negative species-specific behaviors. Using this as an indication of what is a positive or negative reinforcer for a species, let us look at how reinforcement serves to organize innate action patterns into learned sequences of behavior. Some good examples are provided by Eibl-Eibesfeldt.[7]

One of the simplest examples is the way in which the European polecat (*Putorius putorius*) learns to attack prey. In the inexperienced animal, attack behavior is released by the sight of a smaller animal fleeing from it. A polecat which has never killed a rat and is confronted with one will not attack the rat as long as it stands its ground. If the rat flees, however, the polecat will attack it.

One experience of attacking a particular type of prey is enough to teach the polecat to attack that prey whenever confronted by it. A polecat which has once attacked a fleeing rat will then attack any rat it meets, whether the rat runs away or not. This type of imprinting, which would be very difficult to explain in terms of a drive-reduction theory of motivation, becomes just another case of learning through reinforcement, if Glickman's theory is correct. The stimulus of the fleeing rat calls out the response of attack behavior. Because the release of strong approach instincts is highly reinforcing, the stimulus-response connection of rat-attack is greatly strengthened through the one learning experience, and rats thus come to call out attack in the future. Finally, the reason that the learned response does not extinguish is that it goes on being reinforced by the release of the attack mechanism each time the polecat confronts a rat.

Direct evidence that the release of attack behavior is reinforcing for a predator is provided by Roberts and Kiess.[8] When they electrically stimulated a cat's brain in a part of the hypothalamus associated with predatory attack, the cat would learn a maze for the reinforcement of being able to attack a rat. Their study shows not only that attack behavior is reinforcing for a predator, but also that the activation of a motive is necessary before it can serve as a basis of reinforcement. Under normal circumstances, it would be environmental stimuli, rather than electrical stimulation, which would arouse the attack behavior in the cat.

Nest building in the rat provides a more complex example of how innate reinforcement mechanisms organize sequences of behavior.[9] After digging a burrow, the experienced rat makes use of a number of fixed action patterns in nest building. They include grasping nesting material, biting it free, depositing it in a heap, splitting it with the teeth, scratching in the center of the heap, and pushing the nest material toward the edges. When Eibl-Eibesfeldt observed the nest building of inexperienced rats, he found that they employed these same movements but not always in the most effective sequence. They employed pushing motions, for example, before they had collected enough nesting material for this activity to be of any use. The learning that takes place during the first experience of nest building thus seems to be largely a matter of learning the sequence in which to use various innate movement patterns.

If the release of fixed action patterns is reinforcing, this process would explain how the movements would come to be organized in the proper sequence. The rat would try various movements in a trial-and-error fashion, but any given fixed action pattern could only be completely released when the correct environmental stimuli were present. When trial and error happened to create the adequate stimuli for the release of one of the steps in nest building, the release of that step would be reinforcing. On the basis of that reinforcement, the animal would learn to employ that particular step under those particular stimulus conditions. Forming the nesting material into a cup, for example, would become the learned response to the presence of a considerable pile of nesting material, for only with this environmental support could the behavior be adequately acted out. As in the case of the attack behavior by the polecat, the learning which takes place as rats learn to build nests becomes understandable if we assume reinforcement mechanisms which do not depend on the satisfaction of homeostatic drives.

EFFECTS OF HORMONES

The operation of many reinforcement mechanisms is influenced by *hormones,* chemicals released into the bloodstream by the *endocrine glands.* Special endocrine-secretiatory tissues include the pituitary, the gonads, the thyroid and parathyroid glands, the adrenal cortex and adrenal medulla, and the placenta and corpus luteum in pregnant women. The chemicals produced by these glands influence many aspects of adaptation, but there is generally not a simple correspondence of one gland to one form of behavior. Most hormones have a number of effects, and generally more than one hormone is involved in any given item of behavior. The maintaining of pregnancy, for example, involves hormones from the *pituitary,* the *corpus luteum,* and the *placenta.*

There are also a number of different ways in which hormones may act. They may be necessary during development for the growth of a given organ or the organization of a behavior pattern. Sexual hormones, for example, not only influence the development of secondary sexual characteristics but also serve to organize the fixed action patterns involved in sexual behavior. Hormones may also act on existing structures, as thyroid influences the rate at which cells carry on metabolism. When they do this, they may have effects which are fairly general throughout the body, or they may act on certain structures selectively. As these structures can include both reinforcement mechanisms in the brain and other endocrine glands, the interactions of neural and endocrine mechanisms are often difficult to disentangle. As we shall see when we look at emotion, the endocrine system is especially involved in the processes by which a person's ideas about reality influence his physiological reactions to it. They thus provide one more example of the ways in which man creates the world to which he reacts.

The most important motivational effects of hormones probably come about through their acting on reinforcement centers in the brain. We have already considered one example—the reproductive behavior of ring doves—which probably operates in this way. As we have seen, the presence of a courting male stimulates ovarian development in the female. The hormones released by the ovaries then cause the female to build a nest, probably through acting on reinforcement centers within the central nervous system.

STRESS REACTIONS

In human beings, the study of hormones has led to a radical change in ideas about how physiological and psychological variables are related to one another. Not only may psychological states result from physiological processes, but physiological states may result from psychological processes. The study of stress reactions, initiated with the work of Hans Selye, has resulted in a growing awareness of the interactions among the endocrine system, the divisions of the nervous system, other body tissues, and the environment.[10] The picture which emerged has made fundamental changes in our views of how the organism adapts to its environment and of the meaning of health and disease.

Selye's work originated with an observation he made as a young medical student. He noticed, as many had before him, that diseases look pretty much alike in their early stages. While the field of medicine rejected this early stage of just being sick as of no interest since it did not aid in diagnosis, it struck Selye as being significant in its own right.

Although he did not follow up his observation at that time, it occurred to him again years later when he discovered that quite diverse noxious agents called out similar reactions from the body. Again he decided that these nonspecific reactions, like the syndrome of just being sick, were worthy of study in their own right. Despite discouragement by colleagues who felt he was wasting his time, he set out to study the body's general reactions to severe stress, calling these reactions the *general adaptation syndrome.*

This syndrome is called out by such diverse threats to the organism as burning, severe cold, infection, or psychological conflict. It has both adaptive and maladaptive consequences. Basically, it changes the relationship between the pituitary secretion *adrenocorticotropic hormone* (ACTH) and the *corticosteroid hormones* produced by ACTH stimulation of fatty globules on the adrenal glands.

The corticosteroids play important defensive roles in enabling the body to deal with many different kinds of threat. They are involved, for example, in walling off the sites of invading destructive microorganisms and in initiating and controlling the process of inflammation. Normally, the ACTH stimulation of the corticosteroid hormones is regulated by the presence of the hormones themselves in the blood, so that their level is kept relatively constant. In the general adaptation syndrome, this feedback mechanism is somehow circumvented, so that the corticosteroids are maintained at very high levels. Despite the useful functions played by these hormones in dealing with short-term stress, prolonged reliance on this mechanism can lead to such symptoms as high blood pressure, enlargement of the heart, ulcers, allergies, kidney inflammation, and ultimately, death. This is illustrated in one of Selye's studies on the effects of exposing rats to prolonged cold.[11]

One hundred rats were put into living quarters kept at near-freezing temperature. After two days, ten animals were sacrificed and their physical changes noted. The corticosteroid-producing fat bodies on their adrenal glands had been consumed, and their adrenals were enlarged by the process of making more corticosteroids. Their thymus glands were decreased, and they all had stomach ulcers. This represents the initial "alarm reaction" stage of the general adaptation syndrome.

Rats in this stage of the adaptation syndrome are less able to stand cold than other rats not as yet exposed to stress. Selye put some rats which had been in the cold living quarters, together with some rats which had been living in a normal environment, in a still colder room. The rats which had been living in the cold room stood the lower temperature less well than those which had not.

After a longer period in the cold room, however, the rats seemed to adapt to the cold. Rats which had been living for five weeks in the cold room were found to be better able to withstand the still colder chamber than were rats put straight there from a normal living environment. This resistance to cold, however, was bought at a cost. Rats kept in the cold chamber eventually died of exhaustion from their constant dependence on the general adaptation syndrome.

Because psychological stresses can cause reliance on the general adaptation syndrome just as physical ones can, Selye's research helps us to understand some of the ways in which psychosomatic symptoms may be caused. While these symptoms are developed through the effects of psychological stress, their physical consequences are just as real and just as debilitating as if they were caused by some other factor.

Selye's work on stress, then, reveals how the psychological interpretation of stimuli may have important physiological consequences. Through the action of the corticosteroid hormones on reinforcement mechanisms, there may also be important motivational and emotional consequences of arousal of the general adaptation syndrome. We shall return to this topic and look at some studies of the relationships among environmental stress, psychiatric symptoms, and the general adaptation syndrome, when we consider emotion later in this chapter.

To summarize so far, we see that a picture of how motivational systems are organized is just beginning to emerge from psychological and physiological research. Generally, these systems are based on reinforcement mechanisms which have proved adaptive in the evolution of the organism. They are located in the hypothalamic and limbic areas of the brain; they have mechanisms for both initiating and terminating the motivated behavior; and they are often partially under hormonal control. Finally, they both serve as a basis for, and are modified by, those learning processes which give such great flexibility to human behavior.

Some Specific Motives

THIRST

The homeostatic drive of thirst illustrates the general properties of the motivational systems we have been considering. It is obviously adaptive for the organism and serves as a basis for learning. It has separate mechanisms for initiating and terminating the motivated behavior; it involves a reinforcement mechanism in the hypothalamus; and it utilizes hormonal as well as neural control of behavior.

Even before psychologists learned what mechanisms initiated and terminated drinking behavior, it was clear that separate mechanisms were involved. First, it was demonstrated that water entering the stomach was not necessary to the terminating of drinking. A dog with a *fistula* which prevented the water from entering the stomach still drank an amount of water proportional to, but somewhat in excess of, its need. Then it stopped drinking.[12] After a time of not drinking, the animal would again drink the same amount of water. This suggests that the drinking behavior is started by a mechanism dependent upon the body's need for water, but it may be temporarily inhibited by a mechanism not depending on fluid absorption.

The separate mechanisms for initiating and terminating drinking are shown even more directly by the results of placing water directly into the stomach of a thirsty dog without passing it through the dog's mouth.[13] If the dog is allowed to drink immediately after this injection and before the water can be absorbed, it will drink the same amount it would have if the water had not been placed in its stomach. If there is time for the water to be absorbed before the animal is allowed to drink, it will not drink at all. In the former case, the failure of the water to pass through the dog's mouth keeps it from activating the usual mechanism for terminating drinking. In the latter, the water is absorbed and inactivates the mechanism which initiates drinking before the animal has a chance to drink.

One mechanism which initiates drinking and one which terminates it have now been definitely identified. There are suggestions, however, that other mechanisms which are not yet so well understood are involved as well. There is one area of the hypothalamus which responds to an increase in the osmotic pressure of the blood (which in turn depends on the ratio of salts to liquid in the blood and hence increases with thirst). This center not only initiates drinking behavior; it also releases an *antidiuretic hormone* into the bloodstream. The antidiuretic hormone has a specific action on the kidneys, causing them to remove water from the urine and thus to conserve body fluids.

A mechanism which terminates drinking behavior was discovered by Zotterman.[14] It is a nerve fiber in the tongue which responds to salt and to water in the following ways: The fiber has a high spontaneous rate of discharge, and is thus constantly sending nerve impulses to the central nervous system. When salt or a hypertonic (salty) solution is placed on the tongue, the fiber increases its rate of firing. When water or a hypotonic (nonsalty) solution is placed on the tongue, the fiber decreases its rate of firing. The fiber thus provides a basis for the control center in the hypothalamus to judge when sufficient water has passed through the mouth to make up a given fluid deficit.

Unfortunately, from the viewpoint of simplicity, there seem to be other control systems as well. There is a different center in the brain which has effects on both eating and drinking. There are also indications that drinking may be initiated by a low volume of blood as well as by an increase in its osmotic pressure, and that it may be inhibited to some extent by a high volume of stomach contents. These overlapping systems may be adaptive for the organism by ensuring that a function as vital as fluid maintenance is not totally dependent on the functioning of any one mechanism.

HUNGER

The hunger drive illustrates the incompleteness of our understanding of even some of the most basic human motives. Two brain centers are known; one of them stimulates eating behavior, the other inhibits it. The exact way in which they function, and how the control system sometimes breaks down, however, are less well understood.

Schachter and his colleagues have, in recent years, carried out a series of interesting studies on highly obese people.[15] These studies reveal that people who develop serious overweight problems differ not only in how much they eat but even more in the conditions under which they eat. Let us consider one of the studies.

In order to measure eating behavior without making their subjects self-conscious, Schachter, Goldman, and Gordon presented the study as one dealing with taste preference.[16] Subjects were asked to rate the taste of five kinds of crackers, eating as many of them as they needed in order to be sure of their ratings. The dependent variable which was actually being measured was the number of crackers each subject ate.

The effects of two variables on eating were investigated in the study, for both normal and obese subjects. Some subjects tasted the crackers after being deprived of food, and others, immediately after eating. Also, some tasted them while in a fear-inducing situation, and others tasted them without the arousal of fear. (Those in the fear-inducing situation expected to receive painful electric shocks in a later portion of the experiment.)

For subjects of normal weight, the manipulations of stomach fullness and amount of fear arousal had the effects which might be expected. They ate less when their stomachs were full than when they were empty, and less when they were frightened than when they were not. (Part of the body's reaction to stressful situations involves decreasing blood flow to the digestive system, so that a decrease in appetite is a normal effect of fear.) The obese subjects reacted quite differently. The obese person would eat slightly more if his stomach was full when the experiment started than he would if it was empty, and a good deal more if he was frightened than if he was not.

From this and other studies, Schachter concluded that the obese subjects ate in response to different cues from those utilized by people of normal weight. Emotions due to quite different causes, such as fear or loneliness, may be attributed to hunger by the obese subject. Furthermore, obese subjects are much more responsive to environmental cues to eating than are individuals without an eating problem. The normal-weight individual will eat about the same amount regardless of the size of helping he is given. If the helping is too small, he will go get more. If it is too large, he will leave part of it. The obese individual, on the other hand, tends to eat the amount that is easily available, regardless of whether it is too much or too little. The obese person who is trying to control his weight needs to stay out of the sight of food.

A similar eating pattern can be created in experimental animals by damaging the center which inhibits eating on each side of the brain. The cause of obesity in humans would be easy to understand if it turned out that obese people had lesions in these motivational areas. This, however, does not appear to be the case. Either there are physiological causes of obesity which are not yet understood, or obesity in humans depends more on how individuals learn to react to their drives than on the physiological drives themselves.

SEX

The modifiability of basic drives through learning, hinted at by studies of obesity, is even more apparent in the area of sexual behavior. While the sexual behavior of many organisms is quite directly under the control of sexual hormones, that of mammals and especially of human beings is much more independent of hormone levels. Sexual behavior is not completely under hormonal control even in birds. Pigeons usually cease mating after castration, but mating may be induced by particularly active female pigeons.[17] As one goes higher in the phylogenetic scale, hormone levels and behavior become less and less associated. In human beings, considerable sexual behavior may continue in the absence of supporting hormones.

The effects of sex hormones on behavior seem to involve not only current activation of structures but also differences in the development of behavior patterns. Animals castrated before maturity do not exhibit sexual behavior, whereas those castrated after maturity may continue to show it. Similarly, capons and poulards behave differently after the same hormone treatment, showing the effects of those hormones present during early stages of development. These and similar observations suggest that many of the more important effects of sexual hormones are caused by their facilitating the organization of fixed action patterns in the brain during development.[18]

AFFILIATION

If a newborn chick is isolated from other chickens, it will utter loud distress cries. If exposed at this period to a moving object, a flashing light, or another chicken, it will make great efforts to approach that stimulus. When it succeeds in doing so, it will cease making the distress cries, and from then on the presence of the object will be able to comfort the baby chick and will serve as a strong positive reinforcer for it. We say, then, that the chick has becomes imprinted on the stimulus.

The motivational mechanisms which lie behind this behavior are highly adaptive for the baby chick. Its cries enable its mother to find it, the imprinting experience causes it to follow its mother, and the physiological arousal it experiences when isolated may even prepare it to cope with dangerous situations. Furthermore, the fact that the imprinted stimulus serves as a reinforcer can make it the basis for other learning.

When a human infant is left unattended, it too will utter loud distress cries. It can be comforted by being held, and it will become strongly attached to the parent figure which holds it. If continually left unattended, on the other hand, it will eventually stop crying, but it will show signs of emotional detachment and grieving. It may stop eating and die.

There are, of course, some differences in the attachment behavior of the chick and the child. The chick, for example, learns to recognize its own mother from among other similar organisms much earlier than does the child. Despite these differences, the attachment behavior of the child is at least as important as that of the chick. Although it was not recognized until quite recently, the reinforcement mechanisms involved in affiliation serve as the basis of much of the learning which the child carries out. The reassurance that the parent gives the child is also important in making the child feel secure enough to explore a new situation. Even an adult, when joining a group of people, will greet each one before feeling secure in the new situation. The research which has been done on affiliation and its importance in human development will be looked at in the next chapter when we consider personality development.

OTHER MOTIVES

The list of innate motives which we have considered is far from complete. The interactions of innate reinforcement mechanisms, hormonal control, and learning are so complex that we are just beginning to understand their role in a few human motives. For many others, we have little or no idea of their physiological bases and consequences. We have noted, for example, that it is positively reinforcing for the young child to experience stimulus patterns which are slightly, but not greatly, different from a schema which he has built up through past experience. Although this mechanism plays a vital role in much human learning, we have absolutely no idea how it works. This is perhaps not too surprising when you consider that, only a few years ago, it was thought that the entire limbic system in the brain was merely a vestigial remnant from the highly developed sense of smell found in lower organisms.

Perhaps closely related to the mechanism which makes variations on familiar patterns reinforcing is the mechanism involved in the need for autonomy. Let us consider an experiment with mice.[19] The mice are kept in a cage in which they have control over the level of illumination. Since mice follow a diurnal rhythm in their lives, they eventually come to change this variable in a regular way at approximately the same time each day. If the experimenter changes the light level before the mice do, however, the mice will change the level back again. The mouse seems to be like the woman in the television commercial—he prefers to do it himself.

The apparent need for autonomy which the animals show in this study could be based on a mechanism which would make the anticipation of future stimulation reinforcing. In that case, the animal would anticipate, when it made an adjustment in the controls, what change in its environment would result. Changes made by the experimenter, on the other hand, would be unpleasant because they were not anticipated. On the basis of introspective evidence, anticipation does seem to play an important role in many human pleasures. If you listen to a piece of music, for example, you can often anticipate each note just an instant before it is played, even though you may not know the piece well enough to reproduce it all from memory. Similarly, in the motor play of young children, the reinforcing factor often seems to be the willing of something, imagining its happening, and then seeing it actually happen.

Whatever their bases, people in all cultures seem to have some motives of affiliation and autonomy; curiosity and aggression; altruism and aesthetic appreciation. In the chapters that follow, we shall try to understand how these motives are developed and transformed in the course of individual socialization. We shall look at the role of early experiences in the development of affiliation, the consequences of developing autonomy, and the interaction of biological and cultural factors in producing a crisis of identity at puberty. While we are ignorant of the biological mechanisms of many human motives, we know a good deal more about their role in the development of the individual person.

One of the most striking things about cultural difference is the way in which different emotions are institutionalized. Among one group, death is an occasion for mourning, while for another, it is a cause for rejoicing. In one culture, the bereaved is expected to feel a little bit sad for three days, and then to forget the deceased and go on with life. In another, the bereaved is expected to show mourning by chopping off several of his fingers and carrying out murderous attacks on anyone who has the bad sense to come near him.

Other motives and emotions differ similarly. Some groups show so little aggression toward others that if it were not for their tendency to develop psychosomatic ailments, they might be thought to be completely lacking in any but benevolent motives toward everyone. Rivalry, competition, and jealousy are highly developed among other groups. Clearly, the human capacity to be molded by one's culture is very great in the area of emotional development.

It is not, however, complete. Some Plains Indians were not fearless warriors, and even the most gentle of people sometimes feel jealousy or anger. Any useful theory of human emotion must be able to account for both these observations. It must show how an emotional experience can be greatly changed by learning, yet can still contain some core which resists too divergent an interpretation.

Emotion is a cognitive interpretation imposed on a physiological state of arousal. As the state of arousal itself depends upon the interpretive processes which are part of perception, thinking and feeling are very closely intertwined with each other. This is perhaps nowhere more clearly demonstrated than in the studies of psychiatric symptoms and physiological stress.

We have noted that the general adaptation syndrome may be called out by either physiological or psychological stress. When it is called out, it leads to an increase in the rate of excretion of certain hormones which are produced in the stress reaction. By taking regular urine samples, and studying the levels of 17-hydroxycorticosteroids, it is possible to accurately measure an individual's physiological stress reaction.

Studies using this technique have demonstrated a clear relationship between the level of an individual's corticosteroids and the amount of psychological stress to which he is being exposed. One study by Bunney et al. is typical.[20] Patients in a mental hospital who had depressive psychoses were tested for daily corticosteroid levels and independently rated on their state of psychological well-being. Experiences of the patients which they reacted to as being severely ego-threatening were also recorded, separately. When the patients were suffering a severe depressive psychotic crisis as observed by the psychological raters, coinciding on later inspection of their case histories with some separately recorded ego-threatening experience such as being told they would not be released from the hospital as soon as they had expected, their corticosteroid levels were discovered to have been almost three times their average level.

Just as one's interpretation of an event as very threatening can increase one's stress reaction, denying the threat can reduce the physiological stress reaction. This seems, in fact, to be one of the functions of the development of psychiatric symptoms. By denying threatening aspects of reality, an individual may protect himself from levels of stress which would be not only highly unpleasant but perhaps even physically dangerous. Although adaptive in the short run, this type of self-protection proves maladaptive in the long run, however. A study by Wolff and his colleagues showing how the denial of reality protects the individual from experiencing stress will be discussed in Chapter 8.[21]

There are, then, some constraints on the extent to which external reality can be reinterpreted. Interpretations which are too far from reality will prove inadequate for predicting what will happen and will deny to the interpreter the benefits of intelligence. What about internal reality? Are there limits on the extent to which a person can reinterpret his emotional arousal? There definitely do seem to be, even though the exact ways in which they operate are not yet understood. First, while a person might attribute his physiological arousal to any of a number of causes, it would be difficult for him to deny its existence completely. This is so because the endocrines released by the stress reaction would cause changes in internal states and in activity level which would need to be explained. A person whose heart is racing, who is sweating profusely, whose hands are trembling, and who cannot sit still for an instant will have difficulty in convincing himself that what he is experiencing is calm relaxation.

What is less clear is the extent to which there are different types of physiological arousal which activate different reinforcement mechanisms and thus facilitate the experiencing of different emotional states. It was once thought that each emotion was caused by its own characteristic physiological state. Studies such as those we have been discussing, and others by Schachter and his colleagues which we shall consider soon, have caused theorizing to swing in the other direction. Schachter and some other theorists now seem to assume that only one type of arousal exists, and that it may be freely interpreted as any strong emotion. We have noted in an earlier chapter, however, that adrenalin and noradrenalin are secreted under different conditions and seem to lead to different types of responses to threatening conditions. It thus might be more reasonable to take a middle position and to assume that more than one type of physiological arousal is possible even though any given type can be given a variety of interpretations.

Some support for this position comes from studies of the functions of different parts of the limbic system. As we have already noted, this system is primarily concerned with the sense of smell in organisms lower on the evolutionary scale, but it is the main center for emotional functioning in man. This transition in function is not so strange as it might appear at first glance, for smells serve as one of the chief bases of motivational and emotional arousal in many animals. Recent studies have shown, for example, that air exhausted from the cage of a frightened rat and piped into the cage of another rat will cause that rat to cower in fear.[22] If emotions are adaptive because they facilitate the expression of motives appropriate to a situation, it would not be surprising that they should have evolved out of the sense of smell, which played a major role in the control of eating, fear, and sexual behavior.

Although there is still considerable disagreement on the functions of various parts of the limbic system, there does at least seem to be a clear differentiation of function between one subsystem composed of a portion called the amygdala and its connections, and another composed of the pathways of the fornix leading into the hippocampus (a structure deriving its name from its resemblance in shape to a sea horse). In cats, stimulation of the former of these subsystems leads to fear, rage, hunger, searching, and attack; that of the latter subsystem, to grooming and courtship.[23] As might be expected, stimulation of the first of these subsystems results in an increase in the secretion of corticosteroid hormones, while the second subsystem seems to inhibit stress reactions. Within these two subsystems, there are suggestions that specific locations are involved in the release of sexual hormones and the activation of specific reinforcement mechanisms. Because of the complexities of the systems being studied and the limitations of research techniques, however, many of the findings are ambiguous.

While there thus do seem to be some constraints on what interpretations can be given to a particular physiological state, the latitude for interpretation is still very broad. This is most clearly shown in the studies of Schachter and his colleagues. Let us look at a pioneering study by Schachter and Singer as an example.[24] Essentially, their study shows that both physiological arousal and a plausible emotional explanation of the arousal are necessary to the experiencing of an emotion.

What Schachter and Singer did was to have a physician inject subjects with either epinephrine or a *placebo*, a dilute saline solution having no physiological effects. The placebo treatment acted as control and enabled the experimenters to be sure that the effects they were observing were not just due to the subjects' knowing that they had been given a drug and feeling that it should have some effect. Some subjects who were given the epinephrine were correctly told what its physical effects would be—shaking hands, a flushed face, and a pounding heart. Others were misinformed as to its effects, being told that it might make their feet feel numb. The prediction was that subjects who were misinformed about the effects of the epinephrine would ascribe their physiological arousal to an emotion caused by their current social situation, while those who knew that the epinephrine caused their arousal would not experience any strong emotion.

An essential part of the experiment, then, was to create different social situations to which the physiological arousal could be ascribed. Two such situations were arranged, one in which the subject might reasonably expect to feel euphoric and one in which he might feel angry. Each involved the use of a confederate who was supposedly also a subject in the experiment. In one situation, the confederate acted in a wild and silly manner, playing a game of basketball with scraps of paper and a wastebasket, making a slingshot, and playing with a hula hoop. In the anger situation, on the other hand, the confederate objected to a questionnaire which he and the real subject were filling out, eventually tearing it up and leaving the room. It was predicted that the subject who was misinformed about the effects of the epinephrine would report feeling the same as the confederate—happy or angry, depending on the confederate's behavior, but that a subject would not report these emotional reactions if he had not received the epinephrine or was correctly informed as to its effects.

In general, the results supported the hypothesis very strongly. In the euphoria treatment, the subjects who had been misinformed about the effects of the hormone not only reported more happy emotion than those who knew the true effect of the hormone—they even behaved differently. The misinformed subjects significantly more often started playing the wild games with the confederates. The subjects in the two treatments, although they were experiencing the same physiological arousal, attributed it to happiness or anger, depending on the social context in which it occurred. Having interpreted the ambiguous stimulus of their physiological state as due to an emotion, they then behaved in a way appropriate to the emotion.

This study goes a long way toward helping us to understand how different cultures can create such contrasting motives and emotions in their members. The individual not only learns different physiological responses to situations, as we noted in the chapter on learning; he also learns different interpretations of what he is feeling. By providing individuals with interpretations of what they are feeling, cultures may call out radically disparate behavior from the same physiological base.

What about individuals whose interpretations deviate too far from reality, however? The person who denies inner reality, for example by saying that he is not angry when he is, and the one who denies external reality by imagining that he will live forever, each may find the real world destroying his interpretations. The one may find himself suddenly and inexplicably carried away by rage, while the other may become so ill that the possibility of death becomes inexorably apparent. We have seen that the denial of reality may protect the individual from physiological stress. Being forced to face it may temporarily cause him great anxiety. This is illustrated in a study by Sachar.[25]

Sachar and his colleagues studied the excreted corticosteroids of psychiatric patients being treated for extreme depression. At the beginning of treatment, they had relatively low excretion rates, for they were not experiencing much physiological stress. They were, however, protecting themselves from stress by the use of reality-denying defenses. During the course of psychiatric treatment, their corticosteroid levels went up as they came to grips with reality and experienced anxiety. By the end of treatment, which was successful in most cases, they had achieved a more realistic orientation toward the world and toward the events which had precipitated their psychological crises. At that time, they returned to low stress levels while no longer showing the denial of reality which they had exhibited before treatment.

The meaning of physiological states, then, depends on how they are interpreted. This is true not only of emotion but also of pain, as is shown by two further studies. One of them was done by Nisbett and Schachter.[26] They gave inert pills to their subjects. They told half of them that these pills would cause hand tremor, accelerated breathing, and other symptoms which are commonly ascribed to a state of fear. They told the other half of the subjects that the pills would cause symptoms unrelated to those caused by fear. They then asked the subjects to expose themselves to as high a level of electric shock as they could endure.

Their prediction was based on the interpretations the subjects would make. They reasoned that the subjects would all have physiological arousal through fear of the shock. Those subjects who correctly attributed their symptoms to the shock would probably be less willing to experience high levels of shock than those who thought that their symptoms were merely caused by the pill. The prediction was upheld, for the subjects who attributed their fear-symptoms to the pills exposed themselves to four times the intensity of shock that the other subjects were willing to endure.

The other study is even more dramatic, although its results must still be regarded as tentative. To what extent is the pain of a fatal illness due to the meaning of that pain? If the individual has not yet faced the possibility of death, the pain may be more unbearable because of what it symbolizes to the dying individual. One study, done by Gary Fisher, provides strong evidence that psychotherapy oriented to helping dying individuals face the possibility of death can dramatically reduce the pain which they experience.[27] Terminal cancer patients in the study were often able to go for days without pain-reducing drugs, after working through some of their emotional reactions to dying.

The Measurement of Motives

It is of considerable interest to try to determine how the social motives of the adult develop. In many practical situations, however, it is more useful to measure his motives without worrying too much about where they came from. To some extent, it is possible to learn about a person's goals and aspirations by asking him about them. There are two limitations to this approach, however. The person may not be consciously aware of some of his motives, and he may not be willing to tell you about some of them. For these reasons, his statements are usually not taken completely at face value. Instead, they are tested against observations on how he actually behaves and against inferences drawn from his production of fantasy material. This last approach is that taken in projective tests. Let us look at one of the most widely used of these, the *Thematic Apperception Test* (TAT) devised by Henry Murray.

The Thematic Apperception Test is based on the idea that individuals will interpret ambiguous situations in terms of their own beliefs, values, and interests. An individual taking the test is asked to make up a story about the persons shown in each of a score of pictures. The stories he tells tend to reflect both his needs and his perceptions of the nature of his environment.

The test consists of twenty pictures, differing somewhat with the age and sex of the person who is being tested. There are a number of advantages to using known stimuli, such as the pictures, to stimulate the fantasy production. Through the use of stimuli related to important social motives and conflicts, the person's fantasies can be led into areas which will provide a more complete and systematic picture of motivation than would emerge from completely unguided fantasy during the same period of time. Also, it is important to know the stimulus which started the fantasy production because things in the pictures which are not mentioned are often as significant as those which are responded to. Ignoring the main features and concentrating on a minor detail of a picture can be an indication of conflict over the motives apparently being acted out in the part of the picture which is ignored.

The interpretation of the TAT is too complex to be discussed in a brief introduction such as this. Moreover, it is not always equally rewarding with all subjects, since the telling of brief conventional stories may enable an individual to take the test without revealing much about himself. At other times, however, a story will touch on central problems and adjustments of the individual. One such example is given by Holt, who uses it to outline the basic ideas in the interpretation of the test. Let us look briefly at the story and refer to Holt for a more detailed discussion of it.[28]

In the card which Holt uses in his example, "An adolescent boy looks straight out of the picture. The barrel of a rifle is visible at one side, and in the background is the dim scene of a surgical operation, like a reverie-image." The story told about it by a young college man, here called Nailson, was as follows:

> Gee, it looks like a young fellow (pause). Oh, fellow is about fifteen, I guess. It's (pause). He's either seen or read about some operation in which the patient has gone through all kinds of tortures, and he decided he's going to become a doctor. He's going to fix things, they're not going to happen like that any more. These are old doctors, very old, long time ago, I guess. They're going to town, probably no ether or anything else. The kid was probably just a young baby at the time, maybe. Looks like he had a nightmare or two. And (pause) that determined his life for him. He's going to spend his whole time trying to be a doctor and not have any more operations like this. He's going to (pause). Well, it could be that he's something like Bliss or some one of the great doctors that invented anaesthetics, something to bring ease to the patient during the operation. Probably spend his whole life trying to develop something like that. Anyway, he's going to be a doctor, he's not going to have anything like this happen again.[29]

While a number of things could be noted in the young man's story, such as his not mentioning the rifle, his confusion about the boy's age, and even that the boy is going to spend his time trying to be a doctor, let us look at just a portion of the story. The subject says, "He's either seen or read about some operation in which the patient has gone through all kinds of tortures," and immediately follows this with "and he decided he's going to become a doctor." What he appears to have said at this point is that the boy is going to become a doctor so that he can torture people. The rapidity with which the subject denies this by saying, "He's going to fix things, they're not going to happen like that any more," suggests that this same thought is going through his mind and supports rather than denies the interpretation.

Most stories are not so revealing as this one. Nailson had gone through a period of overt sadism, during which he tortured the animals on his father's farm. After that, he had become very concerned over the welfare of the animals and had taken over all the slaughtering on the farm so that it would be done as humanely as possible. This particular mode of handling a motive, appearing to act on just the opposite motive (humaneness) while giving covert expression to the denied motive (sadism), in this case by taking pleasure in the slaughtering, is called *reaction formation*. It is the same mechanism as that shown by the hero of the story.

Can behavior in social situations actually be predicted by tests such as the TAT? Yes, though certainly not perfectly. Let us look at an experiment by Birney, Burdick, Caylor, O'Connor, and Veroff [30] as an illustration, first describing it as it appeared to the subject and then as it appeared to the experimenter. The subjects arrived at the laboratory in pairs, since each original subject had been told to bring a friend as a fellow subject. It was explained to them that one of each pair (the encoder) would have the task of putting messages into a code and that the other (the decoder) would have the task of translating the code messages back into English. The encoder would be scored on how many of the messages he managed to put into code within a limited period of time, and the decoder would be scored on what proportion of the code messages he received he managed to decode within a limited period of time.

For each coder, the task proceeded smoothly for the first few trials. After the second and third trials, he was shown scores which indicated that his decoder was not keeping up with him very well, and after the fourth trial, he received a message from his partner asking him to "Please slow down." At this point, he had to decide whether to make the best score he could by continuing to work fast, or to help his partner by slowing down. (Since the partner was being scored on the proportion of code messages decoded, the fewer code messages there were for him to decode the easier it was for him to make a high score.) Finally, on the last trial, the coder was told that his partner would not have to decode the messages coded on that trial. (This was to see how fast the encoder could really go.)

The reader may have guessed by now that the experiment was rigged, for otherwise how could we know what messages the coder's partner would send him? In fact, there were no decoders. Each person was told that he was the coder and his partner was the decoder, and the message to slow down came from the experimenter. The purpose of this deception was to place each subject in the same rather common conflict situation—a situation where the person must decide between achieving the most that he can himself or helping a friend. (For the good student, the conflict is likely to occur whenever there is a course examination. Should you review for the exam with a friend who has less good notes although this will help him more than it helps you, or should you leave him to founder, and study on your own?)

The experiment thus presented the subject with a conflict between an *achievement* motive and a motive of *affiliation*, or maintaining close relations with others. Predictions were made on the basis of measures of these motives which had been taken before the experiment began, using a technique which is similar in principle to the TAT. It was predicted that subjects who were high in need for affiliation but not high in need for achievement would slow down, and that those who were high in need for achievement but not high in need for affiliation would continue working rapidly. No predictions were made for subjects who were high in both needs or not high in either.

At this point, the complicating factor of sex must be mentioned. The norms in our culture generally develop more achievement motivation than affiliation motivation in men, and less achievement motivation but more affiliation motivation in women. Because of this, situations must arouse stronger affiliation motivation to make men resolve conflicts in terms of affiliation than to make women do so. In the present experiment, the affiliation motives were not sufficient to make the men deviate from their desires for achievement—they did not slow down to help their partners. The women, however, often did so. Of the women with strong affiliation motives and weak achievement motives, three-quarters of them slowed down. Of those with strong achievement motives and weak affiliation motives, only a quarter did so. These results are highly significant, although prediction of course is still not perfect—the wrong prediction was made for a quarter of the women. This inaccuracy should not surprise us, for our measures of motives are not perfect and there are other complicating factors. Prediction might have been better, for example, if we had known how close friends the individual pairs of subjects were.

Summary

Living organisms engage in self-motivated activities. Human personality development begins with biological systems of motivation. Motivational systems include arrangements for both starting and stopping an activity such as eating. They use innate mechanisms, which are greatly modified by developmental experiences. The reinforcement mechanisms, in particular parts of the brain which control various motivational systems, also serve as bases for learning. Many motivational systems are partly under the control of hormones secreted by ductless glands.

The hypothalamus and the limbic system are the parts of the brain most concerned with motivation and emotion. The pleasure centers discovered in the limbic system are part of the reinforcement mechanism of the learning process. What activates them seems to vary from species to species. Much evidence shows that engaging in innate behavior patterns which enhance an animal's survival in its native habitat is pleasurable to the animal. The same neural mechanisms which are involved in reinforcement in the learning process are involved in the release of positive and negative species-specific behavior. Innate action patterns are engaged in because they are rewarding in themselves. They are organized into complex behaviors as the animal discovers that reward, such as food or the warmth of a nest, results from engaging in them in a certain sequence in the appropriate environment.

Hormones can control the growth and activity of organs involved in motivational systems, can effect general physiological states, and can act upon other endocrine glands and reinforcement mechanisms in the brain. Physiological reactions to psychological events are a potential consequence of this interaction. The general adaptation syndrome discovered by Selye is a physiological reaction to stress that can be triggered by both emotional and physical trauma, for example.

The motives of thirst and hunger have been extensively studied. The basic control system of thirst is understood, although additional control systems also govern it. Hunger seems so complex that learned interpretations of physiological stimuli, as contrasted with simple innate physiological drives, must play a crucial role. The effect of hormones in facilitating the organization of fixed action patterns in the brain during development is well illustrated in the sexual motivational system, and the affiliative motivational system illustrates the contribution of emotion to physical development. Not all motivational systems are known, nor their biological mechanisms understood. Experiments with the mouse suggest the existence of an innate motive of autonomy. This may be related to anticipation being intrinsically rewarding.

Emotion is a cognitive interpretation imposed on a physiological state of arousal. The state of arousal itself depends upon the interpretive processes which are part of perception, and thinking and feeling are therefore very closely intertwined. Threatening aspects of reality which might induce a dangerous stress reaction may even be interpreted in a distorted way to reduce the threat and therefore the stress. Both physiological arousal and a plausible emotional explanation of the arousal are necessary to the experiencing of an emotion. Similar arousals may be interpreted very differently. This means that a person's learned cultural environment can provide him with some of the emotions which he experiences by giving him plausible explanations for his physiological states.

Motives, also, can be interpreted by an individual in such a way that their nature is distorted or concealed. Projective tests are designed to provide clues to such reinterpreted motivation. Experiments which put people in situations where one motive can be satisfied only at the expense of another allow some measurement of individual differences in kinds of motivations.

Notes and Acknowledgments

1. These examples are discussed by Irenaus Eibl-Eibesfeldt in *Ethology, the Biology of Behavior*. New York: Holt, Rinehart and Winston, Inc., 1970, pp. 24–26.
2. Lehrman, D. S. "The presence of the mate and of nesting material as stimuli for the development of incubation behavior and for gonadotropic secretion in the ring dove." *Endocrinology*, 1961 (68), pp. 507–516.

3. Deutsch, J. A., and A. D. Jones. "Diluted water: An explanation of the rat's preference for saline." *Journal of Comparative and Physiological Psychology,* 1960 (53), pp. 122–127.

4. Olds, James. "Pleasure centers in the brain." *Scientific American,* October 1956.

5. Glickman, S. E., and B. B. Schiff. "A biological theory of reinforcement." *Psychological Review,* March 1967 (74), pp. 81–109.

6. Glickman, S. E., and R. W. Sroges. "Curiosity in zoo animals." *Behaviour,* 1966 (26), pp. 151–188.

7. Eibl-Eibesfeldt, Irenaus. "The interactions of unlearned behavior patterns and learning in mammals," in the symposium *Brain Mechanisms and Learning.* Springfield, Ill.: Charles C Thomas, Publisher, 1961, pp. 53–73.

8. Roberts, W. W., and H. O. Kiess. "Motivational properties of hypothalamic aggression in cats." *Journal of Comparative and Physiological Psychology,* 1964 (54), pp. 187–193.

9. Eibl-Eibesfeldt, Irenaus. "The interactions of unlearned behavior patterns and learning in mammals." Op. cit.

10. For an interesting introduction to Selye's work in this area, see Hans Selye, *The Stress of Life.* New York: McGraw-Hill Book Company, 1956.

11. Ibid., pp. 88–89.

12. Bellows, R. T. "Time factors in water drinking in dogs." *American Journal of Physiology,* 1939 (125), pp. 87–97.

13. Adolph, E. F. "The internal environment and behavior: III. Water content." *American Journal of Psychiatry,* 1941 (97), pp. 1367–1373.

14. See Deutsch, J. A., and A. D. Jones. Op. cit.

15. Schachter, S. "Cognitive effects on bodily functioning: Studies of obesity and eating," in David C. Glass (Ed.), *Neurophysiology and Emotion,* proceedings of a conference under the auspices of the Rockefeller University and Russell Sage Foundation. New York: Rockefeller University Press and Russell Sage Foundation, 1967, pp. 117–144.

16. Schachter, S., R. Goldman, and A. Gordon. "The effects of fear, food deprivation and obesity on eating." Unpublished manuscript, 1967, discussed in S. Schachter. Op. cit.

17. Carpenter, C. R. "Psychobiological studies of social behavior in Aves: II. The effect of complete and incomplete gonadectomy on secondary sexual activity, with histological studies." *Journal of Comparative Psychology,* 1933 (16), pp. 59–98.

18. Recent research on this topic is summarized in Richard P. Michael (Ed.), *Endocrinology and Human Behavior,* proceedings of a conference, London, May 1967. New York: Oxford University Press, Inc., 1968.

19. Kavanau, J. Lee. "Automatic monitoring of the activities of small mammals," in Kenneth E. F. Watt (Ed.), *Systems Analysis in Ecology.* New York: Academic Press, Inc., 1966, pp. 99–146.

20. Bunney, W. E., John W. Mason, John F. Roatch, and David A. Hamburg. "A psychoendocrine study of severe psychotic depressive crisis." *American Journal of Psychiatry,* July 1965, pp. 72–80.

21. Wolff, Carl T., Stanford B. Friedman, Myron A. Hofer, and John W. Mason. "Relationship between psychological defenses and mean urinary 17-hydroxycorticosteroid excretion rates: I. A predictive study of parents of fatally ill children." *Psychosomatic Medicine,* 1964 (26), pp. 576–591.

22. Valenta, John G., and Marilyn K. Rigby. "Discrimination of the odor of stressed rats." *Science,* August 1968 (161), pp. 599–601.

23. MacLean, Paul D. "The limbic brain in relation to the psychoses," in Perry Black (Ed.), *Physiological Correlates of Emotion.* New York: Academic Press, Inc., 1970, pp. 133–135.

24. Schachter, Stanley, and Jerome Singer. "Cognitive, social, and physiological determinants of emotional state," in R. J. C. Harper et al. (Eds.), *The Cognitive Processes: Readings.* Englewood Cliffs, N.J.: Prentice-Hall, Inc., 1964, pp. 426–449.

25. Sachar, Edward J., John M. Mackenzie, William A. Binstock, and John E. Mack. "Corticosteroid responses to psychotherapy of depressions: I. Evaluations during confrontation of loss." *Archives of General Psychiatry,* April 1967 (16), pp. 461–470.

26. Nisbett, R. E., and S. Schachter. "The cognitive manipulation of pain." *Journal of Experimental Social Psychology,* 1966 (2), pp. 227–236.

27. Fisher, G. "Psychotherapy for the dying: Principles and illustrative cases with special reference to the use of LSD." *Omega,* 1970 (1), no. 1, pp. 3–15.

28. Holt, Robert R. "The thematic apperception test," in Harold H. Anderson and Gladys L. Anderson (Eds.), *An Introduction to Projective Techniques.* Englewood Cliffs, N.J.: Prentice-Hall, Inc., 1951.

29. Ibid., p. 184. By permission of the author.

30. Birney, R., H. Burdick, J. Caylor, P. O'Connor, and J. Veroff. Research summarized as chap. 6 of Edward L. Walker and Roger Heyns, *An Anatomy for Conformity.* Englewood Cliffs, N.J.: Prentice-Hall, Inc., 1962, pp. 54–68.

David Gahr

SIX

PERSONALITY DEVELOPMENT

Introduction

PERSONALITY

What is personality, and where does it come from? Psychologists use the term to refer to the behaviors and adaptations which are characteristic of a given person and which remain relatively stable over time. The same person's behavior will differ from one situation to another, yet it will have some characteristics that will mark it as distinctively his. One person, for example, may react to the environment as threatening and another may perceive it as benign. Similarly, one

169

may exhibit a strong need for social approval in a variety of circumstances while another seems to be without such a need. Because each of these individuals shows the given characteristic in many different situations, it is regarded as a part of his personality.

The expression of personality involves the operation of each of the types of basic process which we have considered thus far in the book. A person may act in a characteristic way because of how he perceives his environment or because of the ways in which he has learned to express his motives. In either case, his way of adapting to his environment is learned, although heredity may set some limits on the adaptations which he is capable of learning. The processes of learning, thinking, perceiving, and being motivated, which we have separated for purposes of analysis, are intimately bound up with one another in the development of personality.

In the last chapter, we looked briefly at the ways in which tests may be used to describe the current functioning of a personality without consideration of how that personality has developed. In this chapter and the next one, we shall examine the processes by which personality develops. In doing so, we shall consider some developmental processes to be healthy and others to be pathological. This necessitates taking a position on what one values rather than simply on questions of fact. What *is* does not tell what *should be*, and applying knowledge always involves making ethical decisions. Because the distinction which psychologists make between normal and pathological personality functioning serves as the basis for the applied field of clinical psychology, we should try to make our value choices as explicit as possible in making this distinction.

NORMALCY

First let us consider the ways in which the word "normal" is *not* used in this book. It is not being used to mean either similar to everyone else or "adjusted" to one's society. Because people differ in their capabilities, experiences, and value choices, what is normal for one person may not be normal for another. Similarly, the possibility must be kept open that one's society should be changed rather than adjusted to. "Normal" should thus be defined in a way which allows for a variety of kinds of normalcy, and which does not classify everyone who is trying to change his society as being sick.

Consider the case of George Jackson, the author of *Soledad Brother*.[1] Under a law which was based on a view of criminals as being "sick" and needing to be confined until they are "cured," Jackson was sent to prison for an indefinite period (up to life imprisonment) for stealing $70. Becoming more and more of a revolutionary as he was turned down for parole again and again, he was killed in a conflict between prisoners and guards after he had served eleven years in prison, seven of them in solitary confinement. Was he "sick," or was the society which kept him there "sick"? We should not define "normal" in a way which allows only one possible answer to this empirical question.

In this book, normal development will be considered to be that development which best enables the individual to realize his potentials. At first glance, this definition does not seem to help much. If a person has a potential to be a murderer or sadist, should this potential be realized? It would seem that healthy potentials and unhealthy ones still need to be distinguished.

Distinguishing them does seem to be possible, however. If human development is looked at in various cultures, it is possible to distinguish stages of child development which are rather similar despite cultural differences. The earliest period of socialization, for example, always seems to involve creating a social bond between the infant and at least one other human being, and the next stage involves some development of autonomy in the infant. Completion of the developmental tasks of these stages moves the child on to the stage which normally follows, and it also prepares him to deal with a wider variety of environmental conditions than he could handle before. Moving through these developmental stages will thus be considered to be normal development.

Some cultures, however, may foster different types of development. A child may be routinely teased and frustrated during weaning in a given culture, for example, and the rage reaction which he learns may then be utilized when, as an adult, he engages in warfare. Because this type of socialization prepares the individual to play only a specialized role rather than to deal with a broad range of environmental contingencies, it is not regarded as normal development despite the dependence of some cultures upon it.

As may be seen from this example, the authors of this book are not adopting the stance of cultural relativism, according to which cultures may be judged only on their own terms. Instead, they are adopting, at least for themselves, a value position according to which it is possible to judge some cultures to be better for their participants than others. The reader, of course, may wish to make a different choice on this issue. The way in which he views child development, and the ends for which he believes psychology should be applied, will depend on the choice he makes.

The process of learning sexual identity may serve as a final example of how the authors' definition of "normal" development applies in a concrete case. Genetically, sex is influenced by the relative number of X or Y chromosomes present. It used to be thought that all females had two Y chromosomes and all males one X chromosome and one Y chromosome. However, it has now been found that an excess of chromosomes is fairly common, and that quite a number of people have combinations such as XXY, XYY, or XXXY. Some such combinations result in an accentuation of the characteristics of one sex, while others produce individuals with less marked sexual characteristics than most people show. On a genetic basis alone, we can distinguish several human sexes.

Two other factors also influence human sexuality, however. One is the person's sex as perceived by others. It too is not so unambiguous as might be thought. A male with undescended testes, for example, may be incorrectly identified as a female at birth. Finally, there are the things the individual has learned in the area of sexual behavior, including motivations, behaviors, and a conscious conception of his or her sexual identity. These often have more powerful effects on the individual than the genetic component.

Now, what is normal sexual development for an individual will differ depending upon the age at which he is viewed. Looking at a young child, it is easy to assume that socialization into the sex role for which his genetic component best qualifies him represents normal development. However, for an adult who has already acquired a strong sexual identity, normalcy may involve adjusting to that identity even if it is at variance with both his genetic component and the dominant practices of his culture.

This example may serve to illustrate one final aspect of the authors' approach to the concept of normalcy. It is their belief that the clients of psychologists, as human beings, must have maximum freedom to make their own ethical decisions and to define the goals of their treatment. From this point of view, a psychologist treating an adult homosexual should make no a priori judgment as to whether his client should adjust to his homosexuality or try to change it. Instead, he should leave the answer to that question to be discovered by the individual as he examines himself through the process of therapy. This view is based on the assumption that if the proper environment is provided, personality development will spontaneously occur.

Stages of Development

In this chapter and the next, the development of personality will be presented as a process which takes place in stages. To some extent, these stages are artificial abstractions from a continuous process of development. At any given moment in a person's life, some of his actions may reflect a higher level of personality development than others. Similarly, a threat to the person may cause him to return to an earlier mode of adjustment, a process known as *regression*. Personality development, in this respect, is similar to the development which a child shows in learning to walk up stairs. When this art is first being mastered, the child may sometimes walk and sometimes crawl. Even after he reaches the point where he usually walks, a particularly steep flight may cause him to resort to crawling again. Despite these complications in the course of his development, we have little hesitation in identifying crawling up stairs as one stage, and walking up stairs as a different and later stage.

Personality theorists similarly have little hesitation in identifying relatively discrete stages in the child's psychological adjustment to the world. What evidence is there in support of their theorizing? Basically, the evidence is of three kinds. First, there is the similarity of the stages perceived by theorists who base their hypotheses on quite different kinds of data. Thus it is some argument in favor of recognizable stages that Erik Erikson and Jane Loevinger distinguish quite similar stages, although Erikson bases his on similarities of development in different cultures and Loevinger bases hers on paper-and-pencil tests given to women and girls in the United States.[2] Second, there is direct evidence from studies, such as Loevinger's, which have tested large numbers of individuals at different developmental levels. This evidence essentially shows that people may master earlier developmental tasks without mastering later ones, but that they do not master later ones without having mastered earlier ones. Finally, there is evidence from the effects of psychotherapy. Especially significant is that on the therapy given by Marilyn Menta and others to children who are, without physical explanation, in that state of speechless withdrawal called autism. Reasoning that these children may have failed to accomplish the first developmental task of forming a strong emotional bond with another human being, Menta successfully initiated therapy with this as the principal goal. She achieved some significant breakthroughs in treating this therapeutically very difficult condition.[3] It provides additional illustration of the theory that one stage of development is necessary before the individual can tackle the tasks of the next level.

Consider, for example, the first two stages. In the first, the child develops attachment to other people, and in the second, he turns away from others to assert his autonomy. Superficially, the second stage appears to be the opposite of the first. In reality, this is not so, however, for the first is necessary before the second can be experienced. The confidence which the child develops through having the close relationship in the first stage seems to be a necessary preparation for the development of the autonomy of the second stage.

The stages of personality development have thus been regarded as Hegelian in nature after the philosopher Georg Wilhelm Friedrich Hegel's description of historical continuity. Hegel's novel theory of history was that violently contrasting stages of existence alternated with periods when the contrasts were merged to create entirely new states of reality. In a similar kind of process, the child's attachment to others, and the antithesis of his autonomy, lead to a synthesis in which he can be close to others without being too dependent on them.

The stages which will serve as the organizing schema of this and the next chapter are taken from Erik Erikson's influential book *Childhood and Society*.[4] While these stages agree in general with those proposed by Loevinger and her colleagues, they are in better accord for the earlier stages than for the later ones. Because failure to complete them has more devastating consequences for the individual, the earlier stages are more apparent and less ambiguous. The sequential nature of the stages is much more clear for the early stages which will be considered in this chapter, than it is for the later stages, which will be explored in the next. Here we shall look at personality development from birth through the learning of moral standards, and conclude with a section on ways of coping with anxiety. The processes examined in this chapter seem to be clearly sequential. In the next chapter, we shall consider processes of identity development in the more mature individual. While we shall discuss these processes in the order in which they usually occur, it is much less clear that they must appear in that order.

BASIC TRUST OR BASIC MISTRUST

As we have stressed, the first developmental task which the infant must accomplish in the area of personality development is the establishment of a close relationship with another human being. This first relationship is very important for two reasons: The emotional learning which takes place in it will color later emotional responses; and it is through social reinforcement that most human learning takes place. The acquisition of language and culture is reinforced not through the reduction of homeostatic drives, but through the social responses of other human beings. If these responses do not acquire the ability to reinforce behavior through the development of social relationships, the child will not learn to speak. It is for this reason that, as Breger has noted, an asocial child is like a hairless polar bear, for it lacks the primary adaptive advantage of its species.[5]

Whereas the first social relationship must be learned, innate reactions and reinforcement mechanisms which form its bases are present from birth. These innate bases of affiliation include clinging, sucking, crying, following, and smiling. They help to form the relationship both by calling out certain parental behaviors, as crying and smiling do, and by providing reinforcement for the child, as clinging and sucking do. Contrary to what earlier theorists believed, clinging seems to be a more important basis of reinforcement than sucking is.

The role of clinging in establishing the first social relationship was made clear in an experiment with monkeys, done by Harry Harlow.[6] Because his experimental manipulations were found to have unanticipated results as well as the ones he had predicted, they led him into an extensive and productive program of research. The initial study was designed to test the idea, popular at that time, that it was the pairing of the mother's presence with reduction of the child's hunger drive which made her presence become a reinforcer for the infant. Harlow believed, instead, that cuddling on a soft object was innately reinforcing for the infant and did not have to be learned. To test which of these explanations was correct, Harlow raised baby monkeys with surrogate mothers. One of the surrogate mothers was a simple wire frame, while the other was covered with soft terrycloth.

To test the relative importance of feeding and cuddling, Harlow gave each baby monkey two mothers, one made of wire and one made of cloth. A nursing bottle was attached to the wire mother, and the amount of time the baby monkey spent on each of the mothers was timed. As Harlow had anticipated, the monkey spent only enough time on the wire monkey to empty the nursing bottle. Much of the rest of the time it spent cuddling on the cloth mother, suggesting that clinging and "contact comfort" were a major basis of the mother-child relationship.

Merely spending time on the cloth mother, however, did not show definitely that the baby monkey had formed an enduring social bond with her. To demonstrate this, Harlow devised other types of experimental tests. In one of them, for example, a baby monkey raised with the surrogate mothers was exposed to a fear-inducing situation, either with or without the presence of the wire or cloth mother. If no surrogate mother was present, the baby monkey would cower in a corner, hide its eyes, and rock back and forth. Its behavior was no different when the wire mother was present. If, however, the cloth mother was present, the baby monkey behaved quite differently. In this case, it first clung to the cloth mother. Then, apparently gaining confidence from this experience, it approached the fear-inducing stimulus. This ability of the surrogate mother to comfort the baby monkey and instill confidence in it in a strange situation demonstrates that the baby had formed a true social relationship with the cloth mother, for this is one of the main functions which such a relationship serves.

The unanticipated consequences of the experiment were discovered when Harlow tried to use the monkeys from the study as breeding stock after they had matured. Even the most experienced and skillful partners were unable to get them to mate, for they reacted to other monkeys with the fear and rage usually shown toward strange objects. As ethological studies have shown, recognition of another animal as belonging to the same species is not usually innate, but is based on imprinting experiences which activate innate reinforcement mechanisms. Harlow's monkeys, imprinted on cloth mothers, did not show normal instinctive behavior toward their own kind. When some of them were bred through artificial insemination, they also failed to show normal maternal reactions to their offspring.

Harlow's most recent research in this area deals with the use of baby monkeys as therapists for monkeys raised on cloth mothers.[7] Three-month-old female monkeys, raised on cloth mothers but with contact with other baby monkeys, can apparently cure older monkeys which have been raised without peer contact. Although normally raised baby monkeys would reject the older social isolates, the young monkeys raised with a combination of surrogate mother and peer contact cling strongly to them despite all attempts by the older monkey to repel their advances. Preliminary evidence suggests that the older monkeys eventually learn to form social bonds with the persistent youngsters and can be cured of their abnormal behavior.

Research on autism in human beings suggests that all Harlow's results in this area apply directly to people as well as to monkeys. Autism is a term generally used by psychologists for that kind of behavior disorder in young children characterized by hyperactivity, negativism, failure to form normal social attachments, and, as we mentioned earlier, failure of the child to acquire speech. It is often diagnosed when this failure becomes apparent.

The central role which failure of attachment plays in the development of autism is shown in the reaction of the autistic child to normal human contact. He will go to great lengths to avoid this contact, covering his ears to avoid hearing someone speak to him, averting his head to avoid looking into a person's face, and struggling violently to escape if picked up. Other symptoms are related to motoric rigidity, need for sameness in the environment, and negativism. They include walking on tiptoe, rhythmic rocking and twirling, and engaging in any activity except the one requested by an adult. While screaming with rage is common, normal crying is absent, and the child often has stronger apparent attachment to an inanimate object than to any human being.

Fortunately, great progress is now being made in the understanding and treatment of this disorder. Especially striking results are being obtained by the rage-reduction technique described in a book edited by Louis Breger. It is the one used by Menta, and it forms the basis for much of this discussion.[8] This technique uses a cycle of emotional arousal, physical holding, and ultimate relaxation to establish a social bond between the patient and the therapist. Earlier attempts to treat the language failure of autistic children through conditioning techniques succeeded in teaching them words which were specifically reinforced, but largely failed to bring them to the point where they would spontaneously develop further language on their own. By developing those reinforcement mechanisms usually employed in language acquisition, the rage-reduction technique is able to lead the autistic child back into the path of normal language development.

The theory which is involved sees a stress-to-relaxation cycle as basic to establishing the mother-infant social bond, and it views any-thing which interferes with this normal cycle as implicated in the ori-gins of autism. Holding is the basic procedure by which the infant is comforted, but the nature of the holding depends on the cause of its crying. If he or she is weeping, with sobs and tears present, nur-turance and protection are called for. Screams of rage, of high inten-sity and often without tears, call for firmer physical mastery of the in-fant.

Both parents and infants differ in how they react to contact with one another, and autism generally seems to develop out of an interac-tion of parental and child characteristics. As research by Shaffer and Emerson has shown, there are innate differences in how infants react to being held.[9] Some infants cling, while others aggressively assert their independence from birth. An uncertain parent who immedi-ately puts the baby down as soon as he shows any signs of struggling may fail to establish a strong social bond with the infant. A more confident and persistent parent, on the other hand, like the monkey therapists in Harlow's study, may refuse to take no for an answer and succeed in socializing even a hyperactive child. As the greater prevalence of autism among males and among firstborns could be explained by the uncertainty of inexperienced parents on how to react to an aggressive child, or by damage to the child's innate mo-tivational mechanisms with a more difficult birth, it is hard to assess the relative contributions of parental and infant characteristics to the development of autism. The success of therapeutic techniques with autistic children, however, would seem to indicate that their symp-toms, even if the effects of birth injury are involved, can be overcome by persistent efforts at socialization. Research in cultures utilizing birth techniques resulting in considerably less trauma to the infant than those employed in our own culture may soon reveal what role the birth process plays in this syndrome.

Autistic symptoms may develop not only because a social bond was never established in the first place, but also through its being disrupted at an early age. The initial bond between infant and parent usually develops in about six months, and any prolonged separation from the parent after that time can call out a loss reaction. As James Robertson has graphically illustrated in a film about a young child who was hospitalized for an operation, this reaction to loss involves three stages.[10] In the first, or protest, stage, the child cries, screams with rage, and frequently requests the absent parents. The second, or despair, stage is characterized by deep feelings of loss and depression and by increasing social withdrawal. Finally, the child becomes detached and socially unresponsive. At this point, he or she will be quite cold to the parents if reunited with them. It is important for them to realize that active efforts on their part may be necessary to reestablish social relations with the child. If the child is not reunited with the parents, and if no other human being manages to develop a strong social bond with the child, he will progressively show the symptoms of withdrawal and retardation associated with long-term institutionalization. While the use of language will not be lost if it has developed before the separation, language and social skills will become much more retarded than perceptual and motor skills.

In the earliest stage of development, then, the child normally forms a close relationship with another human being. This relationship conditions emotional reactions so that he learns to react to others with pleasure and confidence or to experience fear and anger in their presence. His acquired feelings of pleasure in human company serve as the main incentive and reward for learning language and human culture, and are thus the basis for all future social development. For this reason, active therapeutic steps must be taken if the relationship either fails to develop or is broken through loss. Through a successful first relationship, the individual develops the confidence to become more autonomous in the next stage of development.

AUTONOMY OR SHAME AND DOUBT

The young child has no sooner established a first social relationship than he is threatened by the demands which the parent makes. The second major developmental task, and by no means an easy one, is for the child to reconcile his own increasing need for autonomy with society's demands for compliance. If this task is successfully accomplished, the child will find pleasure in attaining self-control. If, on the other hand, socialization at this stage is too traumatic, the child's impulses and behavior will become divorced from each other. Behavior will conform to society's demands, at least when there is danger of being caught. Unsocialized impulses and unsatisfied dependency needs, however, will seriously trouble the individual, who will not take pleasure in his own behavior.

Shame is not a major method of social control in our culture. It is so soon replaced by guilt that its importance in socialization is easily overlooked. For the child undergoing toilet training, however, it is a major fact of life. Lapses of training do not lead, as they would for an adult, to strong feelings of guilt. Instead, they result in the unpleasant experience of being shamed by an adult. Actions are therefore viewed by the child in terms of what consequences are likely to result from them. The two- or three-year-old is quite clear as to which is worse, doing wrong or appearing to do wrong. It is being found with wet pants that is bad, not the act of wetting them.

In the normal course of socialization, two factors are on the parents' side at this stage. As the work of Bandura and others has shown, children spontaneously copy the actions which they see others perform.[11] Furthermore, as we noted in the chapter on motivation, autonomy, or acquiring control over one's fate, seems to be innately reinforcing. There are thus forces which make the child acquire control over his own behavior and use it to conform to his culture even without direct tuition on the part of parents. As autonomy can also be asserted by defying parental desires, and dependency needs may prompt the child to do so in order to test whether the parent really cares, the parent sometimes has difficulty remembering these forces toward socialization when confronted with the "terrible two-year-old."

The normal course of development may be disrupted if socialization is so harsh as to make awareness of his impulses threatening to the child. Loevinger, studying ego development in girls and women, has distinguished both three substages within this period of development and adult symptoms stemming from problems with them.[12] The earliest substage is characterized by considerable dependency and a preoccupation with bodily feelings; the second, by a concern with manipulation of others and with self-protection; and the third, by conformity to external rules and groups. Many of the diagnostic signs of unresolved conflicts at these various stages are similar in children and adults. Thus the first of the substages is characterized in children by temper tantrums and preoccupation with bodily functions, especially functioning of the bowels. Adult problems stemming from this stage are probably related to unmet dependency needs in childhood. They are again expressed through temper tantrums and concern with bodily feelings, although now sexual feelings predominate over bowel functioning. For adults with serious problems rooted in this stage, sex remains solely a bodily function rather than an emotional and social relationship.

Problems at both the second and third substages are related to a conflict between unsocialized impulses and external authority, but the two differ in terms of relations to peer groups. Traumatic socialization of impulses, such as the aggressive impulses normal during the assertion of autonomy, may make the child feel threatened merely by his awareness of having those impulses. He will attempt to force awareness of them out of consciousness while at the same time compulsively complying to the harsh demands made on him. His compliance, however, will be purely expedient, and based not on any real desire but only on a fear of punishment. His interpersonal style will, as a child or as an adult, be manipulative, exploitative, and concerned with gaining advantage. If he has had satisfactory experiences with peer groups, he may identify with them and express his exploitativeness and hostility primarily toward outgroup members. In doing this, he will show compulsive conformity to his peer groups. If he lacks even this identification with a limited reference group, he will show a desire to beat the world on his own, thus revealing his problems with the second substage.

If, on the other hand, impulses are not harshly socialized, the child will not have so great a conflict between his overt behavior and his inner desires. He will be able to participate much more fully in social groups, and his motives will be transformed and socialized through his participation during the third substage. Rather than having an irreconcilable conflict between his public and private selves, he will be in the fortunate position of being able to express his private self in public. Completion of the third substage will leave him an autonomous and independent person, yet able to identify with others and motivated to act toward them in positive ways. He will be prepared for the third major stage of development, in which an adult conscience is acquired.

Before looking at the third stage of development, however, let us consider an interesting application of some of the research on ego development which we have been considering. Marguerite Warren was impressed by the possibilities in Loevinger's research for understanding and treating delinquency. *Delinquency* is a term which covers a wide variety of behaviors engaged in for even more diverse reasons. A person may steal, for example, to conform to a peer group engaged in stealing, to express hostility against the authority structure of society, or to obtain objects which symbolize love and affection to him, as well as for many other reasons. If delinquency is so varied in both cause and behavior, does it make any sense to treat all offenders in the same way?

Assuming that it does not, Warren and her coworkers instituted in California an experimental treatment program relating to stages of ego development.[13] On the basis of tests similar to those used by Loevinger, individuals were divided into the three major categories of "asocial," "external structure," and "internalized standards." Those classed as "asocial" had problems stemming from the earliest stage of ego development, which we have characterized as the stage of developing basic trust. They had strong, unsatisfied dependency needs, and used delinquent behavior as a cry for help and affection. The "external structure" individuals had not succeeded in developing autonomy. They tended to conform to delinquent peer groups or to whoever had the most power at the moment. Many of them had the orientation of attempting to manipulate society without identifying with other people, a type of behavior which has been described as one of the outcomes of difficulty with this stage. Finally, the "internalized standards" group had successfully completed both the first two stages, but had problems of guilt and anxiety stemming from the third major stage.

The experimental treatment program was designed to provide each individual with help that filled his own particular needs. Individuals in the "asocial" group had their dependency needs met by being provided with a very supportive environment, usually in a foster home. Those in the "external structure" group had external structure provided, largely through group therapy. Finally, the problems of the "internalized standards" group were worked on through psychotherapy, for these problems came closer to being the type of neurosis for which this therapy was designed. In any case, the individuals in the experimental treatment project remained in the community instead of being institutionalized.

The effectiveness of the program was assessed by comparing the individuals in the experimental program with those receiving the usual institutional treatment traditionally given by the state. Over a period of five years, the experimental program showed itself far superior to the usual treatment program, and the experimental group committed less than half the number of parole violations occurring in the control group. The program, however, was more effective with individuals with some types of problems than it was with those having other types. Its most striking success was with the "asocial" group. The need of individuals in this group for a warm and supportive social relationship was not usually met by the rules and scheduled reinforcements of institutional treatment, and a marked improvement was apparent when this relationship was provided in a foster home. There were only a third as many parole violations in the experimental group as compared with the control group, for individuals in this category. The experimental program was only slightly more effective than traditional treatment for the "internalized standards" group, perhaps because adequately dealing with the neurotic problems of this group would require an amount of individual therapy which would exceed the financial resources of governmental programs. Finally, considerable improvement in prognosis resulted from the experimental program as it was applied to those needing "external structure."

By their very size, large-scale institutions tend to be unresponsive to human needs, a topic to which we shall return in a later chapter. Prisons, hospitals, and juvenile treatment facilities are usually so badly understaffed that little can be provided in the way of treatment. This results both in their acquiring large populations of inmates who are provided with little other than custodial care, and in their inability to attract first-rate staff. Warren's research shows how much more can be accomplished in many cases by treatment in the community and, most important, by treatment that meets the needs of the individual.

INITIATIVE OR GUILT

One aspect of human experience which is important to understanding personality is the experience of conflict. In many situations, one part of us seems to want one thing and another part seems to want something else. Although some other theorists were also interested in the experience of conflict, it was probably Freud who did most to make it central to the understanding of personality.[14] Freud noted that when he listened to the many conflicts which his patients experienced, he became aware of three types of psychological process which often conflicted with one another. One was an awareness of a desire, without consideration of the consequences of expressing it. A second was an awareness of likely consequences of an action, and the third was a person's feeling about how he ought or ought not to behave. He called these processes *id*, *ego*, and *superego* respectively. Consider the case of Benjamin in the movie *The Graduate*. When Mrs. Robinson began acting seductively toward him, he was sexually attracted to her. This would be classed as id. At the same time, he had a strong feeling that it was wrong to have an affair with a married woman old enough to be his mother. These moral concerns would be considered superego. Finally, he was involved in calculating the chances that he would get caught and how he could arrange for the possible affair safely. Because of their concern with reality, these thoughts would be called ego.

We have seen where two of these types of process come from. Although modified by experience, Benjamin's sexual drive was innate. His awareness of realistic consequences of actions, and his calculation of how to manipulate the world to his own advantage, we have seen develop through his experimentation with life and his attempts to become autonomous. Where, however, did he develop the third type of process, which judges actions to be right or wrong regardless of what consequences they might realistically have?

Although its major development comes during the third developmental stage, the earliest origins of conscience go back to the stage of basic trust. We have noted that one of the main functions served by the first social relationship is to relieve the infant of feelings of helplessness and terror. When an adult's basic drives are frustrated, he knows that he will be able to satisfy them later. Similarly, when the adult confronts a strange situation, he does so with the confidence which comes of having explored and surmounted strange situations in the past. As we saw both with Harlow's monkeys and with autistic children, the young child lacks these bases of competence and confidence, and unless comforting is available, he experiences overwhelming feelings of terror and desolation. These feelings are referred to as *traumatic anxiety*.

Because the young child is solely dependent upon adults for the relief of these feelings, any threat of abandonment or loss of love by the parent will cause the child to reexperience these intolerable feelings. Not only actions, but impulses and feelings in the child which result in serious threat or punishment by the parent, become intolerable to the child through being associated with the experience of anxiety. Even at an early age, the child begins forcing out of consciousness awareness of these impulses and feelings.

Unless discipline is quite harsh and traumatic, however, relatively little of the conscience is laid down during these earliest stages. The young child who is developing autonomy usually has little awareness of the limits which the world will ultimately impose on him. As he develops control over himself and learns to manipulate others, he seems unaware of there being anything he cannot do. At this stage, omnipotence is often an important theme in dreams, and playing at being a king or queen is a favorite role in games.

It is primarily through learning that he is not omnipotent that the child develops a conscience. The development of autonomy is necessary before this lesson can be learned, for if motives are expressed only in fantasy, it is possible to go on imagining oneself to be all-powerful. Acting on the basis of his motives is what brings the individual up against his realistic limitations.

In ascribing the origins of conscience to infantile sexuality, Freud seems to have been partially correct. Competition with the parent of the same sex for the affection of the parent of the opposite sex is, in most families, doomed to failure, and this failure is clear evidence to the child of the limitation of his power. The awareness of powerlessness which results from this Oedipal rivalry, like that arising from other sources, causes the child to reexperience the feelings of anxiety created by his earlier helplessness. Again, as in an earlier stage, these unpleasant feelings can be reduced by forcing the forbidden impulses out of awareness. Besides this negative basis of conscience, however, there is also a more positive basis. By identifying with the more powerful parent and becoming like him, the child can take vicarious pleasure in the parent's experiences. Furthermore, taking on the characteristics of the parent much as a member of a totemic group acquires the characteristics of his totem animal, he can see himself replacing the parent by being, in the future, what the parent is now. The more affection the child feels for the parent, and the easier it is for the child to take pleasure in the parent's accomplishments, the more the conscience will be based on these positive forces rather than on harsh repression and anxiety.

To recapitulate, we see that anxiety plays a basic role in the origin of superego processes, and that violation of the conscience leads to anxiety. By internalizing the standards of the more powerful parent, the child reduces his anxiety and obtains vicarious satisfaction. If the standards of the parent are reasonable and realistic, the child will learn ways of expressing his impulses without experiencing guilt and anxiety. If the standards are traumatically presented, the mere existence of basic human drives will be anxiety-inducing for the individual, and neurotic problems will result.

To illustrate the process of conscience development which we have been considering, let us look at some individuals who behaved in ways which would be utterly abhorrent to most people and, to a considerable extent, to themselves also. These individuals were undergoing psychiatric treatment for serious and repeated abuse of their children.[15] Two facts about them should make clear at the start that the common preconceptions about such individuals are unfounded. First, it might be imagined that a person who would seriously attack a child has no conscience. Instead, the parents of battered children are found to have very harsh and strict consciences. Second, it might be imagined that a person who has experienced the pain and terror of being a battered child himself would, no matter what else he might do, treat his own children with love and kindness exclusively. Instead, it turns out that to a notable extent the parents who batter children are those who were battered children themselves. Let us look at their personality development and see if we can better understand the processes which have made Jane Loevinger propose that "One must do what one has suffered" is a basic principle of human behavior.[16]

The battered-child syndrome was first discovered by radiologists who noted that the x-rays of some children showed evidence of repeated fracturing of the skull and long bones although there was no explanation in their medical histories of how these injuries had been incurred. Study of these cases revealed a long history of assault on the child by one or both parents, a fact which had not previously come to light because of the extreme reluctance of society to interfere with how parents rear their children. In classical Greece, parents who did not want a child were supposed to put it to death within three days of its birth. If it was kept over three days and shown to other people, they were supposed to try to keep it alive. Ancient Rome, on the other hand, gave every father the legal right to sell his children into slavery or put them to death not only before they were legally of age but throughout their lives. Our own society similarly has few safeguards to the rights of children.

Because of the sanctity of the home, it is difficult to obtain accurate statistics on child abuse. There are three main ways in which it tends to be discovered: through police investigation of neighbors' complaints, through the observations of welfare workers, and through dubious medical histories obtained by hospitals. Each of these sources tends to turn up a different class of cases. Police are most likely to discover cases of a single murderous assault on a child, which have causes somewhat different from those of repeated attack. (They are most frequently carried out by a male who is left in charge of a stepchild.) Welfare workers discover the child abuse of low-income individuals but not that of those who are wealthier, and the socioeconomic status of the cases uncovered by a hospital will be a cross-section of its clientele. To the extent that a judgment can be made from the data now available, child abuse is unrelated to socioeconomic class, religious preference, or ethnic origin. It is found as frequently among the rich as among the poor, among the educated as among the uneducated, and among males as among females.

Psychiatric treatment of parents of battered children, such as that carried out by Steele and Pollock, has revealed certain personality problems which the parents are liable to show, as well as the encouraging extent to which they can be helped by psychiatric treatment.[17] While the parents studied fell in a wide variety of categories when classified according to traditional psychiatric diagnostic categories (a system of categories increasingly distrusted by psychologists and psychiatrists alike), they showed similar personality dynamics when viewed in terms of the developmental stages which we have been considering. Let us look at their development in some detail.

We have noted that problems with the earliest stage of ego development, that of basic trust, may be revealed in later life as unsatisfied dependency needs. These were very strong in the parents treated by Drs. Steele and Pollock at the University of Colorado School of Medicine. Having been exposed to sudden and violent abuse and rejection by their own parents, they had not been able to develop the trust and confidence which should be the result of the first stage of ego development. As adults, they were still seeking the support and mothering which they had not experienced, and they looked for it both from their spouses and from their children. As one of them put it,

> I have never felt really loved all my life. When the baby was born, I thought he would love me; but when he cried all the time, it meant he didn't love me, so I hit him.[18]

The feelings of loneliness and rejection experienced by the parents made them especially prone to attack a child when the circumstances of their lives were especially threatening. Another of the cases, that of Larry, serves as an example. As a young man, Larry had not been very popular with women and had been extremely dependent upon those who would date him. His fiancée agreed to marry him but never showed up for the wedding. Weeks later, he heard that she had married someone else. That marriage did not last, and later she made up with Larry and did marry him.

Larry was also only marginally successful in the world of work. He was employed in construction and was sometimes laid off when things were slow. On one of these occasions, he told his wife that he had been laid off, and she walked out of the house without saying a word, making him again feel rejected as he had when she had stood him up and married another. When one of the children began crying and he was unable to comfort the little girl, he attacked her instead.

The unsatisfied dependency needs of the parents are accentuated by contact with children, for this contact brings back memories of their childhood and causes them to reexperience the feelings of terror, helplessness, and aloneness which they experienced then. Their children, by having their parents dependent upon them and by being threatened with attack if they do not meet the parents' needs, have similar emotional experiences and the pattern is transmitted to another generation.

Often the children do meet the dependency needs of the parents, bringing about a situation which has been described as role reversal because the child cares for and nurtures the parent, but they do so at a great cost. Instead of being able to freely express his or her impulses, and to learn to express them in a socially acceptable manner during the stage of autonomy, the child forces out of consciousness those impulses unacceptable to the parent. As a simple matter of survival, the harsh demands of the parents are incorporated into the child's personality. Because the child's desires do not go away even in the face of the severe and premature conscience which is developed, he or she is left with great conflict between unmet needs and desires on the one hand and an overly harsh and anxiety-inducing conscience on the other.

The extent to which the parent has learned to deny having certain impulses causes serious difficulties in the handling of those impulses. It is normal for a father or mother to be annoyed with a child from time to time. A parent who is aware of his own impulses will express them before they grow too strong, or remove himself from the situation until he feels less angry. The parent who was a battered child identifies any unhappiness of the child with what he experienced as a child, and therefore finds the child's crying intolerable. Like Larry, he finds inability to satisfy the child unbearably frustrating, yet cannot admit his aggressive feeling to himself, for he would then be identifying with the hated image of his parent. He also feels jealousy of the child, for nobody ever comforted him when he was a child. Because he does not recognize his anger until it becomes over-powering rage, he does not remove himself from the situation, and he suddenly attacks the child.

Attacks on children, whether by the mother or the father, thus seem to come about because the parent suffers a serious neurotic conflict between an unrealistically harsh and demanding conscience and unmet infantile needs. As might be expected under these cir-cumstances, the parent also lacks any secure sense of identity, for many personality processes are outside of consciousness, and acts which were motivated by unconscious processes may be difficult to rationalize. An effort is made to rationalize them, however, and is often partly successful. While the parent may suffer guilt at attacking the child, the seriousness of the attack is often minimized, and the at-tack is justified as being a necessary part of the socialization of the child. Having been brought up in a strict conventional moralism, the parent can justify that to spare the rod is to spoil the child, and that the punishment is for the child's own good. One more example from Steele and Pollock should make the mechanism clear:

> Henry J., in speaking of his sixteen-month-old son Johnny, said, "He knows what I mean and understands it when I say 'come here.' If he doesn't come immediately, I go and give him a gentle tug on the ear to remind him of what he's supposed to do." In the hospital it was found that Johnny's ear was lacerated and partially torn away from his head.[19]

While the examples from Steele and Pollock's work do much to help us understand how behavior is passed from generation to gen-eration, it is well to remember that in some ways they present a one-sided picture. Two bases of superego development have been men-tioned, the negative basis of fear and the positive basis of vicarious pleasure. The processes of conscience development we have seen in battered children represent the first of these. Where socialization is less harsh, the pleasure of seeing oneself as similar to a loved one may be an equally important, and a far more positive, basis of the superego. As a result, the superego has two parts. The conscience, which we have been discussing, represents internalized prohibi-tions. The ego ideal, on the other hand, is an internalized and idealized picture of what one would like to be and become. Whereas the former is more apparent in neurotic behavior, the latter plays a very important role in the development of cultural skills, which is the next stage of ego development.

Mechanisms of Defense

Personality development is not complete with the development of the superego, and in fact continues throughout the individual's lifetime. There are two ways, however, in which its fundamental aspects may be regarded as laid down by the time the superego is formed. One is that the three types of personality process among which conflicts are most often noticeable have all been developed. The other is that symptoms which develop later usually call out again conflicts with which the individual has struggled before, when they were being dealt with during the stages we have already considered. This does not mean that nobody who has had a satisfactory childhood can develop problems as an adult. Experience with combat neurosis during the Second World War made amply clear that even the healthiest individual may develop symptoms under sufficiently strong situational stress. Instead, it means that the ways in which situational pressures are interpreted and reacted to will depend upon experience with earlier developmental stages. This being so, the end of the third stage seems the most reasonable place to consider the ways in which the various personality processes may conflict with one another and the strategies which the individual can use to cope with the conflicts.

The idea of defense mechanisms has long ago found its way into popular thought, and one individual will often speak of another as "rationalizing" or "projecting." Not everyone, however, has recognized what it is that defense mechanisms defend against: the experience of anxiety.

Anxiety is an unpleasant emotional state similar to fear. It differs from fear, however, in that its cause is not so immediately apparent. If an individual caught in a severe earthquake experiences nausea, trembling, and the other symptoms of extreme fear, his state is clearly attributable to the situation he is in, and it would be classed as fear. If another individual experiences these same symptoms when there appears to be nothing in the situation to be afraid of, his state would be considered anxiety. Often, a person experiences a combination of the two. A situation which is realistically fear-inducing may also call up memories of fear and helplessness experienced at an earlier age, and thus arouse anxiety as well as fear.

As we have noted, anxiety is originally called out by the helplessness of the infant, and it is reduced by his being able to depend upon another. Any threat of loss of this other's love is thus anxiety-inducing. Later, when important others have been incorporated into the individual as his conscience and ego ideal, any indication that he has violated or would like to violate their dictates will be anxiety-inducing. The less basic trust the individual has developed, and the harsher the socialization processes by which the superego was formed, the more easily anxiety will be aroused.

Despite their differences, cultures generally provide some way for expressing virtually all human motives. As Henry Murray has noted, the child must learn the proper time, place, mode, and object for expressing his motives.[20] As we noted in discussing the battered child, an individual who has been socialized early and severely may learn to feel guilt, not at certain ways of expressing motives, but at having them at all. As sexual and aggressive motives are those most likely to be harshly socialized in our culture, let us take as a hypothetical example an aggressive impulse.

Suppose that for some reason someone had strong hostile impulses toward a colleague with whom he had to associate regularly in the course of his work. If he adjusted to the situation by deciding to act on the basis of the impulses, he would fear the feelings of guilt which he knew would follow his actions. This fear of punishment by the superego is called *moral* anxiety. If the impulses were sufficiently antisocial, he might also fear the punishment which society would inflict on him for his behavior, a fear known as *reality anxiety*.

On the other hand, it is likely that he would not plan either to murder his colleague or to commit mayhem on him, but instead, would plan to check his impulses and behave in a socially acceptable manner toward him. In choosing this course of action, however, he would be running a risk that his impulses would prove too strong for him and that on some future occasion they might get out of hand and cause him to act in the way he had decided not to act. Fear of this possibility would be called *neurotic anxiety*.

Hypothetical examples in the area of defense mechanisms may inadvertently reveal the hidden motives of authors. At the risk of our perhaps revealing antisocial impulses of which we are only partially aware, let us continue the example to illustrate one of the defense mechanisms. Of the three types of anxiety, reality anxiety, or fear of the real world, would seem to be the easiest to cope with. If we suffer from uncontrollable hostile impulses, we must admit that we have a problem, for no matter where we go or what we do, there is always the danger that they will get out of hand. If, on the other hand, we can convince ourselves that it is not we but a part of our environment which is at fault, then the problem seems easier—we have only to avoid that aspect of our environment to keep out of trouble. Thus, if we had hostile impulses, say, toward Dr. X, we could conceal our unacceptable impulses from ourselves if we could convince ourselves that it was he who was aggressive. If he said "Good morning" to us when we arrived at work, we could question the way in which he was saying it and see his statement as hostile and provocative. We could thus convince ourselves that we were not hostile, but that this person behaved in a manner that would cause a saint to lose his temper. By seeing our own unacceptable impulses in others rather than ourselves, we would be able not only to conceal them from ourselves, but also to convince ourselves that we merely had to avoid contact with Dr. X in order to lead a happy and well-adjusted life. This mechanism of explaining what one is feeling by ascribing attributes to another is called *projection,* and like all defense mechanisms it serves to protect the ego from anxiety.

Among the defense mechanisms, a central role is played by *repression*—the forcing and keeping of perceptions out of awareness. This is true because all defense mechanisms involve distortion of reality, so repression must be used with each of them to keep the individual from being aware of the material which is being distorted. In the example of projection just given, for example, the mechanism can work only if the individual manages to keep his hostile impulses from awareness. Or consider the mechanism of *rationalization,* the giving of reasons other than the real one to account for behavior by the individual because he cannot consciously admit the real one. We have already seen an example of this mechanism. Parents explain their abuse of children by saying that the children must be punished to be properly socialized, while denying their own aggressive impulses. This mechanism obviously would not succeed in reducing anxiety unless repression were also used to keep the aggressive impulses from consciousness.

Many defense mechanisms could be listed, and any list involves problems of classification, for individual examples often show a mixture of mechanisms. It is thus perhaps more accurate to think of a process of ego defense rather than of a number of discrete mechanisms. Consider, for example, a prejudiced teacher who never calls on the one black child in her grade school class to recite. She may believe that she is doing him a favor by protecting him from the embarrassment of being unable to answer a question in front of his white classmates. If asked why she thinks he is not able to answer the questions correctly, she may declare that it isn't prejudice which makes her think that, but only that he lacks the "cultural advantages" of some of his classmates.

Several mechanisms of ego defense might be involved in this one example. If the teacher actually is expressing hostility toward blacks in a disguised manner, her behavior might be called *displacement*, the turning of a drive against a substitute object. Rationalization would also be involved in giving a reason other than the real one for her behavior, and also repression in keeping her true motive from consciousness. Finally, because she manages to express a forbidden motive (hostility) while appearing on the surface to be motivated by the opposite motive (concern for the other's well-being), the behavior might be considered as an example of reaction formation, for that is how this mechanism is defined. There are many possible ways of classifying the techniques which people invent to protect themselves from anxiety. There is thus no one definitive list of defense mechanisms, but rather a varied process of defense.

There have been a number of attempts to test the theory of defense mechanisms experimentally. However, because different individuals do cope with anxiety in a wide variety of ways, and because the experimenter would not want to arouse a great deal of anxiety in any case, tests have been difficult to devise. Misunderstanding of the theory also sometimes led to inappropriate tests, as in the early studies on repression. As Sears has pointed out, many of these studies were "completely irrelevant to the problem," for they dealt with whether pleasant or unpleasant experiences are better remembered.[21] According to the theory of ego defense, it is not whether an experience is pleasant or unpleasant which determines whether it will be subject to repression, but whether or not it is anxiety-arousing. If two college students spend the weekend quite differently—one studying for an exam and the other getting drunk and seducing the wife of a friend—it is quite possible that the second might have a more pleasant weekend than the first, but it is the second rather than the first who might be anxious to forget what he has done. An experiment on repression must thus compare memory under anxiety-arousing and non-anxiety-arousing conditions.

A more extended theoretical treatment of this idea and relevant experimental data are provided by Rosenzweig.[22] His study was similar to one done by a student of Lewin's named Bluma Zeigarnik. According to Lewinian theory, the forming of an intention to carry out some action involves setting up a force within the personality directed to that end. Zeigarnik reasoned that if that were true, uncompleted tasks should be better remembered than completed ones, and she did a series of experiments to demonstrate such differential memory.[23] Giving children a series of tasks to work on, she did indeed find that those they were forced to leave before completion were better remembered than those they were given enough time to complete. (The design was of course counterbalanced so that each task was sometimes completed and sometimes not completed. We thus know that the results were not just due to some tasks being more noteworthy than others.) One other thing which Zeigarnik noticed was that subjects who saw the experiment as a memory test and thus as a measure of their personal merit tended to reverse the trend and remember the completed tasks best. This is what would be expected on the basis of repression. For these subjects, failure to complete tasks would be evidence of their having little personal merit and would be anxiety-inducing. They would be able to reduce their anxiety by forgetting tasks which they had not been able to complete and by exaggerating how well they had done.

This psychoanalytic hypothesis was directly tested in experiments by Rosenzweig. Using tasks similar to those employed by Zeigarnik, he ran different groups of subjects under threatening or nonthreatening instructions. Sometimes the subjects were told that the experimenter merely wanted to learn how long the tasks took so that he could use the tasks in later experiments. These subjects were not threatened, and they showed the Zeigarnik effect—they remembered the uncompleted tasks better than the completed ones. The other subjects were given instructions which implied that failure to complete the tasks was evidence of low intelligence. Since it is part of the ego ideal of most people that they have at least average intelligence, these instructions made failure to complete the tasks subject to repression. Rosenzweig found that, under these conditions, the subjects remembered more of the completed than of the uncompleted tasks.

There are, of course, individual differences in how easily people are threatened and how frequently they resort to repression as a defense. One more recent study not only reproduced Rosenzweig's results on the effect of instructions on repression but also showed that volunteers for experiments showed less repression than subjects who had to participate as a part of a course requirement.[24] People who lack confidence in their own abilities and are easily threatened are less likely to volunteer.

Cognitive Dissonance

Closely related to the theory of defense mechanisms, but considerably more productive of research, is Festinger's theory of *cognitive dissonance*.[25] Let us look at a study done within the framework of this theory, and then consider the theory itself. The study, done by Walster and Prestholdt, concerns forming an impression of a stranger.[26] Subjects are asked to make judgments of how much an individual deserves to receive welfare payments on the basis of case-history material provided by the experimenter. The information provided is intentionally made quite unfavorable so that the subject will judge the recipient not really to be very deserving. Later, after the judgment has been made, additional information is provided. This information indicates that one of the persons who had provided information about the case had not been telling the truth. If the damaging testimony from this one informant is not believed, the recipient really is very deserving of the welfare payments. The subjects are thus given a chance to make a new judgment about the case after the new information has come to light.

The extent to which the person revises his judgment in the light of the new information depends upon the experimental conditions. In one treatment, subjects are told that their judgments will actually be used by the caseworker dealing with the cases and will probably influence what welfare payments the individuals receive. In another treatment, subjects do not believe that this practical use is being made of their information.

When the subject believes that no use is being made of his judgments, he acts as you might expect him to. He not only makes his second judgment more favorable than his first; he even tries to make up for his previous harshness by judging the person more favorably than he would have if he had never received the unfavorable information. This is not so if the subject believes the first judgment has already been transmitted to the welfare worker. In that event, the subject is committed to the first judgment and does not change it even when it turns out to have been based on erroneous information. He judges the recipient to be as undeserving as he had when the damaging information was presented as valid.

From the point of view of defense mechanisms, we might analyze the experiment by noting that it is anxiety-inducing for an individual to violate his conscience, and that injuring an innocent person usually would involve doing this. This violation of the conscience could be dealt with in a number of ways. In some circumstances, it might be possible to undo the injury. In others, it might be possible to deny to the self that the violation had ever taken place and to rationalize the behavior. From this standpoint, the experimental subjects who maintain their unfavorable judgments are rationalizing their initial decisions by finding other unfavorable aspects of the recipient to justify them. Let us look at the theory of cognitive dissonance to see how it predicted the results.

The theory is called a cognitive theory because it deals with cognitions, the ideas and relationships among ideas which exist in the mind of an individual. Each idea that a person has about something, such as "I like chocolates," is an element in the theory. Furthermore, each element has one of three relationships to each other element—they are either consonant, dissonant, or irrelevant to one another. Take, for example, the elements "I like chocolates" and "Alan always wears his Oxford tie." It is difficult to see any relationship of any kind between these two ideas. The liking for chocolates is not influenced in any way by Alan's sartorial habits, and the two elements are simply irrelevant to each other.

Elements are dissonant if, given the assumptions of the individual, one belief is inconsistent with the other. To use one of Festinger's favorite examples, consider the person whose mind contains the elements "I smoke" and "Smoking is bad for health." For most people, these elements would be dissonant because they also believe that they should avoid doing things which are bad for their health. For a person whose goal in life is to end it as rapidly as possible, the elements would be consonant rather than dissonant, for it would then be perfectly consistent for the person to smoke because it is bad for his health.

While dissonance may be aroused by inconsistent perceptions, it is generally aroused in sufficient amounts to be important only in situations where one of the elements is a perception of the person's own behavior. If we believe that lawns are watered during dry weather and we perceive a sprinkler soaking someone's lawn while it is pouring down rain, the two perceptions would theoretically arouse a slight amount of dissonance. This dissonance, however, could be resolved very easily. We could decide that the owner of the lawn had started his hose and left for the day, not knowing that it was going to rain. The amount of dissonance would be slight because the matter is unimportant to us and because there are few other elements keeping us from changing our beliefs in the area. In perceptions of our own behavior, on the other hand, dissonance may be high and difficult to reduce. What we do is important to us, behavior is often difficult to change, and perceptions also have a stubborn resistance to change. It would be difficult for the authors of this book to believe that they never fought if in fact they were at that moment shouting violently at each other, for example.

Dissonance is thus most often aroused in situations which involve an individual's perceptions of his own decisions and behavior. When aroused, it acts as a motive which can cause an individual to change not only his perceptions of the world but also his actions in order to reduce the dissonance. The amount of dissonance a person feels because of engaging in a given behavior is a function of the number of dissonant elements relating to that behavior, the proportion of the elements relating to it that are dissonant, and the importance of the various elements. Suppose that you have just spent a great deal of money for an automobile and, since you have driven it, there is no way you can get the money back. The amount of dissonance this purchase will cause you will depend on how many ideas you have supporting the decision you made and how many you have going against it. The perception that the radio does not work very well will not cause much dissonance if you perceive that the car is mechanically perfect, a pleasure to drive, spacious, and satisfactory in other ways. One dissonant element might cause you a good deal of discomfort, however, if that element is the perception that your friends all regard the car as a risky purchase.

The factors influencing the amount of dissonance felt also imply ways in which dissonance may be reduced. Adding new consonant elements by seeking out information praising your new car, or by building social support for your decision, could reduce the dissonance resulting from your automobile purchase. Discovering new things to like about the car and deciding that the ones you dislike are less important would also help. Deciding that you really have never had any choice about the matter—that you needed a car for your job and that this one was too good a bargain to be turned down—would also serve to reduce your dissonance.

To return to Walster and Prestholdt's study, we see that the experimental condition was designed to arouse dissonance while the control condition was not. When your negative judgment about the welfare recipient has already been transmitted to the caseworker, dissonance exists between any perception you might have that you have wronged the person and your belief that you do not believe in hurting others for no reason. There are a number of ways in which you might reduce this dissonance. You might convince your friends of this position, making yourself even more confident that it was correct. Or you might do what is easiest to do under the conditions of the experiment—reevaluate the ambiguous information about the recipient to see it as being as negative as you originally judged it. If the person really is undeserving, then you have not done any wrong and need feel no dissonance. The subjects who were committed to their initial judgment, because it was too late to undo its influence, tended to reduce their dissonance in this way.

A very impressive amount of research support for dissonance theory has accumulated over the last few years, and we shall return to the theory again when we reach the topic for which it has the most important implications, that of attitude change. For now, however, let us merely note that the theory is somewhat less ambiguous than defense mechanism theory, and to a great extent predicts the same results. In a psychoanalytic theory of ego defense, anxiety is aroused by any indication that a person has violated, or is liable to violate, the dictates of his superego. In dissonance theory, dissonance is aroused by any indication that a person's behavior is inconsistent with his beliefs and values. There seems to be little difference between these two causes of disquietude other than the words used to describe them.

The two theories also seem to be quite similar in the ways in which the individual defends himself against anxiety or dissonance. It is difficult to make a comprehensive list of defense mechanisms according to either theory, but repression, projection, and rationalization in the one theory and the avoidance of dissonant information, addition of consonant elements, and reevaluation of alternatives in the other theory certainly seem to have much in common. By describing strategies of self-deception in more precise terms and by providing a wealth of experimental evidence on them, Festinger and his colleagues have made an important contribution to clinical as well as to social psychology.

Summary

Personality as defined by psychology refers to those characteristic behaviors and adaptations which the individual exhibits fairly uniformly over time. Personality is developed as a consequence of learning, thinking, perceiving, and being motivated. Development of the individual may be hampered and distorted by various traumas and deprivations, and the resulting personality may be abnormal. In this book, an abnormal personality does not signify an "unadjusted" one, or a "different" kind of person; it means a personality that is unable to deal with life's various complexities to the extent that one's potential should have equipped one to do. In this definition, individuals may be said to have been given an abnormal personality by their culture if that culture overspecializes them for frenzied, outgroup violence or for disassociated passivity. Here, the view of therapy for personality abnormality is that it should help the individual receiving it to realize his potential for the richest possible life as an autonomous individual by increasing his freedom of choice and action.

Personality can be seen as developing by several identifiable stages of growth. A variety of approaches have identified a first stage, consisting of need for closeness and dependency, and a second stage, involving the development of autonomy around age two, as a result of the confidence learned in stage one. Emotional learning during these first years is crucial not only for later emotionality but also for the learning of speech. Social closeness is the reinforcement for attempts to learn language and culture. The innate mechanisms which precede and lead to this social learning include clinging, sucking, crying, following, and smiling.

Harlow's work with infant monkeys reveals a greater importance for clinging than for sucking. When these innate bases of affiliation do not, because of deprivation, lead to further social contact, as for Harlow's experimental infant monkeys, grave developmental abnormalities occur. The monkeys fail to develop the capacity for sexual behavior or social response, and they are without maternal behavior when they do give birth after artificial insemination. Persistent juvenile monkeys can teach them to make social bonds, however, even after maturity.

Human infants who have been deprived of close social contact, for example by institutionalization, suffer grave abnormalities also. Children who have never learned to speak because of failure to develop primary social bonds can be helped by a therapeutic sequence of emotional arousal and close holding that leads to secure autonomy.

In the second stage of personality development, the child needs to learn how to reconcile his growing need for autonomy with the needs of society. The greatest danger for this stage is that when his impulses conflict with society's standards for behavior, he may be made to feel such severe shame and guilt that the very awareness of his impulses may become threatening enough to make him consciously deny their existence. Loevinger has distinguished three substages within this period as well as characteristic adult difficulties which result from developmental problems occurring in each of them. If this and the previous stage are successfully completed, however, the child will be confident about expressing his private self in public, will feel competent as an individual, and will be able to identify with others and be motivated to act positively toward them.

In the third stage, the adult conscience is developed. Methods of internal conflict resolution for dealing with anxieties appear; they will be characteristic of the adult personality. The successful autonomy of the second stage is threatened now by awareness of sexuality in the self and others, feelings of rivalry with parent figures over objects of sexual love, and attendant feelings of powerlessness. The typical developmental solution to the problems of this age is to identify with a powerful parent and vicariously share with that person the pleasures of adult competence and power. The incorporation of this idealized personality, or superego, into one's own self means acquiring a set of internalized prohibitions and standards and an ego ideal, or a picture of what one would like to become.

As in the previous stage, harsh socialization is likely to result in such shame and guilt over impulses that they may be kept from consciousness. Great anxiety will then be the consequence of these impulses threatening to reach conscious awareness.

We have seen that sources of anxiety can be incorporated into the personality during early stages of childhood. Memory of early helplessness can be reawakened by fearful experiences at any time of life, creating anxiety also. When harsh socialization has made an individual feel guilt not only at certain ways of carrying out his innate motives but also at having them at all, anxiety will be very severe. Ways of protecting the ego from this kind of anxiety include certain characteristic methods known as defense mechanisms. Projection (attributing one's unacceptable impulses to another), repression (forcing and keeping perceptions out of awareness), rationalization (ascribing behavior to motives other than the forbidden one), displacement (disguising a drive by turning it against a different object), and reaction formation (convincing oneself that a motive is actually its opposite) are a few of these. Viewing these processes of ego defense from the point of view of cognitive dissonance as developed by Festinger gives some experimental evidence about these personality mechanisms, which were originally described by psychoanalytic theory.

Notes and Acknowledgments

1. The material on Jackson presented here is taken from an excellent article on him by Tom Gaddis, who also wrote *Birdman of Alcatraz.* The article, "San Quentin: What Went Wrong," has unfortunately had only limited circulation, appearing in *Northwest,* a magazine supplement of the Portland, Oreg., Sunday *Oregonian,* on August 29, 1971.
2. See Erik H. Erikson, *Childhood and Society.* (2d ed.) New York: W. W. Norton & Company, Inc., 1963; and *Identity: Youth and Crisis.* New York: W. W. Norton & Company, Inc., 1968.
   Loevinger, Jane. "Theories of ego development," in Louis Breger (Ed.), *Clinical-Cognitive Psychology, Models and Integrations.* Englewood Cliffs, N. J.: Prentice-Hall, Inc., 1969, pp. 83–135.
   Loevinger, Jane. "The meaning and measurement of ego development," in David F. Wrench (Ed.), *Readings in Psychology: Foundations and Applications.* New York: McGraw-Hill Book Company, 1971, pp. 295–299.
   Loevinger, Jane, and R. Wessler. *Measuring Ego Development I: Construction and Use of a Sentence Completion Test.* San Francisco: Jossey-Bass, 1970.
   Loevinger, Jane, R. Wessler, and C. Redmore. *Measuring Ego Development II: A Scoring Manual for Women and Girls.* San Francisco: Jossey-Bass, 1970.
3. Zaslow, Robert W., and Louis Breger. "A theory and treatment of autism," in Louis Breger (Ed.), *Clinical-Cognitive Psychology, Models and Integrations.* Englewood Cliffs, N. J.: Prentice-Hall, Inc., 1969, pp. 246–291.
4. Erikson, Erik H. Op. cit.
5. Zaslow, Robert W., and Louis Breger. Op. cit.
6. Harlow, Harry F. "The heterosexual affectional system in monkeys." *American Psychologist,* January 1962 (17), pp. 1–10.

7. Harlow, Harry F., Margaret K. Harlow, and Stephen J. Suomi. "From thought to therapy: Lessons from a primate laboratory." *American Scientist*, September-October 1971 (59), pp. 538–549.

8. NOTE: Aspects of this technique used for therapy of autism have been misapplied, and also have been grossly misused by people without adequate training, acting in the role of therapist. Situations in which improperly trained people act in a therapeutic role are extremely dangerous.

9. Shaffer, H. R., and P. E. Emerson. "The development of social attachments in infancy." *Monographs in Social Research in Child Development*, no. 3, 1964 (29).

   Shaffer, H. R., and P. E. Emerson. "Patterns of response to physical contact in early human development." *Journal of Child Psychology and Psychiatry*, 1964 (5), pp. 1–13.

10. Robertson, James. *A Two Year Old Goes to Hospital* (film.) Condon. Released in the United States by New York University Film Library, 1953.

11. Bandura, Albert, Dorothea Ross, and Sheila A. Ross. "A comparative test of the status envy, social power, and secondary reinforcement theories of identificatory learning." *Journal of Abnormal and Social Psychology*, 1963 (67), pp. 527–534.

    Bandura, Albert. "Vicarious processes: A case of no-trial learning," in Leonard Berkowitz (Ed.), *Advances in Experimental Social Psychology*. Vol. 2. New York: Academic Press, Inc., 1965, pp. 1–55.

12. Loevinger, Jane. "The meaning and measurement of ego development." *American Psychologist*, 1966 (21), pp. 195–206.

13. Warren, Marguerite Q. *The Community Treatment Project after Five Years*. Sacramento, Calif.: California Youth Authority, Division of Research, 1967.

14. Useful and readable books for obtaining an elementary knowledge of psychoanalytic theory are:

    Brenner, Charles. *An Elementary Textbook of Psychoanalysis*. Garden City, N. Y.: Doubleday & Company, Inc., Anchor Books, 1955.

    Thompson, Clara. *Psychoanalysis: Evolution and Development*. New York: Grove Press, Inc., 1957.

    Freud, Sigmund. *An Outline of Psychoanalysis*. New York: W. W. Norton & Company, Inc., 1949.

    Freud, Anna. *The Ego and the Mechanisms of Defense*. New York: International Universities Press, Inc., 1961.

    Good, brief accounts are also given in:

    Hall, Calvin, and Gardner Lindzey. *Theories of Personality*. New York: John Wiley & Sons, Inc., 1957.

    Cofer, C. N., and M. H. Appley. *Motivation: Theory and Research*. New York: John Wiley & Sons, Inc., 1966.

15. Helfer, Ray E., and C. Henry Kempe (Eds.). *The Battered Child*. Chicago: The University of Chicago Press, 1968. Especially important is the article by Brandt F. Steele, and Carl B. Pollock. "A psychiatric study of parents who abuse infants and small children," pp. 103–147.

16. Loevinger, Jane. "Theories of ego development." Op. cit., p. 106.
17. Steele, Brandt F., and Carl B. Pollock. Op. cit. Relevant excerpts from this chapter are included in David F. Wrench (Ed.), *Readings in Psychology: Foundations and Applications.* Op. cit., pp. 331–360.
18. Steele, Brandt F., and Carl B. Pollock, in Ray E. Helfer and C. Henry Kempe (Eds.). Op. cit., p. 336.
19. Ibid.
20. A good, brief account of Murray's theoretical position is given in Calvin Hall and Gardner Lindzey. Op. cit.
21. Sears, R. R. "Functional abnormalities of memory with special reference to amnesia." *Psychological Bulletin,* 1936 (33), pp. 229–274.
22. Rosenzweig, S. "An experimental study of 'repression' with special reference to need-persistive and ego-defensive reactions to frustration." *Journal of Experimental Psychology,* 1943 (32), pp. 64–76.
    Rosenzweig, S. "The investigation of repression as an instance of experimental idiodynamics." *Psychological Review,* 1952 (59), pp. 339–345.
    Rosenzweig, S. "The experimental study of repression," in Henry A. Murray (Ed.), *Explorations in Personality.* New York: Science Editions, John Wiley & Sons, Inc., 1962, pp. 472–490.
23. Zeigarnik, Bluma. "Über das behalten von erledigten und unerledigten Handlungen." *Psychologische Forschugen,* 1927 (9), pp. 1–85. An English description may be found in Dorwin Cartwright (Ed.), *Field Theory in Social Science.* New York: Harper & Row, Publishers, Incorporated, 1951, pp. 6–20.
24. Green, Donald Ross. "Volunteering and the recall of interrupted tasks." *Journal of Abnormal and Social Psychology,* 1963 (66), pp. 397–401.
25. A very readable description of Festinger's cognitive-dissonance theory may be found in his article by that title in *Scientific American,* October, 1962.
    For a fuller account, see Leon Festinger, *A Theory of Cognitive Dissonance.* New York: Harper & Row, Publishers, Incorporated, 1957.
    For recent experimental studies utilizing the theory, see J. W. Brehm, and A. R. Cohen, *Explorations in Cognitive Dissonance.* New York: John Wiley & Sons, Inc., 1962.
26. Walster, E., and P. Prestholdt. "The effect of misjudging another: overcompensation or dissonance reduction?" *Journal of Experimental Social Psychology,* 1966 (2), pp. 85–97.

Orlando Jimenez

SEVEN

GROUP
PARTICIPATION
& IDENTITY

Introduction: The Transformation of Society

From the end of the Civil War until the start of the Great Depression, the United States underwent a period of rapid industrialization which altered virtually all aspects of our lives. During this period the mechanization of agriculture transformed us from a rural to an urban country; improved methods of transportation created national markets and led to the consolidation of industries; and the development of the automobile drastically altered the nature of the city. These material changes, however, were in some ways less important than the social changes which accompanied them. The wave of industrialization also made basic changes in the nature of work, authority, education, the family, and socialization. Because the next stage of personality development introduces the individual to the world of work, we need to learn more about these changes before we continue with the study of individual development. Let us look at Robert and Helen Lynd's classic studies of industrialization in Muncie, *Middletown* and *Middletown in Transition*.[1]

The Lynds studied Muncie in the 1920s and 1930s, and used historical research to discover what the town had been like in 1890. In 1890, glass jars, the chief product of Muncie, were made by a crew consisting of two men and three boys. First, a boy, called the gatherer, stuck an iron pipe into the caldron of molten glass and brought it out with a glob of glass on the end. He passed it to one of the two adult blowers, who blew it into a mold—a process taking, on the average, three breaths and 25 seconds. The "taking-out boy" removed it from the mold, and the "carry-in boy" took it and put it in the annealing oven. As the three boys could keep two adult glassblowers supplied with materials, the crew of five people could produce about 200-dozen quart jars a day. Some additional labor, usually provided by women, was involved in smoothing out imperfections in the jars.

The glassblowing crew in the 1890s worked a long day. Except in midsummer when the hours were shortened, the crew worked from 7:00 until 5:00, with time off for lunch and several short rest periods during the course of the day. Working close to furnaces and pots of molten glass is always hot, and during a midwestern summer there were some days when work had to be discontinued because of the heat. State laws forbade employing boys of younger than twelve years of age for longer than 10 hours a day, but these laws were not strictly enforced. Statistics from 1892 show that, at that time, just over 40 percent of the employees of Muncie's leading glass works were under the age of twelve.

In 1890, however, a machine was developed which could produce glass jars mechanically, and it was soon adopted by the factories of Muncie. Some figures on productivity should make clear why. In 1890, twenty-one men and twenty-four boys manning an eight-pot furnace could turn out 1,600-dozen jars in a day. With the machines, eight men and no boys could turn out 6,600 dozen during the same period of time.

Eight boys and no men could have done the same. Although

blowing jars was a highly skilled craft, and a man's skill continued to increase throughout his working lifetime, tending the machines was a task that anyone could learn in a short time. The young were actually better at it, in fact, for they were quicker. Under these circumstances, child labor might have driven adult labor off the market, as had happened earlier in the industrial revolution in Britain. It did not happen because the adults banded together and passed laws which required the young to attend school until the age of fourteen.

Although compulsory education came about largely to protect adult jobs, this goal was not its only source. Also involved were shifts in status and power within the community which made formal education much more important in attaining high social status than it had been before. The boy who entered a glass factory in the nineteenth century could look forward to rising in a stable hierarchy of skill and authority. Well-developed craft unions enforced apprenticeship requirements and gave the greatest prestige and authority to those men who had spent decades developing their skill. The skilled glassblower, like the skilled craftsman in many another craft, was the equal in social status of any but the most successful entrepreneur. Furthermore, he could become an entrepreneur by developing and enlarging upon his skills. Early tractors, automobiles, and airplanes were created, not by large teams of industrial designers, but by skilled mechanics who often had little formal education.

The mechanization of industry destroyed this hierarchy of skill and prestige. The older workers, who had been in greatest demand because of their skill, were unable to compete with younger men, who could work faster and were willing to do so for less money. The authority and prestige of the old craft unions were undermined by the increasing irrelevancy of the skills upon which they had been based, and the young looked on older workers not as models to be emulated but as people who were obsolete. Young workers, immigrants, women, and minority-group members began competing successfully for jobs from which they had formerly been excluded by the apprenticeship requirements of the old craft unions. The previously dominant group fought back. Immigration was largely closed down at the time of the First World War and, as we shall see in the chapter on prejudice, minority-group members were actively discouraged from becoming part of the industrial work force. By and large, however, the skilled craftsmen passed into obsolescence.

With the youngest workers most in demand, a boy who entered

industrial employment could no longer look forward to rising in his occupation. There was not even any way, other than regular attendance, in which he could excel in performing his duties, for the machine did an equally good job every time. Almost his sole chance of upward social mobility was through education. By going through high school or even to college, he might hope to escape the machine and enter a world where skill and initiative would be rewarded.

The mechanization of industry changed the family almost as much as it changed occupational prestige. Education and industrial employment necessitated geographic mobility, and it became much less common for several generations of a family to live together in the same house. The rising employment of women outside the home reduced their ability to socialize their children in adult roles at the same time that mobility removed other adult models. Increasingly, the education of children was taken over by the formal educational system. As better transportation enabled the young to seek entertainment outside the home, and as the authority of parents was undermined by their technological obsolescence and ignorance of those things the children were learning, the prestige structure of the family was inverted much as that of industry had been.

In preindustrial societies, technology may remain virtually unchanging for hundreds of thousands of years. Where this is so, authority is usually given to the elders of the group, for by living longer they have acquired more wisdom. Children are socialized into adult roles by observing adults perform them, and by practice starting at an early age. Toys are small replicas of adult tools, and play centers on practicing the skills of the adult. Long before sexual maturity, the child is ready to test himself against his ego ideal by starting to play an adult role. Dorothy Lee gives an example:

> When Standing Bear decided to join in the tribal buffalo hunt, on his own for the first time, his step-mother seriously requested him to save her the kidney and the skin. Standing Bear describes the hunt: "All I could hear was the roll and rattle of hoofs of the buffalo as they thundered along. . . I realized how small I was. I really was afraid of them. Then I thought about what my step-mother had said to me about bringing her a kidney and a skin, and the feeling that I was a man, after all, came back to me." He was eight years old.[2]

Although the United States in the nineteenth century was quite unlike a stable, traditional culture, socialization into adult roles was still carried out at a relatively early age through direct tuition by adult models. The girl was not only taught what it meant to be a woman by her own mother in her own home, she was also provided with aunts, cousins, and perhaps a grandmother as examples of the variety of womanhood. The tasks she had to perform were meaningful, for she saw others carrying them out and understood how they would ultimately give her the authority which her elders enjoyed. Similarly, the boy working at the glass factory learned what it meant to be a man from the older workers. Several times a day, the skilled glassblower who was the head of the crew called a halt to the work, and one of the boys was sent out with two pails on a pole to buy beer. Listening to the men and testing his developing skill against theirs, the boy became a man among men.

In our modern industrial society, things are quite different. Kept in a state of artificial financial dependence, the child goes to school to learn skills which his elders do not have, to prepare himself for an occupation which may not exist yet. Unable to test himself against reality, he can only hope that he will be able to come to terms with an adult role when the time comes. Faced with the conflicting demands of his culture, he may not develop the security which comes from mastering the technology of his culture, but instead may seek ways to escape from the feelings of failure and inferiority which the culture inspires in him.

Success, Failure, and Aspiration

INTRODUCTION

In forming the ego ideal, the child has set goals for what he would like to be and become. Will he ever be able to achieve them, however? This is the major problem which concerns him as he attempts to develop competence in culturally and personally valued skills. Lacking the confident sense of identity of adulthood, he is extremely dependent on how others see him, when forming an impression of himself. His experiences with groups, first the small group of his family and then school groups, are therefore crucial at this stage. If he is accepted and valued by them, he will adopt their positive attitude toward himself. If he is rejected by them, whether because of difference in values, lack of skill, physical handicap, or the color of his skin, he will suffer from a pervasive sense of inferiority. Conformity is such a marked feature of peer-group relations during the grade school years precisely because of this dependence of the individual on others' conceptions of him. If these conceptions are negative, he will, as soon as he is able, seek out and adopt the ideals of other groups which are more accepting of him. Let us look at these early stages of identity formation in more detail.

BIRTH ORDER AND ASPIRATION

The content of the ego ideal depends to a great extent on how parents interact with the child, and this interaction tends to depend on the child's position in the family.[3] Firstborn children are given more parental attention of both a positive and a negative kind. More time is spent in talking to them, more effort is made to explain things in terms they can understand, and higher aspirations are set for their achievement. These higher expectations are also transmitted through more punishment and stricter enforcement of rules. As a result of these positive and negative pressures, firstborn children tend to be considerably more adult-oriented than later children. They conform more to adult expectations, are extremely responsive, and set high goals for themselves in adult-valued activities, such as intellectual achievement. They are more likely than later-born children to graduate from college, and far more likely to achieve fame, especially for intellectual accomplishment. That these results are not simply due to parents' spending more money on the education of the first child is shown by the achievement of last-born children who are considerably younger than their next oldest sibling. These children, born quite a few years after the last birth in the family, resemble firstborn rather than later-born children in both personality and achievement.

With the exception of the children born after a long interval, later-born children tend to turn their attention to areas which are valued more by peers and less by adults. (This may be partially through hesitation to compete with older siblings in areas where the older is most deeply involved.) They are more likely to excel in athletics than firstborn children. They also do well in tasks which call for impulsiveness and risk taking.

SOCIAL COMPARISON IN PEER GROUPS

Having formed an ego ideal largely through interaction within the family, the child will then develop it through play. Perceiving oneself as conforming to idealized roles is reinforcing, and cultural skills can be practiced in play without the threat involved in undertaking them in real-life situations. Basic to this process is a comparison of oneself with others. The goals and standards which have been learned are highly ambiguous, and it is by comparison with peers that the individual evaluates the extent to which he is living up to his superego.

Under normal circumstances, individuals compare themselves with others whom they perceive to be similar to themselves. Studies during the Second World War showed that such comparisons led to some unforeseen results. Contrary to what most people would expect, soldiers stationed near home during their training were more dissatisfied than those stationed far away, and black soldiers stationed in the North liked the army less than those stationed in the South. Both these findings were related to the people with whom the soldiers compared themselves. Soldiers undergoing training near home compared themselves with high school friends who were not in the army. Their army life looked pretty bad by comparison. Those stationed farther from home compared themselves more with fellow soldiers who were as badly off as they were. Similarly, black soldiers might find the army not much worse than civilian life in the Deep South. When they contrasted themselves with black warworkers earning high pay in Northern cities, the army looked much less attractive.

When undertaking a task, an individual usually sets a goal for himself. This goal, which is what he hopes to achieve on a particular trial, is called his *level of aspiration*. It is usually influenced quite a bit by the groups with whom the individual compares himself. If an individual who has never undertaken a certain task is told the performance of some particular group and then asked how well he hopes to do, he will set his goal in relation to the performance of the group. If it is a group of people whom he would expect to excel him at the task, he will set his goal below their performance. If, on the other hand, the group is composed of individuals whom he would expect to be less skilled than himself, he will set his goal above their performance. Not very surprisingly, high school seniors expect to do better on an English test than eighth-grade students but less well than college English majors.

If the individual has attempted the task in the past, he will usually set his goal just a little above his usual performance, although his target may still be influenced by comparison with others. What the individual experiences as success or failure will depend not on some absolute measure of his performance but, rather, on how it compares with his level of aspiration. Is 140 a good game in bowling? It depends on how well you usually bowl and with whom you compare yourself.

THREAT AND DOWNWARD COMPARISON

Experiences of failure cause the individual to set his level of aspiration in a way which will defend him from anxiety. This, paradoxically, may be done by setting the goal either very low or very high. Suppose that you habitually bowl with individuals who usually roll around 140 on a game. Your own score is generally around 100. If you set your level of aspiration in the normal way, basing it both on your reference group and on your own past performance, you might aspire to a score of 120. Because this score is considerably higher than you usually achieve, you would repeatedly experience failure. How could you keep from undergoing this failure?

One way would be to ignore how well the others do and set a low level which you can be quite sure of reaching. You might decide that you will try to get 90, or will concentrate on rolling the ball without its going in the gutter. By setting this very low level of aspiration, you can experience success—as long as you keep from thinking about the scores the others obtain. Unfortunately, they may not be willing to let you ignore how their score compares with yours. Another, less obvious way of avoiding the experience of failure is to set an unrealistically high level of aspiration. You may decide that you are going to bowl a perfect game, getting a strike with each ball. When you fail to achieve this goal, you can take comfort from the fact that none of your friends achieved it either. By concentrating on your failure to reach an impossibly high goal, you can avoid thinking about your failure to reach a less high one.

As studies by Jucknat and by Pauline Sears have shown, both of these defensive techniques are employed by children who have repeatedly experienced failure in school.[4] One of the most important faults of our educational system is that it is structured in such a way that many children do experience failure. Whether they respond by dreaming of impossible successes or by setting a level of aspiration so low that others, teachers, fellow classmates, and above all, parents, will inevitably judge its achievement as a failure, they cannot invest their egos in striving to do well. This in turn makes it more probable that they will fail again. Eventually, they decide that they cannot do schoolwork, and they seek other activities and groups which will not give them repeated experiences of failure.

The vicious cycle of failure, lowered aspiration, and further failure in the school can also take place in the home. A recent study of how parents interacted with children who had a history of delinquency showed that they never praised the children and that they expected the worst of them and spent a good deal of time criticizing them.[5] When the parents were told, in a training program designed to improve their parenting, that they should praise those aspects of the child's behavior they did approve of, many found it difficult to find anything they did like about the child. Is it any wonder that their children sought out groups which would be more accepting of them?

The way in which threat influences the choice of whom people compare themselves with was investigated in a recent study by Hakmiller.[6] Each subject was led to believe that she had scored high in a test of the amount of unconscious hostility she felt toward her parents. To some subjects, this trait was described in positive terms as leading to independence and maturity. To others, it was described very negatively as leading to both antisocial behavior and personal problems. Each subject was then given a chance to find out the score of one fellow subject. As predicted, those who were threatened by having been led to believe that they had a very undesirable quality compared themselves with individuals who would be expected to have even more of the undesirable quality. Those who were not threatened compared themselves with individuals more like themselves. By concentrating on how they compared with individuals who were even worse off than themselves, the threatened individuals were able to reduce their anxiety. Similarly, in real-life situations, an individual may protect himself against anxiety by seeking out reference groups and activities which will make it easier for him to compare himself favorably with others.

The experiment we have just described raises some questions about the use of deception in psychology experiments; not because it is unusual in its use of deception, but rather because it is a fairly typical deception experiment. In it, the subjects were told the true nature of the situation at the end of the experiment, and gave no evidence of being particularly disturbed. But isn't it possible that they were more disturbed than they cared to reveal? If not, one wonders to what extent the experiment really threatened their self-esteem. That is, after all, a presumably quite disturbing experience. Psychologists are currently debating the ethics of such experiments. Proponents of deception argue that it is necessary to the experimental study of human behavior and does not really hurt anyone. Its opponents maintain that a belief in scientific inquiry shoud be subject to ethical considerations just as any other belief should, and that there are better methodologies for understanding human beings than laboratory experimentation anyway. The way in which the controversy is resolved will have a great influence on the shape of the field in the future.

The Development of Independence

WAYS OF RELATING TO GROUPS

In the preceding section, we have seen three different ways in which individuals may relate to groups. First, the individual who has not yet formed a stable impression of his own competence may be highly dependent on them. He will need to conform to the group in order to maintain a favorable view of himself and to protect himself against anxiety. Second, the individual who is unable to meet the standards of a particular group may react by rejecting it and seeking other groups which are more supportive. He may need to reject all aspects of the group he is moving away from in order to keep its rejection of him from being threatening. Finally, the individual who has had successful experiences with groups may develop the self-confidence to become more independent of them. Of these three processes, the first two are largely counterparts of each other. The individual who is most dependent on his reference group for his conception of himself has the strongest need to contrast "we" and "they," and to combine compulsive conformity to his own group with the expression of hostility toward others. We shall therefore save the discussion of expression of hostility toward outgroups until the chapter on prejudice, and concentrate here on the differences between individuals who conform more or less to their ingroups.

RESEARCH ON CONFORMITY

While we have seen that a good deal of conformity is normal during the grade school years, one needs to be able to act independently of groups by the time adulthood is reached. Most of the research on conformity has used college-age or older subjects, and has focused on situations where conformity is not a rational response—that is, where the individual can conform only by denying his own perceptions or violating his values. Let us look at a representative study.

The basic design of conformity experiments is well illustrated by the research of Asch, who did much to stimulate the study of this area.[7] Asch believed that you could only speak properly of conformity if you could show that the group could make the individual act in a different way from the way he otherwise would. If a number of friends all order their steaks rare when they go out to eat, this unanimity does not necessarily mean that they are conforming to one another. They may just have similar tastes. If, on the other hand, a new member of the group who has always preferred well-done meat starts ordering rare steak, his act is more convincing evidence of group influence. Asch thus created a situation where the group pressures clearly differed from what the behavior of the subject would normally be. He did this by giving subjects easy tasks to perform, and then instructing a majority of them to give the same incorrect answer on a number of the tasks.

The subjects in Asch's experiments were brought together to participate in an experiment on perceptual judgment. On each trial, one standard line and three comparison lines were presented, and the task of each subject was to tell which comparison line was of the same length as the standard. The perceptual task was easy, and subjects in a control group where there was no deception made almost no errors. In the experimental groups, however, all the subjects except one were confederates, instructed to give certain agreed-on incorrect answers on some of the trials. Since the one naïve subject was always seated so that he would give his judgments last, he was preceded on each of these critical trials by the unanimous choice of an incorrect alternative. His conformity score was the number of trials in which he also chose this incorrect alternative.

In a typical experiment, which employed seven confederates, considerable conformity was found. While 26 percent of the subjects made no incorrect judgments despite the group pressure, the remainder ranged from one to eleven errors out of the twelve critical trials. In variations on the experiment, two other interesting findings emerged. Whereas the amount of conformity depended upon whether one, two, or three individuals gave the same incorrect judgments, a larger group had no more effect than the three confederates did. Still more interesting, the provision of merely one other individual who gave correct judgments greatly reduced the effects even of a majority of seven. The unanimity of the judgments seems to be a critical factor in group pressure.

PERSONALITY FACTORS IN INDEPENDENCE AND CONFORMITY

In the last chapter, we saw some of the consequences to the individual of internalizing moral standards which are unrealistically high and harshly punitive. We noted that he would tend to suffer from anxiety because of difficulty in living up to these standards; that, in fact, the mere existence of some human motives would be anxiety-inducing for him; and that he would try to cope with his anxiety by employing repressive defenses and denying the nature of his motives to himself. This pattern of anxiety and defense has two important consequences for an individual's conformity to his reference groups. The first is that he, more than other people, will be made anxious by disagreeing with these groups. Not only will he have greater need of group support to deal with his great tendency toward anxiety, but he may even unconsciously interpret his disagreement with the group as hostility toward it, for his parents may have interpreted disagreement that way in the past. The second consequence of his pattern of anxiety and defense is that he will be less in contact with his own emotions and may not even realize when he wants to disagree with the group. Both of these two consequences of a harsh superego will increase the individual's conformity to his reference groups. The second consequence, through making him unaware of his own emotional reactions and those of others, accounts for the research finding that people who conform more have less psychological sensitivity and perceptiveness.

Support for this view of conformity as the result of repressive types of ego defense is found in an interesting study by Breger. His theoretical approach was psychoanalytic:

> Conformity is conceptualized as stemming from a more pervasive ego-defensive process, centering around the repression of hostility, and consisting primarily of the ego defenses of repression, denial, reaction-formation, and turning against the self. . . .The assumption is made that individuals who conform when faced with group pressure do so because at some level of awareness they perceive opposition to the group as an act of defiance and aggression which arouses anxiety and calls into play one or more of the above defense mechanisms. . . .As is characteristic of all defense mecha-

nisms, these involve an unwarranted overgeneralization on the part of the individual employing them such that situations not necessarily involving hostility (e.g., giving an accurate judgment in an Asch situation) are reacted to on the basis of this latent perception.[8]

Two predictions were made from this theoretical orientation, and both were supported by the results of the experiment. The first prediction was that if high conformers suffer anxiety from feeling aggressive, then they should tend to express aggression in a disguised, rather than a direct, manner so as to avoid the anxiety which would result from being aware of their aggressive motives. This hypothesis was tested by means of the Thematic Apperception Test. As we saw in an earlier chapter, subjects taking this test tell stories about pictures. In these stories, hostility may be expressed either directly (through one character's attacking another) or indirectly (through horrible things happening to a character without anyone's being responsible for them). Breger counted as "defended hostility" those instances in which characters were injured, blinded, or killed by fire, flood, famine, and other impersonal forces. As predicted, subjects who conformed more on a conformity task showed more instances of "defended hostility" and fewer direct expressions of hostility in their stories than independent subjects.

The second prediction was that subjects who conformed more would express less aggression against an authority figure in a situation where aggression was a reasonable response, because of the great anxiety which would result from their going against their harsh superego processes. This hypothesis was tested by giving the subjects an impossible experimental task (placing pegs in a pegboard without letting them touch the sides of the holes), and then criticizing them for not performing it rapidly. At the end of this frustrating experience, a confederate tried to induce each subject to be critical of the experimenter. As was predicted, the subjects who were willing to criticize the experimenter were those who had conformed less in the conformity task. Breger's study thus shows a relationship between excessive conformity and the use of repressive techniques of ego defense.

Another interesting study illustrating the relationship between anxiety and conformity was done by Darley.[9] If individuals conform to groups because not doing so is anxiety-inducing for them, then anything which raises their level of anxiety should increase the amount of conformity. Darley contrasted the amount of conformity of subjects who were waiting to participate in an experiment which would involve their being subjected to severe electric shock with that of subjects who were not. The result, which Darley viewed more in social learning terms, was that considerably more conformity was found in the group anticipating the shock.

To summarize the chapter so far, we find that the extent to which an individual is able to accomplish the developmental task of becoming an independent member of society depends on three main factors. The first, which cannot be studied experimentally, is the extent to which the culture provides a meaningful structure of roles and adequate models and groups by means of which the child can be socialized into the culture. The second is the extent to which the individual has the experience of success, an experience which depends both on the aspirations which he brings to his groups and on the ways in which peers and authorities in these groups respond to him. The final factor in developing independence is having reasonable internal standards which leave the individual conscious of his own motives and free from anxiety in expressing them. If these factors are favorable, the individual will reach maturity with secure foundations of an adult identity.

Maturity, Culture, and Identity

CULTURAL AUTHORITY AND IDENTITY

The arrival of physiological maturity radically alters many of the bases of the individual's sense of identity. His skills and coordinations, the size and appearance of his body, and most strikingly, his motives and emotions are all suddenly different. If he doesn't look the same, or feel the same, or act the same, who is he? Arriving at a satisfactory answer to this question is the next major goal in the development of the individual, and his culture plays a significant role in this process.

Identity and culture are inextricably bound together. Culture is an organized system of values and expectations, and it is to a great extent the way in which the individual sees himself as realizing those values and relating to those expectations which gives him his identity. In a sense, the individual and the culture share a similar problem—that of being able to integrate diverse elements into a meaningful whole. A hint at this patterning of culture is given by the following quotation:

> When the buffalo died, the Sioux died, ethnically and spiritually. The buffalo's body had provided not only food and material for clothing, covering, and shelter but such utilities as bags and boats, strings for bows and for sewing, cups and spoons. Medicine and ornaments were made of buffalo parts; his droppings, sun dried, served as fuel in winter. Societies and seasons, ceremonies and dances, mythology and children's play extolled his name and image.[10]

Cultures expect different things of different people, and of the same people under different circumstances. Yet, despite the diversity of expected behaviors, individuals must in some way be motivated to carry them out. This is so because members of a society are interdependent, and one member must rely on another member's carrying out certain expected behaviors.

Individuals are assigned to positions and motivated in a variety of ways. Each position recognized by a culture, whether it is mother, cousin, shamen, or advertising executive, is called a *status*. The behavior expected of an occupant of that position is called a *role*, and the rewards and punishments used to induce the occupant of the position to perform the role are called positive and negative *sanctions*. Individuals may be assigned to statuses on the basis of characteristics over which they have no control, a process known as *ascription*. In preindustrial societies, age, sex, and kinship are usually among the most important bases for assigning individuals to various positions. In industrialized societies, achievement is often a more important determinant of the positions to which an individual is assigned, although no society relies solely on achievement for assignment of statuses. While you may win your wife, you have to accept the sister-in-law your brother happens to marry.

Besides differing in how they assign individuals to positions, cultures differ in how they motivate them. In a society in which individuals of the same age and sex do pretty much the same thing, training in this role may start at birth. In societies where there is more diversity of role, where roles are changing, and where individuals need special skills to achieve certain statuses, the motivation to play the role cannot be built in during childhood. In this case, the motivation must either be selected for at a later stage of development and heightened through special socialization experiences, or else adherence to the role must be enforced through the use of positive and negative sanctions.

Berger has used the terms "man in society" and "society in man" to distinguish the two main ways of obtaining compliance to cultural expectations.[11] "Man in society" reminds us of all the groups and organizations which the individual participates in and which may apply sanctions to him if he deviates from these expectations. How would society react, for example, if a minister started advertising commercial products on television? Although his doing so would not be illegal, he would probably find himself criticized by his family, shunned by his neighbors, rejected by his colleagues, and ultimately relieved of his ministerial duties.

Most ministers, however, would never think of making television commercials. This illustrates the other aspect of social control, that of "society in man." To a very great extent, individuals are assigned to roles and socialized into them in ways that make them want to act in the manner that the role demands. Different roles and organizations vary in the extent to which they assume that individuals are internally motivated to perform their duties or that they need to be induced to do so through positive or negative sanctions. Etzioni, for example, has classified organizations on the basis of whether the authority used is primarily coercive, utilitarian, or normative.[12] Coercive organizations, which use threat of punishment as the main basis of motivation, include prisons, prisoner-of-war camps, and those mental hospitals which provide little but custodial care. Utilitarian organizations base motivation mainly on the hope for economic reward, and they include most businesses and industries in our culture. Normative organizations use membership, status, and the intrinsic value of playing a role to internally motivate the occupant of a status. They include religious and professional organizations and universities, among others.

Each of these orientations on the part of an organization tends to call out a corresponding response from the members of the organization. Coercive authority alienates the individual from the organization, whereas utilitarian authority is likely to cause him to adopt a stance of rational calculation and to try to get the greatest reward for the least effort. Normative authority, on the other hand, may cause the individual to internalize the values of the organization as moral principles and to be motivated to carry them out whether he is rewarded or punished for doing so.

As Etzioni's analysis makes clear, societies can most effectively motivate individuals to perform roles by socializing them in a value system which will result in their finding the performance of the roles intrinsically rewarding, and then by honoring them for their performance. This type of normative authority is, in fact, the most important basis of motivation in preindustrial societies. When a Hopi performed a ritual correctly, or a Dakota set out on a war party, or one Kwakiutl bested another in a potlach, he acted not so much through hope of gain or fear of punishment as through a desire to perform a role which had been incorporated into the ego ideal and which was supported by an integrated system of values and religious beliefs.

Although normative authority is most effective, it is not always possible. As societies evolve more complex patterns of roles, it becomes more difficult to create an integrating set of values which will motivate diverse individuals to perform differing roles. Somehow, the modern industrial society must make the museum curator honor the traditions of the past but the aircraft designer be willing to discard them, the businessman compete on the basis of economic self-interest but the politician put the good of his constituents above his personal gain. Since motivation for such disparate roles cannot be accomplished by imparting the same absolute values to all, it tends to be done by providing them with different socialization experiences and by relying more on utilitarian and coercive authority.

These shifts in the basis of authority in industrialized societies have both positive and negative consequences for the individual. On the other hand, the diverse expectations involved in his playing various roles may give him problems of identity. On the other hand, his very doubts about his identity may increase his freedom. Social institutions are created by the perceptions and actions of human beings, and therefore they can be changed by human beings. Yet they can impress the people who are part of them as being permanent and existing independently of human action. The alienation of a man from his society may force him to analyze this paradox, and he may then be capable of initiating effective change in unsatisfactory cultural institutions. Social phenomena are then not immutable constructions against which he is of necessity powerless.

SEXUAL IDENTIFICATION

With the coming of physiological maturity, the individual is prepared to take on an adult sex role. In every society, among the most important statuses distinguished are those of child and adult, male and female. The ease with which the child takes on the appropriate adult sex role will be a function of three things—the similarity of child and adult roles, the presence of appropriate sex models, and the provision of special socialization experiences to mark the transition from childhood to adulthood. Let us look at the operation of the three factors in a study by Rodgers and Long.[13]

Murphy Town and Crossing Rocks in the Out Island Bahamas are similar very small towns with one important difference. The men in Crossing Rocks make their living by fishing, and are gone from home day and night between 80 and 85 percent of the time. Murphy Town was similar until about ten years ago, but now industrial development has replaced fishing as the primary source of employment. The two towns thus resemble one another except that the male children of Murphy Town grow up in the presence of adult male models while the boys of Crossing Rocks seldom see an adult male.

To study the effect of this disparity, Rodgers and Long first looked for an item of behavior on which boys and girls in Murphy Town reliably differed. Although there seemed to be marked divergences in aggressive behavior, they were difficult to observe systematically. The researchers therefore selected a matter of artistic preference suggested by research in other cultures. Given a choice between a rounded figure and an angular one, the majority of the girls in Murphy Town chose the predominantly curved shape and a majority of the boys chose the angular one.

Having found this not-too-obvious test of sexual identification, the researchers then administered it to the boys of Crossing Rocks. As anticipated, most of them chose the rounded figure, as long as they were fifteen years old or younger. What happened at the age of fifteen? At that time they were taken out fishing with the men.

There is a great difference between the behavior expected of boys and of men in Crossing Rocks. As the boys reach the age of manhood, their fathers become quite concerned that they will become "sissies," and they look forward to the opportunity to teach them to be men out fishing. The first year an adolescent goes fishing, he still prefers carefree play with younger playmates and will sneak off to join them if he can. He is beaten to make him work and he goes through a year of "mooning," a period characterized by apathy and passive aggression toward adult males. At the end of this year, he has usually acquired an adult-male identification. Men of Crossing Rocks, sixteen or more years old, prefer the angular figure just as those of Murphy Town do. Because such a drastic change of role is required between childhood and adulthood, not all boys do make the transition—some retain a predominantly feminine identification. They do not remain Out Island fishermen, but migrate into the larger cities.

Adult sexual identification may thus be acquired in either of two ways. The child may form an identification with a same-sexed model at an early stage, and progressively acquire appropriate behavior patterns as he nears maturity. If the culture is supportive of this pattern, and if no marked discrepancy of behavior need occur between childhood and adulthood, the transition may occur quite easily with little necessity for special socialization to bring it about. If, on the other hand, the child is primarily identified with the parent of the opposite sex, and if the culture requires a radical reorientation of behavior at maturity, strong socialization pressures will be needed to bring this change of identity about. As Whiting, Kluckhohn, and Anthony showed in an earlier study, traumatic socialization experiences at puberty are used primarily by those cultures which radically reorient the individual at that time. Radical socialization techniques, however, have their limitations. Because they require the individual to deny much of his or her previous identity, they can reorient behavior only at the price of anxiety and repression. They lead to a less well-integrated personality than can be achieved by more gradual socialization techniques, and they have a high rate of failure.

Finally, there is the possibility that a new generation may create a new conception of adulthood. Thus far, we have looked at cultures as if their integration were a static one. In industrialized societies, this is clearly not the case. As technological innovation brings continuous change, new patterns are created by the assimilation of elements from diverse cultural traditions. Old authority structures are undermined, and elders who are the victims rather than the masters of their technology become less appropriate models for superego formation. Under these circumstances, peer groups may become experiments in the creation of new cultural identities.

Social Origins and Socialization

SOCIAL CLASS AND SOCIAL POWER

In describing the socialization of individuals into adult cultural roles, we have spoken, thus far, as if this process were quite similar for everyone. This is, of course, a gross oversimplification. The way in which an individual encounters the authority structure of society obviously depends a great deal upon that individual's sex, color, ethnicity, and wealth. Various segments of society differ in their wealth, power, and prestige, and these differences are transmitted from generation to generation. Although there is considerable disagreement about the extent to which an individual can change his position in society, there is no disagreement that people start from different positions and that some positions are more desirable to be in than others.

There is at present considerable theoretical disagreement in the field of sociology over the origin and significance of social class.[14] Until recently, the most widely held view was that the differential reward of different positions, which is basic to social class, serves adaptive functions for societies. It was thought that some positions required greater effort and skill from their incumbents than did others, and that the greater rewards associated with these positions were necessary to ensure that their more difficult roles would be adequately performed. Because this tenet is part of a theory which argues that social institutions generally exist because of the functions which they serve for society, it is called the *functionalist* position.

The antifunctionalist position holds that social-class differences exist because some positions give people more power than others, and that this power is then used to obtain greater rewards. An early statement of this position in fiction was George Orwell's *Animal Farm*. In that work, the farmyard animals band together and carry out a successful revolution against the farmer. After the revolution, they give the pigs some authority to help coordinate things. By the end of the book these animals have managed to obtain all the power and prestige formerly enjoyed by the farmer, and the farm is just as much of a dictatorship as it was before the revolution. Although *Animal Farm* was intended as a comment on political developments in the Soviet Union where the dictatorship of the proletariat gave signs of becoming simply the dictatorship of the dictator, it is also a general theory of social-class differences. It sees these differences not as a way of ensuring that difficult societal tasks will be performed, but, rather, as a failure of the society to establish effective controls over the use of power.

The antifunctionalist approach allows us to see how power differences among people in a society cause individuals who are being socialized into adult roles to have diverse experiences with the authority structure of their society. Sociological studies have indicated, for example, that children from wealthy and powerful families receive less punishment for the same juvenile offenses than children from working-class homes do.

As we noted in the introduction to this chapter, formal educational institutions have over the years become more and more important in determining occupational opportunity. It is therefore especially important to see how educational experiences are influenced by social-class origins. Two studies which throw some light on this question were conducted by August Hollingshead and Edgar Litt.

Hollingshead's book *Elmtown's Youth* is one of the classic studies of American communities conducted before the Second World War.[15] Selecting a relatively stable midwestern town with only one high school, the author made an exhaustive study of the nature of social-class distinctions and the ways in which they influenced the life experiences of high-school-aged youth. First he studied what social-class distinctions were actually made by residents of the community. On the basis of these distinctions, he assigned individuals to social-class levels ranging from I (highest) through V (lowest). He found that individuals from similar social-class backgrounds tended to associate more with one another than did individuals from different social-class backgrounds, and that each extracurricular activity group at the high school tended to draw participants from a particular social-class level. Social-class origins also influenced the advice given the student on what classes he should take, the advisers reasoning that students who could not afford to go to college should be given practical skills rather than college-preparatory courses.

The most striking difference, however, was in the way that a student's background influenced how the school's disciplinary rules applied to him. In cities with many schools, the most harsh discipline is often applied in schools in the least wealthy areas of the city. The stern discipline is justified on the basis that it is necessary to control the children. Because the severe discipline makes them rebellious, this becomes a self-fulfilling prophecy. Consider the following example from Hollingshead, which is especially clear because both students were at the same school:

> The following Wednesday morning, Frank Stone, Jr. (class I), parked his father's Cadillac in front of the high school at a quarter after eight, climbed out leisurely, picked up his notebook, and walked into the office and casually remarked, "I guess I'm late again."

> The principal looked hard at him and spoke firmly, "What's the story this time?"

. . ."*I didn't wake up, I guess.*"

"*This time you are going to detention like everyone else.*" *He wrote young Frank an excuse, placed his name on the detention list, and, as he handed him the excuse, said, "This means one hour in detention. I want to see you there at three-fifteen tonight.*"

Frank Stone did not go to detention, however, and the principal called his father. The principal told the superintendent what he had done and left for a choir rehearsal. When Mr. Stone brought his son in, the superintendent met Frank and asked:

"*Haven't you gone home yet?*" *Young Frank, burning with rage, retorted, "Mr. (Principal) made me come back for detention. Dad is really sore.*"

The superintendent talked with Frank, and had him wait for a while in his outer office (not the detention room). Some days later he explained to the researchers:

"*I did not want to put young Frank in the detention room with the rest of the kids; so I sat him there in the outer office and I deliberately worked around in my office until about five-thirty. Then I came out and said, 'Frank, I guess you have been there long enough. You go on home and let's not have any hard feelings.' I talked to his father later about the whole thing, and I think we have come to an understanding.*"

Following this incident, many class I and class II students managed to avoid being sent to detention when they were late. "Boney" Johnson, a class IV boy, did not fare so well. His English teacher refused to admit him late to class, so he went to the principal's office for an excuse.

Before "Boney" could say a word, he barked, in a sarcastic tone: "So my pretty boy is late again! I suppose it took you half an hour to put on that clean shirt and green tie! (The principal arose from his desk, walked around, and looked at Boney's trousers and shoes and went on.) Ha, you have your pants pressed today! I suppose you took a bath last night, too. New shoes, and they're shined."

Like Frank Stone, Boney tried to skip detention. He, however, did not succeeed in getting out of the building.

The Superintendent rushed out of his office and stood at the head of the stairs. The principal pushed and shoved "Boney" up the stairs as he repeated, "You can't get away with that stuff." As they neared the top, "Boney" broke from his grasp and started down the hall toward the side door. The Superintendent blocked his path, and "Boney" ran upstairs. The principal leaped and grabbed him by the coat collar with his left hand. "Boney" turned and started to fight. The principal spun him around, seized the visor of his cap with his right hand and yanked it down over his eyes.

While "Boney" was fighting to get the cap off his face, the principal hit him three times with the heel of his hand on the back of the neck near the base of the skull. "Boney" cursed, struggled, and hit in all directions. Soon he broke free and ran towards the Superintendent, who shook and slapped him three or four times. Both men then grabbed him by the arms and shook him vigorously. The Superintendent angrily screeched, "You're going out of this building. You're never coming back until you bring your father and we talk this over." [16]

Boney Johnson did not come back to school. Rather than face a continued denial of his identity as a human being, he dropped out. The prevalence of such cases among those who do not finish high school has led researchers in the area to stop referring to "dropouts" and to start calling them "force-outs." Further cases, described by Jonathan Kozol, also illustrate how social institutions teach different attitudes to individuals from observably different backgrounds.

POLITICAL SOCIALIZATION

Because differences which have traditionally been referred to by the term *social class* are largely differences in the relationship of the individual to power and authority within the society, it is especially interesting to see what individuals with dissimilar social origins are taught about power and authority. A pioneering study in this area was done by Edgar Litt, who investigated what high school students learned in the civics courses offered in three suburban communities.[17] These communities were selected because each was relatively homogeneous in terms of social class. There was an upper-middle-class community which he called Alpha, a lower-middle-class community which he called Beta, and a working-class community which he called Gamma. Some of their characteristics are shown in Table 7-1, where, it will be noted, one of the most striking differences is in voter turnout. This difference is in line with national trends. The higher an individual's socioeconomic status, the more likely he is to vote.

To find out whether the nature of the community influenced what children were taught about politics in its schools, Litt looked at three things: the attitudes of community leaders in the three communities, the contents of the textbooks used in civic education courses in the three school systems, and the attitude changes shown by students who took the courses in the three communities. Let us look first at the textbooks.

Table 7–1 *Socioeconomic and political characteristics of Alpha, Beta, and Gamma*

CHARACTERISTIC	ALPHA	BETA	GAMMA
Percent of working force in professions	*38*	*15*	*7*
Median family income	*$5,900*	*$4,250*	*$3,620*
Median voting turnout (percent) for five gubernatorial elections	*67.8*	*43.8*	*32.1*

SOURCE: Litt[18]; from U.S. Bureau of the Census, *General Characteristics of the Population: Massachusetts, 1960,* and Secretary of State, *Compilation of Massachusetts Election Statistics: Public Document 43,* Boston: Commonwealth of Massachusetts, 1950–1960.

Litt content-analyzed all the civic education textbooks from each of the three communities for the preceding five years, using the following categories:

1.   Emphasis on citizen political participation—*references to voting, norms of civic duty, political activity, and the effectiveness of citizen action in influencing the behavior of public officials.*

2.   Political chauvinism—*references to the unique and national character of "democracy" or "good government" as an American monopoly, and glorified treatment of American political institutions, procedures, and public figures.*

3.   The democratic creed—*references to the rights of citizens and minorities to attempt to influence governmental policy through non-tyrannical procedures.*

4.   Emphasis on political process—*references to politics as an arena involving the actions of politicians, public officials, and the use of power and influence contrasted with references to government as a mechanistic set of institutions allocating services to citizens with a minimum of intervention by political actors.*

5.   Emphasis on politics as the resolution of group conflict—*references to political conflicts among economic, social, and ethno-religious groupings resolved within an agreed-upon framework of political rules of the game.*[19]

The results of the content analysis are shown in Table 7–2.

From the content analysis, we may see that all of the textbooks emphasized the democratic creed and that none of them had any significant amount of chauvinistic material. However, only in Alpha and Beta was activity emphasized. Only in Alpha was there any significant emphasis on the political process or conflict resolution, the two types of material which probably best serve to give a realistic picture of how politics really works. Also noteworthy was the increase in unclassified material as we go down the socioeconomic

Table 7-2   *References on salient political dimensions in civics textbooks (in percent)*

POLITICAL DIMENSION	ALPHA	BETA	GAMMA
Emphasis on democratic creed	56	52	47
Chauvinistic references to American political institutions	3	6	2
Emphasis on political activity, citizen's duty, efficacy	17	13	5
Emphasis on political process, politicians, and power	11	2	1
Emphasis on group conflict-resolving political function	10	1	2
Other	3	26	43
Totals	100	100	100
Number of paragraphs	(501)	(367)	(467)

SOURCE: Litt [20]

scale. This material may perhaps be most accurately described as a recitation of historical facts which do not illustrate any principles, but which can be memorized.

The differences in the textbooks were partially, but not completely, in line with differences in what the leaders of the communities thought should be taught in civic education courses. Only in Alpha did a majority of the leaders feel there should be emphasis on the process of politics or its conflict-resolution function, so this important difference in the textbooks did reflect the attitudes of community leaders. However, leaders in all the communities thought there should be an emphasis on participation (they would probably not be leaders if they did not believe in participation), and this emphasis was lacking in Gamma texts. Also, a number of leaders in both Beta and Gamma felt that chauvinistic material should be included.

The variations in the textbooks thus reasonably well reflect the variations in the communities. Did they have any effect on the students? With one exception, students in the three communities changed in the directions we would expect from the textbooks to which they were exposed. The exception is belief in political participation, which was not significantly changed in any community. The students' belief in all communities, however, increased in the democratic creed and decreased in political chauvinism. Reflecting the differences in the textbooks, only the students in Alpha came to see politics as involving people and power and as resolving group conflict. Different attitudes were in fact taught to students from different social-class backgrounds. As Litt concludes:

> In sum, then, students in the three communities are being trained to play different political roles, and to respond to political phenomena in different ways. In the working-class community, where political involvement is low, the arena of civic education offers training in the basic democratic procedures without stressing political participation or the citizen's view of conflict and disagreement as indigenous to the political system. Politics is conducted by formal governmental institutions working in harmony for the benefit of citizens.
>
> In the lower middle-class school system of Beta—a community with moderately active political life—training in the elements of democratic government is supplemented by an emphasis on the responsibilities of citizenship, not on the dynamics of public decision making.
>
> Only in the affluent and politically vibrant community (Alpha) are insights into political processes and functions of politics passed on to those who, judging from their socio-economic and political environment, will likely man those positions that involve them in influencing or making political decisions.[21]

We thus see that there may be external as well as internal obstacles to the achievement of an adult identity. In an imperfect world, social institutions do not make identities equally available to all.

Summary

Fundamental changes in society during the century of industrialization just past radically altered the process of development of the individual. Mechanization of work has made those skills gained with age and experience of little value to society and seldom of significance to the wage-earning capacity of the individual possessing them. Specialization and organization of industrial activity have reduced the chances children have to learn adult roles by watching adults.

Individuals in preindustrial society begin to prepare for adult responsibility long before sexual maturity by watching and practicing the skills of the adult members of their community. In such a society, becoming a man or woman usually means gradually preparing for a role similar to that of one's early childhood ego ideal. In an industrialized society, on the other hand, a child is prepared by school to play a role which he may never have seen performed, against which he has personally never tested himself, and into which he steps after an artificially dependent life as a student. Yet personality development has certain needs which are the same regardless of whether he is in an industrialized or a preindustrial society. The child judges himself by how well he is succeeding in achieving his ego ideal, and he uses the acceptance of his family, school, and peer groups as evidence of this achievement. Often the relationship between his own ego ideal, the standards by which society is actually judging him, and the tasks he is given to perform will be so meaningless as to be chaotic, but if he receives enough accepting encouragement of one kind or another, he may develop enough self-confidence to achieve personality growth. If he obtains less than a viable measure of self-confidence from environmental responses, he will try to find groups which are more supportive or to manufacture them in his imagination.

The development of an adult personality enables a person to set standards for his own behavior rather than to need to see himself through others' eyes as much as a child does. However, the person who has not formed a stable impression of his own competence may be forced to depend on others' evaluation of him even after the normal developmental period of such dependency has passed. Such a person will tend to have a willingness to deny his own perceptions, to ignore his own emotional reactions, and to be unaware of the emotions of others. He will be especially vulnerable to conformity demands by peers or authority figures.

An individual who has been given a fear of his own motives and emotions through harsh socialization will have an especially great need for group support in order to deal with his consequent anxieties. He will be fearful of offending his reference groups in adulthood as he did his parents in childhood, and he will tend to practice exaggerated conformity.

Even in adulthood, each person's cultural environment provides him with many standards and expectations for his own behavior which are continuously learned throughout life by simply living in the culture. Culture is a product of the effort made by individuals and by groups of individuals living together in society to create a meaningful pattern out of raw life, which is composed of incredibly diverse and unpredictable elements and events. People living together in society for a long time evolve cultural explanations which make life more predictable; they include expectations about how individuals with certain characteristics in common will act. Each culture has categories of behavior predictability, though they will be somewhat different in each culture. The categories are statuses, and the behaviors typically expected of a person occupying a status comprise a role. While a status may be actively desired and worked for, individuals may also be stereotyped by their society—a process called ascription—into statuses on the basis of characteristics over which they have no control, such as age, sex, kinship, or physical characteristics. People are motivated to act as expected for their status by positive and negative sanctions, or rewards and punishments, practiced by their society. When a person is playing a role he has grown into by living up to his ego ideal and in which he is supported by a complex system of religious and other values, he is said to conform by normative authority. In industrialized societies, where status and role tend to be very temporary and diverse for an individual, utilitarian authority, or the system of rewarding the individual with financial and social security for playing a role in such a way as not seriously to upset the learned cultural expectations of others, is usually seen. However, industrialized societies can also resort to coercive authority, such as the punishment for stepping out of a narrow range of expected behavior, found in prisons and many custodial systems and institutions.

Adult sexual identification is highly influenced by cultural experience. If a child does not form an identification at an early stage with a member of the sex which his culture considers appropriate, or if there is a large behavioral change expected of him by his culture between childhood and adulthood, he may be subject to very powerful socialization procedures intended to effect his sexual identity.

On the threshold of adulthood, a person can be prevented from achieving adult personality because of differences in social power which exist between himself and others, produced by social-class behavior. Whereas functionalist theories of society once saw social class and resultant inequity in social power as useful characteristics of a healthily functioning society, this book takes a more recent antifunctionalist position, stressing the pathology of social customs which prevent the growth of individuals to adulthood.

Notes and Acknowledgments

1. Lynd, Robert S., and Helen Merrell Lynd. *Middletown* and *Middletown in Transition*. New York: Harcourt, Brace & World, Inc., 1956 and 1937.

2. Lee, Dorothy. "Cultural factors in the educational process," in *Perspectives on Educational Administration and the Behavioral Sciences.* Eugene: The Center for the Advanced Study of Educational Administration, University of Oregon Press. © University of Oregon, 1965.
3. Clausen, John A. "Family structure, socialization, and personality," in Lois Wladis Hoffman and Martin L. Hoffman (Eds.), *Review of Child Development Research.* New York: Russell Sage Foundation, 1966, pp. 1–53.
4. Jucknat, M. "Leistung, Anspruchsniveau und Selbstbewusstsein." Untersuchungen zur Handlungs und Affectpsychologie: XX. Kurt Lewin (Ed.), *Psychologische Forschungen,* 1937 (22), pp. 89–179.
   Sears, Pauline S. "Levels of aspiration in academically successful and unsuccessful children." *Journal of Abnormal and Social Psychology,* 1940 (35), pp. 498–536.
5. Research on this topic is being conducted by Irene Kassorla of the North Ridge Hospital, North Ridge, Calif. Some of it is portrayed in her film "Bridge to Communication," produced by the North Ridge Hospital Foundation.
6. Hakmiller, Karl L. "Threat as a determinant of downward comparison." *Journal of Experimental Social Psychology.* New York: Academic Press, Inc., 1966 (2), Suppl. 1, pp. 32–39.
7. Asch, Solomon E. "Effects of group pressure upon the modification and distortion of judgments," in E. Maccoby et al. (Eds.), *Readings in Social Psychology.* New York: Holt, Rinehart and Winston, Inc., 1958, pp. 174–183.
8. Breger, Louis. "Conformity as a function of the ability to express hostility." *Journal of Personality,* 1963 (31), p. 248. By permission of the publisher.
9. Darley, J. M. "Fear and social comparison as determinants of conformity behavior." *Journal of Personality and Social Psychology,* 1966 (4), pp. 73–78.
10. Attributed by Erik Erikson, in *Childhood and Society,* to C. Wissler, "Depression and Revolt." *Natural History,* 1938 (41), no. 2, page not found.
11. Berger, Peter L. *Invitation to Sociology: A Humanistic Perspective.* Garden City, N.Y.: Doubleday & Company, Inc., Anchor Books, 1963.
12. Etzioni, A. *A Comparative Analysis of Complex Organizations.* New York: The Free Press, 1961.
13. Rodgers, William B., and John M. Long. "Male models and sexual identification: A case from the Out Island Bahamas." *Human Organization,* Winter 1968 (27), no. 4, pp. 326–331.
14. For a discussion of this and related controversies, see Robert W. Friedrichs, *A Sociology of Sociology.* New York: The Free Press, 1970.
15. Hollingshead, A. B. *Elmtown's Youth.* New York: John Wiley & Sons, Inc., 1949.
16. Ibid., pp. 188–191. By permission of the publisher.
17. Litt, Edgar. "Civic education, community norms, and political indoctrination." *American Sociological Review,* February 1963 (28), pp. 69–75.
18. Ibid., p. 70. By permission of the publisher and the author.
19. Ibid., p. 70. By permission.
20. Ibid., p. 72. By permission.
21. Ibid., p. 74. By permission.

PART TWO

THE PSYCHO- LOGICAL PERSPECTIVE APPLIED

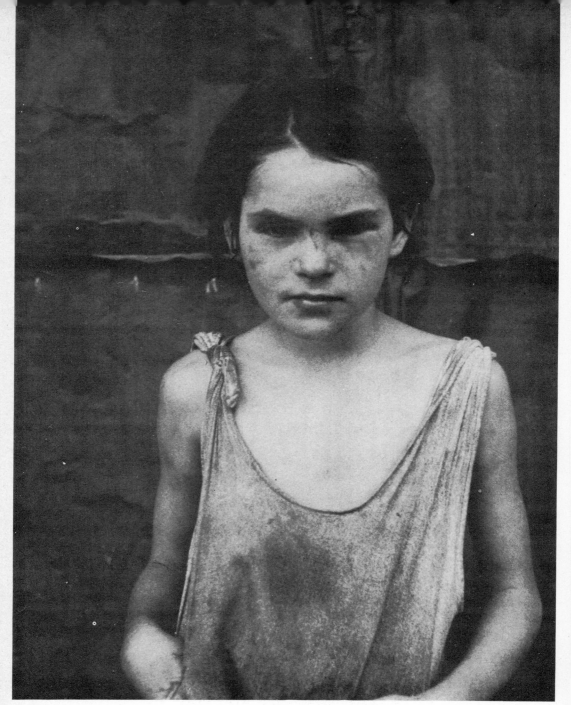

Dorothea Lange. Permission of Oakland Museum.

EIGHT

STRATEGIES & SYMPTOMS

Introduction

VIEWS OF MENTAL ILLNESS

Individuals whose mental processes seem bizarre and maladaptive to other members of their culture have been regarded in a variety of ways in the past hundred years. One way has been to consider them as suffering from specific disease entities, an approach which led to attempts to classify the diseases and to find specific causal agents responsible for them. A second, pioneered by Freud, was to see them as suffering from unconscious conflicts, a view which made the goal of therapy to make the unconscious conscious. While the mental health movement took its views partially from the preceding two orientations, it laid more emphasis on the idea that the individual was not adjusted to his culture. It thus viewed the individual's problem as one of learning things which would make him do what his culture required. Most recently, existential and *neoanalytic* approaches have stressed the need for the individual to control his own destiny and live up to his own potentials.

Each of these views has been partly accurate, and each has contributed new insights into what, for lack of a better term, we may still continue to call mental illness. The disease entity model was a definite advance over considering the patient to be possessed by evil spirits or to be showing insufficient will power. In regard to a few patterns of symptoms, it is quite accurate. The symptoms which develop from untreated syphilis, from a long-term insufficiency of B vitamins, or from noxious agents, such as mercury or airplane glue, may properly be regarded as specific medical syndromes. A much larger number of mental symptoms are psychological rather than physiological in their origin, but may show some physiological consequences. As we have seen in an earlier chapter, psychological stress can cause a variety of psychosomatic symptoms, to which the medical model is partially applicable.

Applying the disease entity model can, in other cases, be completely inappropriate and can subtly imply things which are not true. It can, for example, lead to a search for a nonexistent specific causal agent, suggest that cure will come about through physical rather than psychological methods of treatment, and result in the neglect of social factors in the sufferer's environment. Defining a person as a "patient" in relation to an expert, the "doctor," may lead to his being cast in a passive-dependent role which does not enlist his aid in getting well.

The psychoanalytic view that unresolved conflicts underlie the formation of psychological symptoms is the dominant one in psychiatry and clinical psychology, and it has perhaps been the most productive insight of any of the views considered here. However, it too neglects important aspects of the individual's situation. Freud lived and worked at a period in history when faith in human rationality was high. Although he might seem at first glance to be the irrationalist *par excellence*, the treatment method which he devised still shows the effects of nineteenth-century rationalism. Psychoanalytic therapy helps the individual to become aware of impulses which he has previously been keeping from consciousness. It is assumed that when he does become aware of them, he will be able to guide his behavior in a more rational manner. In other words, the assumption is made that ideas are the source of behavior, and that to change behavior, all that is necessary is to change the ideas.

There is, of course, evidence that changing ideas does change behavior, as we have seen in studies of learning. There are, however, other ways of altering behavior which are neglected in classical psychoanalytic therapy. Teaching the individual new skills, providing him with groups which will support him in new behaviors, and restructuring institutions, such as hospitals, are ways of bringing about change in individuals which are neglected in a traditional psychoanalytic approach.

Although the mental health approach did turn attention to the individual's relationship to his social environment, its emphasis was one-sided. To a great extent, it defined its goal as making the individual "adjusted." This term implied a value judgment, for it indicated that the individual should change to fit in with his society rather than change that society. Since the Second World War, the view that society may need basic changes has become more common, and "personal and social adjustment" has ceased to be the clear goal of treatment of the individual that it once seemed to be.

It has to a great extent been replaced by *self-actualization*. This term implies that the main purpose of psychotherapy is to enable the individual to achieve goals which he sets for himself rather than ones which are set for him by society. This approach is fairly compatible with at least the first two of the other approaches we have been considering, for the individual cannot really be in control of his own destiny unless he frees himself from disease and addiction, and unless he becomes conscious of his own motives.

The view taken in this book is that the goal of psychotherapy is to help the individual achieve the goals which he sets for himself. The concept of a psychological symptom will be used to mean a maladaptive attempt to achieve one's goals.

ATTEMPTS TO ADAPT

Although he may not always be conscious of making a choice, each person selects, to some extent, his own strategy in seeking after happiness. How much, for example, should a person permit himself to care about another person? One who remains indifferent to others guards himself against pain and disappointment. Enduring loneliness and isolating oneself from others, as Freud observed, are the surest safeguard against the unhappiness that may arise from human relations.[1] To achieve the positive satisfactions which come from having close relations with another person, one must take the fundamental risk of loving and being loved. It is a risk because the person upon whom one becomes dependent may prove undependable. The lover who has just been rejected experiences great anguish. In the song, Frankie wouldn't have shot Johnny if he hadn't been "her man." Yet only involvement with the real world can bring gratification of our impulses. There are many ways of avoiding taking a chance on real-life gratifications. Some of the major ones are the use of drugs and intoxicants, development of forms of gratification which cannot be easily frustrated by the outside world, and escape into fantasy. Under stress, each way of adjusting may develop into well-developed symptoms. The occasional use of alcohol may become alcoholism. The person who takes pleasure in music may so completely escape into this world as to neglect all else. The person who daydreams may come to spend the greater part of his life in the world of fantasy.

In a sense, then, mental disorders develop as unsuccessful attempts to cope with life. The symptoms people suffer, unpleasant as they may be, develop as the person's attempt to protect himself against something he sees as being worse. Although they may not be adaptive, symptoms are an attempt to adapt.

Let us look at a strategy which, at first glance, seems completely improbable—that of seeking failure. It can be observed in many situations. One example is cited by John Holt in *How Children Fail*.

> *Can a child have a vested interest in failure? What on earth could it be? Martha, playing the number game, often . . . does not understand, does not want to understand, does not listen when you are explaining, and then says, "I'm all mixed up."*[2]

To a person who fears failure, not trying and taking failure for granted can be less threatening than investing effort and perhaps failing anyway. More than that, being punished can help to relieve guilt. Without punishment, the person must face the fact that he feels bad because of his own guilt about what he believes are his shortcomings. If he is punished, however, it is possible for him to convince himself that he feels bad because of the punishment rather than his own guilt. Externalization of the guilt relieves some of the anxiety, and it may even be possible for the person to convince himself that the punishment was undeserved. "I hate myself" can thus become "My wife does not understand me."

This particular mechanism seems to be a central one in alcoholism, and it is thus important to the alcoholic that he find someone to play the role of "persecutor." A good example of this is given by Eric Berne in *Games People Play*—in this example the protagonist is known as "White":

> In one case a female alcoholic in a therapy group participated very little until she thought she knew enough about the other members to go ahead with her game. She then asked them to tell her what they thought of her. Since she had behaved pleasantly enough, various members said nice things about her, but she protested: "That's not what I want. I want to know what you really think." She made it clear that she was seeking derogatory comments. The other women refused to persecute her, whereupon she went home and told her husband that if she took another drink, he must either divorce her or send her to a hospital. He promised to do this, and that evening she became intoxicated and he sent her to a sanitarium. Here the other members refused to play the persecutory roles White assigned to them; she was unable to tolerate this antithetical behavior, in spite of everyone's efforts to reinforce whatever insight she had already obtained. At home she found someone who was willing to play the role she demanded.[3]

Neurosis

Some of the mechanisms which an individual may use to defend himself against anxiety have been presented in earlier chapters. All people make some use of such defenses, but most people do not need to employ them a great deal. As we move from occasional anxiety, routinely handled by mild defenses, to debilitating anxiety and well-developed symptoms, we pass over the hazy boundary between mental health and *neurosis*.

Neurotic symptoms all seem to be effects of anxiety, or ways of acting out impulses that cause anxiety, or attempts to cope with anxiety. Still, there is a great deal of variety in the particular symptoms developed. One individual may experience anxiety directly, with feelings of panic and dread and physical symptoms such as heart palpitation and muscular tremor. Another may not complain of anxiety, but, instead, may show selective memory loss and physical symptoms which mimic those of a physical illness. Each person has his own idiosyncratic pattern of symptoms, and even the classification of the patterns is a matter of some doubt. Although there is thus no such thing as a typical neurotic pattern, one example from Malamud may give some impression of the way in which neurotic symptoms may represent an attempt to adapt.[4]

Following a minor accident, a 28-year-old married man was admitted to a hospital, claiming that the accident had made him blind. Since physical examination could reveal no injury which would have caused blindness, he was referred to the psychiatric department for an interview. There it was discovered that he had suffered the accident while on the way to the hospital to see his wife and newborn first child. He explained to the psychiatrist that since he was now blind, his first duty would have to be to divorce his wife as he could not keep her tied down to a blind man. Further interviews indicated that the man's symptoms made sense in terms of both his childhood and his current situation. His mother had been extremely domineering and his father submissive. The son had thus strongly resisted his own dependency longings, for giving in to them would symbolize unwilling submission to his mother's domination. He left home and resolved never to marry. Eventually, he became so involved with a woman that he did marry her, but with the agreement that they would never have children. When she became pregnant and was unwilling to have an abortion, he saw his escape closed. Psychosomatic blindness was a last-ditch fight to escape, although he was not consciously aware that that was what his blindness was. (Discussions with the psychiatrist about his background and its implications for his marital situation brought about a cure of his blindness, and continued therapy with both the patient and his wife resulted in a much improved marriage. It is unfortunate that not all patterns of symptoms are so easily understood.)

That the development of symptoms may serve a real function for the individual is most clearly shown in a study by Wolff et al.[5] This study differs from most studies of psychological disturbance in that it was predictive and that the individuals were studied while they developed the symptoms rather than after they had become disturbed. Wolff studied the parents of children who were dying of leukemia, an experience which often has very serious consequences for the mental health of the parent, as we shall see in looking into the causes of psychosis. Wolff predicted that those parents who actively faced the reality of the child's dying and dealt with the psychological stresses involved as they presented themselves would show the physiological general adaptation syndrome as measured by higher levels of excreted corticosteroid hormones. Those parents who developed psychological (reality-denying) defenses against this threatening perception of their child's dying were expected to have lower stress-corticosteroid symptoms. By assessing, by psychological methods, the degree to which each parent was facing the reality of the impending death, he estimated their level of corticosteroid excretion. His predictions were upheld by the evidence. The student will remember, from the chapter dealing with endocrines, that the general adaptation syndrome puts a severe physiological strain on the organism.

Neurotic symptoms have been variously classified. A typical categorization is that of Lazarus,[6] who lists *anxiety state, hysteria, obsessive-compulsive reactions, neurotic depression,* and *psychosomatic disorders.* Under anxiety states are included not only simple anxiety but also *asthenic reaction,* characterized by feelings of fatigue which the person assumes to have an organic basis; *hypochondriacal reaction,* with anxiety focused on particular physical symptoms; and *phobic reaction,* with fear of some particular type of situation or object. Each of these types of reaction represents an attempt to explain the anxiety that the person feels. Of course a person would feel upset if he had some physical basis for being so fatigued that he could not work, had a serious illness, or was exposed to a dangerous threat from outside. By ascribing his anxiety to one of these causes, the individual explains it to himself and makes it less threatening.

Under hysteria are classed *conversion reactions,* in which anxiety is transformed into a physical symptom such as paralysis or blindness, and *dissociative reactions,* in which some of the individual's memories are split off from consciousness. The young man in the motor accident mentioned at the beginning of this section is an example of the former reaction, and cases of multiple personality exemplify the latter. While the dissociative reaction is not common, and the alternation of separate, well-developed personalities is actually quite rare, the disorder is still especially interesting because of the light which it throws on the role of unconscious processes in neurosis. Two cases which have been described at length are that of Christine Beauchamp, studied by Morton Prince[7] before the publication of Freud's first major work and thus uninfluenced by psychoanalytic theory, and the more recent case of Eve.[8]

A CASE STUDY

Prince's study is a psychological classic, and even today is perhaps as interesting a book as the introductory student may find to read. Who could resist a book which begins:

> *Miss Christine L. Beauchamp, the subject of this study, is a person in whom*

several personalities have become developed; that is to say, she may change her personality from time to time, often from hour to hour, and with each change her character becomes transformed and her memories altered.[9]

The book is not only exciting, however; it is also the work of a patient and skeptical investigator. Over the years that he treated Miss Beauchamp, Prince conducted many small experiments to test his hypotheses about her case. It was only reluctantly that he came to believe that it was a true case of alternating. His skepticism adds to the convincingness of the description.

The Miss Beauchamp who came to Prince for treatment was a proud, sensitive, diligent, and self-sacrificing young lady—a model in many ways of what society applauds. If she had not suffered from headaches, insomnia, bodily pains, and fatigue, she might have been thought highly successful. As it was, she remained an outstanding student despite her difficulties, which she avoided imposing on her friends. One appreciates Prince's difficulty in trying to do psychotherapy with a woman whose attitude was, "I have never been in the habit of talking about my private affairs."[10]

Prince treated Miss Beauchamp for her physical symptoms by using hypnotic suggestion, with the usual amount of success. Each symptom could be temporarily cured in this manner, but either it or a similar one would recur. Miss Beauchamp's personality under hypnosis was no different from her waking personality.

Then one day another personality appeared under hypnosis. At first, Prince considered it merely another hypnotic state, but ultimately it became clear that this particular state differed in mood, interests, abilities, and memories from the Miss Beauchamp Prince knew. The alternating personality, who eventually took the name of Sally, sometimes controlled the activities of Miss Beauchamp, and at the end of these periods Miss Beauchamp had amnesia for what had happened during them. "Sally," however, did not have amnesia for the periods when "Miss Beauchamp" was the dominant personality.

The first clue that Sally represented a different portion of the personality from Miss Beauchamp was that Sally referred to the conscious Miss Beauchamp as "She." Miss Beauchamp referred to the conscious Miss Beauchamp as "I." Here is an exchange between Prince and Sally on the subject of "She."

"You are She," *I said.*
"No, I am not."
"I say you are. . ."
"Why are you not She?"

"Because She *does not know the same things that I do."*
"But you both have the same arms and legs, haven't you?"
"Yes, but arms and legs do not make us the same."[11]

Miss Beauchamp did not know who "She" was:

"Well, you know who you are?"
"Yes, Miss Beauchamp."
"Exactly. You have got over the idea of being different from other persons—that there is a She?"
(Surprised and puzzled) "What She? I do not know what you mean. . . ."
"You used to tell me that you were not Miss Beauchamp."
"I did not."
"That when you were awake you were a different person."
(Remonstrating and astounded) "Dr. Prince, I did not say so."[12]

Sally differed from Miss Beauchamp in many ways. She was impulsive, childish, and enthusiastic. She spent the last of Miss Beauchamp's money on candy and gorged herself, regularly made dates with a man who did not at first know of the existence of the staid personality of Miss Beauchamp, played practical jokes on her friends, smoked and drank. She then left Miss Beauchamp to awake with a hangover and amnesia for the previous day! Sally also differed from Miss Beauchamp in one instantly apparent way. Sally spoke with a bad stutter, whereas Miss Beauchamp was completely free of it.

The relationships of the various personalities shown by Dr. Prince's patient are not easy to describe. Any person may be reminded by some sensation of something he has not thought about for years, and memories and feelings which have been, in a sense, unconscious may come back. Under the influence of these memories, he may show insights which he would not normally show, remembering, for example, what it is like to be a four-year-old. The process might strongly influence both his feelings and his behavior. Miss Beauchamp seems to have differed from this normal type of alternation of consciousness by (1) having kept many aspects of herself from expression because they did not live up to the high ideals which she had for herself, and (2) allowing these aspects to become sufficiently organized and autonomous, partly through experiences with hypnosis, to come to the fore. In a sense, the development of Sally was a stage in the cure of Miss Beauchamp, for the unconscious aspects of her personality first found expression as secondary personalities and were then integrated into a new and more complete self.

That the processes involved in the formation of secondary personality states, such as Sally, are essentially similar in kind to processes taking place in all people does not mean that all people have submerged secondary personalities. In most people, unconscious processes are simply that—isolated processes. They are not organized into a secondary personality. From the rare case, such as that of Miss Beauchamp, where they are organized, we may gain interesting insights into the nature of the self. Sally was not only able to produce various neurotic symptoms in Miss Beauchamp, such as obsessive thoughts which Miss Beauchamp did not know the origin of. She was also able to give much more complete accounts of her dreams and experiences than most people can give. The following is Sally's report of how Miss Beauchamp lost some money. Miss Beauchamp did not yet know that it was lost at the time Sally told about it:

> She yesterday received a letter from a photographer. She had it in her hand while walking down Washington Street, and then put it into her pocket (side pocket of coat) where She kept her watch and money (banknotes). As She walked along She took out the money and tore it into pieces, thinking it was the letter from the photographer. She threw the money into the street. As She tore up the money, She thought to herself, I wish they would not write on this bond paper.[13]

The case of Miss Beauchamp also illustrates the rather artificial nature of the distinctions made among different types of neurosis, for she showed all the types at one time or another. She had attacks of anxiety, obsessive thoughts, compulsions to act in bizarre ways, and physical symptoms with psychological causes. She suffered from depression to such an extent that she almost succeeded in killing herself. Clearly, we should not think of patterns of symptoms as discrete disease entities but as varying mechanisms which may be shown by the same person. Rather than classifying types of neurosis, we need to study the dynamics of the individual case.

A Psychosis: Schizophrenia

Besides neurosis, there are a number of other varieties of mental disorder. Some are clearly the result of organic deterioration or damage of the brain. Others are as poorly defined as *character disorder*, a category which includes alcoholism, drug addiction, and an apparent ability to not live up to the expectations of society without feeling guilt. Also familiar to most people are *psychosomatic disorders*, symptoms such as ulcers and high blood pressure, which are real organic illnesses even though they result from psychological stress.

Within this broad range of types of disorder, *schizophrenia* is especially important to understand. It is one of the *psychoses*, serious disorders which involve major disturbances in the perception of reality, in speech and thought, and in mood and social relations. It is also quite a common disorder in our culture, accounting for approximately half the hospital beds which are occupied by psychiatric patients.

Psychoses are generally divided into schizophrenia, in which the disturbance involves thought processes, and *manic-depressive psychosis*, in which the emotions are more disordered. While there does seem to be some tendency for symptoms to cluster into syndromes, we have also seen that the categories also do represent a good deal of oversimplification. Some individuals have patterns of symptoms which have some of the characteristics of schizophrenia and some of those of manic-depressive psychosis. There is probably about as much oversimplification in summing up a person's pattern of symptoms by calling him a schizophrenic or a manic-depressive as there would be in summing up all of his attitudes by calling him a Christian or an atheist. Any particular description of symptoms is thus an idealized model which no particular case would fit.

Perhaps the most striking symptom of schizophrenia, and one which is shown very frequently, is a basic disturbance of the use of language. Words, rather than being selected so that they make communication possible, are combined on the basis of idiosyncratic and illogical associations, or common associations that are out of place in that particular communication. This may lead to varying amounts of language disturbance from slightly idiosyncratic use of language to a *word salad* which is completely incomprehensible.[14]

Concept-formation tasks show similar disturbances of the thinking of schizophrenics. If asked to classify objects, they will do so in idiosyncratic ways which are difficult to describe. A knife might be classed with an apple, an orange, and a banana because it could be used to peel the apple. Similarly, the experimenter and furniture in the room may be classified along with the experimental objects. These and similar types of distortion have led some investigators to conclude that the basic problem in schizophrenia is a failure of attention processes, and consequent inability to exclude irrelevant material from consciousness.[15]

Loss of contact with reality is shown in a variety of ways. Delusions, unshakable beliefs that are clearly mistaken, are held by many schizophrenics. These may take many forms, with feelings of being persecuted, delusions of grandeur, and sexual delusions the most common. Disordered perceptions are shown in responses to projective tests such as the Rorschach, and sometimes in distorted perceptions of one's own body. One study found that, unlike other people, most schizophrenics are unable to recognize photographs of their own bodies.[16]

Besides showing disturbance of language and thought, schizophrenics show changes in their emotions and behavior. Their emotions often seem inappropriate, with the person showing great anxiety or rage for no apparent reason. Certain other emotions seem to be blunted, so that joy and sadness are absent even when they would be appropriate. An experience of great emotional meaning, such as the death of a parent or child, will be described with no apparent feeling. This emotional withdrawal mirrors a social withdrawal from the world. One common early symptom of schizophrenia is a withdrawal from normal social contact with others.

The wide variety of symptoms described do not all develop at the same time, and the course of symptom development differs from one person to another. In some cases the onset of symptoms is fairly sudden, they are clearly related to extraordinary stresses on the individual, and the individual is depressed and confused. These individuals are unlikely to have well-developed delusions. Their illness is clearly a reaction to specific stresses, and the chances of their recovering are relatively good. Because their symptoms are clearly related to a reaction to particular stresses of life, these individuals are frequently described as having *reactive* schizophrenia. On the other hand, some individuals develop their symptoms more gradually over a longer time, and the symptoms are not so clearly related to extraordinary stress. Perhaps because they have a longer period in which to develop secondary symptoms in the attempt to understand the effects of the primary ones, they are more liable to develop systematic delusions. These individuals generally were less well adjusted before the onset of their symptoms and have a less good chance of recovering. Because their symptoms reflect processes which have continued for a considerable period of time, they are sometimes described as showing *process* schizophrenia.

Rogler and Hollingshead, in a study which throws a great deal of light on the origins of schizophrenia, provide a good example of its onset in a Puerto Rican family. Although the woman, whom they gave the pseudonym of Mrs. Padilla, was expecting another child, her husband was keeping a mistress.

". . .when the birth pangs began my husband could not be found. He had put on his guayabera *(fancy shirt) and gone out into the street. The midwife had to be rounded up. (The midwife delivered twins to Mrs. Padilla in their one-room shack.) Two days after the birth my husband went out into the street again. He was not concerned at all about my condition. In addition to having to care for four children, I was not feeling well at all."*

Mr. Padilla rejected the twins, which hurt Mrs. Padilla; to complicate the situation, one of the twins was not healty; he vomited black and green fluid. Mrs. Padilla became so distraught she took the baby to the municipal hospital. The doctor recommended that the baby be left there, and although Mrs. Padilla wanted to stay with the infant she was told that she could visit the child only twice a week.

One day she went to visit the infant and left a sister to care for the other children and to look after the house. She related:

"When I returned from the hospital I found the house in a turmoil My sister was sitting in the middle of the mess reading a cheap novel. I became very angry. I grabbed a broom and began to hit her. I threw her out of the house. Then I became very sleepy and I went to bed and I woke up late at night. It was only then I realized what I had done."

(Mrs. Padilla had knocked her sister unconscious and thrown her out of the house. The unconscious girl was lying in the muddy street when a neighbor revived her.)

After ten days the baby was brought home from the hospital in a city-owned ambulance, but Mrs. Padilla worried still more because he had diarrhea and continued to vomit. When ten more days passed and the child did not appear to be improving, Mr. Padilla insisted that they consult a curandera *(folk healer) who prescribed castor oil. . . .*[17]

The parents gave the child castor oil, and the child died. At that time Mrs. Padilla became psychotic.

A THEORY OF SCHIZOPHRENIA

The evidence on what causes schizophrenia is still so unclear that it is possible for intelligent and well-informed people to see the disorder as being due to a wide variety of factors. Different theorists have viewed it as being entirely due to hereditary factors, as being a failure of motivation resulting from inadequate childhood training, as a breakdown of the ego resulting from a disturbed relationship to the parents in early childhood, as a result of social disorganization in modern industrial society, and as a disorder of thinking resulting from inconsistencies between verbal and nonverbal communication. Even this list does not exhaust all the theories which have been proposed. Moreover, various combinations are possible, so that the disturbance can be seen, for example, as having a genetic basis but as being aggravated by certain environmental conditions. Each of the theoretical approaches has some evidence to support it, and no theory is able to account for all the evidence. The theory to be presented here should therefore be viewed as incomplete and speculative even though it is consistent with a number of research findings. Even an incomplete explanation, however, represents substantial progress over what was known about the disorder a decade or two ago. Since a great deal of research is now being done on schizophrenia, it is quite possible that in a few years we shall have a much more comprehensive explanation of it.

It would seem that any explanation of schizophrenia would need to account for at least three things: who develops the disorder, when he develops it, and the particular symptoms he develops. Although we shall see that the situation a person is in at the time he develops the disorder has a good deal to do with his becoming psychotic, yet there are people who come through adverse circumstances without becoming psychotic. The difference needs to be explained. Similarly, the person who does become schizophrenic does so at a particular time, often after many years of an apparently normal adjustment to life. Why does it happen at this time? Finally, some people become so severely disturbed as to be classed as psychotic, but their symptoms are not those of schizophrenia. Why do some people develop one disorder and some people another? Until we can answer these questions, we cannot say that we really know the causes of schizophrenia.

In some ways, the immediate reasons for becoming psychotic at a particular time are the easiest to study. When a person develops schizophrenia, there are many people around who can be easily located and asked to report on what happened to him at the time. It is much more difficult, however, to get adequate reports on childhood events which have occurred many years before. Let us therefore start with the easiest question to answer, the events which push a person over the brink into schizophrenia. These may help to give us insight into the nature of the disorder, and may hint at the answers to the other questions.

When schizophrenia is developed. An especially informative study is the one by Rogler and Hollingshead from which the example of Mrs. Padilla was taken. By studying schizophrenics who were still living with their families, they could be certain that the symptoms they were studying were characteristic of the illness and not reactions to having lived in a mental hospital. Furthermore, they were able to match a control group to the sample of schizophrenics so that they could discover the ways in which the psychotics differed from other individuals living under the same conditions.

The study was carried out in the slums and public housing projects of Puerto Rico, an environment in which schizophrenics generally continue living with their families. The first step was to locate a sample of schizophrenics, an undertaking which involved visiting 300 families and obtaining psychiatric diagnoses on 55 individuals. Because of the extremely good cooperation obtained by the researchers, no person who was asked to undergo a psychiatric examination refused to do so. In this way, twenty families were located in which at least one spouse was schizophrenic. Another twenty families, chosen from adjacent residential areas, were similar to the first group except that they contained no psychotic members. The two groups of families were then intensively studied and compared.

The results were striking. The study revealed few differences in the childhood experiences of the sick and well individuals, and virtually no differences in their adjustment to life prior to the crises which culminated in the illness. Up until about a year before becoming ill, schizophrenics did not show social withdrawal, difficulty in earning a living, or interpersonal conflicts with others. They were normal insofar as individuals living a marginal existence in a slum can be normal.

What did distinguish the schizophrenics from the nonschizophrenics was a series of crises which threatened each schizophrenic's conception of himself and with which he could not cope. This was most clearly demonstrated in the relationship between schizophrenia in women and the death of a child. As Rogler and Hollingshead put it:

> The death of children is linked significantly to the mental status of the mother. Twelve children died in seven families. Ten of the twelve deaths were in families in which the mother is suffering from schizophrenia. Six of the seven families who have faced the death of a child are in the sick group. All deaths preceded the onset of mental symptoms in the parents.[18]

For a woman who is a mother, her self-conception probably depends more upon her ability to care for her children than upon any other factor. The death of one of the children represents a failure which destroys the purpose of life. A massive denial of reality is one of the few alternatives left open. Similarly, for a man, ability to support his family is probably the role most necessary to preserving his good opinion of himself. It is therefore not surprising that difficulty in earning a living is one of the factors associated with the onset of schizophrenia in men. In that event, however, it is more difficult to say whether the symptoms of schizophrenia or the economic difficulties came first, for the two augment each other. A person who is out of work for reasons not associated with personal symptoms may develop symptoms, and the symptoms may make it more difficult for him to find work.

In many ways, the observations of Rogler and Hollingshead suggest that a vicious cycle is involved in the development of schizophrenia. Continued stresses, such as illness and unemployment, reduce the person's ability to cope with the world. Reactions to the stress, such as Mrs. Padilla's beating her sister, estrange others and cut the person off from normal sources of consolation and social support. Finally, some especially threatening event pushes the person over the brink of being able to face reality. From that point on, symptoms develop in an attempt to understand the effect of other symptoms. A person who is unable to remember things because of repression, for example, might imagine a physical explanation of the symptom.

The interaction of stress and the disturbance of interpersonal relations are reflected in the variety of factors which Rogler and Hollingshead found to be associated with the onset of schizophrenia:

> *Systematic comparisons of the six types of perceived personal problems reported by the sick persons (and families) with those of the well persons (and families) demonstrate that each of the diagnostic family types in the sick group encountered many more problems than the well families during the problematic year. There are more economic difficulties and more severe physical deprivation in the sick than in the well families. There are far more interspouse conflicts among the sick families than the control families; difficulties with members of the extended family are more frequent and more severe. The sick families report more quarrels and fights with the neighbors. There are more physical illnesses in the schizophrenic families. Finally, more sick persons than well persons, male as well as female, note a disparity between their own perception of the difficulties they encountered and the ways they think their spouses viewed these same problems. Stated otherwise, the schizophrenic men and women think their spouses do not understand the personal difficulties they face, as well as the men and women in the control group do. In general, the person who is diagnosed as suffering from schizophrenia perceives himself as bombarded by a multiplicity of personal and family problems he is not able to handle. The behavioral evidence shows, however, that he struggles to solve them by every means available to him.[19]*

The final and precipitating cause of schizophrenia thus seems to be a threat to a person's conception of himself which is so pervasive and overpowering that he must escape from it into fantasy. This does not, however, solve the problem of why some people seem to break down more easily under stress than others. The underlying causes leading to these individual differences still need to be investigated.

Who develops schizophrenia.   There is now reasonably convincing evidence that individuals inherit characteristics which make them more or less likely to develop schizophrenia. Early studies seemed to show inherited factors to be much more important than now thought and virtually to determine whether any given individual would become schizophrenic or not. These studies, however, had serious methodological errors, many of them pointed out in an excellent review of the literature by Jackson.[20] One study, for example, concluded that there was a genetic factor in schizophrenia because schizophrenia ran in families. But the researcher used a family history of schizophrenia as one of the bases for deciding that an individual was schizophrenic! A great deal of confusion also stemmed from early studies of identical twins. One study referred to twins who were "separated," and many people thought that the investigator meant that they had been separated early in life. Since there was a very strong tendency for both the twins to have schizophrenia if one of them did, this seemed to show the importance of genetic factors. Actually, the investigator merely meant twins that had been separated for at least five years before becoming schizophrenic. Since they averaged thirty-three years of age at that time, the "separated" designation clearly did not mean that they had not been reared together.

More recently, there have been better-controlled twin studies, including a study of quadruplets, each of whom developed some schizophrenic symptoms.[21] Similarity in individuals born as multiple births, however, does not necessarily point to hereditary factors, for these individuals also share an intrauterine environment during pregnancy, and this environment may well not be adequate in the case of multiple pregnancies. One of the best-controlled of currrent studies on the causation of schizophrenia, in fact, points to the importance of complications during pregnancy and birth. This study, which is being conducted by Sarnoff Mednick, differs from many other investigations on schizophrenia in that it focuses on individuals as they are developing schizophrenia rather than simply looking at their histories after they have developed it.[22]

Mednick is carrying out a long-term study of 200 children of schizophrenic mothers. On either genetic or social grounds, these children are more likely than other children to develop schizophrenic symptoms. After eight years of the study, twenty of them have done so. Mednick found that the histories of these twenty children were characterized by serious complications of pregnancy and birth that seemed to have resulted in damage to the hippocampal area of the brain. Innate predispositions to schizophrenia, whether genetically or environmentally caused, may be a result of abnormalities of motivational and emotional systems in the hippocampus.

Because of the possible role of pregnancy and birth factors in causing similarities between twins, studies of foster children are perhaps most informative on the matter of genetic factors in schizophrenia. One of the most convincing of these was done in Denmark by Kety and his colleagues.[23] In one portion of their study, they looked at thirty-three children, adopted during the first month of life, who showed signs of schizophrenia, and a matched control group of thirty-three adopted children who did not. They found that of the schizophrenic children, thirteen had a biological relative who showed signs of schizophrenia, whereas only three of the control children did. This study would be perfectly convincing on the existence of a genetic predisposition toward developing schizophrenia if it were not for one possible complicating factor. We have already seen how early researchers were more likely to diagnose an individual as schizophrenic when there was a history of schizophrenia in his family. What about the adoptive parents of the children in Kety's study? Did any of them know that the child they were adopting came from a family with a history of schizophrenia? If they did, it would probably have made them much more likely to identify characteristics of the child as symptoms of schizophrenia, and to behave differently toward him accordingly.

If the evidence for innate factors is strong, so is the evidence for the importance of the early social environment. A child with a schizophrenic mother is approximately three times as likely to develop schizophrenia as is one with a schizophrenic father. In fact, a child with a severely disturbed mother is likely to develop schizophrenia even if the mother suffers from manic-depressive psychosis or alcoholism rather than schizophrenia. These and similar observations suggest that the early social bond between the mother and child is particularly important in the development of schizophrenia. Where genetic, prenatal, or birth-injury factors play a major role in the causation of schizophrenia, they may well do so by influencing the nature of this relationship.

What symptoms are developed. Except in the case of the development of process schizophrenia in early childhood, where the precipitating cause may be difficult to discover, the precipitating cause of schizophrenia seems to be an overwhelming threat to the self. What alternative does the person have besides becoming schizophrenic? Not everyone who becomes psychotic does become schizophrenic, even though it is the most common psychosis in our culture. Let us look briefly at the other major psychotic reaction, manic-depressive psychosis. Then we will pay some attention to environmental factors which tend to accompany one set of symptoms, schizophrenia; and ones which accompany the other set, manic-depressive psychosis.

Manic-depressive psychosis involves two syndromes which seem, at first glance, to be exact opposites of each other. The manic is bubbling over with energy and good humor. His mood is one of boundless optimism and enthusiasm, and he throws his energy into one ambitious project after another, although he never finishes any of them. His behavior is characterized by wild silliness, with an inability to sit still. His clowning and joking would be enjoyable if he did not carry them so far, but he is liable to have more sexual and aggressive content to his humor than society will tolerate. Thinking is not disordered as in schizophrenia, although his thoughts jump rapidly from one topic to another and there may be a good deal of grandiosity in both thought and behavior. An example of manic behavior which illustrates both its wildness and its sexual and aggressive content is a university professor who began to punctuate the points in his lecture by throwing articles of clothing at his students.

Psychotic depression, on the other hand, involves the opposite of many of these characteristics. Movements are slow and occur rarely. The individual's mood is one of black despair. Rather than the self-pity which may characterize neurotic depression, the depressed psychotic has a pitiless hatred of himself which may lead to suicide. In some ways, however, the depressive is like the manic. He has a similar inability to concentrate, and he may have similar delusions. The two disorders are classed together because some individuals alternate between the two states, lending support to the view that mania is a way of trying to ward off depression by throwing oneself into other activities.

Manic-depressive psychosis differs from schizophrenia in both the cultural circumstances and family situations in which it occurs. Schizophrenia occurs in conditions of cultural disorganization. It is seldom found in nonindustrial cultures unless they are undergoing rapid change after contact with industrial cultures. It has an especially high incidence in the center of the American city where that area is a melting pot for different ethnic groups, but it does not have an especially high incidence in the central areas of older European cities which are not trying to assimilate new minority groups. Similarly, schizophrenia occurs in disorganized families, as we have seen. Manic-depressive psychosis, on the other hand, occurs in cultures and families which are, in some senses at least, well integrated.

Schizophrenia seems to involve an identity crisis which may be brought about by threats to the self in maturity, which may also reflect doubts about the self stemming from living in cultural anomie, and which may even go back to problems of the initial formation of the self in infancy. The blotting out of reality and the escape into fantasy shown in schizophrenia are the crudest and most primitive defense, and may be learned in response to threats occurring at such an early age that no more adequate methods of coping with anxiety have yet been learned.

The following example of childhood schizophrenia, taken from Erik Erikson, gives an idea of the extreme inadequacy of the early socialization which has been observed more often in schizophrenia than in manic-depressive psychosis. In this case the family disorganization was due to the mother's being quarantined but remaining within the home, and she was able to observe and describe with unusual clarity the situation that preceded the baby girl's illness.

> Her mother told me that Jean's extreme disorientation had begun after the mother had become bedridden with tuberculosis. She was permitted to stay at home in her own room, but the child could speak to her only through the doorway of her bedroom, from the arms of a good-natured but "tough" nurse. During this period the mother had the impression that there were things which the child urgently wanted to tell her. The mother regretted at the time that, shortly before her illness, she had let Jean's original nurse, a gentle Mexican girl, leave them. Hedwig, so the mother anxiously noticed from her bed, was always in a hurry, moved the baby about with great energy, and was very emphatic in her disapprovals and warnings. Her favorite remark was, "Ah, baby, you stink!" and her holy war was her effort to keep the creeping infant off the floor so that she would not be contaminated by dirt. If the child were slightly soiled, she scrubbed "as if she were scrubbing a deck."

*When after four months of separation Jean (now thirteen months old) was
permitted to re-enter the mother's room, she spoke only in a whisper. "She
shrank back from the pattern on the chintz on the armchair and cried. She
tried to crawl off the flowered rug and cried all the time, looking very fearful.
She was terrified by a large, soft ball rolling on the floor and terrified of
paper crackling."*[24]

In babyhood the manic-depressive, on the other hand, appears
to have an adequate socialization up to the time when he begins to
find that independent movement is getting him into trouble. Then he
learns that he is rejected or accepted by the adults of the family according to extremely forceful standards which have little or nothing
to do with him as an individual. The manic-depressive patient tends
to have been successful in childhood in living up to the stereotyped
patterns of behavior visualized by the strongest of the adults who
reared him, and it is only when he must face the quite different and
more complex demands of adulthood and society at large that he has
the catastrophic reaction of manic-depressive psychosis. This is illustrated in a study by Gibson[25] comparing the family backgrounds of
manic-depressives with those of schizophrenics. The study concludes that families of manic-depressive patients make stronger efforts to raise or maintain their social prestige, have stronger aspirations that the patient will raise the family prestige, and are more concerned about what various social groups think of them. Similarly, the
families were characterized by strong envy among the children,
which the future manic-depressive responded to by failing to utilize
his individual and personal abilities to the utmost. The pressure was
great on the child both to maintain a traditional way of life and to
succeed in terms of it.

These observations on the families of manic-depressives fit in
well with cross-cultural indications of the incidence of the disorder.
It is common in well-integrated traditional societies which would be
expected to be successful in transmitting their beliefs and values to
the new generation. Among the Hutterites, a religious group with
highly integrated communal living arrangements, for example,
manic depression is more than four times as frequent as schizophrenia.[26]

This is just about the opposite proportion from that generally
found in the United States. Manic-depressive psychosis thus does
seem to occur more often in well-integrated cultures and families,
whereas schizophrenia characterizes disorganized cultures and families.

We have thus arrived at first approximations of the answers to our three questions of which persons develop schizophrenia, when they develop it, and why they develop the symptoms which they do. The answers suggest that the people who are most likely to develop it are those who, for either innate or social reasons, were least well integrated into a family and homogeneous culture during early childhood. These individuals seem to develop schizophrenia as a result of repeated threats to the self with which they are unable to cope. Finally, their symptoms represent both the immediate effects of escape into fantasy and the development of explanations of what is happening to them. As research on schizophrenia continues, these answers will undoubtedly be modified in many ways.

The Effects of Psychotherapy

SOME METHODOLOGICAL CONSIDERATIONS

Every field of knowledge seems to have myths which grow up around its history. The history of any field is not of great interest to most people, yet everyone knows something about it. The result is that, through a process similar to rumor transmission, there grows up a history of the field as it "should" have happened. Psychology, too, has a history similar to the history of England presented in the humorous book *1066 and All That*.

One of the tenets of this fictitious history of psychology is that Freud was the first person who was interested in unconscious processes. From the study of Miss Beauchamp done by Morton Prince before he was familiar with Freud's work, we have been able to see that this was not so. Here we must turn our attention to a second item of pseudohistory which asserts that "Eysenck demonstrated in the 50's that psychotherapy does not work."

What Dr. H. J. Eysenck[27] did, in an article in 1952 and a popular paperback book in 1953, was to compare four groups of patients. Two of these groups received psychotherapy, one was a "control" group consisting of neurotics admitted to state mental hospitals, and the fourth was another "control" group consisting of individuals receiving disability payments for neurosis treated by general practitioners. Eysenck found that within each of these groups, about two-thirds of the patients were "cured." From this he concluded, not that it had been demonstrated that psychotherapy was worthless, but that it had *not* been demonstrated that psychotherapy was of value. This was an understatement, for if we look at the methodology of the comparison, we may easily see that *no conclusions of any kind* may be drawn from the figures presented.

In an excellent review of the literature on learning-theory approaches to psychotherapy, Breger and McGaugh[28] break down the common methodological errors in evaluations of psychotherapy into (1) *sampling biases,* (2) *observer biases,* and (3) lack of *experimental controls.* Let us look at these three general types of research weakness, for the figures presented by Eysenck exemplify all three types.

On the matter of sampling, the various groups which Eysenck compared are so different from each other that it is very difficult to compare them. Eysenck assumed that the patients at state mental hospitals must be the most disturbed initially, as no one in his right mind would allow himself to become a patient in such an institution. The argument does have some force. Equally likely, however, is the possibility that individuals become patients in state mental hospitals if their behavior shows a sudden and radical change—in other words, if their illness would be classed as reactive rather than process. Such individuals have a higher probability of rapid recovery than individuals whose disturbance is longer in developing and less clearly a reaction to specific circumstances. The main thing is that we just do not know what types of patients the three populations represent, and thus cannot make meaningful comparisons among them.

A more important difficulty is that of observer biases. Instead of concluding that two-thirds of neurotics will be cured no matter what type of treatment they receive, perhaps we should conclude that two-thirds of the people treating others will assume that they have "cured" these others regardless of the amount of improvement shown. State mental hospitals do not like to spend money on custodial care. If they can get a patient back into the community, they will do so. As an indication of this, let us look at the control group in an experimental study of therapy done by Fairweather. The control group represented psychiatric patients who were discharged by a veterans' hospital after receiving the usual therapy offered by that institution. They were probably roughly comparable to the discharged patients in Eysenck's comparison and were carefully studied six months after discharge. At that time it was found that:

46% had been rehospitalized some of the time.
62% were unemployed.
14% were living with their wives.[29]

These few figures should help in the interpretation of what it means to be "cured" if the criterion of cure is being discharged from a mental hospital.

Psychoanalytically oriented psychiatrists have generally set much higher standards of mental health. Some of those discussed by Jahoda in *Current Concepts of Positive Mental Health* are: "resistance to stress," capacity for "independent behavior," "perception free from need distortion," and "adequacy in love, work, and play."[30] The "cured" group above could hardly be considered cured by these standards.

Perhaps the least meaningful figures were those from the medical practitioners who had no special training in psychiatric diagnosis or therapy. They considered that they had helped two-thirds of their patients. Although they may have done so, it is difficult to know.

The greatest problem in Eysenck's comparison, however, is the problem of experimental control. A commonly held ideal of experimental psychology, a field which Eysenck would like to see clinical psychology emulate, is that experimental and control groups should differ from one another in only a limited number of known ways. It is adherence to this ideal which makes it possible to draw some conclusions about the differences found between the groups. We have seen that the groups compared by Eysenck differed in the populations from which they were drawn and in the criteria of being "cured." They also differed in a variety of ways in the therapy which they had received. Neither the patients at the state mental hospitals nor those going to general medical practitioners were allowed to continue without help of any sort. The therapies which were used were almost as various as the practitioners: Drugs, occupational therapy, control of the environment, electric shock, stern lectures, and sympathetic listening were probably all employed—in what proportion no one can tell. It may well be that if a wide range of procedures is tried on neurotic patients, many of them will improve. Without better experimental control, it is impossible to tell why.

THERAPEUTIC APPROACHES

While Eysenck's article obviously did not prove that psychotherapy was ineffective, it did point out the complete inadequacy of the studies which had been done to evaluate its effectiveness. In the 1970s, more than twenty years after Eysenck wrote, the evidence is much more conclusive. There are now quite a few studies showing the effectiveness of a given form of therapy under a given set of circumstances, and also a large number of studies pointing out conditions which make the therapeutic process more or less effective. We still lack studies which adequately evaluate the relative effectiveness of different therapeutic approaches, however. To see why this is true, we must look at the differences among some of the major approaches to therapy.

Although there are almost as many approaches to psychotherapy as there are psychotherapists, any given approach may be reasonably well characterized by noting the types of problems it is meant to deal with, the setting in which it is carried out, the goals of treatment, and the main methods used in working toward those goals. Let us consider each of these characteristics in turn.

One of the main differences existing among the therapeutic approaches is the generality or specificity of the *problems* with which they are meant to deal. Perhaps the most specific in its objectives is *desensitization therapy,* an approach designed to deal with a person having a negative emotional reaction to one object or situation, such as a fear of snakes or of public speaking. The therapy deals with this reaction by providing emotional reassurance while the person encounters or imagines stimuli more and more closely related to the feared one. (It is thus rather similar to the process of breaking a horse to the saddle by first putting a very light blanket on his back, and then gradually working up to a saddle and rider.) Somewhat less specific of goal are *behavior modification* approaches designed for such tasks as to make a child respond to social reinforcers or model his behavior on that of a parent. Most general is the approach of psychoanalysis, for it attempts to deal with general personality characteristics and overall adaptations to life.

The specificity of a therapist's approach will influence his choice of client. The more specific approaches are generally considered useful with people who seem to be functioning adequately except in one specific way. Broad, generalized therapeutic approaches are most often employed with clients who have definite neurotic or psychotic symptoms. (One exception to this practice would be the use of specific conditioning techniques to try to get psychotic patients to pay attention to other people so that broader therapeutic approaches might then be employed.)

The therapist's approach also influences how he diagnoses his client. A therapist who usually employs a technique designed to bring about specific changes of limited scope may see a phobia, for example, as an isolated problem which can best be treated by desensitization therapy, and a person who usually treats broader problems may see a phobia as a symptom of more general difficulties.

The *settings* in which therapy is carried out differ in the amount of contact between client and therapist and in the amount of control which the therapist has over the client's social environment, as well as in whether therapy itself is carried out in a dyadic (two-person) or a group situation. Perhaps the greatest recent change in conceptions of therapy is that more and more people have moved away from a conception of psychotherapy as something which takes place only through contact between a client and a therapist. While this type of relationship is very important in many approaches to therapy, most therapists today would also ascribe great significance to the social environment in which the individual spends the rest of his time. Sometimes this environment becomes the main agent of therapeutic change, as in sensitivity-training groups. At other times it is manipulated to be supportive of therapeutic changes initiated in other ways, as we shall find described when we look at a study by Fairweather later in this chapter. The extent to which the social environment is used as a therapeutic agent cuts across other differences in therapeutic approach. Group psychotherapy grew out of psychoanalysis, for example, but training parents to change the social environment of the home is a technique emphasized by those who see behavior modification as a major goal.

Perhaps the most important difference among approaches to psychotherapy, and the one which is sometimes emphasized to the neglect of the other differences we have been discussing, is the main *goal* of the therapy. This is usually either to change a person's perceptions and give him greater insight into his own motives, or to change his behavior. The former is the main goal of psychoanalysis, and it was the goal in the two studies involving psychotherapy which we have so far discussed. Sachar and his colleagues in their treatment of depressed patients,[31] and Steele and Pollock in their therapy with parents of battered children,[32] had as their main goal what Freud referred to as "making the unconscious conscious." While this also resulted in physiological changes in Sachar's patients and behavioral ones in Steele and Pollock's, these changes were seen as being subsidiary to changes in the patients' views of themselves and their world. These therapeutic approaches would therefore be classed as *insight therapies*.

Behavior therapies, on the other hand, have the changing of behavior as their main goal. This may be either internal behavior, as when desensitization therapy is used to modify a physiological stress reaction, or external behavior. Just as insight therapies may also change behavior, behavior therapies may also increase insight. Patterson, for example, has trained parents to change their behavior toward their children.[33] While this is intended as a program of behavior modification for the children, it also undoubtedly increases the insight of the parents into how they were treating their children before the therapy began.

There is some tendency for therapists who set broad goals for therapy to conceptualize those goals in insight terms, and for those who set more limited goals to view them in terms of behavior modification. Psychotherapists who want to change large areas of a person's behavior, instead of specific bits of it, tend to use insight therapy because increased insight has the same advantage as intelligence in general—it is applicable to a wide variety of situations. It changes behavior across a broad spectrum of the person's personality. Therapists who set more limited goals, on the other hand, are more likely to try to change certain specific behaviors of their clients. As with all general statements, there are exceptions: Some group-training procedures, for example, attempt to change the overall adjustment of the participants by influencing specific behaviors in a group, and sometimes insight therapies are used for pursuing limited therapeutic goals.

Finally, therapists differ in the *methods* which they employ. The main techniques used are the reinforcement of some behaviors (including verbal behaviors indicative of insights) and the interpretation of the client's statements or behaviors. Behavior-modification techniques assume that the therapist knows what behaviors are desirable and that he can change them through the use of reinforcement. Traditional psychoanalysis also assumes that the therapist knows a great deal more than the client, although in this case his knowledge is of the unconscious significance of the client's thoughts, which he interprets to the client. In contrast to both these approaches is the type of *nondirective therapy* advocated by Rogers, in which interpretation is limited to the rephrasing of what the client has said. Largely under the influence of nondirective therapy, modern psychoanalysis has also become less directive than Freud's techniques were. It is interesting to note that one study has found interpretations of moderate depth (in which the therapist extends the patient's insight only a little way) to be more effective than either superficial or deep interpretation.[34]

While there are therapeutic approaches which exemplify almost every possible combination of characteristics on the four variables we have considered, some combinations are much more commonly found than others. The four broad categories of therapeutic approach which are most frequently found are psychoanalytically oriented therapy, behavior modification, nondirective therapy, and sensitivity training. Psychoanalytically oriented therapists generally set broad goals, work in a dyadic situation, and use interpretation as their main therapeutic technique. Behavior therapies are most strongly contrasted with this approach, for they usually set limited goals; they may use a group or even a teaching machine as a therapeutic agent; and they use reinforcement as the main therapeutic tool. Nondirective therapy, on the other hand, is quite similar to psychoanalytically oriented therapy in all respects except therapeutic technique. It stresses the importance of the therapist's maintaining "unconditional positive regard" for the client and refraining from deep interpretation.

Sensitivity training, like psychoanalysis, is a term which in everyday language has come to cover a multitude of different things. Group-training techniques initially grew out of an interaction of Freudian psychiatry and Lewinian group dynamics. They were systematically employed and evaluated at the National Training Laboratories in Bethel, Maine, and at some other centers, including Teachers College, Columbia University. As in the practice of psychoanalysis, fairly clear standards were set as to who was qualified to employ the techniques. As group techniques became popular, however, the term was extended to apply to any conscious effort by a group to change its members. These efforts, often carried out with untrained leaders or no leaders at all, have been shown by recent research frequently to have very bad effects on some participants.[35] It is thus important to note that the term as used here, and in the evaluation study to be discussed later in the chapter, applies only to the efforts of trained personnel, such as the Fellows of the National Training Laboratories.

Sensitivity training, defined in this way, sets broad goals for changing both the perceptions and the behaviors of its participants. It utilizes interpretation more than reinforcement in doing so, and it is usually employed in situations where the social environment can be utilized as a therapeutic agent on almost a full-time basis.

This brief overview of different approaches may give some idea of why a simple study could not prove that one approach was better than another. The first problem in doing such a study is that there are just too many different kinds of therapists, and that they differ from one another in their training and skill as well as in their theoretical orientations. The main problem, however, is that different therapies are intended to do different things. How appropriate the therapeutic task is to each of the therapies being compared will largely determine which one comes out as "best." This is well illustrated in a study by Paul,[36] which is sometimes cited as showing that behavior modification is more effective than insight therapy. Paul compared the relative effectiveness of desensitization therapy and insight therapy in reducing anxiety at having to speak in public. While both the treatment groups improved significantly more than an untreated control group, the desensitization group showed greater reduction in fear of public speaking than did the insight group.

It is not surprising that the desensitization group showed more improvement than the insight group in this study, for both the therapeutic objectives and the criteria by which the two therapies were evaluated were appropriate to the desensitization approach and inappropriate to the insight approach. Treating a specific fear in a normal population is not the use for which insight therapy was designed. It is, instead, intended to carry out broader objectives—at the cost of a good deal of time. Given its objectives, it should also be evaluated on how well it reduces the individual's anxiety in a wide range of situations, not just at speaking in public.

In fact, the really surprising thing about Paul's results is that the insight group showed any improvement at all. The individuals in this group had only five hours of therapy, and it did not concentrate particularly on the public-speaking issue. Yet they showed a significant decrease in anxiety at public speaking. Since the goals of the therapy were general, this would seem to be an indication that the subjects probably showed notable decrease in anxiety in many other difficult life tasks—a truly phenomenal change for only five hours of therapy. By contrast, members of the desensitization group seemed to have changed more on the specific issue of fear of public speaking, but since the therapy was specific to that issue, there is no reason to think that they showed change in any other respect.

In other words, which therapeutic technique turns out to be most effective depends primarily on how the therapeutic task is defined and evaluated. There probably is no one best technique for all people and all purposes. If your sole therapeutic goal is to reduce fear of public speaking, for example, then desensitization therapy is probably the most effective way of achieving your goal, just as Paul's study indicates.

FACTORS INFLUENCING SUCCESS

In evaluating the success of psychotherapy, we need to compare the improvement shown by those who receive it with that shown by individuals who, for one reason or another, are unable to do so. Individuals who cannot obtain help from a psychotherapist usually seek it from other sources—from medical doctors, ministers, and friends. For this reason, and because the life circumstances which precipitated their crises may well change with time, these untreated individuals often show improvement with the passage of time. When the improvement of therapy clients is compared with the improvement of these "control" individuals, we discover that therapy is not an unmixed blessing. The clients of some therapists improve more than those individuals receiving only informal help, while those of others improve less.[37]

That therapy, broadly defined, can lead to negative as well as positive changes means that it is especially important to see what factors will make it more or less successful. One of the most significant elements seems to be the amount of training and experience of the therapist. In general, well-trained therapists help their patients to improve most. Informal change agents with no training are next most helpful to those who seek aid from them, and poorly trained therapists are least helpful to their patients.[38] How are these results to be interpreted?

Perhaps an analogy will assist in interpreting them. Imagine three individuals with appendicitis who sought help, respectively, from a well-trained surgeon, from an individual with some slight knowledge of surgery, and from one with no knowledge of it. It would not be surprising if the well-trained surgeon operated and his patient recovered, if the individual with slight knowledge operated and his patient died, and if the completely untrained individual did not operate, giving his patient a reasonable chance of getting well anyway. This is the result analogous to that found in the area of psy-

chotherapy. Perhaps the explanation of the result is that the therapeutic relationship, like surgery, can be a very powerful force toward
change in the individual. When this force is utilized by someone
who does not know what he is doing, he is more likely to do harm
with it than good. We have already noted this possibility in looking
at the effects of sensitivity training conducted by untrained individuals.

An extremely interesting study which may help to clarify why
some therapists actually interfere with the recovery of their clients
was done by Richard Cutler.[39] Ideally, therapists should be able to
perceive the problems of their clients accurately and respond to them
in ways that are motivated by the needs of the client rather than the
needs of the therapist. Cutler studied the possibility that unresolved
conflicts in the therapist led to inaccurate perception of his client and
inappropriate action by the therapist. Although only two therapists
were studied, the results were extremely suggestive.

Areas where the therapist had unresolved conflicts were identified by comparing the therapist's own ratings of the extent to which
he showed various characteristics with the ratings made of him by
nine judges who knew him well. Large discrepancies were taken as
an indication of unresolved conflict. If, for example, the therapist saw
himself as very low in submissiveness while others saw him as high
in this characteristic, the discrepancy would be considered an indication of unresolved conflict in that general area. It was predicted that
in areas where the therapist had unresolved conflicts, he would (1)
consistently misperceive how much his own behavior showed those
characteristics about which he had conflict, (2) misperceive the extent
to which the client's behavior showed those characteristics, and (3)
act in ways which were motivated more by his own need to defend
his ego than by the therapeutic task. These predictions were strongly
supported by the data. To the extent that therapists misperceive their
clients and act toward them in ways that are motivated by their own
problems, it is not surprising that some "therapy" is found to have
negative effects.

A number of other factors besides the training and experience
of the therapist have now been shown to influence how effective the
therapy is likely to be. An excellent summary of these factors has
been published by Rosalind Dymond Cartwright, who concluded
from her survey of the literature that:

> . . . We now seem to have reached some consensus that the quality of the
> therapeutic relationship is important in all treatments. The elements of an

effective relationship seem to include: motivational, affective, perceptual, and cognitive factors. (a) For the motivation to be sufficiently strong to outweigh competing motivations, the patient should be pretty uncomfortable and self-dissatisfied. The therapist should be motivated to work hard at helping. How he translates his devotion to this task most effectively is still a matter of conjecture. (b) Affectively, the qualities of warmth, respect, and acceptance of the partners for each other seem crucial. (c) Perceptually, role clarity of each partner and role differentiation between them seems important. The more consensus there is between the partners on the expected behaviors of each, the more likely it is to work. (d) Cognitively, the therapist must be able to understand his patient. The patient must be able to supply the information necessary for the therapist's understanding. Not all patients are such "good catches." Some therapists seem able to convert the poor bets into more workable patients. The literature seems to show that either the very inexperienced or the highly experienced can do this.[40]

Thus far, we have concentrated on the conditions under which therapy is or is not successful for it is important to realize that not everything called therapy is necessarily beneficial. This concentration, however, probably gives an overly negative picture of the state of the art at this time. As was noted earlier, there are now many studies showing particular therapeutic processes to be effective under certain conditions. Let us look at two such studies, one dealing with severely disturbed, hospitalized patients and the other dealing with individuals who are normally well adjusted. While they differ in other ways, the studies are similar in that both use group processes as a change technique and both employ more adequate criteria of change than most studies.

The first study, by Fairweather and his colleagues, explored the effects on hospitalized patients of participating in task-oriented, problem-solving groups. Life in a hospital usually requires the patient to play a dependent role which may ill prepare him for life outside of the hospital. The experimental treatment program which Fairweather and his colleagues introduced rewarded the patients for playing a more normal, adult social role. As they put it:

In the traditional program, all problems regarding the patient are taken up with him as an individual matter. His role is very clearly a subordinate one in which he relies upon the staff for their final decisions without any voice about possible courses of action. On the other hand, the social system of the small-group treatment program clearly delineates the patient's role as that of participant in group discussion and recommendations. Although the final decision regarding such recommendations rests with the staff, each patient's task group has the responsibility and is rewarded for recommending realistic and meaningful courses of action for each of its members, with particular emphasis on daily living and future plans.[41]

Conditions were carefully controlled so that differences between the treatment and control groups could be clearly attributed to the experimental treatment program, and the two groups were studied in a variety of ways. Two general findings clearly emerged: (1) The experimental treatment program led to better adjustment on the part of the patients after they left the hospital. Those who had participated in the small-group program were significantly more likely to be employed, to talk with other people, and to have friends after leaving the hospital than those who had not. (2) Adjustment after leaving the hospital had very little relationship to the measurements taken while the patient was in the hospital. Most important, it had almost no relationship to whether the patient's attitudes toward the treatment program were positive or negative. If the treatment program had been evaluated in terms of the attitudes of the patients to it, rather than by their adjustment to community life, its effectiveness would not have been discovered. Since some studies of the effectiveness of therapy have relied on patients' statements about how much they have been helped, this is important to note.

Miles's study differs from Fairweather's in dealing with a group of individuals with normal psychological adjustment rather than a severely disturbed population.[42] It is similar, however, in the careful attention to providing relevant control groups and adequate criteria of change. The experimental group was composed of thirty-four elementary school principals who attended a two-week training laboratory in human relations. Their change was evaluated not just through self-report techniques and ratings by the laboratory staff, but also by their associates on the job. In follow-ups after three and eight months, they were found to have become more sensitive to the needs of others, more egalitarian in their ways of doing things, and more skillful as leaders, as a result of the laboratory experience. This is impressive evidence of the effectiveness of sensitivity training when it is performed by qualified individuals. It is also interesting to note what did, and what did not, correlate with change by the participants. Long-term change was unrelated to personality factors. However, individuals who were more secure in their jobs changed more. Most important, there was no relationship between how much an individual perceived himself as having changed and how much he had changed according to external judges. *Those who expected to change the most through taking the program actually changed the least.* These results underline the importance of developing objective criteria in evaluating psychological change rather than relying on the individual's own report. As such criteria are developed, psychotherapy may for the first time be really adequately evaluated.

Summary

Mental illness can be the culmination of earlier attempts to protect oneself from serious anxiety. The defense mechanisms used may take all of one's energy and attention, leaving one unable to cope with the rest of reality. Escalation of resulting problems and symptoms may result in mental functioning which is anything but adaptive but which nevertheless arose out of attempts to adapt.

Mental illness can also be the result of tissue degeneration, nutritional deprivation, poisoning, and other physical agents of neurochemical and anatomical change. It is difficult to classify mental disorders because of confusing origins and overlapping categories of symptoms.

The state of disability in which one suffers some impairment of function but can still perceive most aspects of reality is called neurosis. Problems in coping may arise from the debilitating anxiety itself, but are usually compounded by the difficulties caused by the forms which one's defensive mechanisms have taken. The sufferer may have transformed his anxiety into a physical symptom such as paralysis, called a conversion reaction, or split some of his memories off from consciousness in a dissociative reaction. These symptoms are classed as hysteria. He may suffer a serious chronic fatigue, or the conviction that he has a grave physical disorder, or a terrible fear of something. These are varieties of anxiety states. He may have obsessive-compulsive reactions or neurotic depression, and may experience psychosomatic disorders which are true physical ailments caused by the wear and tear of too-long reliance on the general adaptation syndrome. The complex dynamics of each person's set of symptoms make it impossible to put a simple classificatory label on a particular individual.

A much more serious degree of mental disturbance is the psychosis. Two syndromes, or clustering of symptoms, are recognizable in this category—manic-depressive psychosis and schizophrenia. They involve major disturbances in the perception of reality, in speech and thought, and in mood and social relations.

The origins of schizophrenia may well lie in a combination of disordered perceptual learning, disrupted personality growth in early childhood, and overwhelming stress as the individual later attempts to cope with his environment. There appear to be innate differences which make some individuals more likely than others to develop schizophrenic symptoms under stress. Genetic factors alone, however, do not seem to be sufficient to cause schizophrenia. Experimental tests of these hypotheses are so difficult to design and carry out that they remain only suggested explanations, at the present time. For example, the degree of stress a person is under can be assessed to some extent, while he is under study, by measuring the corticosteroid output in his urine, but how do you retroactively measure his childhood traumas to compare them with those of a control group?

Manic-depressive psychosis has two characteristic, alternating states. During the manic phases of this disorder, the sufferer can be so wild with silliness or exultation that he is dangerous to himself and others, and during the depressive phases so full of self-hatred and black despair that suicide is possible. The phases can exhibit similar delusions and incapacity for organized thought. This type of psychosis tends to be found more frequently than schizophrenia in traditional authoritarian unchanging communities, whereas schizophrenia is more found in areas of social upheaval and disorganization.

Different types of psychotherapy have not only different methods and points of view, but may also have different goals. Most psychotherapeutic treatment for mental disorders proceeds on the assumption that it should make the person better able to meet stress, more capable of independent behavior, and more able to perceive without need-distortion. It should also make the person better able to engage in life processes, such as love, work, and play, and even find peace in his own dying at life's end.

Development of an agreed-on set of objective criteria for evaluating psychological change is a necessary first step before meaningful comparison of psychotherapeutic methods is possible.

Notes and Acknowledgments

1. An excellent discussion of strategies in adaptation to life makes up the second chapter of Sigmund Freud, *Civilization and Its Discontents*. Garden City, N. Y.: Doubleday & Company, Inc., 1958.
2. Holt, John. *How Children Fail.* New York: Pitman Publishing Corporation, 1964, p. 3. Used by permission of the publisher.
3. Berne, Eric. *Games People Play.* New York: Grove Press, Inc., 1964, p. 78. Used by permission of the publisher.
4. White, Robert W. *The Abnormal Personality.* New York: The Ronald Press Company, 1956, pp. 263–264.

5. Wolff, C., et al. "Relationship between psychological defenses and mean urinary 17-hydroxycorticosteroid excretion rates: I. A predictive study of parents of fatally ill children. II. Methodological and theoretical consideration." *Psychosomatic Medicine,* 1964 (26), pp. 576–609.

6. Lazarus, Richard S. *Adjustment and Personality.* New York: McGraw-Hill Book Company, 1961, pp. 337–347.

7. Prince, Morton. *The Dissociation of a Personality.* New York: Longmans, Green & Co., Inc., 1913.

8. Thigpen, C. H., and H. M. Cleckley. *The Three Faces of Eve.* New York: McGraw-Hill Book Company, 1957.

9. Prince, Morton. Op. cit., p. 1. Used by permission of David McKay Company, Inc.

10. Ibid., p. 9. By permission.

11. Ibid., p. 27. By permission.

12. Ibid., pp. 28–29. By permission.

13. Ibid., p. 80. By permission.

14. Maher, B. A., K. O. McKean, and B. McLaughlin. "Studies in psychotic language," in P. J. Stone, D. C. Dunphy, M. S. Smith, and D. M. Ogilvie (Eds.), *The General Inquirer.* Cambridge, Mass.: The M.I.T. Press, 1966.

15. McGhie, A., J. Chapman, and J. S. Lawson. "Effect of distraction on schizophrenic performance." *British Journal of Psychiatry,* 1965 (111), pp. 383–398.

16. Arnhoff, F. N., and E. N. Damianopoulos. "Self-body recognition and schizophrenia." *Journal of General Psychology,* 1964 (70), pp. 353–361.

17. Rogler, Lloyd H., and August B. Hollingshead. *Trapped: Families and Schizophrenia.* New York: John Wiley & Sons, Inc., 1965, pp. 194–195. Used by permission of the publisher.

18. Ibid., pp. 171–172. By permission.

19. Ibid., pp. 409–410. By permission.

20. Jackson, Don D. (Ed.) *The Etiology of Schizophrenia.* New York: Basic Books, Inc., Publishers, 1960.

21. Rosenthal, D. (Ed.) *The Genian Quadruplets.* Basic Books, Inc., Publishers, 1963.

22. Mednick, Sarnoff A. "Breakdown in individuals at high risk for schizophrenia: Possible predispositional perinatal factors." *Mental Hygiene,* 1970 (54), no. 1, pp. 50–63.

23. Kety, S. S., D. Rosenthal, P. H. Wender, and F. Schulsinger. "The types and prevalence of mental illness in the biological and adoptive families of adopted schizophrenics," in D. Rosenthal and S. S. Kety (Eds.), *The Transmission of Schizophrenia.* London: Pergamon Press, 1968, pp. 345–362.

24. Erikson, Erik H. *Childhood and Society.* (2d ed.) New York: Copyright 1950 ©1963 W. W. Norton & Company, Inc., 1963, pp. 196–197. Used by permission of the publisher.

25. Gibson, R. W. "The family background and early life experience of the manic-depressive patient." *Psychiatry,* 1958 (21), pp. 71–91.

26. Eaton, J. W., and R. S. Weil. *Culture and Mental Disorders.* New York: The Free Press of Glencoe, 1955.

27. Eysenck, H. J. *Uses and Abuses of Psychology.* Baltimore: Penguin Books, Inc., 1953.

Eysenck, H. J. "The effects of psychotherapy: An evaluation." *Journal of Consulting Psychology,* 1952 (16), pp. 319–324.

28. Breger, L., and J. McGaugh. "Critique and reformulation of 'learning-theory' approaches to psychotherapy and neurosis." *Psychological Bulletin,* 1965 (63), no. 5, pp. 338–358.

29. Fairweather, George. (Ed.) *Social Psychology in Treating Mental Illness.* New York: John Wiley & Sons, Inc., 1964, p. 164.

30. Jahoda, M. *Current Concepts of Positive Mental Health.* New York: Basic Books, Inc., Publishers, 1958, pp. 41, 47, 49, and 55.

31. Sachar, Edward J., John M. Mackenzie, William A. Binstock, and John E. Mack. "Corticosteroid responses to psychotherapy of depressions. I. Elevations during confrontation of loss." *Archives of General Psychiatry,* 1967 (16), pp. 461–470.

32. Steele, Brandt F., and Carl B. Pollock. "A psychiatric study of parents who abuse infants and small children," in Ray E. Helfer, and C. Henry Kempe (Eds.), *The Battered Child.* Chicago: The University of Chicago Press, 1968, pp. 103–147.

33. A good example of Patterson's approach may be found in Gerald R. Patterson, Shirley McNeal, Nancy Hawkins, and Richard Phelps. "Reprogramming the social environment," in Roger Ulrich, Thomas Stachnik, and John Mabry (Eds.), *Control of Human Behavior: From Cure to Prevention.* Vol. 2. Glenview, Ill.: Scott, Foresman & Company, 1970, pp. 237–248.

34. Speisman, Joseph C. "Depth of interpretation and verbal resistance in psychotherapy." *Journal of Consulting Psychology,* 1959 (23), pp. 93–99.

35. This research by Dr. Irvin D. Yalom is briefly described in *Science News,* May 15, 1971 (99), no. 20, p. 333.

36. Paul, G. *Insight vs. Desensitization in Psychotherapy.* Stanford, Calif.: Stanford University Press, 1966.

37. Cartwright, R. D., and J. L. Vogel. "A comparison of changes in psychoneurotic patients during matched periods of therapy and no-therapy." *Journal of Consulting Psychology,* 1960 (24), pp. 121–127.

38. Cartwright, Rosalind Dymond. "Psychotherapeutic Processes." *Annual Review of Psychology.* Palo Alto, Calif.: Annual Reviews, 1968, pp. 124–416.

39. Cutler, Richard. "Countertransference effects in psychotherapy." *Journal of Consulting Psychology,* 1958 (22), pp. 349–356.

40. Cartwright, Rosalind Dymond. Op. cit., p. 412. Used by permission of the publisher.

41. Fairweather, George (Ed.) *Social Psychology in Treating Mental Illness.* New York: John Wiley & Sons, Inc., 1964, p. 31. Used by permission of the publisher.

42. Miles, Matthew B. "Changes during and following laboratory training: A clinical-experimental study." *Journal of Applied Behavioral Science,* July 1965 (1), no. 3, pp. 215–242.

Allan Alcorn, from an exhibit at the Phoenix Gallery.

NINE

ATTITUDES & ATTITUDE CHANGE

The Nature of Attitudes

Because man responds to the world in terms of his ideas about it, understanding how he views the world is an important help in predicting his behavior. This fact has led psychologists to the study of beliefs, attitudes, and values. Let us look at some examples, and then analyze them to see just what these terms mean.

Caroline Ware, in her study *Greenwich Village, 1920–1930*, discovered three different patterns of marriage among the residents of this New York City area.[1] The population of the area was composed of a number of distinct groups. First there was the art colony which made the area famous, composed both of productive artists and of others who had chosen a bohemian way of life. This colony, however, was superimposed on a population of local residents who had no particular interest in art nor any attraction to bohemian ways. Some of these residents were fairly recent immigrants from Italy, Ireland, or Germany, drawn there, as the artists originally were, by the low rents. (These rents rose as the area became fashionable, driving most of the real artists out.) More of the residents were families for whom Greenwich Village was an area of second settlement, moved into after they had lived long enough in America to be able to afford to leave the downtown tenements where they had settled first.

The members of these various cultural groups differed, by and large, in most aspects of their lives—how they earned their livings, educated their children, and spent their leisure. The differences in their marriage patterns are a good illustration of what we mean by an attitude.

A central thesis of the bohemian way of life was that sexual partners should not be tied to each other by legal or financial bonds, but should be free to dissolve their union whenever either of them felt like it. Marriage was seen as a temporary union between equals, and husband and wife were expected to share equally in the financial support of the family, in housekeeping chores such as cooking and dishwashing, and in the care of children if there were any. Because the bohemians believed in giving all possible psychological and educational advantages to their children and this created those binding ties of marriage which they were trying to avoid, they also tended to avoid having children. Ware interviewed the residents of 452 apartments typifying this approach to marriage, and found a total of only 31 children.

The most striking contrast to the bohemian pattern of marriage was the patriarchal form practiced especially by recent immigrants from Spain and Italy. If bohemian marriage was viewed as a temporary alliance between two individuals, patriarchal marriage was seen as a permanent union between two families. Since this was the case, marriages were arranged between families rather than resulting from a pattern of dating and courtship. Ware interviewed twenty-two Italian-American wives whose marriages fitted the patriarchal pattern, and found that only three of them had ever had a date with a man other than the one they married.

Most other aspects of the patriarchal marriage differed from those of the experimental marriages of the bohemians. Children were desired in large numbers, were expected to obey their parents, and were required to add to the family income from quite a young age. The father was the head of the family, woman's place was supposed to be in the home, and there was a double standard of sexual morality. Men were expected to have extramarital sexual affairs to prove their masculinity, while an entire family would be dishonored if a woman had an affair either before or outside of marriage.

The third major marriage pattern, that of courtship and romantic love, was intermediate in many ways between the other two. It was the dominant pattern in this country during the first half of this century, although it has now been somewhat modified by incorporating elements from the experimental marriage pattern. Each of the three patterns had its own strains and contradictions. The romantic love pattern was dependent on husband and wife feeling as if struck by a thunderbolt every time they looked at each other, and this feeling did not always survive decades of marriage and child rearing. The patriarchal form required every man to have affairs with women to prove his masculinity, but demanded the male relatives of any woman to kill any man who dishonored her. The experimental marriage required the wife to provide the best possible environment for the children while also having an income-producing career and remaining attractive to a husband who could leave her at any time. It required the husband to sacrifice everything for his art while also paying high tuition for his children's education at private progressive schools.

Despite these internal strains, each type of marriage formed a coherent pattern. If you asked a practitioner of any of the three types to give his or her ideas about marriage, you would not get a disorganized collection of separate opinions—that marriage should be a temporary experiment but that the couple should have many children to support them in their old age, for example. Instead, their opinions would have a structure. Given certain fundamental assumptions, other elements of the pattern follow. For example, if marriage is regarded as a union between families, it cannot be dissolved simply because two partners to that union, the husband and wife, are dissatisfied with each other.

The existence of this type of organized pattern of opinions is what we mean when we speak of a person's having an *attitude* toward something. An *opinion*, on the other hand, is only a single element, such as "Women should have independent interests outside the home." An opinion may or may not be part of an attitude, and there are many subjects we have no attitudes about. Most of us have an attitude toward marriage, but only isolated opinions about military strategy during the Civil War.

Opinions and attitudes combine both beliefs about the way things are and judgments about how they should be. People who differ about whether marriage should provide for women's having careers often differ on how necessary such activities are to a woman's happiness. An advocate of patriarchal marriage, on the other hand, might also argue that woman's place is in the home whether she is happy there or not, for he would see that role as instrumental to the fulfillment of certain values which are ultimately sanctioned by his religious faith. It is because attitudes are organized, and because they are made up both of beliefs about the world and of value judgments, that they exert a powerful influence on behavior.

A person's behavior being influenced by his attitude toward something, however, depends upon his having an attitude toward it. Consider the realm of political behavior. One person may have only isolated opinions about politics. At one moment, he may be a champion of the view "That government governs best which governs least," and at another, he may be equally strong in demanding that the national government establish a uniform curriculum in every public school in the country. Not thinking much about politics, he may never stop to consider whether his views are consistent. More common is the person who has a few well-developed attitudes in the political realm. His political ideas will be organized around these central attitudes, but there will still be some inconsistencies in his thinking and some aspects of political life which he has never bothered to relate to the attitudes he does hold. Finally, a few individuals have well thought-out, comprehensive systems of attitudes in the political realm. These comprehensive world views, called *ideologies*, are important even though they are relatively rare. That is because, as Agger and his colleagues have shown, those who hold them are most influential in the political process.[2]

Attitudes and Behavior

The word "attitude" originally meant a physical posture. Because assuming a certain posture prepares one to carry out a particular action, its meaning was extended to cover those thoughts and feelings about something which prepare us to act in a certain way toward it. Conceived in these terms, attitude is not the only cause of behavior but, rather, is a readiness to act in a certain way under appropriate conditions.

If this is so, then there are some conditions when attitude will predict behavior and other conditions when it will not. Consider the case of the conspirators who killed Julius Caesar. Each had organized thoughts and feelings about Caesar which prepared him for his action. Yet, if you had looked at the behavior of any one of the conspirators prior to the assassination, you would have found that it differed markedly from that dictated by his attitude, for he acted in a friendly way toward Caesar and tried to conceal his murderous intent. His true attitude would be expressed only in circumstances which were relatively free of strong situational pressures, in this case fear of punishment.

Although knowing the attitude of each conspirator might have enabled us to predict his behavior only imperfectly, it might have been of more help than merely observing behavior. The day-to-day behavior of the conspirators toward Caesar might have given us as little basis for predicting the assassination as it gave Caesar himself. If we did want to predict from behavior alone, we would probably do well to concentrate on those nonverbal behaviors which are least under conscious control. This approach would be especially advisable if we could not induce the conspirators to tell us their true attitudes.

Behavior, then, can be best predicted from attitudes when three things are true. First, the person must have relevant attitudes and must know what they are. If he has never thought about his attitude toward something, or if ego-defensive processes make him conceal his feelings from himself, attitude will be a less useful predictor of behavior.

Second, the behavior we are predicting must take place in circumstances where the actor is not exposed to overwhelming pressure to act in a given way. If a person holds a gun on you and tells you to give him your money, your attitude toward contributing money to others will be of little use in predicting your behavior. To some extent, situational pressures may be taken into account by predicting differences in how various people will act instead of by considering the absolute level of one person's behavior. Suppose one person believes in giving to charity and another doesn't. Strong social pressures may cause even the former individual to make some contributions, but for any given level of pressure, the latter individual will probably contribute more than the former.

Finally, if attitudes are to predict behavior, we must have adequate measures of those attitudes. A number of attitude-scaling techniques have been devised to ensure that the questions asked will adequately reflect each individual's attitude.[3] Careful attention must also be paid to the question of whether the person is telling the truth when he answers the questions. He can be counted on to do this only if the interviewer establishes adequate rapport with him, if the interviewer is careful to give no clues revealing his own feelings about the matter, and if the questions deal with matters about which the person being interviewed has no particular reason to lie.

Despite these limitations and cautions, attitude measurement can be a powerful tool in understanding behavior. This seemed so obvious to early workers in the field that they tended merely to assume the validity of their instruments rather than to demonstrate it. It is only recently that fairly adequate studies have started to show that attitudes can in fact predict real behavior. Let us look at one of them.

The study, by Goodmonson, deals with a topic of current interest.[4] With the corneal transplant a commonplace operation and the heart transplant becoming one, medicine is rapidly approaching the point where availability of organs will be a major factor in its ability to save life. How willing are people to leave their internal organs to others at death? Is it possible to predict, from attitude tests, who will be willing to donate their organs?

Goodmonson did a study to find out. It differs from almost all other studies of the validity of attitude scaling in that she tried to predict real behavior of importance to the subjects. At the end of the study, she asked each person to sign a card leaving his organs to medicine at death, and to put this card in his or her billfold or purse. A number of her subjects did so. Under Oregon law, the existence of such a card at the time of a person's death gives the attending physician the right to take a person's organs for transplant purposes. It is hard to imagine a study which would put a person's expressed attitudes to a more stringent test.

From an attitude test administered earlier, Goodmonson was able to predict with some accuracy the persons who would donate their organs. This was probably so because her study almost completely met the conditions under which attitude will be a good predictor of behavior. She obtained frank answers on the attitude scale by having subjects take it anonymously, only asking them later to reveal their identities. Both the attitude measure and the measure of the subject's behavior were carefully devised. Only one condition fell short of being close to optimal for maximizing the relationship between attitude and behavior. Some of the subjects may not have thought enough about organ donation to have a clearly defined attitude on the subject.

As well as giving the subjects an attitude scale which measured their general favorability or unfavorability toward organ donation, Goodmonson also had her subjects tell how they would respond if they were asked to do a number of things in the area of organ donation. These behavioral intention questions closely paralleled the actual behavioral measures which were taken later. (One item, for example, asked whether they would accept literature telling more about organ transplants. Later, under different circumstances, they were offered a piece of literature, and their acceptance or refusal of it was one of the behavioral measures.)

The responses regarding behavioral intentions were found to predict actual behavior just about as well as the attitude scale. What, then, is the value of sophisticated attitude-scaling techniques? Why not just ask people what they would do?

The answer lies in the generality of what is found out from the attitude measure. The behavioral intention statements were very specific to the behaviors which were going to be observed and could predict only them. The attitude scale dealt with much more general feelings in the area of organ transplants, and could predict hundreds of different behavioral measures as well as it predicted the ones in the study. It is because they are of help in predicting so many different behaviors that attitudes are worth studying.

Bases of Attitude Change

INTRODUCTION

Studies of interpersonal attraction have indicated that people are attracted to others who help them achieve their goals, who conform to the norms of their reference groups, who reduce their anxiety, and who symbolize their values. These four categories of attraction apply not only to other people but to the objects of our attitudes generally. They function to serve our needs and so may be called, respectively, the *instrumental* function, the *group-affiliation* function, the *ego-defensive* function, and the *value-expressive* function.[5] An automobile which is instrumental in helping a person achieve his goal of driving downtown is a good automobile, while one which breaks down and frustrates his goal achievement is not. It is an even better automobile if it serves a group affiliation function by making him the envy of his friends, or if it expresses the value he places on a clean environment by being smog-free. It might even serve an ego-defensive function if he imagines himself escaping from all the cares and troubles of his life in it. In that instance his attitude toward it, while sick, will be very positive.

Attempts to induce a person to hold a positive attitude toward some object generally involve trying to convince him that the object serves one of these four functions for him. Buying the encyclopedia will enable you to achieve your goal of helping your child obtain high grades in school. Drinking X brand of scotch will make you one of that exciting group of people who are pictured in the advertisements as sun-bathing on the Riviera or skiing in the Austrian Alps. Using Y deodorant will relieve you of all the anxieties which you feel on social occasions, and voting for Z will show that you are proud of your city, state, or country.

These four functions can also be seen in the appeal of social movements. Consider Hitler's appeal to the German people.[6] Germany had entered the First World War with an expectation of rapid and complete victory. Throughout the early portion of the war, the German people heard reports only of victories, and they were by no means prepared for defeat when it came. The defeat, moreover, resulted in a disastrous peace treaty involving reparations payments which crippled the German economy. The combined effects of the war destroyed the value of the German currency. By 1923, one American dollar would buy over 3 billion German marks. The crippling inflation was followed by the Great Depression of the thirties. By 1932, production in Germany had fallen to half of what it had been in 1929, and half the population was estimated to be living at close to a starvation level.

Conditions such as these give rise to what have been called *revitalization movements*. A revitalization movement is one which provides a new interpretation of the nature of the society, supports it by appeals to a reinterpreted and often mythical cultural history, and furnishes a vision of a utopian future toward which the society can strive. Whether religious or secular, it gives its participants a new identity as instruments of the future.

The two main ideologies which proposed alternate interpretations of conditions in depression-torn Germany were Communism and Hitler's National Socialism. (The latter, of course, became progressively less socialistic as it achieved power.) Both of these ideologies had an explanation of what the country was experiencing, advocated a course of action to deal with the situation, and offered a vision of a more perfect society which could result. From the Communist point of view, the Depression of the 1930s was a natural consequence of the capitalist system, it could be remedied by controlling industrial output through governmental decision rather than considerations of profit and loss, and this change could lead to a society in which men were truly equal and wars no longer necessary. From the Nazi point of view, both the peace treaty at the end of the First World War and the Depression were caused by an international conspiracy of Jewish bankers, the situation could be remedied by taking action against this group and against anyone lacking in national patriotism, and these steps could lead to a victorious Germany's assuming the leadership of Europe. Although it was a near thing, this latter ideology triumphed.

From this rather oversimplified view of Nazi ideology, it is clear that the ideology convinced its followers of both its instrumental and value-expressive functions. Not only would Hitler lead his people to victory and prosperity, but in doing so, he would enable the German people to show those qualities of bravery, loyalty, strength, and purity which made up the best portion of their cultural heritage. This appeal to past values was carried out by a reinterpretation not only of German history, but also of the personal histories of the leaders. The myths of Hitler's youth, like those surrounding other national heroes, portrayed him as symbolically embodying the struggles and aspirations of his people.[7]

The ego-defensive function was appealed to by blaming the people's troubles on someone other than themselves. A person's anxiety at not being able to cope with his environment was reduced both by attributing his difficulties to hostile agents of an alien conspiracy and by encouraging him to rely on an all-good and all-powerful leader who would care for his needs. Finally, through Nazi youth organizations, the members of the movement were provided with supportive reference groups to maintain them in their new ideology.

While different ideologies vary in their specific content and also in how realistic they are, they are similar in the functions of attitude to which they appeal. The person who wants to keep things the same, as well as the one who wants to change them, will have a system of beliefs and values which serves to organize his cognitive world and glorify his own role in it. Let us therefore turn our attention away from mass movements and consider how attitude change comes about under more normal circumstances.

CONTROL OF INFORMATION

People change their attitudes for any number of reasons. They also find other people trying to change their attitudes for them, for this is one of the everyday social skills which we all possess. It is developed by certain individuals into a fine art. However, scientific study of techniques of persuasion has greatly increased the effectiveness with which it can be carried out. This raises the serious issue of how much scientists are responsible for the uses to which their findings are put. While we know that the science of persuasion is used for beneficent purposes such as reduction of intergroup conflict, it is also used for cynical control of people by whoever has the means to arrange the controlling. A study of it should start by pointing out the fact that the effectiveness of persuasion will depend to a great degree on the proportion of information received which is under the control of the communicator. The easiest way to persuade is to have control of all sources of information.

ATTENTION

Since most communicators do not have such control, their first problem is to make potential recipients pay attention to their messages. This is easiest to do in face-to-face contact, but that medium is extremely expensive of time. Printing is relatively cheap, but most printed messages are thrown away unread. Radio and television messages are probably most effective when they are so brief that the message is over before the recipient has time to turn his set off. Because of the low level reached in political campaigns when no message can be over 10 seconds long, serious questions are now being raised about the effects of modern means of communication on political institutions.

Even if a message is heard or read, it may not be thoughtfully considered by the recipient. The recipient is likely already to have an attitude about the object of the communication, and that attitude will be related to other attitudes held by the recipient. Cognitive structures are organized, and changing one part of the structure may create imbalance with other parts. Forces toward balance thus usually resist change.

This organized nature of attitudes is well illustrated in research by Milton Rosenberg, who considered how attitudes are organized around values.[8] In the first stage of the study, he measured the attitude positions of a large number of undergraduate students on the question of whether members of the Communist party should be allowed to address the public. He also measured the importance of a wide range of values for these individuals and the extent to which they saw allowing members of the Communist Party to speak as furthering or hindering the achievement of those values. His prediction was that there would be a strong relationship between seeing a course of action as advancing an important value and endorsing that course of action. This prediction was strongly borne out by the data. The students who saw their values as being furthered by allowing members of the Communist Party to speak favored doing so, and those who saw their values as hindered by this policy generally did not.

Even more interesting was the second part of the study. Using individuals who could be deeply hypnotized as subjects, Rosenberg looked at the effects of experimentally changing an individual's attitude toward some topic of importance to him. The first part of the study had shown that we endorse attitudes which we see as furthering our values and disagree with those which we see as blocking them. What will happen if our attitudes are changed under hypnosis so that we now endorse an attitude which we see as being in opposition to our basic values? Two ways of resolving the inconsistency are possible. We could change the value, or we could change our beliefs about the relationship between the attitude and the value. Both these types of reactions were found. Some subjects changed their values to make them more consistent with the attitudes they had acquired under hypnosis, and others maintained their previous values but no longer saw their attitudes as being related to their more general value position. Rosenberg's study is one of the more striking demonstrations that our attitudes are organized around our values and that a change in our cognitive structure necessitates other changes to restore consistency.

This being so, recipients of messages which are in discord with their present attitudes may systematically avoid paying attention to them. This was suggested in an early study by Ewing.[9] Using a persuasive message which went against the existing attitudes of most of his subjects, he began the message with one of two different sentences. One of them correctly suggested what the message was going to argue, while the other implied that it would take the side of the issue agreeable to the subjects. The group members who received the misleading beginning sentence, which implied that the message was going to agree with their attitudes, paid more attention to it. They remembered it better, and were more convinced by it, than the group members who realized at the start that the message was going to disagree with their views.

Despite Ewing's study, research has not consistently supported the hypothesis that a person selectively exposes himself to information which supports his own position. Perhaps the main reason is that there are conditions under which it is easier to maintain one's beliefs by refuting opposition arguments than by trying to remain ignorant of them. A study by Lowin illustrates this way of dealing with potential imbalance.[10]

Using as subjects political partisans during the Johnson-Goldwater presidential campaign, Lowin gave each subject a pamphlet of political arguments. The pamphlets differed in two ways. Some of them contained arguments agreeing, and others presented arguments disagreeing, with the subject's own position. Further, some pamphlets contained arguments which were implausible and easy to refute, while others contained much more telling arguments. At the end of each pamphlet was a form which the subject could use to send for additional material if he so desired.

Lowin's suggestion was that attitudes can be maintained not only by learning arguments supporting one's own position but also by learning and refuting opposition arguments. He therefore predicted that the subjects who received easily refuted opposition arguments would send for more information, just as those who received difficult-to-refute supporting arguments would. This prediction was supported by the data. The subjects showed, by sending in requests for more information, that they desired strong arguments supporting their own positions or weak arguments supporting the other side. Weak arguments on one's own side and strong ones on the other side were much less in demand.

If we look at the discrepancy between the support for selective exposure found in field studies and the lack of support for it often found in laboratory studies, we see that the two situations differ in the ease with which attitudes may be maintained. The individual in a real-life situation, unless he is so deeply involved in the issue that he must know and refute opposition arguments, can usually maintain his beliefs most easily by paying attention only to information supporting his own position. In doing so, he supports the selective-exposure hypothesis. The subject in the laboratory experiment, on the other hand, is under some social pressure to become aware of arguments opposing his own position. By learning them in order to refute them, he fails to follow the selective-exposure hypothesis. From this point of view, selective exposure to supporting arguments may or may not be found, depending on the circumstances. What will be found in all cases is the resistance to attitude change which results from the individual's attempts to maintain his cognitive structure.

TIMING

When is a persuasive message most effective? Is it best to get your argument in first, before the recipient has heard the other side? Or is it better to have the last word, so that he will not have time to change his mind after hearing your message?

The answers to these questions are complex because there are two factors which interact in determining when an initial or a final presentation is most effective. These factors are the role played by initial information in the interpretation of later messages, and the course of forgetting over time. Let us consider each in turn, and then look at how they interact under various conditions.

We have already seen how perception involves the interpretation of stimulation by the perceiver. Solomon Asch investigated this process of interpretation in a variety of studies.[11] In some, he presented subjects with a quotation and asked them to interpret its meaning. Some of the subjects were told the actual author of the statement, while for others it was incorrectly attributed to a different famous person. Asch found that the interpretation of each statement was influenced by the subject's opinion of its supposed author. "A little rebellion," for example, had quite a different meaning when attributed to Thomas Jefferson or to Karl Marx.

From results such as these, Asch reasoned that similar interpretation of meaning must go on in the perception of persons. If the things we learn first about a person provide the context for interpreting later impressions, they should be especially influential in determining our impression. Asch tested this idea in a number of experiments in which subjects were asked to form an impression of a person from a list of adjectives describing him. He found that adjectives coming later in the list were interpreted in the light of those coming earlier. A word such as "humorous" has quite a different meaning when applied to a person who has already been described as "warm" than it does when applied to a person who has been described as "cold." Further studies by Kelley[12] and by Luchins[13] also demonstrated that interpretation goes on, although Luchins showed that warning the subjects not to jump to conclusions too hastily will keep them from being overly influenced by the first impression.

Asch's finding that the first message has an advantage over later ones has generally stood up in persuasion research also, if the persuasion attempt deals with a subject the recipient is uninformed on at the start of the study. This initial advantage of the first message is often overcome, however, by the longer time the subject has to forget it. We have already noted that the course of forgetting is very rapid at first, and then progressively more gradual. Suppose that a person receives a persuasive message, and then is given a counter message a week later. If he is tested immediately after receiving the counter communication, he will show a *recency effect*—that is, he will be more influenced by the second communication than by the first one. This is because he will have lost more of the effect of the original message through forgetting over the week, and will not have had any time to forget the counter message.

A *primacy effect*—greater influence from the first than from the second message—may be created by changing the time relationships a bit. If the original message is immediately followed by the counter message, and if testing of the effect is then delayed for a week, a strong primacy effect will result. In this case, forgetting will have influenced the two messages equally, and the greater initial impact of the first message will be allowed to show clearly.[14]

Now we can answer the question of whether it is better to come first or last in the attempt to persuade someone. If he will have about equally long to forget both persuasive attempts before taking the action they are trying to influence, there is a definite advantage to having the first word. If he will have slightly longer to forget the first communication than to forget the second one, the initial and final positions will be about equally desirable. Finally, one persuasive attempt may come long before the recipient's action, while the other will come just before it. In this instance it is far better to have the last word.

MENTION OF OPPOSITION ARGUMENTS

If you do come first in trying to persuade someone, should you just state your case or should you also mention opposition arguments and try to refute them? Research results so far seem to support the following generalizations:

1. If the recipient of the message does not know the other side of the case and you do not think he will be exposed to it in the future, it is most effective to mention only arguments supporting your position. If he already knows arguments opposing your position, you should attempt to refute them.[15]
2. If the recipient of your message agrees with your position but you know he will be exposed to a counter argument later, then forewarning him against that argument will often increase his resistance to it.[16]
3. The more familiar the recipient is with the counter arguments which will be used, the less help you should give him in refuting them. If he is not familiar with them, you should provide him with arguments against them. If he is familiar with them, he will best bolster his position by thinking up his own arguments against the opposition position.[17]
4. Even if you do not know what arguments will be used against the recipient's position, you can still help him resist them. Providing him with arguments against some attacks which might be made on his position will increase his resistance to persuasion even if different arguments come to be used.[18]

THE SOURCE OF THE MESSAGE

The psychologist William McDougall, who lived from 1871 to 1938, originally referred to his approach to psychology as "behaviorism." It is said that when he heard that John Watson also called his approach "behaviorism," he stated, "If he's getting on, I'm getting off," and promptly modified the name of his system. Whether or not this actually happened, it is true that there are certain people, institutions, and ideas which we desire to be associated with and others which we would rather not be. We tend, in ways described by *balance theory*, to see those to whom we are attracted as being in agreement with us, and those whom we do not care for as disagreeing with our views.[19]

This tendency of perception has important consequences for persuasion. Because imbalance is involved in disagreeing with a communicator to whom one is attracted, the recipient may change his opinions to agree with an attractive communicator. The main factors influencing the effectiveness of various communicators are, in fact, the ones we would expect them to be from balance theory. Individuals are most influenced by those they like, those whom they perceive as being expert in the field discussed, and those they perceive as similar to themselves. These three variables tend, of course, to go together. We are attracted to those we believe to be similar to ourselves, and of course we tend to perceive ourselves as holding opinions which would be supported by expert knowledge.

Another factor related to the expertise of the communicator is his disinterestedness. If he seems to have something to gain by convincing us, we may doubt that the message represents his true opinion. An interesting study on this point has been done by Walster, Aronson, and Abrahams.[20] They presented messages arguing that the courts should have either more power than they have now, or less. Each message was sometimes presented as a statement made by a district attorney and sometimes as a statement made by a convicted criminal. As predicted, messages were especially persuasive when arguing against the apparent self-interest of the communicator. The district attorney was especially effective if he argued that the courts should be made weaker, whereas "Joe the Shoulder" was especially believed when he argued that the courts should have more power.

Powerful as the immediate effects of expertise are, they are not always long-lasting. This was demonstrated in a classic study by Hovland and Weiss.[21] In it they exposed subjects to a number of persuasive messages, each one identified as coming from either an expert source or a less expert source. For three of the four messages used, the subjects who thought that the message came from the high-prestige source were more convinced by it. This effect was not lasting, however. When the subjects were tested again four weeks later, an interesting finding emerged. The subjects who had received the communication from the expert source had moved back toward their original position during the intervening time. Those who had received it from the low-credibility source showed more attitude change in the direction advocated by the message during the four-week interval. By the time of the retest, the persuasive effects of the high- and low-credibility sources were found to be equal.

Hovland and his colleagues reasoned that this strange finding might be caused by the subjects' remembering the messages and thinking less about their sources as time went on. Kelman and Hovland tested this idea in a study similar to Hovland and Weiss's, but with one important addition.[22] They found that when they reminded the subjects of the source of each message before the delayed test of attitude change, the expert source again became much more persuasive than the less expert source. These results suggest that propaganda may be effective because people remember its message longer than they remember its unreliable source, and thus find themselves more and more convinced by it with the passage of time.

THE MESSAGE AS PROPAGANDA

As we have already noted, persuasive messages try to imply that the action they advocate will enable the recipient of the message to achieve his goals, affiliate with his reference groups, express his values, and feel free from anxiety. The techniques by which this is done commonly involve the use of emotional words, unstated assumptions, and faulty logic. While the techniques are too numerous to review here, two points about the content of messages seem especially worth considering.

First, messages deceive as much by what they fail to say as by what they do say. The way a message emphasizes a certain portion of information gives other facts by implication. "I don't have school next Monday" implies that there is school all next week except Monday. A candidate for the Senate saying "I have a very high regard for your organization's goals!" implies that he will vote to pass bills that implement those goals. He may know that his party's leadership has no intention of letting any of those bills get passed for four years, but to tell you that would only ruin his campaign point, so he doesn't.[23]

Second, messages persuade largely by manipulating the context in which important facts will be interpreted. Consider, for example, a military action in which large numbers of civilians are killed. It is possible, in describing such an event, to stress the innocent nature of the victims and the hideousness of the event. Or it is possible to concentrate on the necessity of killing to carrying on warfare and the difficulty of distinguishing between enemies disguised as civilians and true civilians. Depending on how it is presented, the same incident may be seen as an atrocity or a normal part of war.

A study of this subject was done by Helge Mansson.[24] Objectively, the 1968 killing of civilians by North Vietnamese at Hue and the killing of civilians by American troops at My Lai were very similar incidents. But were they perceived as the same? Could the way in which they were perceived be manipulated by how each event was described? Using excerpts from news stories, Mansson created a high-justification and a low-justification account of each event. Two hundred subjects participated in the study. Fifty each received the high-justification account applied to Hue, the high-justification account applied to My Lai, the low-justification account applied to Hue, and the low-justification account of My Lai. After reading the account, each subject rated the event as genocide, an atrocity, terrorism, a normal war action, an isolated incident, an official policy of the power which carried out the action, or a pure propaganda story.

One result of the study is easy to anticipate. Regardless of the level of justification in the account read, American citizens see the United States as less at fault than an enemy power. Six subjects rated the Hue incident as genocide and twenty-three considered it an atrocity. No subjects saw the My Lai event as genocide, and only nine considered it an atrocity.

Some effects of the presentation were also apparent. Those who received the high-justification account of My Lai were much more likely than those receiving the low-justification account to feel, for example, that the civilians involved were at least partially responsible for their own deaths.

Ego defense, however, limited the extent to which the subjects could change their attitudes as a result of the messages. To a very great extent, they rejected information about the My Lai incident, rating press releases as much less reliable about it than about Hue. It is really quite striking that any effect of the messages could be observed, since the subjects had both some knowledge of the events before participating in the study and very strong reasons for wanting to believe certain things regardless of the content of the messages read. When the communicator has control over a greater portion of the information the recipient receives on an issue, manipulation of the context can cause a greater change in how an event is interpreted than was seen in this study.

SELF-PERSUASION

In discussing forewarning, we noted that a person who has been warned that his beliefs will come under attack bolsters them by thinking up new arguments to support his position. This activity on the recipient's part is probably one of the main reasons why discussions often have little impact on a person's position. In many discussions, each person spends the time while the other person is talking in thinking of new arguments to strengthen his own position rather than in listening to the other person's statements. Under these circumstances, it is not surprising that each may come away from the discussion more convinced than ever of the rightness of his views.

If this is true, the most effective means of persuasion should be those which cause the recipient to think of arguments opposing his position rather than those supporting it. One way of doing this is suggested by dissonance theory. If you can induce a person to act in a way which is counter to his beliefs, he may change his beliefs in order to justify his actions.

Another possibility is suggested in research by McGuire. He reasoned that people usually hold inconsistent beliefs, often of a wish-fulfilling nature. It is possible for them to do so partly because they do not think about them at the same time. If this is so, then just inducing them to consider the beliefs together might lead to an increase in the consistency of their views.

In a series of related studies, McGuire demonstrated that this was the case.[25] His basic design involved giving people questionnaires containing elements of syllogisms and asking them to assign probabilities to the statements. Inconsistency was shown by assigning the conclusion of the syllogism a probability lower than the product of the probabilities of the two premises. Let us consider an example.

Suppose that you consider it highly likely that the public health authorities will stop anything that seriously threatens public health. Suppose that you also believe that the beaches in your city are so polluted that swimming there constitutes a serious threat to public health. From these two premises, it follows that the public health authorities will probably stop the swimming at the beaches. If you enjoy swimming at the beaches, it is quite possible that you will not believe this conclusion even though you believe the two premises that lead to it.

Testing the initial beliefs of his subjects, McGuire found that the extent to which they believed the conclusion of a syllogism was only partially related to the extent to which they believed its premises. Their acceptance of any conclusion was also related to how desirable that conclusion seemed to them. That is, the subjects believed that desirable events would take place and that undesirable ones would not to a greater extent than was justified by their belief in the premises the events might follow from.

McGuire then tested the beliefs of the subjects a second time a week later. Although the subjects had not been exposed to any persuasive attempt, their beliefs were significantly more consistent than they had been before. Apparently, just answering the questionnaire the first time made them more aware of inconsistencies and caused them to change their attitudes in order to eliminate them. In a process similar to that involved in psychotherapy, the subjects had become more logically consistent.

These results suggest that asking questions may be one of the most effective ways of bringing about attitude change. It is very difficult for an unrealistic set of beliefs about the world to be consistent, for experience constantly provides observations which do not fit the preconceived ideas. If an individual can be made to examine his beliefs rather than to feel threatened and made to defend them, he can develop more realistic views of the world.

MEMBERSHIP GROUPS AND REFERENCE GROUPS

Most of human life is lived in groups. A person is not socialized by society, educated by a school, or introduced into the world of work by a company. Instead, his experiences are with a family, a series of school classes, and a work crew or office staff. His conception of who he is depends primarily on how these groups view him, and the pressures which they bring to bear on him are the strongest forces in changing or maintaining his attitudes.

There may be differences, however, between the groups to which a person actually belongs and those he cares about. Those he belongs to may have some influence on him even without his caring about them, for he may not realize that the ideas which he obtains from them are not shared by other groups to which he aspires. Those he aspires to may influence him to the extent that he knows what they believe, but their influence will be limited by his knowledge of their beliefs. A study by Ellis illustrates this, and illustrates, as well, another way in which group membership can influence an individual—the devastating effects of group rejection.[26]

Ellis's study was done at Stanford University. As is well known, Stanford is an institution with very high academic standards and equally high tuition fees. Both these factors tend to skew the distribution of students attending the school in terms of their social origins. Not only must students come from quite wealthy families to be able to pay Stanford tuition; they must also be able to meet the entrance requirements. Wealthy suburban schools and private preparatory schools give their students an education which makes them much more likely to get into Stanford than they would be if they had attended, for example, a public school in a ghetto. The result is that it is primarily individuals from upper-middle- and upper-class backgrounds who go to Stanford. About ten years ago, when Ellis did his study, he found that only 11 percent of Stanford students came from a lower-middle-class or working-class background. The vast majority of the American population, of course, falls into these categories.

Some students, however, obtain scholarships to Stanford. These scholarships account for the 1 percent of Stanford students who come from a working-class background. What sort of people are they, and what happens to them when they reach Stanford?

The scholarship students are an even more highly selected group than most Stanford students. The average scholarship student was not only at the top of his high school class in terms of grades and aptitude scores; he was also a recognized student leader. Often he was either the captain of the football team or the president of the student body. Sometimes he was both.

Furthermore, he had prepared for Stanford in another way. Aspiring to become a Stanford student, he had to some extent taken on attitudes typical of the social groups who attend that school. This *anticipatory socialization* was limited, however, by his knowledge of those groups. When he arrived at Stanford, he was in for two severe shocks.

The first was that the work was more difficult than he had imagined. Coming from a school in which he had been competing with some students who had academic aspirations and some who hadn't, he was unprepared for the competition in an institution with a highly selected student body. Even more devastating, he was usually rejected by the other students. The anticipatory socialization was not adequate to make him fit in with the upper-middle-class students at Stanford, and he was significantly more likely to be identified as a social isolate by his dormitory counselor.

Even though the scholarship students had been selected because they had outstandingly healthy personalities and were student leaders, they developed personality problems at Stanford. Rejected by the other students, significantly more of the scholarship students were identified as personally disturbed by the time they graduated. Even a well-adjusted individual may be seriously upset by group rejection. Fortunately, many of the scholarship students who did graduate went on to graduate schools. There they were more likely to find reference groups which would value their intellectual achievements regardless of their social attitudes.

GROUP ACCEPTANCE

While rejection by an important reference group has devastating effects upon the individual, acceptance into a group holding different beliefs and values from those of the individual may be an important source of attitude change. This is dramatically illustrated in a study carried out by Newcomb at Bennington College from 1935 to 1939. Bennington was, at that time, a very atypical academic institution, for the faculty believed that "one of the foremost duties of the college was to acquaint its somewhat oversheltered students with the nature of their contemporary social world."[27] While the women at Bennington, like the Stanford students in Ellis's study, came from prosperous and politically conservative homes, they encountered, unlike the Stanford students, a faculty who saw it as their social duty to communicate to them their own progressive political beliefs.

In performing this duty, they were apparently very successful, for the political views of the women changed a great deal while they were at Bennington. This is best illustrated by the way in which women who had been at the school varying numbers of years voted in a mock presidential election in 1936. While 62 percent of the freshmen supported the Republican candidate, a proportion which reflects the political preferences of the families from which they had come, the percentage fell to only 14 percent for those women who had been at the school more than two years. These results are illustrated in Table 9-1.

The dramatic change shown by students at Bennington was probably largely due to its being a small, isolated, and cohesive community. The student body at that time numbered only about 250 women, and the college community was so self-sufficient that there was no need for the students to go off campus—it had its own store, post office, beauty parlor, and recreational facilities. These conditions all favored the development of the college community as the major reference group for the students.

Nevertheless, not all of the students changed their attitudes. A comparison of those who did and those who did not will give some indication of what the change process was. When they arrived at Bennington, women from politically conservative families were faced with a conflict between the attitudes of their parents and those of

Table 9-1   *Votes in the mock election (in percent)*

VOTED FOR	FRESHMEN	VOTE BY JUNIORS AND SENIORS
Republican	62	14
Democrat	29	54
Socialist or Communist	9	30

SOURCE: Newcomb[28]

their teachers and friends. This conflict could be resolved in a number of different ways.

In general, it is satisfying to find that those we like agree with us on important issues and disturbing to find that they disagree with us. For Bennington women who were attached to both their parents and the college community, it would be disturbing that they would need to disagree with one or the other on political issues.

One way of dealing with the conflict would be to remain unaware of it. Some women did this. Some, who had a few close friends who shared their own conservative political beliefs, managed to remain unaware of how few people at Bennington agreed with their views. Others adopted Bennington's more progressive ideology but did not realize how strongly their parents disagreed with this point of view.

Another possible solution is *differentiation*. In differentiation, a part of an attitude object is split off from the rest and evaluated differently. It is the solution suggested by statements such as, "It's always a pleasure to talk to Bob except when he talks about fishing." The negatively evaluated fishing Bob is split off from the rest of him, and it is possible to reject this portion of him while accepting the rest.

There were two ways in which the Bennington woman could resolve her conflict by differentiation. One was to decide that Bennington was a wonderful place in all other ways, but that the people there had some rather weird ideas about politics which just had to be disregarded. The other way was to decide that one loved one's parents but that they had lived sheltered lives and did not understand about politics, so their ideas on that subject simply had to be ignored. Each of these solutions was used by some Bennington women to deal with their imbalanced cognitions.

Whether or not any given Bennington woman changed her political opinions, then, depended on how she related to her parents and to the college community. If she accepted her parents as a reference group for politics and limited her participation in college political activities, she remained politically conservative. If she rejected her parents or accepted them but not as a reference group for politics, she was able to participate in campus political interests and to take on a new set of political attitudes.

One of the things which makes the Bennington study so interesting is that Newcomb did a long-term follow-up of the women after they left the school.[29] Twenty years after they graduated, he managed to find and interview almost every one of the women who had participated in the original study for three or more years. The results are quite striking.

Most people would expect that when the women left Bennington, they would go back to the attitudes held by their families and by themselves before going to college. At most, it might be expected that they would become old liberals—maintaining attitudes which had been liberal in 1940 but failing to develop comparably liberal positions on contemporary issues. Neither of these was the outcome. The majority of the women not only had maintained the progressive orientation which they had developed at Bennington—they had adopted comparably liberal positions on contemporary issues. They favored Medicare, for example, and the admission of mainland China to the United Nations.

This result was even more striking, considering the fact that most of them were rather well off financially. Three-quarters of the women had incomes of over $20,000 per year in the early 1960s, and two-thirds of those who were parents had paid tuition to send their children to private schools. Their voting pattern, however, was very different from that of most people with these financial characteristics. In the United States generally, 75 percent of the voters with the income and religious preferences of the Bennington graduates chose Nixon over Kennedy in the presidential race of 1960. Yet, of the Bennington graduates, only 40 percent preferred Nixon. Furthermore, that 40 percent was largely made up of those women who had been most politically conservative when they left Bennington.

The relationship between political orientation while at Bennington and presidential vote in 1960 is shown in Table 9-2. While the women were at Bennington, they took an attitude test of political and economic progressivism, or PEP for short. If they are divided into the quarter of the sample who were most progressive, next-most-progressive, and so on through the quarter of the sample who were most conservative while at Bennington, it is apparent that the test predicted their vote twenty years later quite well. Of those who were least conservative while at Bennington, only three out of thirty-three voted for Nixon twenty years later. Of those who were most conservative while at Bennington, twenty-two out of thirty-three

Table 9–2 *Presidential preferences in 1960, according to quartiles of PEP scores on leaving college in the late 1930s*

PEP QUARTILE	NIXON PREFERRED	KENNEDY PREFERRED	TOTAL
1 (least conservative)	3	30	33
2	8	25	33
3	18	13	31
4 (most conservative)	22	11	33
Total	51	79	130

SOURCE: Newcomb[30]

voted for Nixon. Under the conditions of Newcomb's research, attitude tests really can predict behavior.

The interesting question, though, is why the women changed less in the twenty years after leaving Bennington than they did in their four years at college. The answer again seems to lie in how they related to their reference groups. While at Bennington, the majority of the women had been placed in an environment where their previous political beliefs had little support. After leaving Bennington, they were able to select groups which supported their political ideology. Especially important in this respect were the men they married, for the family is one of the most important reference groups for most people.

The husbands of the women who went to Bennington turned out to be an unusual group. They had highly paid jobs, and half of them had gone to Ivy League colleges, yet to a great extent they shared their wives' political preferences. There was even a highly significant correlation between each husband's voting record over the period from 1940 to 1960 and his wife's political-progressivism score before marriage. By selecting husbands who agreed with their political beliefs, the Bennington women were able to form reference groups which supported those beliefs after they left Bennington. Even though they also found support from political groups outside the home, women who married conservative men were much more likely to become more conservative themselves. On the whole, the Bennington women maintained the political attitudes which they had acquired at college because those attitudes caused them to select reference groups which maintained them in political progressivism.

SOCIAL NORMS

Some of the attitude change which Newcomb observed in the original Bennington study would probably have taken place even if the students had related to one another only as isolated individuals. The forces toward change were greatly increased, however, by their interacting in small, informal groups. When members of a group reach a decision on how a situation should be reacted to, the resulting norm becomes a powerful influence on its members. Let us look at how norms are formed and why they are so influential.

As we have already noted, a norm is an expectation which applies to all members of a group and is enforced by sanctions. Norms are powerful largely because members of the group will usually enforce them whether they are personally happy with them or not. Consider, as one early study did, the question of whether a student-living organization should serve white bread or whole wheat bread. Initially, a sizable proportion of the group favored each alternative. Eventually, after much discussion, the matter was decided by taking a vote. Because the group members believed in abiding by a majority decision, the vast majority then came to favor the alternative which had won the vote.

If someone had immediately tried to reopen the question of what kind of bread should be served, he probably would have met with considerable hostility. This suggests that one of the main reasons why group members abide by and enforce group decisions is to avoid the conflict which would result from always reopening every question. The power which this gives to norms is illustrated in a study by Merei.[31]

Merei first observed boys in a free play situation and noted that each spontaneous group tended to be dominated by one boy. When this boy made a suggestion, it was carried out. If he took a toy from another boy, his action might be resisted by the boy he was taking it from, but would not be resisted by other group members.

Merei then formed the less dominant boys into small groups from which the dominant boys were excluded. Each group was allowed to meet for several hours in a special room where new toys were available. By the end of this time, they had developed favorite games which they played with the toys.

Each formerly dominant boy was then reintroduced into his group. Instead of being able to assert his dominance as before, he was now forced to conform to its traditions. He engaged in the activities which the group had established in his absence, but his own suggestions were either ignored or modified to conform to the group norms. Because all members of each group defended its traditions, very few of the formerly dominant boys were able to reestablish themselves in authority over their groups.

Once a group norm has been established, it is highly resistant to change. Individuals who privately disagree with the norm may publicly conform to it, with the result that all members of the group underestimate how widespread the dissatisfaction is. Consequently, group members may go on conforming to a norm which no longer represents majority sentiment in the group.

This characteristic of norms results in the paradoxical situation that it is sometimes easier to change groups of people than it is to change individuals. One member of a group may resist change because of believing that he would be negatively sanctioned for going against the group norm. If the entire group can be led to discuss the norm, each individual who wants to change can get the support of seeing others start to change also. This was demonstrated in a series of studies by Lewin and his colleagues, in which it was found that food preferences could be changed more effectively through group-decision techniques than through individual-persuasion situations.[32] The present-day group-dynamics movement originated in these studies.

SOCIAL CHANGE THROUGH NORM FORMATION

From the point of view of the person who is trying to carry out persuasion, deciding that individual attitudes are often determined by group norms merely pushes the problem back one more step. If individual attitudes can be changed by changing group norms, how can group norms be changed? Let us look at some examples and see if we can get some hints as to the answer to this question.

The student who goes from class to class is exposed each day to one of the problems of university organization. Each academic field is taught as if no other field existed. Lectures in psychology contradict principles given in anthropology, while those in economics do not agree with either. Each faculty member's knowledge of related disciplines is about as many years out of date as his college degree, and the student is left to try to make sense out of the resulting confusion. Isn't there any way in which a university might encourage faculty members to learn more about fields other than their own?

The problem is essentially one of norm formation. For administrative purposes, faculty members need to be assigned to units of fairly small size. Each of these units develops norms which will facilitate the achievement of individual and group goals. Individuals are then rewarded or punished to the extent to which they conform to the group norms. If the school is a small one and has a department of general social science, generalists will best conform to the norms and will be most rewarded. If the school is huge and has an entire administrative unit devoted, for example, to survey-sampling techniques, the person whose work is most narrowly specialized in this area will be the one who is most rewarded. Changing the structure of the organization will change the norms. If a large university is divided into a number of small colleges, the departments will be small enough so that each can be given a broader scope. This will solve the problem of overspecialization but will create different problems in its turn. However the core of an administrative unit is defined, there are some areas of inquiry which will be marginal to that definition and which will be slighted by the developing norms. In a department of biochemistry, it is the general biologist who becomes the marginal man.

This example suggests an answer to our question of how to create different social norms. It is largely done by combining people into groups in various ways so that particular concerns will become central to each group. That such structuring can be effective shows that much social change is essentially a process of creating new coalitions. The dean who changes the administrative structure of the university, the union organizer who tries to convince workers that they have much to gain by banding together despite their differences, and the sensitivity trainer who brings together a new group for the purpose of personal development all have in common that they are trying to change people by combining them in ways which will favor the development of certain norms.

We have suggested that the goals of any organized group will be partly those which it was officially organized to carry out and partly personal goals of its members. An academic department can again serve as an example. Most departments are organized primarily for teaching, with research playing a much more minor role. Individual faculty members, however, know that research publication is what counts if they should ever want to move to another job. Because they do not want to be dependent upon one employer for the rest of their lives, they, as a group, redefine their purposes. By giving major weight to research publication when evaluating one another, they make it possible for each of them to pursue his individual goals as well as the official goals of the organization. Ego defense being what it is, this is usually accomplished by ideological development which stresses that the best researchers make the best teachers.

Implicit in this discussion is the importance which the instrumental function plays in attitude development. The extent to which individuals adopt organizational goals, for example, will depend largely on whether they perceive those goals as being compatible with their own personal goals. The most crucial role of persuasive communication in attitude change may well lie in persuading individuals that group activities will or will not enable them to achieve personal goals.

One of the most striking demonstrations of how perceived instrumentality may be manipulated to bring about personal change was carried out by Muzafer and Carolyn Sherif in a series of studies at a boys' camp.[33] In the first stage of the research, they observed which boys were starting to form friendships with which other boys. Next, they set up two clubs within the camp, assigning boys to them in such a way as to separate as many of the newfound friends as possible. This was done so that the results in the next stage of ingroup formation would clearly not be caused by the assignment of friends to the same group initially.

The second stage was that of ingroup formation. This was carried out by giving the two clubs separate living quarters and by staging series of competitive games and contests between them. In each of the contests, the winning team was given a reward—such as ice cream—while the losing team got nothing. This structured the situation in such a way that the members of a person's own team facilitated his achievement of personal goals, whereas the members of the other club frustrated his goal achievement. As would be expected from the instrumental function of attitudes, this resulted in the boys' developing positive attitudes toward members of their own club and negative attitudes toward members of the other team. Although

roughly two-thirds of friendship choices were of members of the opposite club at the start of stage two, over nine-tenths of the
friendship choices were of members of one's own club by the end of
this stage.

In fact, the experiment created many of the phenomena of
group prejudice. The members of each club developed norms glorify-
ing members of their club and vilifying members of the other one.
They put up posters expressing hostility toward members of the
other group, and sometimes expressed that hostility in a more direct
manner, such as by smearing the other group's eating table with
honey and other food. Each club also developed distorted perceptions which exaggerated its own achievements. The Sherifs found
great differences in the perception of how long a tug-of-war lasted,
for example. The losing team thought that it had held out for a very
long time before being defeated, while the winners believed that
they had overpowered the other team in no time at all.

Just as perceived instrumentality was able to create hostility between the clubs, it was also able to make the members become
friends again. To do this, the Sherifs created a series of situations in
which an important goal could be achieved only by the cooperative
efforts of the two groups. In one case, the water supply of the camp
"broke down" and the members of both clubs needed to find where
the pipe was broken before either would have water. In another, the
truck used to bring food from town failed to start and needed to be
pushed and pulled by the combined efforts of all the boys to start the
engine. Eventually, such techniques succeeded in bringing the
groups together again, although in one of the experiments an athletic
competition with another camp was required to completely overcome the effects of stage two.

REDEFINITION OF IDENTITY

Regardless of how they are carried out, major changes in attitude involve a redefinition of identity on the part of the person whose attitude is changing. In the Sherifs' study, for example, the boys took on
the new identities of "Red Devils" and "Bull Dogs," which they had
never had before going to camp. Let us review two other ways in
which we have seen identity being changed.

One way is through the interpretation of what a person is feeling. In Schachter and Singer's research, we saw how physiological

arousal is given a different interpretation in different contexts.[34] A similar process is probably involved in much religious and political conversion. Both political and religious persuasion is often carried out under conditions designed to create high stress for a long period of time. This stress will result in the type of physiological activation utilized by Schachter and Singer in their study. By the use of an appropriate message, the stress can be interpreted to the listener as patriotic fervor, hatred of the establishment, or the stirring of the voice of conscience. If the hearer does experience conversion, and if this is followed by sufficient group support to prevent backsliding, he may then reinterpret his previous life as a leading up to, and preparation for, his new identity.

The other way in which identity may be manipulated is through the use of dissonance forces. As we saw in looking at the Walster and Prestholdt study in the chapter on personality development, individuals change their attitudes to justify their actions.[35] In fact, the less justification they have for having engaged in the action, the stronger the force toward attitude change will be. This means that a person's conception of himself may be manipulated by getting him to engage in an action for which he has little justification. A study by Zimbardo and his coworkers illustrates this very nicely.[36]

We have already noted that individuals are generally persuaded more easily by communicators to whom they are more attracted than by those to whom they are less attracted. Let us now consider a somewhat different situation. Suppose that two people both engaged in an action which was distasteful to them, one in response to a request by a person he found attractive and the other in response to a request from a less congenial individual. The one who had been influenced by the attractive communicator would experience little dissonance. Although he might have found the action which he engaged in distasteful, he could always justify his behavior by saying he did it because he liked the person who asked him to do it. The person who engaged in the action and lacked that justification would experience more dissonance. He might have few ways of justifying his behavior other than deciding he enjoyed it after all.

Zimbardo et al. used this type of situation to change attitudes toward a much-disliked food. In their experiment, they exposed the subjects to a persuasive communication on the eating of survival foods. For half the subjects, the communicator presented his best qualities so that they would find him attractive; for the other half, he accentuated his undesirable characteristics so that they would find him quite unattractive.

Following the persuasive message, each subject was asked in private by a different communicator to eat a survival food—a fried grasshopper. About equal numbers of subjects did so in each of the attractiveness conditions. As predicted, those who had heard the attractive communicator liked the grasshoppers as little as they had expected to, and the group who had heard the unattractive communicator changed their attitudes and came to like fried grasshoppers better than they had before. Because the identity of a person who would eat something horrible to please someone he didn't like was unattractive to him, each subject took on the new identity of fried-grasshopper-liker.

Because we are constantly called on to act in the absence of sufficient information, dissonance processes have pervasive effects on what we believe and how we view ourselves. In impression-formation studies, for example, they will often cause a primacy effect. If the subject is called on to rate the stimulus person before receiving all information about him, the mere act of making the rating will make him more committed to his initial impression than he would otherwise be. In the area of organizational policy, the effects can be even more important. Once a policy decision is made, the processes which the decision maker uses to justify his action to himself will often blind him to the shortcomings of that policy when new evidence comes in. This process has been well documented by de Rivera in his examination of foreign policy decision making.[37]

Lest this seem too discouraging, it should be noted that attitude change through dissonance processes, like ego-defense mechanisms, can only work if the individual keeps certain aspects of himself from consciousness. The person who was fully aware of his own motives, for example, would eat the grasshopper only if he wanted to. He would suffer no dissonance and would not change his attitudes.

We see, then, that there are at least three ways of changing people's attitudes by creating new identities for them. They can be given new identities by creating new social groups, by reinterpreting what they are feeling, or by changing their behavior in the hope that attitude change will follow. Regardless of how the redefinition of identity is brought about, it is a major aspect of every important social movement. Consider, for example, the following song, written by Meredith Tax. It raises fundamental questions about the nature and origins of male and female identities in our culture, and doing so through the powerfully interpretive agencies of poetry and song it manages in a minimum of words to describe all three of the identity-changing methods we have discussed above.

There Was A Young Woman Who Swallowed A Lie[38]

Tune: There Was An Old Woman Who Swallowed A Fly

There was a young woman who swallowed a lie,
We all know why she swallowed that lie,
Perhaps she'll die.

There was a young woman who swallowed a rule,
"Live to serve others," she learned it in school.
She swallowed the rule to hold up the lie,
We all know why she swallowed that lie,
Perhaps she'll die.

There was a young woman who swallowed some fluff,
Lipstick and candy and powder and puff.
She swallowed the fluff to sweeten the rule,
She swallowed the rule to hold up the lie,
We all know why she swallowed that lie,
Perhaps she'll die.

There was a young woman who swallowed a line,
"I like 'em dumb, baby, you suit me fine."
She swallowed the line to tie up the fluff, . . .

There was a young woman who swallowed a pill,
Might have said "no," but she hadn't the will.
She swallowed the pill to go with the line, . . .

There was a young woman who swallowed a ring,
Looked like a princess and felt like a thing.
She swallowed the ring to make up for the pill, . . .

There was a young woman who swallowed some Spock
"Stay at home mother, take care of your flock."
She swallowed the Spock to go with the ring, . . .

One day this young woman woke up and she said
"I've swallowed so much that I wish I were dead
I swallowed it all to go with the Spock
I swallowed the Spock to go with the ring
I swallowed the ring to make up for the pill
I swallowed the pill to go with the line
I swallowed the line to tie up the fluff

I swallowed the fluff to sweeten the rule
I swallowed the rule to hold up the lie
Why in the world did I swallow that lie?
Perhaps I'll die."

She ran to her sister, it wasn't too late
To be liberated, regurgitate.
She threw up the Spock and she threw up the ring
Looked like a princess and felt like a thing
She threw up the pill and she threw up the line
"I like 'em dumb, baby, you suit me fine."
She threw up the fluff and she threw up the rule
"Live to serve others," she learned it in school
And last, but not least, she threw up the lie
We all know why she threw up that lie
SHE WILL NOT DIE!

Summary

A description of a person's beliefs, attitudes, and values reveals a large segment of his perceived world. Man responds to the world in terms of his ideas about it. Those ideas that are called attitudes refer to broad-ranging phenomena of importance to the individual. They are organized and are reasonably internally consistent. Opinions are ideas which do not follow from a larger cognitive framework and which can be isolated from, and inconsistent with, one's more organized attitudes. A person tends to have opinions, not attitudes, about things he has not thought much about.

As motivators of action, attitudes can tell us something about how a person is likely to react to future situations. This is only true, however, under certain conditions. The person must be aware of his attitude and willing to communicate it to us. The situation in which his behavior is shown must also be relatively free of pressures which might cause him to act in ways which go against his attitude.

The function which attitudes serve, that of organizing the individual's world and giving him a meaningful place in it, implies that when his world changes, he will modify his attitudes in such a way as to re-create meaningfulness. This may require great overall change in specific parts of his beliefs. He will generally restructure his attitudes to make them positive toward people and things which can help him achieve his goals, reinforce his values, conform to his expectations, and reduce his anxiety. People who wish to change the attitudes of others can best do this by finding out what functions the existing attitudes serve for the people who hold them. Designing the change so that these needs will still be met will greatly reduce resistance to change.

Persuasion by appealing to the needs described above is often characterized by the use of emotion-laden words, unstated assumptions, and faulty logic. People who do not want their attitudes changed can learn to recognize such techniques of persuasion. A further technique of persuasion is manipulation of the context in which information is interpreted. The more control the persuader has over the sources of information available, the more difficult it is to avoid his intended effect.

People can change their attitudes themselves by thinking up arguments for the opposing point of view. We do this, for example, to reduce dissonance if we find ourselves acting in a way which conflicts with an existing attitude. If two of our attitudes, which we have kept apart so that we could be comfortable with inconsistencies between them, are then brought together, we may develop new attitudes as a way of dealing with the inconsistencies. We may also spontaneously change our attitudes to make them more realistic. This is easier to do if we are not threatened and thus motivated to defend our attitudes merely to defend our self-identities.

We gain our attitudes partially by our association with groups which we care about. Not only our attitudes but our very feelings of identity depend on some congruence between our attitudes toward ourselves and others' attitudes toward us. The attitudes which others hold toward us may influence us, even if we are not aware of them, by influencing how the others act toward us.

A characteristic peculiar to group behavior is the norm, an expectation which applies to all members of the group and which is enforced by sanctions. In function, it reduces the possible number of conflicts due to differences between members. It is as if well-established groups were able to declare certain things lifted—by habit, tradition, or parliamentary procedure—to a different plane of existence where individual attitudes no longer apply. An environmentally caused change in habit or tradition or a different election outcome can change the norms, but while they are in force they are highly resistant to change by individuals.

So interrelated are one's attitudes and one's identity that changing one drastically affects the other. Moreover, change can be initiated from either direction.

Notes and Acknowledgments

1. Ware, Caroline F. *Greenwich Village, 1920–1930.* New York: Harper & Row, Publishers, 1965. First published by Houghton Mifflin Company, 1935.
2. Agger, R. E., D. Goldrich, and B. Swanson. *The Rulers and the Ruled, Political Power and Impotence in American Communities.* New York: John Wiley & Sons, Inc., 1964.
3. A highly readable description of standard techniques of attitude measurement may be found in Allen Edwards, *Techniques of Attitude Scale Construction.* New York: Appleton-Century-Crofts, Inc., 1957.

    A more comprehensive treatment is William A. Scott, "Attitude Measurement," in Gardner Lindzey and Elliot Aronson (Eds.), *Handbook of Social Psychology.* (2d ed.) Reading, Mass.: Addison-Wesley Publishing Co., Inc., 1969 (2), pp. 204–356.
4. Goodmonson, Courtney Weldon. "Donation of organs for transplantation: An investigation of attitudes and behavior." A thesis submitted in partial fulfillment of the requirements for the degree of Master of Science in Psychology, Portland State University, 1970.
5. This fourfold breakdown represents a modification of a set of categories originally proposed by Daniel Katz, "The functional approach to the study of attitudes." *Public Opinion Quarterly.* 1960 (24), pp. 163–204.
6. For an excellent account of Hitler's appeal written immediately after his rise to power, see H. Cantril, *The Psychology of Social Movements.* New York: John Wiley & Sons, Inc., 1963.
7. See chap. 9, "The Legend of Hitler's Childhood," in Erik H. Erikson, *Childhood and Society.* (2d ed.) New York: W. W. Norton & Company, Inc., 1963.
8. Rosenberg, Milton. "An analysis of affective-cognitive consistency," in M. J. Rosenberg and C. I. Hovland (Eds.), *Attitude Organization and Change.* New Haven, Conn.: Yale University Press, 1960, chap. 2.
9. Ewing, T. N. "A study of certain factors involved in changes of opinion." *Journal of Social Psychology,* 1942 (16), pp. 63–88.
10. Lowin, A. "Approach and avoidance: Alternative modes of selective exposure to information." *Journal of Personality and Social Psychology,* 1967 (6), pp. 1–9.
11. Asch, Solomon E. "Forming impressions of personality." *Journal of Abnormal and Social Psychology,* 1946 (41), pp. 258–290.
12. Kelley, H. H. "The warm-cold variable in first impressions of persons." *Journal of Personality,* 1950 (18), pp. 431–439.
13. Luchins, Abraham S. "Primacy-recency in impression formation," in Carl Hovland (Ed.), *Yale Studies in Attitude and Communication.* Vol. I. *The*

Order of Presentation in Persuasion. New Haven, Conn.: Yale University Press, 1957, chap. 4.

14. Miller, N., and D. T. Campbell. "Recency and primacy in persuasion as a function of the timing of speeches and measurements." *Journal of Abnormal and Social Psychology*, 1959 (59), pp. 1–9.

15. Hovland, Carl I., Irving L. Janis, and Harold H. Kelley. *Communication and Persuasion*. New Haven, Conn.: Yale University Press, 1953.

16. Kiesler, C. A., and S. B. Kiesler. "Role of forewarning in persuasive communications." *Journal of Abnormal and Social Psychology*, 1964 (68), pp. 547–549.

    Freedman, J. L., and D. O. Sears. "Warning, distraction, and resistance to influence." *Journal of Personality and Social Psychology*, 1965 (1), pp. 262–266.

17. Freedman, J. L., and D. O. Sears. Op. cit.

18. McGuire, W. J. "Persistence of the resistance to persuasion induced by various types of prior belief defenses." *Journal of Abnormal and Social Psychology*, 1962 (64), pp. 241–248.

19. For a good description of balance theories, see Roger Brown, "Models of attitude change." *New Directions in Psychology*. New York: Holt, Rinehart and Winston, Inc., 1962.

20. Walster, E., E. Aronson, and D. Abrahams. "On increasing the persuasiveness of a low prestige communicator." *Journal of Experimental Social Psychology*, 1966 (2), pp. 325–342.

21. Hovland, C. I., and W. Weiss. "The influence of source credibility on communication effectiveness." *Public Opinion Quarterly*, 1951 (15), pp. 635–650.

22. Kelman, H. C., and C. I. Hovland. " 'Reinstatement' of the communicator in delayed measurement of opinion change." *Journal of Abnormal and Social Psychology*, 1953 (48) pp. 327–335.

23. *The Propaganda Game*, a WFF 'N PROOF "Game for Thinkers," P.O. Box 71, New Haven, Conn., shows many ways messages mislead.

24. Mansson, Helge Hilding. "The morality of massacres: Song My and Hue." Paper presented at the 1970 Western Psychological Association convention.

25. McGuire, W. J. "A syllogistic analysis of cognitive relationships," in M. J. Rosenberg and C. I. Hovland (Eds.), *Attitude Organization and Change*. New Haven, Conn.: Yale University Press, 1960, pp. 65–111.

26. Ellis, Robert A. "The cognitive failure of the upwardly mobile." Paper presented at the West Coast Conference for Small Group Research, 1964.

27. Newcomb, Theodore M. "Attitude development as a function of reference groups," in E. Maccoby et al. (Eds.), *Readings in Social Psychology*. New York: Holt, Rinehart and Winston, Inc., 1958, pp. 265–275.

28. Ibid., p. 266. By permission of the publisher.

29. Newcomb, Theodore M. "Persistence and regression of changed attitudes: Long-range studies." *Journal of Social Issues*. October 1963 (19), pp. 3–14.

30. Ibid., p. 7. By permission of the author and publisher.
31. Merei, Ferenc. "Group leadership and institutionalization." *Human Relations*, 1949 (2), pp. 23–39.
32. Lewin, Kurt. "Group decision and social change," in E. Maccoby et al. (Eds.), op. cit., pp. 197–211.
33. Sherif, Muzafer, and Carolyn W. Sherif. *Social Psychology.* New York: Harper & Row, Publishers, 1969. A summary of the most basic part of the Sherifs' research which we discuss may be found in David F. Wrench (Ed.), *Readings in Psychology: Foundations and Applications.* New York: McGraw-Hill Book Company, 1971, pp. 300–311.
34. Schachter, S., and J. Singer. "Cognitive, social, and physiological determinants of emotional state." *Psychological Review*, 1962 (69), no. 5, pp. 379–399.
35. Walster, E., and P. Prestholdt. "The effect of misjudging another: Overcompensation or dissonance reduction?" *Journal of Experimental Social Psychology*, 1966 (2), pp. 325–342.
36. Zimbardo, Philip G., Matisyohu Weisenberg, Ira Firestone, and Burton Levy. "Communicator effectiveness in producing public conformity and private attitude change." *Journal of Personality*, 1965 (33), no. 2, pp. 233–255.
37. de Rivera, Joseph H. *The Psychological Dimension of Foreign Policy.* Columbus, Ohio: Charles E. Merrill Books, Inc., 1968.
38. Copyright © 1970 by Meredith Tax. Text as in *Sing Out!*, vol. 20, #3, Jan./Feb. 1971, p. 17. Used by permission of Meredith Tax.

TEN

PREJUDICE

Introduction

It has been noted that racism has a history, a politics, and a psychology. This chapter is entitled "Prejudice" rather than "Racism" because it concentrates especially on the psychological processes involved in denying humanity to others while expressing aggression against them. These processes are much the same whether the target population consists of Indians, women, blacks, or the members of the other team in the Sherifs' studies of boys' camps.[1]

That similar psychological processes are involved in these different cases of prejudice should not blind us to the fact that each of them has its own unique politics and history, and that different behaviors are enacted toward members of different minority groups. These behaviors cannot be understood in terms of individual psychological processes alone, but must be understood also in terms of social and cultural institutions which result in the exploitation or extermination of peoples. The processes of perceptual distortion which were once the main phenomenon studied under the topic of prejudice cannot account for what happened to the Jews in Nazi Germany, the Indians on the American frontier, and black Americans both before and after the ending of slavery. Let us look, therefore, at the history and politics of white racism as an example, before turning to the more general question of the psychological processes involved in prejudice.

THE HISTORY OF WHITE RACISM

Man's ancestors have been hunting, gathering, and making tools from stone for two million years. They have been indistinguishable from contemporary man in terms of skeletal remains for approximately 60,000 years.

During this long history, there have been many technological changes which have had a major impact on man's way of life and on the population density which he was able to attain. The domestication of grains, the smelting of metals, the achievement of the complex social organization of the city, and the discovery that the chemical energy of fossil fuels could be converted into kinetic energy through the use of a Newcomben engine, for example, have all brought about profound transformations in the relationship of man to his environment.

Many of these changes took place so early that we have little way of discovering their history. Moreover, because so few of the world's potential archaeological sites have yet been excavated, there is much history that we may someday know but do not know yet. The relationship of the agricultural revolution and the evolution of cities probably falls into that category. We do know, however, that cities evolved independently at least five times in man's history—at one location in China, two in the Near East, and two in the Americas. Because the location and excavation of early cities have barely been begun, it is quite probable that we may someday discover other instances of the independent origin of cities as well as learning more about the combination of circumstances which made the development of the city possible. Such new learning is made the more likely because the complex social organization of the city proved much better able to conduct warfare than the smaller social aggregates which surrounded it. The cities defeated their neighbors and incorporated their territory, creating empires and imposing their way of life on their inhabitants, who then became citified or "civilized." The early cities, through the creation of empires, thus left extensive archaeological remains.

Whatever the necessary conditions were for creating civilizations, having white skin was apparently not one of them. From the locations of the world's first cities, it would seem that none of them had been created by the "white race." Prior to the advent of the industrial revolution, individuals with light skins were no more wealthy nor more powerful than those whose skins were red, brown, or yellow. Until recently, this has not been made at all clear in the history courses taken by most American college students. Courses in the history of Western civilization, originally devised to supplement courses in world history, were, for many years, taught as if they *were* courses in world history. The histories of civilizations which did not culminate in the creation of the white American were, however, not covered in such courses. This omission made it easier than it otherwise would have been for the student to believe that whites were innately superior and had dominated world history from the time of the Old Stone Age.

This is, however, not history. At the time of the Norman Conquest, the Islamic empire of Ibn Yasin held all of North Africa and was engaged in a 14-year war with the western African empire of Ghana. Ghana was reputed at that time to be able to put an army of 200,000 in the field, 40,000 of them armed with bows and arrows, figures which are credible in terms of Ibn Yasin's difficulty in defeating them. The empires of Ghana, Mali, and Songhay dominated West Africa from the ninth to the sixteenth century, yet are not generally covered in courses in the history of Western civilization. Neither, for that matter, is the empire of Ibn Yasin.[2]

The large-scale conflicts carried on for centuries by western Europeans led to continuous improvement in their techniques of warfare. By the time the Spanish concluded their expulsion of the Moors and went on to the conquest of the New World, the uses of armored horsemen and siege warfare had become extremely sophisticated.

Consider, for example, Elmina Castle, which the Portuguese finished as their major fortress on the Gold Coast in 1560. The castle had walls 30 feet thick, was protected by two moats on the landward side, and possessed 400 cannons. Despite this, it was captured by the Dutch in 1637 by force of arms.[3] When the same highly sophisticated techniques of warfare were turned against peoples without similar military experience or skills, the result was almost a foregone conclusion.

Although a variety of colonial systems were tried by different colonizing powers under various conditions, slavery was a part of many of them from the very beginning, just as it had been in the empires of Greece and Rome. Columbus enslaved West Indians on his voyages of exploration, and he largely exterminated the Indians of Hispaniola when they rose up against the Spaniards who were forcing them to labor in the mines.[4] It was in an attempt to preserve the surviving Indians of this island that Las Casas obtained permission from Charles V for the wholesale importation of African slaves.

Slavery was well known to European countries at the time of the discovery of the New World, and was not confined to Africans. Slavers traded in whatever they could catch or buy, regardless of race, creed, or national origin. In 1652, for example, 270 Scotsmen who had been captured in the Battle of Dunbar were sold in Boston.[5] That the slaves in the Americas came to be largely Africans seems to have been due to two factors. They survived the conditions of the New World better than some other peoples did, and they were available as a result of warfare between African states. It was thus partly a matter of chance that slavery and race became linked in the minds of the colonists.

It was not completely a matter of chance, however. Scholars in European Christendom had, until within a century of the beginning of the Atlantic slave trade, taught a doctrine called *The Great Chain of Being*; and this doctrine had made Europeans ripe for making a connection between slavery and blackness of skin. The Great Chain of Being had been an immensely popular idea with Renaissance men needing reassurance amidst the bewildering expansion of the known world. It was a sophisticated theory, Neoplatonic in origin; but its real power lay in its ability to give the kind of cultural interpretations of reality we discussed in Chapter 7. The doctrine said that divine creation ordained a continuous and descending chain of God-likeness and therefore of legitimate authority. Beginning with God himself, it did not end until it categorized minerals, or rocks! It clearly showed the source of authority which kings held over their subjects, fathers over their children, men over women, and "human-like" men over "animal-like," or primitive, man. While it was already losing popularity in the minds of theological and political revolutionaries during the major European expansion into North America, it lived on in fragments of attitudes and values.

We have already seen how individuals create ideologies to justify their behavior. Both the slave traders and the slaveowners developed a system of thought to justify their actions. Although a high proportion of the slaves died during the long ocean passage, slave captains did not find their profession inconsistent with Christianity. As Alex Haley has pointed out,[6] the hymn "How Sweet the Sound of Jesus' Name" was written by a slave captain while his ship was anchored waiting for cargo. Among the slaveowners, the system of justification revolved around the idea that the slaves were less than human. Because the slaves were largely black and the slaveowners mostly white, the doctrine which developed was one of white supremacy.

The Politics of Racism

THE GROWTH OF THE GHETTO

Just as the history of the African kingdoms is not covered in most humanities courses, the relationships of blacks and whites in the United States following the Civil War are often treated very cursorily in American history courses. The impression sometimes seems to be given in these courses that a brief attempt was made during the reconstruction period to give black citizens their civil liberties, but that it was soon abandoned as impractical. Students holding this view of American history assume that black Americans have been making gradual but steady progress in attaining equal rights since right after the Civil War.

As a demonstration of how commonly this view is held, one of the authors has tried telling his classes that, in Louisiana, there were 1,342 black voters in 1896 and 130,334 black voters in 1904. Although students have been puzzled that the number of black voters should have grown so rapidly, they have not been able to point out what was wrong with the figures. Actually, they are reversed, and should read: 1896: 130,334 black voters; 1904: 1,342 black voters.[7]

The year 1896 was a long time after the Civil War. Most high school American history courses do not stress that American society, in both the North and the South, was quite successfully integrated for over thirty years after the Civil War. At about the turn of the century, black citizens were systematically deprived of their civil rights and forced into segregated facilities. The way in which unequal rights were instituted at that time and are maintained today constitutes the politics of racism.

What happened around 1900 which caused black voters to lose rights which they had enjoyed for decades, and which caused whites to introduce segregated facilities into restaurants, railway cars, buses, and courts of law? At one level of analysis, the change was caused by the breakdown of a coalition of Northerners and liberal Southerners, coupled with a series of Supreme Court rulings upholding segregation. This type of explanation does not make clear, however, why political forces could no longer be marshaled to defend the rights of black citizens in either the North or the South. Some hints on the answer to that question are found in Allan Spear's *Black Chicago*.[8]

We have already noted in an earlier chapter the profound changes in the American way of life which were brought about by the mechanization of industry in Muncie during the latter half of the nineteenth century. These changes reached Chicago a little earlier than they reached Muncie, and led to phenomenal growth in the city's population. The total population of the city went from just over half a million in 1880 to over two million by 1910. The opportunities associated with this growth rate brought many people to Chicago from outside the state and outside the country. Included in this influx were a substantial number of black Americans from the South, causing the black population to increase from about 6,500 in 1880 to about 44,000 in 1910.

The rapid growth of the city created a severe shortage of housing, for not only was more housing needed but many existing homes were being torn down to create room for the expanding industrial district. It was partly the competition for scarce housing which instigated friction between the various ethnic groups in the city. There was some tendency for each group to be concentrated in certain areas of the city, although the segregation of neighborhoods was by no means complete. As Spear points out, black Chicagoans were less segregated from the rest of the city population, up until 1910, than were Italian immigrants.[9]

Prior to 1900, however, competition for housing was not expressed in overt acts of hostility between the black and white residents of Chicago. The city of Chicago was founded by a black man, growing up on the site of a cabin erected by this trader from the West Indies. Despite some discrimination against blacks on the part of whites, relations between the two groups were relatively good until the turn of the century. From then on, they became steadily worse until they exploded in the race riot of 1919 in which thirty-eight people were killed and hundreds were injured.

While competition for housing contributed to the hostility which led up to this riot, competition for jobs was even more important. We have seen how the mechanization of the glass industry in Muncie turned glassmaking from a skilled craft entered through a long apprenticeship into a machine-tending job which could be performed by anyone who was young and strong. Similar changes were taking place in the industries of Chicago and were in large part responsible for its growth. These changes had the effect of making blacks able to compete for industrial jobs.

During the period of the old craft unions, blacks had been effectively excluded from most industrial employment, largely by being barred from apprenticeship programs. Although Chicago in 1900 had a substantial black bourgeoisie, almost 65 percent of male black workers were employed in domestic and personal service trades. When the mechanization of industry eliminated the need for apprenticeships and black workers began to enter industrial employment, it was often as strikebreakers that they were employed. The white discrimination which excluded blacks from almost all industrial unions thus created black strikebreakers. They were specially recruited in the South and brought north on special trains, and they had few compunctions about working outside the unions. There were five major strikes in Chicago between 1904 and 1919. In every one of them black strikebreakers were used, and every one of the strikes failed. Furthermore, the black workers were usually fired as soon as the strike was over.

The use of black strikebreakers fresh from the rural South was strongly disapproved by black leaders in Chicago, who foresaw the trouble which might result from it. It seems to have been a major factor in the increasing violence between blacks and whites which led up to the race riot of 1919.

When the riot did come, the people who were killed were not necessarily either leaders or strikebreakers, but were probably largely those people—black or white—who were badly outnumbered in their neighborhoods. After the violence, no black felt safe in a predominantly white neighborhood, and no white felt safe in a predominantly black one. Because of this, neighborhoods tended to become all black or all white as residents in the minority in that area moved out. The ghetto, which had taken shape during the increasing violence of the early twentieth century, was solidified and made permanent by the disaster of 1919. If Chicago was at all typical of the forces which were molding political thought around the beginning of the century, the competition for industrial employment was a basic factor in the breakdown of political support for the rights of black citizens.

THE DENIAL OF IDENTITY

As Will Herberg has pointed out, all immigrants to the United States underwent changes of identity as they became a part of a new nation.[10] Prior to immigration, a person might think of himself in terms of his occupation, the town he was from, and the extended family he was part of. Often none of these identities would be recognized in his new country. Usually he needed to take a new occupation, at least until he became proficient in English. Distinctions of region and clan were lost on his new associates, and he was classified by them, instead, in terms of his language, nation of origin, and religion. Even his name and country of origin were frequently changed by customs officials. A German who gave his nationality as *Deutsch* was often recorded as being Dutch, and anyone whose name was difficult for the customs official to pronounce or spell was likely to be told that from then on his name was Smith or Jones.

While the first generation of immigrants might cling to identities which they had had for many years before coming here, the second generation was forceably Americanized. The second generation, those individuals who were either born in the United States or came here as young children, attended American schools. Here very strong pressures were put on them not to talk, dress, eat, or act any differently from anyone else. In most instances, they responded by becoming proud of speaking only English and by scorning the foreign customs of their parents. To a great extent, the cultural heritage of their ancestors stopped with the second generation. If, as often happened, the third-generation Americans became interested in what their history had been, they were unable to find out and so created a fictitious heritage which had no more relationship to reality than leprechauns do to the realities of life in modern Ireland. Indians on the West Coast, for example, who traditionally built cedar houses and lived by catching salmon, have now adopted some cultural characteristics of Plains Indians which they saw portrayed in western movies.

This example illustrates another feature of Americanization, which led Herberg to refer to a "transmuting pot" instead of a melting pot. This is that the presentation of American history in the schools has called on everyone to accept the Pilgrims, John Smith, Daniel Boone, and the Alamo as his cultural heritage. Whatever went into the transmuting pot came out white, Anglo-Saxon, and Protestant. To take some examples from black history, most United States history books do not indicate that Balboa had 30 black members of his party when he discovered the Pacific, that Cortez brought 300 to aid in the conquest of Mexico, or that about one-fifth of the population of the Colonies was black at the time of the War of Independence.

While the denial of cultural and personal identity has thus been a part of the experience of most immigrants to the United States, the experience of their descendants has depended on what they have looked like. White indentured servants were often brought over under conditions not unlike those to which black slaves were subjected, and cases are on record in which one-third or fewer of them survived the voyage.[11] The descendants of those who survived, however, could not be physically distinguished from descendants of Roger Williams or Benjamin Franklin. This integration was not available to the descendants of American Indians who were here when Columbus arrived, Spaniards who created a vast empire in the Southwest long before the Protestants arrived, or blacks who were prosperous merchants for many decades before the Civil War. Their descendants continued, generation after generation, to experience the rejection which the children of other immigrants escaped by becoming Americanized.

The denial of personal and cultural identity to these groups is a way of keeping them in subservient positions, and is thus a part of the politics of racism. The nature of this assault on identity is perhaps most clearly revealed in Jonathan Kozol's book *Death at an Early Age*.[12] In it he describes, among other things, the consequences of teaching black children from history books which portray Africans as happy, childlike savages who need whites to lead them, and of whipping the schoolchildren for not showing respect to teachers who call them niggers.

That the assault on identity which Kozol observed is not unique is revealed by studies of the self-conceptions of white and black children. Early studies in this area revealed that black children learned to prefer light skin to dark skin. In contrast, a recent study shows that when black children who attend integrated schools have been exposed to a "Black Is Beautiful" campaign, they prefer their own skin color.[13] Politics and psychology are thus related. Political conditions have consequences for the self-conceptions of individuals, and changes in individual identity are a fundamental part of any major political movement.

THE PSYCHOLOGY OF PREJUDICE

We have briefly mentioned the effects of racism on the psychology of the oppressed. The remainder of this chapter will be devoted to the psychology of the oppressors. Let us survey this area, and then go into it in more detail.

The first point which we should note is that almost nobody feels like an oppressor. Whether he is prejudiced against blacks or whites, males or females, young people or old people, Catholics, Protestants, or Jews, he usually sees himself as responding to a real threat from the group against which he is prejudiced. We have already seen how social comparison is used in the interpretation of emotion, and how the same physiological state can be ascribed to a variety of causes, depending on the person's perception of the situation in which he finds himself. The same process seems to be used by the individual to interpret threats to his autonomous functioning.

Deterioration in the individual's ability to function in his environment is often due to causes which he cannot understand. The fifteenth-century Norse of Greenland who were gradually frozen out by a cold cycle of the earth's climate, or the modern small businessman who is losing his trade because foot traffic is being replaced by automobile traffic in front of his store, share this in common: complex forces are responsible. If there is some person or group to whom the difficulties may be ascribed, this simple explanation may be chosen over a more complex one.

In other cases, failure to understand causes of individual difficulties may be a result of ego-defensive processes. Repressive defenses which keep the individual from being aware of his own impulses, and the use of projection to ascribe one's own unacceptable impulses to others, both seem to be deeply involved in the functioning of prejudice.

Marriage relationships can exemplify the basic elements of prejudicial thought. Individuals often conceal from themselves both the extent to which they give up the capacity for autonomous functioning when they enter a marriage relationship and the extent to which they are thereafter dependent upon their partner. Concealing the realities of marriage from themselves, they attribute the undesirable aspects of their situation to some shortcoming of their spouse, or generalize it to the entire opposite sex.

Women and men possess the power to make each other so dependent, through affection and child-rearing, that they can impair each other's ability to function autonomously for years at a time. Each may then seize upon some easily identifiable characteristic of the other and see that as the sole origin and cause of the predicament. For example, the task-orientation of the man which has developed in our culture has provided the woman with too easy an explanation of her oppression and dependency, leading her to attribute characteristics of domination to all men. Similarly, the sexual attraction of the man to the woman may be projected by him so that he sees all women as seductively trying to entrap him. The male fear of entrapment by female sexual characteristics can be so strong as to pervade entire cultures. Rules about what women may or may not wear in order not to "evilly enflame" men are commonly posted by the village priest in some countries, and the United States Supreme Court recently felt obliged to rule on whether or not the female body is obscene.

The Expression of Aggression

We have seen that prejudicial thinking may develop out of a person's attempt to understand what is happening to him. The more his understanding is hampered by denial of certain aspects of reality, the more prejudicial the thinking which is likely to result. The most virulent forms of prejudice are those which justify to the individual his acting out of aggressive impulses of which he is only partially aware. We have already seen an example of this in looking at the parents of battered children, in an earlier chapter. In the remainder of this chapter, we shall consider this type of prejudice, examining developmental, personality, and situational factors which create or inhibit it.

MILGRAM'S EXPERIMENT

An individual comes to a laboratory in response to a newspaper advertisement for subjects to participate in a study of learning.[14] He is greeted by a thirty-one-year-old man dressed in a gray technician's coat, who introduces himself as the experimenter, and he is introduced to a fellow subject. Both subjects are paid in advance, and then the experiment is explained to them. It is on the effects of punishment on learning. One of them is to serve as the teacher, reading pairs of words to the other, who is to learn them. Slips of paper are drawn, and the individual finds that he has been assigned the role of teacher.

The experiment is then described in more detail. The second subject is strapped into a chair in the adjacent room and electrodes are attached to parts of his body. The "teacher" is taken back into the main room, where he is shown the shock generator with which the "learner" is to be punished for incorrect responses. This instrument bears an engraved panel reading "Shock Generator, Type ZLB, Dyson Instrument Company, Waltham, Mass. Output 15 Volts–450 Volts." It has thirty lever switches set in a horizontal line, ranging in power from 15 volts to 450 volts by 15-volt increments. In addition, each group of four switches has a verbal designation. These designations are: Slight Shock, Moderate Shock, Strong Shock, Very Strong Shock, Intense Shock, Extreme Intensity Shock, and Danger: Severe Shock.[15] The last two switches are simply labeled "XXX."

The teacher is given a 45-volt shock to demonstrate how the

shock generator works, and is instructed to shock the learner each time he makes an error. He is also instructed that with each error, the shock level should be raised by 15 volts. He is reassured that although the shocks can be extremely painful, they will not cause permanent tissue damage. After a few preliminary trials to make sure that the instructions have been properly understood, the experiment begins.

If the teacher continues to carry out his instructions, he will administer increasingly strong shocks to the learner, who will make quite a few errors. The learner will pound on the wall, and then stop answering the questions after receiving the 300-volt shock. The experimenter will instruct the teacher to consider no response to be incorrect and to continue raising the shock level. After 315 volts, the learner will again pound on the wall, and then will not be heard from again, nor will he answer any further questions.

As you may have guessed by now, although none of the subjects did so, the learner is a confederate of the experimenter and is not receiving any shocks. The experiment was designed to see what level of shock the so-called teacher would administer before refusing to obey the instructions of the experimenter.

Clearly, the subject has been placed in a conflict situation. On the one hand, he has been told that he should continue administering greater and greater shocks right up to the maximum on the scale. On the other, there are very strong cultural prohibitions against causing great pain to an unwilling victim, even in the interests of science. How would the subject be expected to react to this conflict? Judging from a sampling of other individuals who, after hearing the experiment described, were asked to predict the outcome, most people would expect the majority of subjects to refuse to give any higher shock once one of the lowest of the four possible levels was reached. No one in this sample expected more than 3 percent of the subjects to go to the maximum shock level.

As may be seen in Table 10-1, the results were very different from these expectations. Out of forty subjects, five refused to give further shock after the learner pounded on the wall and stopped answering questions after 300 volts. Another nine became defiant somewhere between this point and the maximum shock level. More than half the subjects, twenty-six in all, continued to press the switches up to the maximum shock on the scale.

Table 10-1 *Distribution of break-off points*

VERBAL DESIGNATION AND VOLTAGE INDICATION	NUMBER OF SUBJECTS FOR WHOM THIS WAS MAXIMUM SHOCK
Slight shock	
15	0
30	0
45	0
60	0
Moderate shock	
75	0
90	0
105	0
120	0
Strong shock	
135	0
150	0
165	0
180	0
Very strong shock	
195	0
210	0
225	0
240	0
Intense shock	
255	0
270	0
285	0
300	5
Extreme intensity shock	
315	4
330	2
345	1
360	1
Danger: severe shock	
375	1
390	0
405	0
420	0
XXX	
435	0
450	26

SOURCE: Milgram[16]

This continuation did not come easily for them, and there were marked signs of internal conflict. As Stanley Milgram, the experimenter, reports:

> In a large number of cases the degree of tension reached extremes that are rarely seen in socio-psychological laboratory studies. Subjects were observed to sweat, tremble, stutter, bite their lips, groan, and dig their fingernails into their flesh. These were characteristic rather than exceptional responses to the experiment.

> One sign of tension was the regular occurrence of nervous laughing fits. Fourteen of the 40 subjects showed definite signs of nervous laughter and smiling. The laughter seemed entirely out of place, even bizarre. Full-blown, uncontrollable seizures were observed for 3 subjects. On one occasion we observed a seizure so violently convulsive that it was necessary to call a halt to the experiment.[17]

Three facts are significant about this experiment. The first is that individuals are quite inaccurate in predicting how they will react to some situations. Although everyone is confident that *he* would defy the experimenter, few of the individuals actually in the situation did so. Second, the experiment is interesting in giving evidence on the signs of internal conflict. Most important, however, the experiment gives frightening evidence on the extent to which individuals may follow the commands of authority even when those commands require them to violate their own moral standards. To understand these findings, we must digress for a moment and consider a psychoanalytic view of aggression.

CONTROLS ON AGGRESSION

Freud's view of aggression was that it is a drive second in importance only to sex in explaining human behavior. Like sex, it is denied free expression by the demands of society as internalized in the superego, and thus may be repressed and expressed in an indirect manner. As the question of repression is central to the question of aggressiveness, let us consider how a repressed drive may be distinguished from the absence of a drive. If John does not behave in an aggressive manner, is there any way to know whether he is repressing aggressive impulses or simply does not have them?

The first way of making this distinction is in terms of reactions to forces toward change. To draw an analogy, imagine that you are put in charge of a partially completed landscaping project, where a very large tree has been prepared for transplanting. Attached high up on the trunk are a number of taut ropes reaching to other trees. A controversy has arisen as to whether these are very weak ropes exerting no force, or whether they are all that holds the tree up, by attempting to pull the trunk in opposite directions. If the tree is left alone, there may be no way to decide between these views. It is easy to decide the controversy, however, by attaching a stronger cable and attempting to pull the tree over. If the ropes are having no effect on it, it will fall easily. If they are exerting strong forces, you will not be able to pull it over.

Similarly, if a force induced on a personality does not have an effect, it may safely be assumed that there are other forces holding the personality constant, a point which Lewin developed in analyzing social norms.[18] Let us take a social example. Imagine that for some unknown reason you are trying to start a quarrel with a stranger in a bar. First you bump his elbow and spill his beer. Then you criticize him for being so clumsy as to spill the beer on you. Next you complain loudly that he smells so bad that you must move to another seat. In getting up, you grind your heel into his foot. These stimuli represent increasingly strong instigations to an aggressive response on his part, and it would be normal to expect increasingly hostile responses by him to each of your actions. If, on the other hand, you obtain no normal aggressive response from him—if he apologizes for spilling the beer, for being clumsy, for smelling bad, and for having large feet—you can safely assume that he has strong forces within him holding any aggressive impulses in check. The individual with strong defenses against the expression of an impulse, then, will not express the impulse even when we can be certain from the stimulating conditions that it is present, whereas the person who does not employ these repressive defenses will express the impulse freely when circumstances call it out. This difference is illustrated in Figure 10-1.

Figure 10-1 shows the possibility of another, more dramatic demonstration of the existence of repression. Even strong restraining forces may break down under sufficient instigation. Consider another example. You want to discriminate between a man who does not drink alcoholic beverages because he does not care for them and one who does not drink them because he is a reformed alcoholic who keeps himself away from alcohol with great difficulty. Each may re-

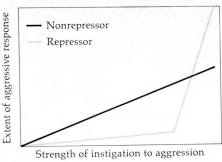

Figure 10–1 *Expression of aggression by people with and without repressive defenses.*

fuse a drink if it is offered to him. What will happen, however, if circumstances exert such strong pressures on the two men that each takes a drink? (To choose a far-fetched example, it might be imagined that they are in a lifeboat on the North Atlantic in midwinter with nothing to drink but scotch.) The man who actually dislikes alcohol should have little difficulty in taking one drink and stopping. The former alcoholic, if he once starts, may well find it impossible to stop.

In other words, repression may be broken down by strong instigation. If it is, the person who has strong defenses to hold his impulses in check will find that the impulses he has been controlling are added to the impulse arising from the situation, and he will thus express the impulse to a much greater extent than the individual who has neither the strong impulse nor the strong defense. It is for this reason that Figure 10-1 shows the person who represses aggressive impulses as behaving in a more aggressive manner under very strong instigation than the person without such defenses. The defenses would not be employed if there were no impulses to be controlled.

Next, the same result might be obtained if it were possible to remove the controls of the superego. In the example of the ropes attached to the tree, it would be possible to see if one was exerting any force by cutting the one opposite it. In the case of the individual, large quantities of alcohol may cause a person to do things that he not only would normally refrain from doing but would normally be unaware of wanting to do.

Finally, impulses which are denied direct expression may make themselves apparent in other ways. They may be expressed in a disguised manner or against a substitute object. The man who apologized when you provoked him in the bar may have incorporated a good deal of sarcasm in his replies, perhaps even without awareness: "I'm *so* sorry." ("Like ---- I am.") "I always spill my beer." ("When some clumsy oaf jostles me.") The provoked man may also go out and express his aggression against someone who is less able to retaliate than you are. Both these tendencies may be apparent in response to a projective test such as the T.A.T. It is the release of aggression against a substitute object that is of the greatest significance in understanding racial prejudice.

AN INTERPRETATION OF THE EXPERIMENT

We are now in a better position to understand two of the results of Milgram's experiment. If people do have strong aggressive impulses which they keep from awareness, we should not be surprised that they cannot correctly anticipate how they will act in a situation designed to give free expression to these impulses. Similarly, it should not surprise us that since these impulses are forbidden, a great deal of conflict and anxiety should be experienced when they are expressed. Why, however, should this particular situation cause people to act on the basis of motives which are usually kept well under control?

Authority figures play an especially important role in a psychoanalytic theory of personality, for the restraining forces of the superego are seen as the internalized voice of authority. Although later theorists have stressed more than Freud did that not solely parents, but also peers, teachers, and other significant figures contribute to the formation of the superego, parents are still generally regarded as its most important sources in most cases. This has two especially important consequences. The first is that the way in which an individual copes with his impulses may be at least partially understood from knowledge of his childhood relationships with his parents, a point which we shall return to when we consider personality factors in prejudice. The second consequence, which has received less attention, is the role which authority can play in freeing the individual from the dictates of his conscience.

Let us return to viewing the individual in Milgram's experiment as subject to conflicting forces. On the one hand, he has aggressive tendencies which are repugnant to him and which he excludes from his consciousness. On the other hand, he has a well-developed moral code which keeps these tendencies constantly in check. Finally, he has the remains of a childlike fear of violating the dictates of authority figures and his peers, and nearly all authority figures will be acting in support of his conscience in restraining him from actions condemned by society. An additional voice of authority added to what he carries inside himself—for example, his employer urging him to greater effort in his work—may do little to make him abide even more closely by the dictates of his conscience, for this force is opposing the strong forces of his impulse. But a voice of authority telling him to do what his conscience considers wrong to do—say, a superior telling him not to bother working hard—may have dramatic effects on his behavior, for this voice of authority undermines the force of the superego which is founded on authority, and encourages him in doing what his impulse wants to do.

This explanation of Milgram's experiment manages to explain the result, while also explaining the obvious fact that people do not do everything that authority figures tell them to do. It does so, however, at the cost of assuming that people often have strong aggressive impulses which are gratified by inflicting pain upon others. Evidence for this view will be provided in the section on situational factors in prejudice. Let us briefly consider one piece of evidence from Milgram's research at this point, however. One of the variations which Milgram[19] ran on his basic experiment was a control group in which the "teacher" chose the level of shock to be administered with no suggestion from the experimenter. As would be expected, the level of shock given was considerably lower on the average than in the experimental condition. Two out of forty control subjects, however, gave the maximum possible shock!

Personality Factors in Prejudice

A PSYCHOANALYTIC APPROACH

The relationship between personality factors and prejudice has been extensively studied by Adorno and his colleagues in their monumental work *The Authoritarian Personality*.[20] While a number of difficult methodological questions are involved in the interpretation of their study,[21] it also has many strong points and is probably the single most informative work in this area. Furthermore, some of its main findings have been supported by more recent research using different techniques. Epstein,[22] for example, studied the relationships among three factors: authoritarianism as a personality characteristic, the amount of displaced aggression a person has toward others, and the social status of the victim of the aggression. Using an experimental situation in which aggression was expressed by the subject's administration of an electric shock to someone instead of merely by verbal expression of attitudes, he obtained results which supported two of the findings of the original studies covered in *The Authoritarian Personality*: (1) Individuals high in authoritarianism expressed more aggression toward the experimental victim, and (2) they turned their aggression toward victims lower in social status than themselves.

In the 990 pages of *The Authoritarian Personality*, there is much more material than can be summarized in an introductory text. In this section we shall look at just a portion of the research, the intensive interview study of forty highly prejudiced and forty relatively unprejudiced individuals, drawn from a broad cross-section of American society and roughly matched on demographic characteristics. The individuals were rated by persons with a variety of theoretical orientations and without knowledge of whether a particular subject was high or low in prejudice.

The overall theoretical view of Adorno and his colleagues, which was highly influenced by psychoanalytic theory, was that prejudice, like other attitudes, develops partially through direct learning and partially as an expression of personality needs. That the former of these two ways is not the only way of acquiring prejudiced attitudes is nicely demonstrated in a study by Hartley.[23] If people are prejudiced against minority groups simply through having learned to be prejudiced against them, they should have no prejudice against a group which does not exist and which they have therefore never heard of. In Hartley's research, subjects were asked social-distance questions about both real and imaginary groups. Some subjects refused to express opinions about "Danerians," "Wallonians," and "Pirenians," but most of them did so without hesitation. Considerable prejudice against the nonexistent groups was found, and in general the people who rejected them most strongly were the same people who rejected real-life groups.

To the extent that prejudiced attitudes are not the result of social learning, but an expression of personality needs, they should be found in individuals who have strong aggressive needs but also strong superego controls on the direct expression of aggression, for it is in this situation that the individual would be likely to turn his aggression against a more socially approved object. Who would we expect these people to be?

As was indicated in an early study of the socialization of aggression,[24] aggressiveness may result from identification with an aggressive parent. A boy with a strict, aggressive, and punitive father would be expected to develop the type of conflict about the expression of aggression which may result in his expressing his aggression against a substitute object. He would develop strong aggressive impulses partially through the resentment he might feel at the punishment which was inflicted on him and partially through the model of successful aggression which was constantly before him. The punishment he received would not make him not identify with his father, but, through the mechanism of identification with the aggressor, would lead to his idealizing him. To the degree that the superego represents an internalization of the parent, the child would develop a moral code which would be as harsh and punitive as the parent.

In contrast to the child with milder and more lenient parents, then, the child with harsh and punitive parents should develop both stronger aggressive impulses and stricter internal controls on the direct expression of those impulses. He should consciously idealize his parents while unconsciously being resentful of them. His aggressive impulses should be anxiety-inducing to him because of his strict moral code, and various defenses would need to be employed in dealing with them. These defenses would make him less in contact with his own emotional reactions and would raise the possibility of his expressing the resentment he was not consciously aware of against substitute objects which were not as strictly outlawed by his moral code as the initial source of the resentment.

Viewing the prejudiced individual as a person who is expressing aggressive impulses against a substitute object thus leads us to make several predictions about him. He should, first of all, have had aggressively punitive parents. He should consciously idealize these parents but unconsciously feel resentment against them, which he expresses indirectly. Finally, he should be out of contact with his own emotional reactions. Evidence that all these characteristics are found in prejudiced individuals gives strong support for this view of the personal origin of prejudice. This evidence is found in *The Authoritarian Personality*.[25]

CHILD DEVELOPMENT AND PREJUDICE

Evidence on the first two of the expectations is provided in Else Frenkel-Brunswik's chapter "Parents and Childhood as Seen through the Interviews." Strongly prejudiced men, significantly more often than less prejudiced ones, describe their fathers as distant and stern rather than relaxed and mild, and their homes as dominated by their fathers. Even more interesting are the kinds of behavior that the child was punished for and the types of punishment used. The first comparison was between punishment for violating rules and punishment for violating principles. As Frenkel-Brunswik puts it:

> In particular, discipline for violation of rules, primarily "moralistic," was contrasted with discipline for violation of principles, primarily "rationalized" (Category 10). As the first of two variables to be considered in this context, the choice between these two opposite alternatives on the part of the parents would seem to be crucial for the establishment of the child's attitude toward what is considered right or wrong: it probably decides the externalization vs. internalization of values. These two types of discipline further imply different resultant attitudes toward authority.
>
> In the first case, discipline is handled as "vis major," as a force outside of the child, to which at the same time he must submit. The values in question are primarily the values of adult society: conventions and rules helpful for social climbing but rather beyond the natural grasp of the child. At the same time this type of value lays the foundation for an attitude of judging people according to external criteria, and for the authoritarian condemnation of what is considered socially inferior.
>
> The second type of discipline invites the cooperation and understanding of the child and makes it possible for him to assimilate it.[26]

In somewhat simpler terms, demands that the child conform to arbitrary rules which he cannot understand are liable to lead to the child's developing a moral code which is similarly arbitrary and ego-alien. Unable to express his impulses directly because of his arbitrary conscience, the child would need to express aggression against substitute objects who could be moralistically condemned on the basis of these principles. This variable again significantly distinguished between the more and less prejudiced subjects, with more prejudiced men and women having been disciplined for the violation of rules rather than of principles.

The most significant variable, however, was the type of punishment used. More and less prejudiced subjects were differentiated at the .01 level of statistical significance by whether the punishment was traumatic or assimilable. The distinction is not merely a matter of the extent of physical punishment, although references to "whipping," "not sparing the rod," and "beating the life out of me" were common in the protocols of the more prejudiced subjects. Also considered in making the ratings was the parents' arbitrariness through not making clear to the child what he or she was being punished for, and their use of threats and methods of punishment with which the child could not cope. Examples of the latter are the following:

> "But mother had a way of punishing me—lock me in a closet—or threaten to give me to a neighborhood woman who said she was a witch . . . . I think that's why I was afraid of the dark."

> "Father picked upon things and threatened to put me in an orphanage."[27]

> "I was kind of temperamental when I was little. I had temper tantrums if I didn't get my way. My mother cured them—she dunked me under the water faucet until I stopped screaming."[28]

We thus see considerable evidence that the use of harsh and arbitrary punishment is an important factor in the development of prejudice. Another possibility, however, must be considered. Is it possible that the more prejudiced subjects are simply prejudiced against their parents as well as against minority groups, and therefore describe them as distant, arbitrary, and cruel? This possibility must be ruled out, for the more prejudiced subjects actually idealized their parents *more* than the less prejudiced, a point which supports a theory of identification with the aggressor. The same individuals who described their parents as "beating the life out of me" could find nothing to say against those parents when asked to describe them. Although holding their parents up to admiration, however, these subjects often found it difficult to pick out specific characteristics to admire:

> One of the outstanding features in the above quotations is the use of superlatives in the description of parents, such as "excellent man in every way," "best in the world," "most terrific person," etc. If more detailed and specific elaborations are made at all, they refer to material benefits or help given by the parents. Where there is no readiness to admit that one's parents have any weakness in them, it is not surprising to find later an indication of repressed hostility and revengeful fantasies behind the mask of compliance.[29]

Some support for the view that the more prejudiced individuals had repressed aggression against their parents was also found in the Thematic Apperception Test protocols of these individuals. An example of such feelings from the interview study is as follows:

F 32: Altogether she thinks her "father is a grand person." When asked whether, since no one is perfect, there were any little faults that she could name, she said that she couldn't think of any. He never drank; well, he swore a little bit. And he was argumentative. (However, in discussing her vocation, subject had mentioned that the father had been willing to finance the education of the boys, but that he expected the girls to stay home and be ladies, so what the girls got they got on their own. In another connection, subject remarked that she had got nothing out of her father. He provided them with the necessities of life, but would not give them anything extra. He never allowed the girls to entertain boys at home. Nevertheless, subject stated that she was closer to her father than to her mother.) When the interviewer broached the topic of her brothers and sisters, subject replied, "I'm right in the middle—don't they say middle children are forgotten children!" When asked if she thought that so, subject closed up, merely remarking that her parents showed no partiality.[30]

The evidence on the final question, whether more prejudiced people are less in contact with their emotional reactions, is less easily summarized, for it was not so much a single factor for analysis by the authors as a constant theme running through a number of separate parts of the study. Perhaps it emerges most clearly in what more and less prejudiced women were looking for in a marriage partner.

... the traits which the typical high-scoring woman tends to desire in men are likewise primarily instrumental in getting the things she wants. They are: hard-working, "go-getting," "energetic," "a good personality," (conventionally) moral, "clean-cut," deferent toward women.

By contrast, low-scoring subjects tend to emphasize as desired traits companionship, common interest, warmth, sociability, sexual love, understanding, presence of liberal values. Sometimes their quest for love is so intense and unrealistic that it becomes a source of disappointment to them.[31]

This divorce of the individual from impulse also comes out, for the men, in the drawing of a dichotomy between "pure" and "bad" women. High-scoring men drew this dichotomy more often than those with low scores, to an extent that would happen by chance only one time in a hundred.

Although not all the predicted relationships were found in the work described in *The Authoritarian Personality*, and although only a very small part of the evidence which was found can be summarized in a brief account, a clear picture does emerge from the overall work that is strongly supportive of a psychoanalytic view of prejudice. While more or less prejudiced behavior may be called out in the same person by different circumstances, and while the object of his aggression may depend on cultural opportunities, prejudice seems to consist primarily of unrecognized aggressive impulses turned against a relatively powerless victim. In this respect, it is very similar to the adult's aggression against children which we have already considered in looking at the battered child syndrome.

Situational Factors in Prejudice

THREAT TO THE SELF

Although different childhood experiences may make a person more or less likely to express his aggressive impulses against a member of a minority group, it is a concrete social situation which calls out those impulses. Prejudice, like rumor, "serves the twin functions of explaining and relieving emotional tensions felt by individuals."[32] When social conditions provide a threat to the self, the emotional tensions are created which are expressed and explained through prejudice. Thus personality differences may help explain who will participate in a lynch mob and who will not, but social forces are the factor which primarily determines when and where lynch mobs will come into being.

Of the various sources of self-esteem available to American men, the occupational role is perhaps the most important. While the family is undoubtedly the most important group for most men, with occupational groups definitely secondary in importance, the peculiarity of the man's occupational role is that his relations with his family are also extremely dependent upon it. The husband and father who is not also the family provider has not only failed in his occupational role; he is unable to play a traditional masculine role in his family, a point which is illustrated by the matriarchal family structure which characterizes many underemployed segments of the population. A threat to a man's means of earning a living is thus one of the most important threats which may be made to his conception of himself and to his role in society.

If hostility to minority groups is displaced aggression in response to frustrating situations, then economic insecurity and threats to employment should be among the major factors calling out this hostility. If a man loses his job, his anxiety about not living up to his self-conception could be both explained by blaming his failure on a minority group and relieved by venting his hostility against them. Evidence in favor of this view is presented by Dollard, Doob, et al.[33] For the years analyzed, from 1882 to 1930, there was a significant negative relationship (a correlation of $-.67$) between the number of lynchings per year and the price for cotton crops. Although individuals do not say that they have lynched another person because the price of cotton is low, the number of such incidents is certainly predictable from this index of economic insecurity.

Even stronger evidence of the role of occupational threats to the self as a factor in ethnic prejudice is provided by a study of World War II veterans carried out by Bettelheim and Janowitz.[34] It is stronger evidence because, in considering a correlation between changes in two variables over time, we must keep in mind that, rather than one causing change in the other, the changes in both might be caused by other historical changes.

Bettelheim and Janowitz based their study on a sample of 150 veterans of the Second World War residing in Chicago. The sample was random except that it excluded former officers, since they would have had quite different experiences in the armed forces, and members of discriminated-against minority groups, since they would be expected to have different prejudices from those of the dominant cultural group. Prejudice was measured in a way which is interesting because it comes closer to measuring prejudiced behavior than many attitude-measurement techniques.

When a person spontaneously tries to convince others that the rights of a particular group should be restricted although the persons he is trying to convince have not even mentioned that group, he is not only reflecting attitudes but also engaging in political behavior against the interests of the group. Bettelheim and Janowitz therefore classified a person as intensely prejudiced against a particular group if he advocated such restrictive actions against the group when he was merely asked about his experiences in the armed forces. Next most hostile in his behavior toward the group is a person who comes out in favor of action against the group only when questioned about it. This reaction was classified as outspoken prejudice. While it represents behavior which is politically hostile to the minority group, it does not contain the degree of hostility which spontaneous behavior does. Classed as less prejudiced than either of these individuals is the person who holds unfavorable views about the minority group but does not favor political action against it. In the study, his views were classified as stereotyped. Finally, a person was classed as tolerant of a particular group if he held only isolated stereotypes, not all of which were unfavorable. Subjects were classified into these four categories with respect to each minority group on the basis of an interview lasting between 4 and 7 hours.

No significant relationship was found between the degree of prejudice expressed against blacks or Jews and a person's position in the social structure at the time he was interviewed. His age, salary, religious affiliation, socioeconomic status, and education had no consistent relationship to his views. Quite a strong relationship emerges, however, when his occupational mobility is examined, as will be seen from Table 10–2.[35]

For 130 of the sample of 150 men, it was possible to find out about their prior civilian employment. They were classified as *upward mobile* if their employment at the time of interview was one or more steps higher on the Alba Edwards socioeconomic scale than their previous employment, *downward mobile* if their present job was one or more categories lower than their previous one, and of course considered to show *no mobility* if the two jobs fell at the same point on the scale. As would be expected from our previous consideration of the importance of a man's occupation to his conception of himself, the most prejudice was shown by those who were downwardly mobile, and the greatest tolerance was found among those who achieved upward mobility.

On one important point, however, Bettelheim and Janowitz obtained results which differed markedly from those of the research described in *The Authoritarian Personality*. When they investigated the reactions of the more and less prejudiced men to the controlling

Table 10-2 *Intolerance and mobility*

	DOWNWARD MOBILITY NO.	%	NO MOBILITY NO.	%	UPWARD MOBILITY NO.	%	TOTAL NO.	%
Anti-Semitic								
Tolerant	2	11	25	37	22	50	49	38
Stereotyped	3	17	26	38	8	18	37	28
Outspoken and intense	13	72	17	25	14	32	44	34
Anti-Negro								
Tolerant and stereotyped	5	28	18	26	22	50	45	34
Outspoken	5	28	40	59	17	39	62	48
Intense	8	44	10	15	5	11	23	18
Total	18	100	68	100	44	100	130	100

SOURCE: Bettelheim and Janowitz[35]

institutions of society, they found that the *least* prejudiced men were *most* accepting of social authority. As they put the matter:

> When acceptance or rejection of the four representative institutions was compared with the degree of anti-Semitism. . . ,it appeared that only an insignificant percentage of the tolerant men rejected them, while nearly half the out-spoken and intense anti-Semites did so. This is in marked contrast, for example, to studies of certain types of college students, in whom radical rejection of authority is combined with liberalism toward minority groups.[36]

It seems unlikely that the difference between the results of Bettelheim and Janowitz's study and the research reported in *The Authoritarian Personality* is actually due to differences in the samples used, for, as has already been pointed out, *The Authoritarian Personality* research was not based solely upon college students. Instead, the difference in results may be due to the type of questions asked. As Frenkel-Brunswik et al. put it, " 'Authoritarian submission' refers to an inability seriously to criticize, reject or actively rebel against one's main ingroup (particularly the family) figures and values."[37] The controlling institutions which Bettelheim and Janowitz obtained reactions to: the Veterans Administration, the political party system, the federal government, and the economic system, probably did not represent the ingroup to their subjects. As "those guys in Washington who run our lives," the controlling institutions which Bettelheim and Janowitz investigated are probably just as good candidates for the displacement of aggression as minority groups.

THE EXPLANATION OF ANXIETY

So far, we have been considering the role of prejudice in expressing aggression. Does it also serve to explain anxiety-causing perceptions? It is easy to see how some stereotypes could do so. The most common stereotypes of Jews found by Bettelheim and Janowitz, for example, are as follows:

> They are clannish; they help one another. . . .
>
> They have money. . . .
>
> They control everything (or have an urge to control everything);
>
> They are running the country. . . .
>
> They use underhanded or sharp business methods. . . .
>
> They do not work; they do not do manual labor.[38]

It is not difficult to see how holding such views could help a person to rationalize his own economic failure. It is more difficult, however, to see how the common stereotypes of blacks could do so. These stereotypes dwell heavily on physical topics, and seem to be related to deeper impulses than economic competitiveness, for the tendency here apparently is to see the minority group as dominated by those impulses which the prejudiced person has difficulty in controlling. This, then, would be a case of projection, with the individual explaining the anxiety which he feels by attributing his own forbidden impulses to others. An excellent experimental demonstration of this method of coping with anxiety was carried out by Bramel, Bell, and Margulis.[39]

Subjects were shown either slides or a movie dealing with the Soviet Union. Half the subjects seeing each were led to believe that high readings on a dial indicated that they were showing physiological fear reactions to the stimuli dealing with the Soviet Union, but not to other stimuli. Through necessarily elaborate deception, their attitudes toward the Soviet Union were measured both before and after exposure to the stimuli without their realizing that this was part of the same study. There were thus four groups of subjects: (1) those who were led to believe that they had shown marked fear responses to very innocuous and peaceful slides dealing with the Soviet Union; (2) those who believed that they had shown fear responses to a film portraying the Soviet Union in a very threatening manner; (3) those who had seen the innocuous slides without being led to believe that the slides had frightened them; and (4) those who saw the threatening film without being led to believe that the film had frightened them.

On the basis of dissonance theory, the experiments predicted that those subjects who thought they had been frightened by the innocuous slides would explain their fear to themselves by deciding that the Soviet Union was actually more dangerous to the United States than they had previously thought. Those who had seen the frightening film were not expected to show this reaction, as they would be able to explain their fear reactions in terms of the threatening nature of the film itself. These predictions were supported by the results. The subjects who were led to believe that they had been frightened by the slides, in comparison with those who were told nothing about their physiological reactions to the slides, changed more in the direction of seeing the Soviet Union as dangerous on the postexperimental questionnaire. They also changed significantly more than the subjects who had seen the apparently more threatening film. This result shows quite clearly that views of the world may change to explain anxiety-inducing self-perceptions.

The predictions of the experimenters were drawn, however, not from psychoanalytic theory but from dissonance theory. In this as in many other situations, the two theories seem to make identical predictions. As the authors of the study conclude:

> Let us consider one final potential alternative interpretation of the experimental results. Suppose that finding an explanation of one's anxiety is itself anxiety reducing. Not knowing the cause of one's emotional state is perhaps a source of discomfort (anxiety), and this discomfort is reduced when the person thinks he has found an explanation for his feelings. This hypothesis is so akin to the dissonance interpretation that it is very difficult to distinguish between the two. Both hypotheses focus upon the discrepancy between one's emotional state (or cognitions concerning it) and the surrounding situation. According to the other hypothesis, the discrepancy produces an uncomfortable state called anxiety, which can be reduced in the same way. It is doubtful whether a profitable distinction can be made at this time between the two approaches.[40]

Prejudice in Attitude and Prejudice in Behavior

In this chapter we have been considering prejudice as an example of the ways in which impulses, perceptions, and behavior interact in social behavior. At the risk of some oversimplification, we might generalize that social conditions influence the pressures brought to bear on individuals and therefore constitute a main factor influencing the amount of prejudice present in the society at a given time and place. Further, individual differences in personality influence how different people are likely to react to these social pressures. Finally, cultural beliefs and values, as expressed in ideologies, influence the choice of targets against whom impulses may be turned. Dissonance theory suggests an additional point—that behavior is not simply the expression of attitudes, but to at least an equal extent, attitudes can develop to justify behavior. Consider, for example, the work of Deutsch and Collins in an observation-study of some public housing projects.[41] Their study was a natural experiment—one in which the experimenters did not create the conditions which they observed but did manage to find conditions such as they would have liked to create for the purposes of the study. They studied housing projects which were similar in the ratio of black to white families, the socioeconomic level of the inhabitants, the nature of the staff, and other relevant variables, but which differed in the pattern of occupancy. Two projects were chosen in New Jersey in which all the black families were housed in one area and all the white families in another. These projects were compared with two similar projects in New York where families were assigned to housing units without regard to color.

Striking differences were found in the behavior and attitudes which developed in the two types of housing project. In the integrated projects, it was common for black and white women to associate with one another and choose one another as friends, while in the segregated project this was virtually unheard of. More interesting, such community norms developed that, in the integrated project, there were social pressures on the two groups to be friendly toward one another, and the norms in the segregated projects specified that they should have nothing to do with each other. As might be expected from this, more than half the white women in the integrated projects reported having developed more favorable attitudes toward blacks since moving to the project, whereas only a small percentage of the whites in the segregated projects did so.

These results might not have been found if hostility between the two groups had been so great that violence had erupted when they were brought together. The Sherifs[42] tested the theory that more contact is the solution to intergroup conflict in their camp study by bringing the two clubs together. A free-for-all fight developed, rather than more favorable attitudes. The difference between these two results is consistent with dissonance theory, which holds that it is not contact as such which changes attitudes, but behavior. In a situation such as that studied by Deutsch and Collins, where minimal social pressure is sufficient to bring about tolerant behavior between two groups, increased contact should bring about more favorable attitudes. In a situation where hostile attitudes are so strong that extreme coercion, such as armed intervention, is necessary to ensure behavioral compliance, no dissonance would be generated and attitude change would not necessarily take place.

We have now seen some of the evidence which shows that the way members of different groups *act* toward each other, and the conditions which lead them to act in those ways, can have important effects on their *attitudes* toward each other. Equally true, but somewhat more difficult to demonstrate, is the proposition that new insights into their own attitudes can have dramatic effects on their behaviors. An incident from a sensitivity group conducted by Dennis Jackson and Walter Klavun may serve to illustrate the point.[43]

Jackson and Klavun were doing prejudice-reduction in industry in Atlanta, Georgia, and William Greaves recorded it on film for his brilliant documentary "In the Company of Men." We will have to rely on description by the written word. The program brought together white supervisors who were unaware that their behavior toward black employees exhibited prejudice, and black men who had left industrial employment because of white racism. In emotional role-playing, these blacks, who had found unbearable their white supervisors' constant expression of dehumanizing stereotypes against them, were allowed to act out for the white supervisors present the kind of humiliating experiences that had driven them from the industrial system. The white supervisors then found themselves playing roles which they had unthinkingly played day after day in real life, with this difference—that now the emotional meaning for the blacks in the situation had been laid bare before them. These emotional meanings had been further clarified by the blacks and whites switching roles, so that the whites had experienced the situations from the blacks' position. Much emotion was generated among the blacks when one white supervisor, who had been as stereotyping as the rest in persistently referring to black workers to their faces as "boy," hesitated while making a long speech to the group of blacks about their work problems. He called them first "you fellows"; paused, and, in an obvious moment of insight, said, "you men."

Summary

When an individual denies humanity to others, it is his own psychological processes which allow him to do so. When such denial is characteristic of an entire culture, including the expression of aggression against those denied humanity, then historical and political processes must be involved also.

Political and social traditions can, without much special effort by any individual, maintain an environment of subjugation, rejection, and destruction for those people who are designated by social norms as deserving of such misfortune. The social ideologies of the times will determine, largely by means of historical interpretation, what characteristics will be recognized as identifying these victims. Political processes will tend to ensure that as long as these people remain both distinguishable and comparatively helpless, they will remain in this category. However, it is the psychological processes of individual people which permit these social phenomena to continue.

Unmanageable feelings of threat to the self can be handled by the person experiencing them in many ways. One of them is to believe that his well-being, his autonomy, or his very life is endangered by the actions or even the existence of certain persons or groups. By attributing dangerous impulses to others, he may explain his own anxiety.

The way in which a person has learned to handle his aggressive impulses is an important factor in prejudice. There is evidence that highly prejudiced individuals often have had parents who used threatening discipline and denied human motives. Their children learned to suppress their aggression except when it became too strong for them to control. When these children become adults, hostile behavior against minority-group members may serve as a less socially censured outlet for their aggression.

When an authority figure condones turning another person into a victim of aggressive acts, a person who usually restrains his aggressive impulses with great difficulty may feel suddenly relieved of the moral imperatives which have kept such behavior in check.

Social arrangements will influence what social behavior is shown. Some arrangements will be less productive of prejudice than others. Reduction in prejudiced behavior through changes in perceptions and feelings may also be brought about by personal insight or learned empathy with others.

Notes and Acknowledgments

1. See Chapter 9, Ref. 33.
2. Davidson, Basil. "Africa and the Beginnings," in Melvin Drimmer, *Black History*. New York: Doubleday & Company, Inc., 1968, pp. 34–55.
3. Mannix, Daniel P., in collaboration with Malcolm Cowley. *Black Cargoes: A History of the Atlantic Slave Trade 1518–1865*. New York: The Viking Press, Inc., 1962, pp. 4–5.
4. Ibid., p. 2.
5. Ibid., p. 87.
6. Haley, Alex. *Black Heritage*. A talk given to the Black Student Union at Portland State University. A tape recording of this talk is on file in the audiovisual department of the Portland State University library.
7. Silberman, Charles E. *Crisis in Black and White*. New York: Random House, Inc., 1964.

8. Spear, Allan H. *Black Chicago: The Making of a Negro Ghetto 1890–1920.* Chicago: The University of Chicago Press, 1967.
9. Ibid., p. 15.
10. Herberg, Will. *Protestant-Catholic-Jew: An Essay in American Religious Sociology.* (Rev. ed.) New York: Doubleday & Company, Inc., 1960.
11. Mannix, Daniel P., in collaboration with Malcolm Cowley. Op. cit., p. 58.
12. Kozol, Jonathan. *Death at an Early Age.* Boston: Houghton Mifflin Company, 1967.
13. Hraba, Joseph, and Geoffrey Grant. "Black is beautiful: A reexamination of racial preference and identification." *Journal of Personality and Social Psychology,* November 1970 (16), no. 3, pp. 398–402.
14. Milgram, Stanley. "Behavioral study of obedience." *Journal of Abnormal and Social Psychology,* 1963 (67), pp. 371–378.
15. Ibid., p. 373. By permission of the author and the publisher.
16. Ibid., p. 376. By permission.
17. Ibid., p. 375. By permission.
18. Lewin, Kurt. "Group decision and social change," in E. Maccoby et al. (Eds.), *Readings in Social Psychology.* (3d ed.) New York: Holt, Rinehart and Winston, Inc., 1958, pp. 197–211.
19. Milgram, Stanley. "Liberating effects of group pressure." *Journal of Personality and Social Psychology,* 1965 (1), pp. 127–134.
20. Adorno, T. W., Else Frenkel-Brunswik, Daniel J. Levinson, and Nevitt R. Sanford. *The Authoritarian Personality.* New York: Harper & Row, Publishers, Incorporated, 1950.
21. See Richard Christie and Marie Jahoda (Eds.), *Studies in the Scope and Method of "The Authoritarian Personality."* New York: The Free Press of Glencoe, 1954.
22. Epstein, Ralph. "Authoritarianism, displaced aggression, and social status of the target." *Journal of Personality and Social Psychology,* 1965 (2), no. 4, pp. 585–589.
23. Hartley, E. L. *Problems in Prejudice.* New York: King's Crown Press, 1946.
24. Sears, Robert R., Eleanor E. Maccoby, and Harry Levin. "The socialization of aggression," in Maccoby et al. (Eds.). Op. cit., pp. 350–359.
25. Frenkel-Brunswik, Else. "Parents and childhood as seen through the interviews," in Adorno, Frenkel-Brunswik, Levinson, and Sanford. Op. cit., pp. 337–389.
26. Ibid., p. 372. By permission of the publisher.
27. Ibid., p. 373. By permission.
28. Ibid., p. 375. By permission.
29. Ibid., p. 343. By permission.
30. Ibid., p. 347. By permission.
31. Frenkel-Brunswik, Else. "Sex, people, and self as seen through the interviews," in Adorno, Frenkel-Brunswik, Levinson, and Sanford. Op. cit., p. 401. By permission of the publisher.
32. Allport, Gordon, and Leo Postman. "The basic psychology of rumor," in E. Maccoby, T. M. Newcomb, and E. L. Hartley (Eds.), *Readings in Social Psychology.* (3d ed.) New York: Holt, Rinehart and Winston, Inc., 1958,

p. 55. Copyright 1947, 1952, 1958 by Holt, Rinehart and Winston, Inc. By permission of the publisher.

33. Dollard, John, et al. *Frustration and Aggression*. New Haven, Conn.: Yale University Press, 1939, p. 31.

34. Bettelheim, Bruno, and Morris Janowitz. "Ethnic tolerance: A function of social and personal control." *American Journal of Sociology*, 1949 (55), pp. 137–145.

35. Ibid., p. 140. Copyright 1949 by *American Journal of Sociology*. By permission of The University of Chicago Press.

36. Ibid., pp. 142–143. Copyright 1949 by *American Journal of Sociology*. By permission of The University of Chicago Press.

37. Frenkel-Brunswik, Else, Daniel J. Levinson, and Nevitt R. Sanford. "The antidemocratic personality," in E. Maccoby, T. M. Newcomb, and E. L. Hartley (Eds.), *Readings in Social Psychology*. (3d ed.) New York: Holt, Rinehart and Winston, Inc., 1958, p. 641. Copyright 1947, 1952, 1958 by Holt, Rinehart and Winston, Inc. By permission of the publisher.

38. Bettelheim, Bruno, and Morris Janowitz, "Ethnic tolerance: A function of social and personal control." *American Journal of Sociology*, 1949 (55), p. 145 (excerpts from Table VII). Copyright 1949 by *American Journal of Sociology*. By permission of The University of Chicago Press.

39. Bramel, Dana, J. E. Bell, and Stephen Margulis. "Attributing anger as a means of explaining one's fear." *Journal of Experimental Social Psychology*, 1965 (1), pp. 265–281.

40. Ibid., p. 281. By permission of the authors and the publisher.

41. Deutsch, Morton, and Mary E. Collins. *Interracial Housing*. Minneapolis: The University of Minnesota Press, 1951. Also in William Petersen (Ed.), *American Social Patterns*. Garden City, N. Y.: Doubleday & Company, Inc., Anchor Books, 1956.

42. Sherif, Muzafer, and Carolyn Sherif. *Social Psychology*. New York: Harper & Row, Publishers, Incorporated, 1969.

43. "In the Company of men," made by, and available from, William Greaves Productions, Inc., 254 West 54th St., New York, N.Y.

Jill Landsdowne

ELEVEN

CREATING EFFECTIVE ORGANIZATIONS

Introduction

On March 25, 1947, in Centralia, Illinois, there occurred one of the worst mine explosions this country has yet known.[1] Of the 142 men who went down the shaft of Centralia No. 5, only 31 returned to the surface alive. The 111 men who did not come back were killed in an explosion that they had expected but had been powerless to prevent. Off and on, conditions had been highly dangerous in the mine for at least five years. Eventually the explosion occurred, as others like it have occurred since.

There were several organizations which could have closed the mine before the explosion took place. The Centralia Coal Company, which owned the mine, or its parent organization, Bell and Zoller, could have closed it. So could the Department of Mines and Minerals of the State of Illinois, or the United Mine Workers, which represented the workers in the mine. That none of them did was not due to bureaucracy, but may instead have resulted from the lack of it.

The word "bureaucracy" is used in two different ways. In everyday speech, it means any large organization. Since organizations get slower and more rigid in responding as they get larger, this definition has led to the belief that bureaucracy is inefficient. As a technical term, however, "bureaucracy" has quite a different meaning. It refers to an organization set up according to certain principles rather than to one of a certain size. Some of these principles are that offices are filled by full-time rather than part-time employees, that the officials make decisions according to rules which can be learned, and that they gather information on the effects of the decisions which they make. For any given size, organizations set up according to these principles are more effective than those established on other principles, such as employment on the basis of kinship or feudal loyalty to a ruler.

The Illinois Department of Mines and Minerals at the time of the Centralia disaster was not a bureaucracy. In a bureaucracy, officials are selected and promoted according to their technical expertise. They are given expert training and freedom from arbitrary dismissal, and they are expected, in return, to make a full-time career of their jobs in the organization. The mine inspectors in the Illinois department, on the other hand, were appointed as part of a political patronage system. They expected to remain in office only until their party lost an election, and they were expected to solicit campaign contributions from the management of the mines they were inspecting. Reports of mine inspectors were filed, but nothing was done to see if their recommendations were complied with.

From this summary it might seem that the Illinois Department of Mines and Minerals was a particularly glaring example of a badly structured organization. Upon inspection, however, many other large-scale organizations are similarly found to violate principles of bureaucratic organization. The first question to which we must address ourselves in trying to understand organizations is therefore that of why individuals who know how to create an effective organization may actually create something else instead. The answer, as we shall see as this chapter develops, is that no one person creates an organization. The various individuals and groups who develop organizations have different goals, some more compatible with the formal goals of the organization than others. The structure which emerges is the result of these competing forces, and it may not be what was desired by any of the participants.

The study of organization thus has many of the elements of formal Greek tragedy. From the beginning the end is seen; nobody desires it, and yet nobody seems able to prevent it. Let us look again at the Centralia explosion. There are two main dangers in a coal mine—coal dust and gas. Several safety precautions can be used to minimize the dangers of explosion. Haulage roads can be sprinkled with water or dusted with rock dust to cover the combustible coal dust. The blasting done to loosen the coal can be confined to the period between shifts, so that relatively few people will be in the mine if an explosion should occur. Similarly, the magnitude of the disaster can be limited somewhat by restricting the number of men working on one shaft of air and thus likely to be involved in the same explosion.

The mine inspector responsible for Centralia No. 5 had complained of conditions there for more than five years before the explosion took place. On February 7, 1942, he reported that the haulage roads needed to be cleaned and sprinkled. He also noted that the practice of tamping down the explosive charges with coal dust instead of with wet clay should be discontinued. Thereafter, he repeated his warnings every three months, adding to them the injunction that the mine should be rock-dusted. At times, his pleas seemed to have some effect. During December of 1944 the mine was cleaned up, but following that it was allowed to get dirty again. Finally, in April of 1945, the mine inspector closed the mine on his own authority for cleanup work. Cleanup work must be done continually to be effective, however, and soon the mine was dirty again.

By the end of 1945, complaints about the mine's condition caused the Mining Board to carry out an official investigation of the mine. The mine managers were told in advance when the inspection would take place, but the mine inspector and workers were not. According to the secretary of the local mine workers union, the inspection team was kept on the main (and cleaner) roads and was not taken back into the dusty parts. Also, riding on railway cars, the team members may not have been as aware of the dust as they would have been if they had walked in it.

After the official inspection failed to find conditions bad enough to shut down the mine, the local inspector no longer dared to close it down himself. The mine workers, who had lost the right to elect their own union leaders in a power struggle during the thirties, did not know where to turn for help. In March of 1946, they appealed directly to the Governor of Illinois to save their lives. Their letter was referred to the Department of Mines and Minerals by a secretary to the Governor, and was probably never seen by the Governor himself. Just over a year later, the explosion took place. More than half the miners who had signed the letter to the Governor were killed in it.

The Centralia mine disaster is not unique in giving this feeling of inevitability. The Chicago race riot of 1919 could be seen coming, as could the violence in Newark in the summer of 1967. The feeling of inevitability, however, may be misleading. While none of these three events could have been prevented, given the political and organizational structures which existed, all of them could have been avoided with different structures.

If man is to survive, perhaps no one thing is more important for him to understand than how organizations function and how they can be changed. In this pursuit, psychology is one of the many fields with a contribution to make. When individuals create organizations, they do so on the basis of their ideas about the nature of man, just as the conceptions of man which developed during the eighteenth-century Enlightenment influenced the drafting of the United States Constitution. What the field of psychology has discovered about human perception, motivation, and development thus has important implications for understanding and creating the kinds of social organizations which we can master, rather than ones which master us.

In this chapter we shall examine some of these implications. First, we shall look at the tasks which organizations must accomplish, whether they are as small as your immediate family or as large as General Motors Corporation. Then, at the end of the chapter, we shall consider how organizations may be designed to best accomplish those tasks.

Small-Group Processes

AN OBSERVATIONAL SCHEME

The study of small groups can serve as a useful introduction to the study of larger organizations. There are two reasons for this. First, as the smallest units in which many social processes can be observed, small groups are the most economical to study. Second, small groups are the building blocks of which organizations are built. As we have noted, the individual in an organization usually has most of his contact with it through a small, face-to-face group. By understanding the dynamics of that group, we can understand much about the functioning of the organization.

The first problem faced by the researcher when he begins to investigate small groups is the wide latitude of interpretation which group processes allow. If you ask several individuals who attended the same group meeting what happened at it, you will get surprisingly different answers. Where one person observes friendliness among the group members, another will perceive veiled competition and hostility. Where one sees nothing but the routine transaction of business, another will see the items on the agenda as questions relating to broader political and social issues. How is it possible to study group processes when even people who observed those processes disagree as to what they were?

The usual solution to this problem is to develop an agreed-on system of observational categories. This involves getting observers to agree on what specific behaviors will lead them to label interaction as "cooperative" or "competitive," "friendly" or "hostile." Different observers are then able to record each instance of behavior which fits in each of these categories, and to come up with comparable results. In developing such an observational system, the nature of the categories will depend on the problem to be studied. Often the first step in developing the category system is to question the participants in the social process being observed so that the observers can become at least as insightful about what is going on as the people they are observing. Categories developed in this way, if used to make systematic observations, may then result in the development of insights which the participants themselves do not have.

In this chapter, we shall organize our observations about organizations around a category system developed by R. F. Bales.[2] This system, called *interaction process analysis*, was devised within the context of an interdisciplinary approach to the analysis of stability and change in different cultures. The categories are thus particularly adapted to looking at the elements that diverse social organizations have in common.

The category system is shown in Figure 11–1. As will be seen, categories 4 through 9 deal with behaviors necessary to getting some

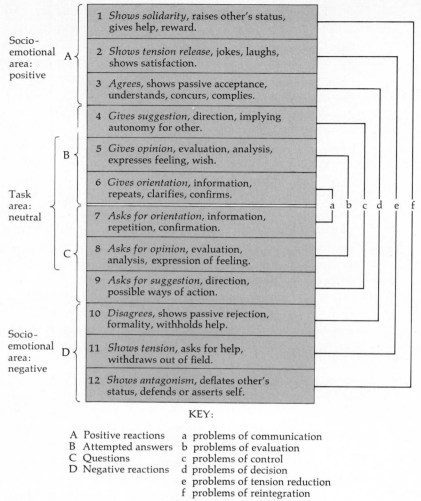

Socio-emotional area: positive — A

1 *Shows solidarity*, raises other's status, gives help, reward.

2 *Shows tension release*, jokes, laughs, shows satisfaction.

3 *Agrees*, shows passive acceptance, understands, concurs, complies.

Task area: neutral — B

4 *Gives suggestion*, direction, implying autonomy for other.

5 *Gives opinion*, evaluation, analysis, expresses feeling, wish.

6 *Gives orientation*, information, repeats, clarifies, confirms.

C

7 *Asks for orientation*, information, repetition, confirmation.

8 *Asks for opinion*, evaluation, analysis, expression of feeling.

9 *Asks for suggestion*, direction, possible ways of action.

Socio-emotional area: negative — D

10 *Disagrees*, shows passive rejection, formality, withholds help.

11 *Shows tension*, asks for help, withdraws out of field.

12 *Shows antagonism*, deflates other's status, defends or asserts self.

a b c d e f

KEY:

A Positive reactions
B Attempted answers
C Questions
D Negative reactions

a problems of communication
b problems of evaluation
c problems of control
d problems of decision
e problems of tension reduction
f problems of reintegration

Figure 11–1 *Bales's categories for interaction process analysis.*[3]

task done. Category 6, for example, is the giving of orientation, and category 7 involves asking for orientation. Orientation differs from opinion, dealt with in categories 5 and 8. Information given is orientation if it can be accepted by anyone hearing it, whereas more controversial material is opinion. "What is the date today?" and "What is the first item on the agenda?" are examples of questions which would usually fall in category 7, the asking for orientation.

As groups attempt to deal with a task, first orienting themselves toward it and then moving on to the stating of opinions and suggestions, they also arouse emotional reactions in their members. A person who suggests one thing may feel hurt and rejected by someone who suggests something quite different. The discussion may become heated, tempers may be lost, and things may be said which will be regretted later. The emotional reactions of the members as they attempt to solve a difficult problem may, in fact, lead to the group's disintegration.

The average small group thus must deal with two major tasks. The first is achieving certain things in its environment, and the second is maintaining the social relations and morale of its members. Categories 1 through 3 and 10 through 12 are relevant to this latter goal of maintaining positive socioemotional relations.

Now let us look at the categories in a different way. Earlier in the book, we looked at four functions which attitudes serve for the individual—the instrumental, value-expressive, ego-defensive, and group-affiliative functions. These functions correspond quite well to the distinctions made in interaction process analysis. The instrumental function is given the most prominence in Bales's scheme, and is differentiated into the six categories in the task area. Group affiliation is reflected in categories 1 and 12, which deal explicitly with the problem of maintaining integration of the group. Problems of ego defense are reflected in categories 2 and 11, in which behaviors indicating psychological tension and its release are coded. Finally, categories 3 and 10 deal with whether one person agrees or disagrees with another, and hence expresses or opposes the values which the other holds. We thus see that the types of behaviors which are categorized in interaction process analysis are, in fact, those which facilitate or frustrate the goals which individuals pursue in a group setting.

PROCESS AS TASK

As a group pursues its two main goals of achieving things in its environment and maintaining itself as a social structure, it must also deal with each of the six types of problem listed in Figure 11–1. Its members must communicate about issues, evaluate alternatives, reach decisions, enforce those decisions through control procedures, reduce the tension of its members, and reintegrate the group when it threatens to break up over substantive disagreements. Failure by an organization to deal with any one of these six tasks can seriously handicap its ability to carry out its intended purposes. The Illinois Department of Mines and Minerals, for example, had problems of communication, evaluation, and control. While failures of communication and evaluation were involved in the fact that higher-level decision makers remained ignorant of conditions in Centralia No. 5, the problems of control were the most serious. The importance of the mine owners as a political force in the state, when combined with a decision-making structure which gave real power to those with the most political influence, made the department in reality unable to enforce safety standards in the mines.

COMMUNICATION

Communication channels are so important to an organization that it is hardly a simplification to say that the structure of the communication channels is the structure of the organization. This is perhaps most elegantly illustrated in a classic study by Leavitt.[4]

Leavitt seated the members of a five-man group around a table with partitions between them. In the center of the table was a message box with slots leading from each person to each of the other seating positions. By opening or blocking slots, Leavitt could control who could send messages to whom. In this way he created four different communication structures: a circle, a chain, a Y, and a wheel. The patterns are shown in Figure 11–2. Note that the patterns do not represent where the participants' chairs were, but only who could send messages to whom. The chain would be the same pattern whether it were straight or curved, for example.

It is possible to analyze each of the patterns which Leavitt used in terms of how many steps it takes for a message to go from each position to each other position. In the circle pattern, for example, there are two positions which can communicate with any given position directly in one step and two positions which can communicate with it in two steps. It is the only pattern in which all members have equal access to communication. As you move from the circle to the chain to the Y to the wheel, you find more and more structural differentiation in terms of access to information. In the wheel, for example, the most central position (C) can communicate with each other position in only one step, while all positions other than C require two steps to communicate with one another.

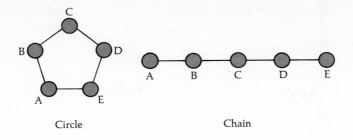

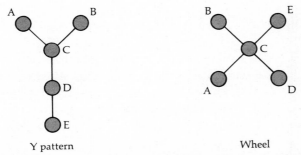

Circle   Chain

Y pattern   Wheel

Figure 11−2 *Communication patterns. (After Leavitt, 1951)*

Leavitt gave the groups tasks which required the group members to communicate with one another. Each group was given sixteen problems, and each of the problems consisted of finding out which one of a number of symbols had been distributed to all the members. The way in which the group was structured was found to have considerable impact on how the problem was solved.

The least centralized groups, such as the circle and the chain, were slowest in solving the problems. They did not operate according to any regular procedure, but just sent messages to one another until someone figured out that he had enough information to solve the problem. Despite their feeling that somehow they had to get organized, the group members generally enjoyed their participation in the experiment.

The most centralized groups, especially the wheel, solved the problems more rapidly. In the wheel pattern, the person at position C emerged as the group leader, as the problem could be solved most rapidly by each of the peripheral members communicating with him and his solving the problem. Despite the efficiency of the centralized groups, however, their members were generally dissatisfied with the communication pattern. Except for person C, the role of each member was reduced to the mechanical one of transmitting information to someone else who had the more enjoyable task of solving the problem.

Leavitt's study illustrates two important features of organization. The first is that a person's position in the communication structure of an organization is the largest single factor in determining whether he will be a leader or an isolate. The second, equally important, is that the performance of routine duties in an organization will often lead to morale problems. We shall see, later in the chapter, how individuals in organizations try to transform their jobs so that they can make decisions rather than operate in a routine way.

While both those findings of Leavitt's study do seem to apply to organization in general, one of his findings does not. We have seen that the most centralized decision-making structure was most efficient in Leavitt's study. This is not always true in more complex organizations, for too centralized a structure can lead to overloading the individuals in the central positions. This was nicely illustrated in a study by Bavelas and Smith.[5]

They gave groups a task much like Leavitt's. Instead of giving printed symbols to each member, however, they gave each one a number of colored marbles. The members' task was to discover what color marble they all had in common.

As long as they used plain marbles, they obtained results similar to those achieved by Leavitt. The most centralized structures, such as the Y and wheel, were most efficient in solving the problems. In the later part of the experiment, however, Bavelas and Smith made the task more difficult. Instead of giving the group members plain colored marbles, they gave them ones mottled with several colors.

To solve the problems with the mottled marbles, the group members had to decide whether the marbles that one person described as salmon and flesh-colored were the same as those someone else called orange and pink. The less centralized groups, with everyone communicating with everyone else, managed to reach some agreement on how they described the marbles and thus to start solving the problems fairly efficiently. In the wheel, however, it was quite different. The man in the central position was inundated with messages describing marbles, asking questions, and making suggestions. On this problem, the centralized structures were least efficient.

This overloading of the decision maker in a centralized structure also has its counterpart in real-life organizations. A company which expands rapidly without adequately decentralizing its decision-making structure will often find its top executives developing psychiatric symptoms from the increased stress. The optimal amount of centralization or decentralization of an organization thus depends both on its size and on the tasks it needs to perform.

EVALUATION OF ALTERNATIVES

We have already looked at one study which shows the importance of group members' developing shared ways of looking at things. In the study by Merei which we considered in the chapter on attitude change, it was shown that developing a shared frame of reference enables a group to resist domination by some outside force, in this case a formerly dominant boy.[6] The task of developing some agreement on how things should be viewed and evaluated is not an easy one in larger organizations. When we look at de Rivera's work on governmental decision making, we shall see that in many areas it is not that governmental policies are misguided, but rather that the _overnment has no policy.[7]

Even when organizations do have policies, it may be apparent that those policies are no longer adequate to the changed circumstances in which the organization finds itself. Because of the difficulty in creating a new consensus, however, leaders may continue to follow old policies even when they would prefer to gain acceptance of new ones. Because the old consensus is reinforced by sanctions, a high price may be extracted for attacking it. The problem of how to develop new views of a constantly changing reality is probably the most difficult one faced by organizational leaders.

Some hints as to the processes which are involved are given by the work of Lewin and his colleagues on changing food preferences.[8] Working during the Second World War, they were concerned with practical problems of how to improve the nutrition of infants and to reduce the wastage of meats derived from internal organs. Forces toward change, such as lectures on the importance of cod-liver oil and orange juice for babies or on ways of cooking kidney and liver, did not result in behavior change. From this, Lewin reasoned that there must be forces opposing the change, probably in the form of social norms on how to feed babies or on what foods are considered fit for human consumption.

If social norms are the force resisting change, then change can perhaps be brought about more effectively by reducing this force against change than by simply adding more forces toward change. Lewin and his colleagues tested this idea by using a group-decision technique as a way of changing social norms.

In a lecture situation, norms cannot be changed because individuals cannot communicate with one another about the ideas given in the lecture. Even if convincing arguments were presented that kidneys could be cooked in ways which made them very appetizing, a woman who merely heard the lecture might still wonder how other people would feel toward her if she served them to her family. If, on the other hand, the members of a group to whom she herself could relate were to decide that kidneys should be served, she would see herself as living up to her new social norm when serving them.

Lectures were thus contrasted with group discussions in their effect on the use of cod-liver oil, orange juice, and new cuts of meat. In all instances, the group-discussion techniques had greater effects. In the case of using new meat cuts, for example, only 3 percent of the subjects tried one of the new cuts after the lecture, while 32 percent of those who had participated in the group discussion did so. The mothers were more willing to give their children orange juice—55 percent did so after the lecture and 100 percent after the group discussion.

These studies by Lewin and his colleagues served as the earliest foundation for the group-dynamics movement which ultimately led to current interest in such techniques as sensitivity training and encounter groups. Their main implication for the functioning of organizations is their indication that the way to obtain support for new policies from individuals is to have those individuals participate in shaping the policies. Failure to consult others is one of the most common causes of the downfall of administrators, as is amply documented in case studies of administrative decision making.

DECISION MAKING

Shared ways of viewing things are important largely because they lead to decisions on concrete actions which should be taken. Decisions differ in the extent to which they are based on knowledge or ignorance of the relevant facts. Another major problem of organization therefore is to devise procedures which will provide decision makers with relevant information without being so cumbersome as to make decision making impossible. This task is very closely related to the previous two. Inadequate communication channels and assimilation of information to shared but inaccurate schemata are probably the two chief causes of misinformed decisions.

Problems of obtaining informed decision making are nicely illustrated in a study by Torrance.[9] Using three-man bomber crews as subjects, he gave them several problems to solve. One of the problems, for example, described the purchases and sales of a man in the horse-trading business. He bought a horse for $60, sold it for $70, bought it back again for $80, and sold it again for $90. The problem was to determine how much money he made or lost.

The answer is that he made $20. Although there are several ways of arriving at this answer, probably the easiest is to note that he paid out a total of $140 and took in a total of $160. The problem is tricky, however, and not all the individuals and groups got it right. The probability that a three-man group would agree on the correct answer was a function of which individuals got it right initially. If the pilot, who was an officer and the aircraft commander, had the right answer, this answer was adopted by the group. If the navigator, who was also an officer, was the only one to have the correct answer initially, the group usually adopted his answer. If the gunner, who was an enlisted man, was the only one to get the problem right initially, the group frequently failed to adopt the correct answer. There are barriers to upward communication which prevent a lower-status individual from communicating unwelcome information to someone of greater status or power.

The magnitude of the barrier to upward communication depended on whether the three men were drawn from the same aircraft crew or from three different crews. The gunner's correct solution was less likely to be adopted if he was participating with the members of his own crew. The fact that the pilot was not only an aircraft commander but his own aircraft commander, in direct authority over him, increased the barrier to communication.

As we shall see when we look at larger organizations, these barriers to upward communications cause distortion of information communicated to decision makers and often make them misinformed without their realizing that they are. Because of this, organizations which want to make informed decisions must use special measures to ensure that dissenting and unpopular views will be communicated to individuals with power. Norms must be developed which will not merely tolerate, but reward, such communications. Some industrial firms, for example, reward not only an individual who makes a valuable suggestion for change but also his immediate superior. Without such a system, the individual who has an idea as to how things might be done better may keep it to himself for fear that, even if the company gives him a bonus for it, his immediate supervisor, seeing a suggestion for change as a criticism of his methods, might make him suffer for it. Rewarding the superior also makes him somewhat more tolerant of innovative suggestions.

CONTROL

To be effective, organizations must not only make decisions but also have some power to implement them. In larger-scale organizations, money and votes are two of the main currencies of power. (The conversion of money into votes is called campaigning and is regarded as a legitimate enterprise. The conversion of votes into money is called corruption and is not.) The power to hire, fire, or evaluate others, and the right of access to information are two other important sources of organizational power.

In small groups, anything which makes one person able to reward or punish another may be regarded as a source of power. If one person is attracted to the other, agreeing with him will be rewarding and disagreeing will cause imbalance. Attraction can thus serve as a basis of influence. This is illustrated in a study by Kurt Back.[10]

The experimental task which Back gave to two-person groups was to write a story about a series of pictures. First, each subject wrote his own story, then the two subjects conferred on what they had seen in the pictures. Then each again wrote his own story. Without the subjects' realizing it, each partner had a different series of pictures, so that each saw somewhat different things. This made the initial stories vary in predictable ways, and made it possible to measure how much each subject influenced the other by how much the stories changed after the conference.

Attraction between the two partners in each group was varied in one of three ways. Some subjects were told that they had been selected in such a way that they were sure to like each other. Others were told that they were competing for a prize, and still others, that their group was going to be used as a model to teach other groups how the task should be performed. For comparison, subjects in the fourth group were not given any basis of attraction to their partners. They were told that the attempt to pair people who would work well together had not been successful because of scheduling difficulties, and nothing was said to them about serving as a model or winning a prize.

The differences which Back found between the high-attraction groups and the low-attraction groups are interesting, and they could not all be predicted on an intuitive basis. Individuals in high-attraction groups made greater efforts to persuade each other, but also resisted being persuaded to a greater extent. In contrast, those in the low-cohesive groups didn't seem to care what they wrote in their stories—each made little effort to persuade his coworker, but was quite willing to compromise if his partner tried to persuade him.

The outcome of the greater involvement in the high-attraction groups was that the individuals reached more agreement than those in the low-attraction groups, and did so by changing their stories in unequal degrees. Because both partners were trying to write the best story possible, one sometimes won the other over completely by the force of his arguments. What compromise occurred in the low-attraction groups, on the other hand, was of a more mechanical nature. The participants split their differences down the middle without much attempt at persuasion.

While participants' behavior was influenced by each of the high-attraction arrangements, the nature of the interaction depended to some extent on the basis of attraction. Where it was based on anticipated liking, the subjects tended to converse about topics unrelated to the experimental task in the attempt to get to know each other better. Those who expected to serve as a model for later problem-solving partnerships were much more guarded, and they interacted the least of the high-attraction groups, perhaps because they were trying not to spoil the favorable picture which the experimenter apparently had of them. Finally, those who were competing for a prize were the most businesslike and involved in trying to persuade each other.

One of the most widely accepted categorizations of social control is that of French and Raven.[11] They list five bases of power. *Reward* power and *coercive* power are self-explanatory. *Legitimate* power stems from a person holding a position which is accepted as giving him the right to make certain decisions influencing others. *Expert* power derives from the expert's ability to give or withhold help, and thus may be regarded as similar to reward and coercive power. Finally, *referent* power, which French and Raven assume to operate in terms of identification, would lead to reward or the lack of it through the operation of forces toward cognitive balance.

The use of power is limited by the extent to which the other individual has counter power. One person's having power with respect to another does not mean that he can influence the other if the other also has power with respect to him. *A*'s ability to use his power to influence *B* can also be limited by *C*'s having power with respect to *B* and using it to counter *A*'s power. Individuals in organizations who are subjected to pressures in one direction can sometimes increase their freedom of action by creating groups which will exert pressures on them in the opposite direction.

With the exception of coercive situations in which an individual is held against his will, the exercise of power is also limited by the willingness of the individual to leave the situation. A threat of firing, for example, means little to a person who has other equally attractive employment possibilities, but means much more to a person who does not. To understand the operation of power in organizations, it is therefore necessary to look not only at the forces which can be brought to bear on an individual, but also at the counter forces which he can mobilize and the other alternatives open to him. Finally, it is necessary to consider what costs he may be willing to pay.

TENSION REDUCTION

As we shall see when we look at the larger organization, failure to deal with the psychological tensions of its members can be a major source of inefficiency in the organization. At first glance, it might seem strange that the course of history is sometimes changed by a major leader's leaving a meeting in a fit of temper or being unable to cope with urgent affairs because he is suffering from debilitating anxiety. Considering the pressures under which such individuals operate, however, it would perhaps be more surprising if they could always cope with them.

In small groups also, the psychological needs of members may interfere with the task functions of the group. This is illustrated in a study of decision-making conferences in business and industry carried out by Fouriezos, Hutt, and Guetzkow.[12]

In their study, observers recorded the interaction of the groups as they dealt with real-life problems. The observational scheme enabled the observer to count the number of behaviors of the group participants which appeared to be expressions of their personal needs rather than attempts to deal with the task. If the group praised one participant for doing some job well, for example, and another member of the group stated that he thought he himself had been doing a good job also, his remark would be counted as the expression of a self-oriented need.

The expression of such needs was found to be related to the presence of group conflict, low group solidarity, lack of satisfaction with the group, and low productivity. These relationships were significant even though the use of diverse real-life groups introduced many other sources of variation and necessitated the use of rather crude measures. The study does not, however, tell what was cause and what was effect. Whether the groups were unproductive because they contained members who expressed neurotic needs, or whether the frustration of belonging to an unproductive and conflict-ridden group called out the expression of the self-oriented needs, is not made clear. Whether the causality worked in one of these directions or in both, however, it is clear that a group must deal with the needs of its members if they are to deal effectively with tasks. Nor should the personal consequences for the group members of failing to deal with their psychological needs be overlooked. As recent research has shown, encounter groups which are run without skilled leadership may cause individuals to bring up problems which the group cannot deal with and may lead to the development of serious psychological symptoms.

REINTEGRATION

Failure to deal with a group member's needs may not only be disturbing for him; it may lead to his leaving the group. Because of the divisive effects of working on a task, groups must constantly make efforts to reestablish themselves as a social unit. This is partially apparent in the course of a meeting. Before any business is started, interaction on irrelevant matters serves to develop group cohesion. After the formal business is over, expressions of solidarity and tension release again serve to reaffirm the interpersonal ties strained by the disagreements during the meeting. The reluctance of group members to subject themselves to the strain of disagreement is often shown by postponement or avoidance of conflict-laden issues. If the members of a decision-making group spend 45 minutes laughing and joking before getting down to business, it is fairly certain that the agenda contains items with a high potential for serious conflict.

Dealing with the socioemotional needs of the group is one of the main tasks of group leadership. This is illustrated in Bales's research, which shows that groups often have a differentiation of leadership, with one leader serving as the main organizer of the group's work and another as the social specialist who provides sympathy, understanding, and emotional support for the members.[13] Traditionally, differentiation of role along these lines has been shown in the American family, with the father cast as task leader and the mother as socioemotional leader regardless of the characteristics and aptitudes of the particular individuals involved.

The group members' understanding of the six tasks of groups, which we have discussed, can lead to better group functioning. A person who is aware of the emotional impact of his actions and who sees the need for dealing with the emotional needs of others can be a more effective group member than one who does not, a proposition which serves as the basis for laboratory training in group processes. While this type of insight may also be useful to an individual in functioning as a member of a large-scale organization, the problems of the larger organization are more complex. Many of them need to be dealt with not only through the development of individual insight but also through structural change. Let us look at examples of organizations which have failed to perform the six tasks which we have listed, and see what clues they provide as to how organizations may be improved.

Achieving Organizational Goals

Social structure is not immediately apparent in small groups. If one person frequently speaks to another, they do not usually think of this occurrence as a communication channel. If there is another person who is popular and tells jokes, he is not conceived of as functioning to maintain the morale of the organization. As an organization grows larger, however, the roles which were performed by individuals in the group require larger social organizations to carry them out. Both creating a system of internal communications and dealing with morale problems within the organization are functions which, in a large organization, will be largely left to specialized parts of the organization.

In this section we shall examine how the six tasks of organization, which we looked at in small groups, are carried out in larger organizations. We shall look at examples of what happens when they are not carried out, and try to see what organizations can do to perform them more effectively. Because organizations are composed both of positions having certain formal relationships with one another and of individuals filling these positions, we shall consider proposals of two kinds. Some of the proposals will concern the institutional arrangements, and others will be suggestions on the orientation of the individuals in the organization.

IMPROVING COMMUNICATION

As a bureaucracy exists in theory, individuals at lower levels transmit information upward in the organization. Those at higher levels, obtaining information on all aspects and parts of the organization, are best qualified to make general policy decisions, which are then transmitted down through channels and are implemented at the lower levels. In theory, this leads to the organization's consistently following policies which are well adapted to its organizational goals and which take account of the variety of conditions it confronts.

Anyone who has worked in a large-scale organization, whether it is a business, union, or governmental agency, is bound to feel somewhat skeptical of this theoretical picture. In practice, the policy decisions made at higher levels are frequently completely unworkable at the lower levels. This problem is handled by modification and reinterpretation of the policy as it is transmitted to lower and lower levels in the organization, so that what is actually done in the field may be quite different from what top decision makers intended. The deviation from official policy is concealed as information is transmitted back up through channels, so that the higher-level personnel are systematically misinformed as to what is actually being done. Because they are misinformed, they do not know that the policies they have established are unworkable, and they continue to make unrealistic decisions. These in their turn are distorted as they are transmitted downward, and the cycle of unworkable decision and official misinformation repeats itself. In many organizations, the discrepancy between official policy and what is actually done is so great that strict adherence to rule is an effective way of crippling the organization. If everyone does exactly what he is supposed to do according to official policy, the organization cannot function. Let us look at a study by Peter Blau and see what light it throws on this phenomenon.[14]

Blau's study dealt with an employment agency in a large metropolitan area. The rules of the employment agency were designed to select the best-qualified applicant for each available position. To achieve this end, the specified procedures called for obtaining detailed information from each applicant. This information was supposed to be kept on file. When the agency heard of a job opening, the procedures called for selecting the best-qualified person for the job from those in the files and sending him to apply for the job.

The department Blau studied, however, was primarily concerned with placing individuals in a clothing industry. In this industry, slack periods alternated with periods of feverish activity. When a company was hiring, it did not want the best-qualified man the next day—it wanted any reasonably qualified person immediately. Employers not only called the employment agency to fill positions; they also placed help-wanted signs on the sidewalk and frequently hired the first person to walk in off the street.

To cope, this department of the employment agency used different procedures from those specified in the regulations. Instead of selecting a qualified person from the files, it selected applicants from those sitting in the office at the moment. Although this might not produce the best-qualified man, it did succeed in getting someone to the employer before the job had been filled. Since there might not be anyone even remotely qualified in the office when notice of a vacancy came in, other modifications to procedure were made. Individuals were scheduled for frequent interviews and were kept waiting in the office for them. This ensured that an adequate pool of applicants would be available. Furthermore, the receptionists who scheduled the interviews also changed the nature of their own jobs. They were supposed to follow rigid rules as to when each person's next interview would be scheduled. Instead, they made judgments about how badly a particular applicant needed work and scheduled the ones they thought to be in greatest need for the most frequent interviews. This transformation of a mechanical task into one involving the exercise of judgment and choice will be seen frequently in organizations.

The procedures followed in the employment agency were adaptive in one sense and maladaptive in another. They coped with the immediate situation which the local agency faced. Because the result was that higher administrative levels were not being informed about policy inadequacies, however, they also had maladaptive aspects. The bad consequences of policy errors at higher levels were not felt, so the errors were not corrected.

Blau's study illustrates what is probably the greatest barrier to communication within organizations, the existence of power differentials. As other studies have shown also, individuals are very guarded in what they communicate to those who have power over them. The bearer of unwelcome news is seldom rewarded, and subordinates have an understandable reluctance to tell their superiors what is wrong with organizational policy.

Although the tendency to distort information passed upward in the organization is understandable, its consequences can be devastating. Policy makers who are told only what they want to hear can get very far from reality, as we saw in the case of the Centralia explosion. What, then, can be done about the problem?

One solution is to limit the power of supraordinates to exact reprisals from subordinates. The king may want to chop off the head of the bearer of unpleasant tidings, but he may be prevented from doing so by a group of powerful barons who insist that this just isn't done. Traditional bureaucratic structures use such devices as hiring on the basis of competitive examinations, granting of tenure in office after a probationary period of service, and the conduct of independent reviews of personnel decisions to limit the dependence of the officeholder on the good will of his immediate superior. The lack of these safeguards was one of the major weaknesses of the Illinois Department of Mines and Minerals.

Although these measures may alleviate the problem somewhat, they are not sufficient to remove it. Some less traditional possibilities must therefore be considered. They are the creation of parallel channels of communication, the decentralization of decision making, and the development of internally directed officeholders. The first of these is often used informally. The school principal may rely on the janitor to give him information which is not passed upward through official channels, and the President may send a special envoy to investigate conditions reported by the Ambassador. These techniques can make some improvement in communications, although they too have weaknesses. The janitor may be a biased source of information, and what he tells the principal about the teachers may be largely a function of how much they mess up their classrooms. Similarly, the biases of the special presidential adviser may be well known, and he may be told what he wants to hear. For important communications, however, two channels are probably better than one.

The decentralization of decision making is based on the idea that if information cannot be given to people who have power, maybe power can be given to people who have information. Because individuals who participate in making decisions are much more willing to carry them out than those who do not participate in making them, a broader distribution of authority within an organization may result in more, rather than less, adherence to official organizational policy.

In the case of the employment agency, decentralization would have meant giving its local departments power to devise procedures for pursuing organizational goals within the context of their own particular problems. Following this approach would have had two major advantages. First, because the modifications in policy which they were actually carrying out would have been officially approved, the local units would have been more willing to report accurately what they were doing. Second, the following of diverse policies by different local agencies could have served as a natural experiment, giving central decision makers much useful data as to what did or did not work under various conditions.

Closely related to the development of more widespread participation in decision making are the selection and development of decision makers who are willing to make sacrifices for the good of the organization. Sometimes the messenger has to risk having his head chopped off, the congressman to risk losing party funds for his reelection campaign, or the official to risk being fired. He will be more willing to do this if the organization is based on normative, rather than utilitarian or coercive, authority. Again Blau's study serves as an example.[15] Attempts to make interviewers more productive by introducing differential rewards based on competitive evaluation actually made them less productive. They became so concerned with improving their ratings that they did so at the expense of those aspects of performance which were not easily measured. A comparable work group whose members were tenured and who operated on the basis of internalized professional standards proved more productive than the group threatened with dismissal. Individuals who are bound to an organization's goals only by the ties of immediate self-interest will deceive the organization when it is to their advantage to do so.

IMPROVING EVALUATION

The evaluation of incoming information by an organization involves, just as does individual perception, the relating of new information to old. The information is assimilated to the schemata of those to whom it is transmitted, with two possible consequences for the organization. One is that the information will be distorted as it is transmitted; the other, that alternatives will be misevaluated when it is ultimately acted upon. Let us look at some examples of these possibilities as presented in Joseph de Rivera's *The Psychological Dimension of Foreign Policy*.[16]

In this book, de Rivera discusses in detail four major policy decisions of the United States government. The examples which we shall look at here are all drawn from the decisions involved in our entry into, and participation in, the Korean war, a subject which has been intensively studied by Snyder and Paige.[17]

Early in June of 1950, the United States Ambassador to South Korea sent a cable notifying the State Department that North Korean forces were massing along the border between North and South Korea, and indicating that they had an overwhelming superiority over the South Korean forces in the area. Although the massing of forces is often a warning of imminent attack, and the Ambassador had a reputation for being a reliable source of information, no particular attention was paid to his message. Even when the attack took place a few weeks later and the United States became involved in the ensuing war, the contents of this cable were not considered. As a result, the strength of North Korean forces involved in the attack was considerably underestimated, and United States policy was based on erroneous assumptions about the ability of the South Korean forces to deal with the attack. What caused this dramatic failure of evaluation of information?

Like many such failures, it was caused by interpreting the information on the basis of erroneous assumptions. Three widely shared beliefs in the United States at that time were that North Korea was a completely captive puppet of the Soviet Union, that the Soviet Union could not develop an atomic bomb until at least 1954, and that it was inconceivable that the Soviet Union would risk war with the United States without atomic weapons. If all these things had been true, the Soviet Union would never have permitted North Korea to attack South Korea, thus risking war with the United States long before a Soviet atomic bomb could be developed. Since it was assumed that they *were* true, the ambassador's message was taken to signify something other than an impending North Korean attack on South Korea.

Some explanation needed to be found for it, however. Since the Ambassador had recently been in Washington requesting additional arms for the South Korean forces, his cable was seen merely as further justification of his budget request. Exaggerating the financial needs of one's own part of an organization is such a normal part of bureaucratic life that the assumption that the Ambassador was doing so was not incompatible with his reputation for honesty. It is so common, in fact, that everyone forgot about his cable. They didn't remember it even when the invasion took place.

Although it is more apparent when information has been incorrectly evaluated than when it has been perceived relatively accurately, the evaluation process *always* involves assimilation to existing schemata. The history of the Korean war abounds in examples. Consider, as illustration, the interpretations made after the invasion had taken place and had been identified as more than a mere border incident:

> The Chairman of the Joint Chiefs of Staff believed that the Soviet Union might try to move into Iran. A high official in the State Department believed that Soviet foreign policy was quite cautious in its expansionism. The President believed that a nation did not become belligerent unless it thought its opponents too weak to fight. Hence, when news of the Korean attack first reached government officials, it was perceived in slightly different ways. The Chairman of the Joint Chiefs of Staff appears to have seen the event as a diversionary move before a major blow against Iran. The State Department official interpreted the invasion as a tentative probing action. The President saw the attack as similar to Hitler's invasion of Czechoslovakia.[18]

From the perspective of history, it is easy to identify erroneous assumptions of an earlier time. It is much more difficult to identify the erroneous assumptions of one's own time, for the principles which are most readily taken for granted are often the ones which are most likely to be wrong. What, then, can be done to minimize the possibility of basing a policy on the misinterpretation of events?

Generally, there seem to be two measures which organizations can take to minimize this danger. One is to establish structures which ensure that minority points of view will be presented; the other is to increase the self-understanding of decision makers. Two ways of ensuring the presentation of unpopular views are to clearly define who should participate in making certain decisions, and to give certain individuals and groups the responsibility of playing the "devil's advocate."

As Snyder and Paige show, the composition of governmental groups making such important decisions as whether or not to go to war is at present unspecified.[19] This not only means that those making the decision are not responsible for it, but also makes it possible for the President to exclude anyone whose opinion he expects to differ from his own. This leeway presents a serious danger that unquestioned assumptions will remain unquestioned.

Simply ensuring that all relevant decision makers are included is not enough to make sure that all points of view will be heard. The phenomenon which we saw operating in Torrance's experiment with the bomber crews operates equally in the United States Cabinet. John Kennedy heard virtually no dissenting views when he decided upon the ill-fated Cuban invasion, although some of the individuals present has private doubts. As de Rivera suggests, it may be necessary to entrust a special organization within the government with the role of presenting opposition arguments to major policy decisions. decisions.

On the other hand, the provision of a devil's advocate within the government might not be an effective way of dealing with the problem. In general, individuals and agencies, when established as independent judges of policy makers, become involved in making policy themselves and lose their independence. If the devil's advocate sometimes succeeds in making a strong opposition case, his recommendations may be accepted and he may become the policy maker he is supposed to be criticizing. For the provision of an opposition case, there is probably no effective substitute for the political process. We shall return to this idea later in the chapter.

The final way of minimizing misinterpretation, already mentioned, is to increase the insight of decision makers. By learning some of the factors leading to erroneous interpretations, they can take steps to avoid them. John Kennedy, for example, learned from the experience of his Cabinet's failure to present strong opposition arguments to the Cuban invasion. He later encouraged meetings of his top advisers without his being present, so that ideas differing from his own might be more freely developed. Similarly, insight into one's own motives and into the diversity of historical precedents can help safeguard the individual against those misinterpretations brought about by ego-defensive processes and by false analogies to a familiar historical event.

IMPROVING DECISIONS

As we have seen, inadequate decisions may be made through ignorance of important information or through misevaluation of the information considered. Equally important failures of the decision-making process are those in which no decision is made, a decision is made prematurely, or a decision is made under conditions which prevent its implementation. Let us consider these possibilities.[20]

The decision-making processes which took the United States into the Korean war involved both a failure to make decisions when they should have been made and premature arrival at a decision when it finally was made. Prior to the North Korean invasion of South Korea, the United States simply did not have a policy with respect to Far Eastern affairs. Both governments and the societies of which they are a part contain many relatively independent centers of power. A government may be considered to have a policy when it can obtain sufficient agreement from these power centers to be able to follow a goal-oriented course of action with respect to a class of events. If, on the other hand, there is little agreement among various groups, and if these groups are powerful enough to prevent the implementation of policy, the government will be reduced to following whatever pressures are strongest at the moment and will be prevented from consistently pursuing any particular set of goals.

This was the situation with respect to Far Eastern affairs prior to the outbreak of the Korean war. While several power centers within the State Department and the armed forces shared some goals with respect to the area, their priorities were quite different. General MacArthur, as Supreme Commander for Allied Powers in occupied Japan, was the ruler of a nation of 83 million people as well as the central figure in decision making within the armed forces and a leader having strong political support from the Republican party. His Far Eastern policy was to use whatever allies were available to limit the territorial expansion of communist governments, avoiding war if possible and risking it if necessary. This differed significantly from the Far Eastern policy of the State Department. Although it too aimed at the containment of mainland China, the State Department policy also had, as a long-term goal, the establishment of friendly relations with the government which had ensconced itself in firm control of mainland China. In order to make this possible in the long run, it wished to avoid too great an American commitment to Chiang Kai-shek, and particularly to avoid supporting him in any direct attack on China. Some individuals within the State Department also had a commitment to further the development of the United Nations.

Where basic disagreement on policy exists, leaders may do one of several things. They may take the issue to the political arena and win support for a position; they may make internal compromises which will gain sufficient support so that some policy can be implemented; they may follow the pressures of the moment without a policy; they may capitalize on favorable events to destroy competing power centers; or they may try to mislead people into believing that the policy they favor is being followed. At the time of the outbreak of the Korean war, the third alternative, of meeting only immediate pressures, was being followed by the Truman administration with respect to the Far East. One practical consequence was that the United States government had no idea what it would do if North Korea attacked South Korea. Some statements by government officials seemed to indicate that the United States would play no role in such a conflict.

When the invasion took place, Truman decided, before meeting with any of his advisers, that it was similar to Hitler's invasion of Czechoslovakia and that North Korea must be stopped. Because he was emotionally committed to this view, the outcome of the several days of meetings which brought about United States intervention was largely a foregone conclusion. Since some of the decision makers opposed such intervention, it was limited initially to supplying equipment to South Korean forces, and reality was distorted to indicate that no American troops would need to be involved. The Seventh Fleet, however, was interposed between China and Formosa, bringing about the commitment to Chiang Kai-shek which had until then been successfully avoided.

The combination of failure to create support for a Far Eastern policy and the making of major decisions under the press of events with little thought for their long-term consequences thus seems to illustrate both the failure of decision making and the arrival at premature closure on decisions. The result of this course of events was that the United States failed to achieve any of its major goals in the area: war was not avoided, the mainland Chinese government was made thoroughly hostile to the United States, and yet the power position of that mainland Chinese government was in no way impaired.

Other examples of failures of decision making abound in any study of large-scale organization. What, if anything, can be done to prevent them?

Various technical changes in the decision-making process have been proposed, and under some circumstances, they might result in improvement. The decisions regarding entry into the Korean war might have been somewhat improved if the Ambassador's earlier cable had been considered so that North Korean forces were not so badly underestimated, if Truman had reserved judgment until obtaining more information, and if a systematic case had been made for some policy other than the one he was proposing.

These technical changes in the decision-making process, however, fail to deal with the main weakness of the Korean decision: the government's lack of agreement on policy before the invasion took place. That lack of policy agreement was in its turn the result of two failures of control—a failure of the government to be able to control armed forces which theoretically exist to implement, rather than to make, policy decisions, and a failure of the people effectively to control the policies of the government.

The differences which existed between Truman and MacArthur were not just technical differences on the best means to reach an agreed-upon end. Instead, they were differences as to what the goals of American policy should be, and as such, they should have been solved by political processes. The failure of the political system to choose a direction for American policy and to give the government the power to pursue that direction was what lay behind the lack of any Far Eastern policy. To some extent, this may have been a failure of political leadership. Truman might have campaigned on foreign policy and made the difference between his policy and MacArthur's so clear to the electorate that he could confidently implement his policy when he came to office. To some degree, however, the failure was not one of leadership but of structure. Authority and responsibility are not so clearly fixed in our governmental system as they might be. Further discussion of this topic, however, lies beyond the scope of an introductory psychology text.

IMPROVING CONTROL

As we have seen, large-scale organizations have two serious problems of control. One of them is represented in Blau's study of the employment agency. Decisions made at higher levels in the organization may be reinterpreted as they are passed down the chain of command, so that the policy which is actually implemented is different from, or even opposite to, the policy decided upon. The other control problem is equally serious, and was anticipated over a century ago by Max Weber when he wrote:

> Under normal conditions, the power position of the fully developed bureaucracy is always overpowering. The "political master" finds himself in the position of the "dilettante" who stands opposite the "expert," facing the trained official who stands within the management of administration.[21]

The difficulty is that the decision makers of larger-scale organizations, whether business firms, unions, or governments, are often able to act independently of, and contrary to, the interests of the larger membership which they supposedly represent. The two control problems are thus the problems of control by the organization and control of the organization.

That large organizations often do not exercise effective control over even the most important actions of their members is immediately apparent from the study of those organizations. Take, for example, the dropping of the second atomic bomb over Nagasaki.[22] Orders to the aircraft crew were that the bomb should be dropped only when the weather was clear enough to drop it by sighting rather than by radar. As the aircraft approached the target, the crew members made a decision that they would drop the bomb even if they had to do so by radar. Because the clouds broke as they reached the target, they did not actually have to disobey their orders to drop it only visually. Their willingness to do so, however, presented in miniature the same problem represented, at a higher level, by General MacArthur's following a different foreign policy from that of the President.

As has already been mentioned, problems of control in the employment agency which Blau studied became especially apparent when a new supervisor introduced a new method of evaluating the work of interviewers. While evaluation of interviewers had previously not been taken very seriously and had been based simply on the number of interviews conducted, the new department head instituted a complex method of evaluation based on eight criteria, including such considerations as the proportion of interviews resulting in placements.

The interviewers in one group had been employed by the employment agency for a considerable time. During the earlier period of their employment, they had developed an approach which, like the overall policy of the employment agency, stressed the goals of recommending the best-qualified man for the job and of providing extensive counseling for applicants. They had become accustomed to working cooperatively toward these goals. Finally, since they had been employed for more than a year, they had tenure with the agency and could be fired only for cause. The new evaluation procedure did not have much impact on their methods of work.

The members of the other group, however, were almost all new employees. They had not had time to establish cooperative ways of working, and they were on probationary, one-year appointments. They were quite concerned to maximize their ratings and devised some ingenious ways of doing so.

Blau used as a measure of competitive practices the extent to which one interviewer was more likely than others to fill the positions he had been first to hear about with applicants he himself had registered. The noncompetitive interviewer might let other interviewers find out about the position so that the best man could be recommended for it. The competitive interviewer could raise his own rating by placing one of his own applicants in the position. Some of the ways of doing so were given by one of the interviewers:

> When you take an order, instead of putting it in the box, you leave it on your desk. There was so much hiding of orders under the blotter that we used to ask, "Do you have anything under your rug?" when we looked for an order.

You might leave an order you took on your desk, or you might leave one you pulled from the box on your desk, even though you made no referral. . . .

Or you might take an order only partially. You write the firm's name, and a few other things; the others you remember. And you leave it on the pad of order blanks. You keep on doing this, and all these orders are not in the box.

You can do some wrong filling out. For instance, for a rather low-salary job, you fill out "experience required." Nobody is likely to make a placement on that except you, because you know that experience isn't required.

Or, if there are several openings on one order, you put the order into "referrals" (file category for filled job openings) after you make one placement. So you have a better chance of making the next placement than somebody else. Time and again, you see four, five openings on one order filled by the same person.[23]

In the more competitive group, the most competitive individuals were the most productive, for they were best at the practices needed for success in that situation. (The most productive of all was a man who dated one of the telephone operators and who had a disproportionate number of calls telling of openings routed to his desk.) In the less competitive group, on the other hand, competitive individuals were excluded by their colleagues from information shared by all the others. They were unable to compete effectively with an organized group, so they were less productive than the others. Because of its better organization, the noncompetitive group was more productive as a whole than the competitive group. The tough line adopted by the new supervisor had the opposite result from that intended, and made the organization less effective in achieving its major goals.

Blau's study suggests, as do many others, that treating individuals with consideration and giving them the maximum possible opportunity to participate in decision making may more effectively motivate them to work for organizational goals than will crude threats or rewards. In more general terms, the most important step toward increasing the internal control of an organization is to design it in such a way that employees can meet both their own needs and those of the organization. This in turn calls for organizational decision makers to be much more aware than they often are of both the professional and personal needs of other members of the organization.

This conclusion is also supported by the research of Irving Janis on the morale of combat units during the Second World War. Janis considered, among other things, the conditions which caused such groups to pursue goals which were markedly deviant from those of the larger organization of which they were a part. His results are paraphrased as follows. Persistently deviant behavior on the part of a local unit tends to be preceded by the following situations: (a) Most men in the unit have specific grievances against the leadership on the next level up, feel their needs are being neglected, that extraordinarily harsh demands have been imposed which menace their personal welfare, and that unnecessary deprivations have been inflicted; (b) the men either see no channel through which they can communicate these things to anyone who could rescue them, or else they think such communication will be useless; (c) they see little or no way that their deviant behavior will get caught; (d) central in the deviant unit are one or more members who communicate disaffiliative feelings about the organization, act against its norms themselves, or fail to prevent others from doing so even though they have the power.[24] Those familiar with *Catch-22* might think of relevant examples.

The two control problems of organization are thus closely related to each other. It is much easier for an organization to retain control of its membership if the members in turn feel that they have some effective control of the organization. This is often not the case. If the executives of a corporation own more than a small percentage of the stock, they, instead of the stockholders as a whole, will probably exercise effective control of it. Union organizations similarly are frequently run by one man for decades without any effective control by the membership. Why is this so common, and what can be done about it?

Part of the answer is given in an article "Union Democracy and Secondary Organization," by Lipset, Trow, and Coleman.[25] It is a study of the International Typographers Union, one of the few large union organizations in which leadership has repeatedly been successfully challenged and in which members have thus retained effective control of the executive. The main question asked in the study is why this union remained democratic when others did not.

The answer lay largely in terms of channels of communication. In most large organizations, the executives have a virtual monopoly on communication about the organization. While they may be required by the courts to furnish others with lists of stockholders, there still remains one important difference between them and others who might want to communicate with the stockholders. The executives can communicate at company expense, while anyone else must do so at his own expense.

Similarly, in unions the executives can use union funds to communicate with the membership. Since their communications present matters in a way supportive of the policies of the union leaders, these leaders are almost impossible to dislodge once they take office.

The existence of channels of communication independent of the decision makers of the organization is thus the first prerequisite for democratic control of an organization. Because decision makers frequently feel that they know, better than the organization membership, what is good for the members, and that the press of events justifies not telling them more than they ought to know, maintaining these channels of communication is extremely difficult. In the case of the typographers union, they existed largely because typographers do a great deal of night work. They therefore live on an odd schedule and associate with members of their own profession more than do most occupational groups. The incredibly numerous social organizations in which they associate with one another serve as parallel channels of communication about union affairs. Because these organizations communicate information about union matters which the union executive might have suppressed, they result in the membership's retaining control of the union.

It is important to note that these secondary organizations do not exist primarily to communicate information about union affairs. Merely having an independent observer within the union executive body who communicates to the membership would probably not be a sufficient source of communication for two reasons. First, he would not be able to judge well enough which things were important to communicate. Second, the membership would not devote time to study his communications if they were not presented in the context of supportive social organizations. Retaining control of an organization thus requires not only channels of communication, but also a pluralistic organizational structure which will make those channels part of a meaningful social structure.

IMPROVING TENSION REDUCTION

Organizations which meet the various human needs of their members will be more successful not only in enlisting the support of those members, but also in reducing the psychological strains of the members. Decision makers, during times of crisis particularly, are subjected to stresses which may seriously impair their functioning.

Let us consider two examples, not of serious impairment of functioning but of the momentary intrusion of personal needs into an important decision-making process. Both are drawn from the meeting of President Truman with his top advisers the day after the Korean invasion began. It was at this meeting that the basic decisions leading to United States intervention in Korea were taken.

After the situation had been presented to the group, President Truman asked each of his advisers to give his views. First, the Secretary of State presented his opinion and recommendations. The President next called on the Secretary of Defense. As de Rivera notes:

> The Secretary said that he had no recommendations to make. This failure to either make suggestions or present a clear view of the military situation, and the Secretary's general lack of participation in the meeting, may be partly accounted for in terms of the Secretary's resentment of the relation between the President and the Secretary of State. He evidently felt that since the Secretary of State had wanted responsibility for Korea, and since the President had favored his request, the Secretary of State could now stew in his own juice for a while.[26]

As we have already seen, this type of intrusion of personal needs reduces the efficiency of a decision-making group. In the case of the Korean decision, the strength of the North Korean forces and the necessary extent of American involvement in order to be effective were both seriously underestimated.

The second intrusion of personal needs took place later in the evening, and is again described by de Rivera:

> Towards the end of the meeting, the Undersecretary of State (formerly Director of the Bureau of the Budget) said, "I'd like to talk about the political aspects of the situation." Reportedly, the President snapped back, "We're not going to talk about politics. I'll handle the political affairs." . . .The Undersecretary of State did not speak again during the meeting and does not appear to have been present at subsequent meetings of the group. Furthermore, months later when the President and his advisors debated the wisdom of pursuing the invaders back into North Korea, no one brought up the question of politics. This was a serious omission, for, as Neustadt has observed, the considerations of politics would have dictated caution and averted the disaster that followed.[27]

Dealing with personal needs is a task for both leadership and the group as a whole. Norms must be developed which encourage the expression of honest emotion while condemning attack on others, withdrawal, or role playing. Decision-making groups in crisis situations are objectively in a situation which arouses strong emotion. As in the case of laboratory groups where emotions are aroused for different reasons, honest discussion of these emotions may lead to deeper understanding among members of the group and to personal growth. If, on the other hand, the group tolerates the dishonesty which is involved in not discussing the true causes of the emotion, it will be prevented from dealing with the realities of the external world because of the deceptions within the group.

While there are no simple rules which will free decision makers of all self-oriented needs, there are principles of developing group norms which will enable the group to deal with those needs. Presentations of such principles may be found in works by Egan[28] and by Schein and Bennis.[29]

IMPROVING INTEGRATION

The final task which organizations must accomplish is integration of their diverse parts. We have already seen how the human need for close social relationships leads to an identification with groups. In organizations, the result is that each part of the organization feels that it is doing the really important work and is distrustful of other groups. This has two important consequences. One is that positions involving coordination between different parts of the organization are stressful as the individual is subjected to incompatible demands from the parts which he must coordinate. Even more important, during times of stress, the individuals playing linking functions are rejected as untrustworthy by each of the parts which they are supposed to be coordinating, with the result that communications between different parts of the organization break down.

If the danger of this type of breakdown is known, however, its occurrence is not inevitable. Universities and cities, in times of potential conflict, may set up special communication groups which maintain a possible channel of communication between mutually hostile groups, and they are able to prevent the spread of rumor which might otherwise take place in the absence of reliable information. Such groups may thus do much to prevent unnecessary conflict.

The problem of integration of an organization, like the other problems we have discussed, is one which may be alleviated both by structural change in the organization and by personal change of the participating individuals. Physical arrangements which will increase the probability of chance interaction, decision-making jobs which require cooperative effort to achieve shared goals, and rotation of personnel through a variety of positions are a few of the techniques which can be used to give one part of an organization more understanding of other parts. Most important of all in solving the problem, however, is knowing that it exists. This is true for each of the problems we have considered. For that reason, the suggested ways of alleviating these problems are not intended as universal cures, and are, in fact, much less important than an analysis of the problems as they exist in a particular organization. As an example of this, let us consider a creative solution of a communications problem.

Status differences present a barrier to communication in the restaurant industry just as they do in other lines of human endeavor.[30] Waitresses take orders from customers. In the past, they used to then speak (or, given the noise conditions, more likely shout) the orders to the cook. The cook was, however, traditionally of higher status than the waitress. The potential was high for misunderstanding and conflict in a system which required a lower-status person to shout orders to a higher-status person, and in many restaurants the waitresses were frequently in tears as a result of it.

The solution was as elegant as it was simple. It consisted of the invention of the rotating wheel on which orders were clipped, which is now in common use. It kept waitresses from shouting at cooks, made it easier for the cook to plan his own activities in an efficient manner, and presented an indisputable record both of what had been ordered and of which order had come in first. By doing these things, it also stopped cooks from shouting at waitresses. The first step in solving problems is understanding what they are.

Summary

Many of the processes which have been described in this book may be seen operating in small groups and larger organizations. External events to which groups must respond are ambiguous, and they are interpreted in the light of what group members have learned in the past. The personal needs of group members are also important in understanding how a group functions. If these needs are not met, the resulting morale problems may lead to the dissolution of the group.

Small groups are especially useful in understanding social organization for two reasons. The first is that many important social processes take place within small groups. A person interacts with economic or educational institutions primarily through participation in a work group or a school class. The second reason is that the small group is the smallest social unit in which many significant social processes may be observed. Caution is necessary in applying the results of small-group studies to larger organizations, however.

Important social processes carried on in groups include communication, evaluation, decision, control, tension reduction, and reintegration. In this chapter, we have seen how an analysis of these processes may help us to understand the functioning of larger organizations.

Notes and Acknowledgments

1. Martin, John B. "The blast in Centralia No. 5, a mine disaster no one stopped." *Harper's Magazine,* March 1948 (196), # 1174, pp. 193–220.
2. Bales, R. F. *Interaction Process Analysis.* Cambridge, Mass.: Addison-Wesley Press, Inc., 1951.
3. Ibid., p. 59. By permission of the author and publisher.
4. Leavitt, H. J. "Some effects of certain communication patterns on group performance." *Journal of Abnormal and Social Psychology,* 1951 (46), pp. 38–50.
5. Experiment done by Alex Bavelas, and S. L. Smith, reported in J. Macy, Jr., L. S. Christie, and R. D. Luce, "Coding noise in a task oriented group." *Journal of Abnormal and Social Psychology,* 1953 (48), pp. 401–409.
6. Merei, Ferenc. "Group leadership and institutionalization." *Human Relations,* 1949 (2), pp. 23–39.
7. de Rivera, Joseph. *The Psychological Dimension of Foreign Policy.* Columbus, Ohio: Charles E. Merrill Publishing Company, 1968.
8. Lewin, Kurt. "Group decision and social change," in E. Maccoby et al. (Eds.), *Readings in Social Psychology.* New York: Holt, Rinehart and Winston, Inc., 1958, pp. 197–211.
9. Torrance, E. Paul. "Some consequences of power differences on decision making in permanent and temporary three-man groups," in A. Paul Hare, Edgar F. Borgatta, Robert F. Bales (Eds.), *Small Groups: Studies in Social Interaction.* Alfred A. Knopf, Inc., 1955, pp. 482–492.
10. Back, Kurt. "Influence through social communication." *Journal of Abnormal and Social Psychology,* 1951 (46), pp. 9–23.
11. French, J. R. P., Jr., and Bertram Raven. "The bases of social power," in D. Cartwright (Ed.), *Studies in Social Power.* Ann Arbor, Mich.: Institute for Social Research, 1959.
12. Fouriezos, N. T., M. L. Hutt, and H. Guetzkow. "The measurement of self-oriented needs in the discussion situation, and their relationship to

satisfaction with group outcome." *Journal of Abnormal and Social Psychology*, 1950 (45), pp. 682–690.

13. Bales, Robert F. "Task roles and social roles in problem-solving groups," in Eleanor Maccoby et al. (Eds.), *Readings in Social Psychology*. New York: Holt, Rinehart and Winston, Inc., 1958, pp. 437–447.

14. Blau, Peter. *The Dynamics of Bureaucracy*. Chicago: The University of Chicago Press, 1955.

15. Ibid.

16. de Rivera, Joseph. Op. cit.

17. Snyder, R. C., and G. D. Paige. *The United States Decision to Resist Aggression in Korea: The Application of an Analytical Scheme*. Evanston, Ill.: Northwestern University Press, 1958.

18. de Rivera, Joseph. *The Psychological Dimension of Foreign Policy*. Columbus, Ohio: Charles E. Merrill Publishing Company, 1968, p. 29. By permission of the publisher.

19. Snyder, R. C., and G. D. Paige. Op. cit.

20. de Rivera, Joseph. Op. cit.

21. Gerth, H. H., and C. Wright Mills. (Eds.) *From Max Weber: Essays in Sociology*. New York: Oxford University Press, 1958, p. 232. By permission of the publisher.

22. See Knebel, Fletcher, and Charles W. Bailey, II. *No High Ground*. New York: Bantam Books, Inc., 1960.

23. Blau, Peter. *The Dynamics of Bureaucracy*. Chicago: The University of Chicago Press, 1955, p. 59. Copyright 1955 by the University of Chicago. By permission of The University of Chicago Press.

24. Janis, Irving L. "Group identification under conditions of external danger." *British Journal of Medical Psychology*, 1963 (36), pp. 227–238.

25. Lipset, Seymour Martin, Martin A. Trow, and James S. Coleman. "Union Democracy and Secondary Organization," in William Peterson, *American Social Patterns*. New York: Doubleday & Company, Inc., 1956, pp. 171–218.

26. de Rivera, Joseph. *The Psychological Dimension of Foreign Policy*. Columbus, Ohio: Charles E. Merrill Publishing Company, 1968, p. 217. By permission of the publisher.

27. Ibid., pp. 222–223. By permission of the publisher.

28. Egan, Gerard. *Encounter: Group Processes for Interpersonal Growth*. Belmont, Calif.: Brooks/Cole Publishing Company, 1970.

29. Schein, Edgar H., and Warren G. Bennis. *Personal and Organizational Change Through Group Methods: The Laboratory Approach*. New York: John Wiley & Sons, Inc., 1965.

30. Whyte, W. F. "The social structure of the restaurant." *American Journal of Sociology*, 1949 (54), pp. 302–308.

GLOSSARY

acceleration principle: the economic principle that slight changes in demand for a consumer good cause great changes in demand for the machinery to make the consumer good.

achievement motive: a desire to accomplish things which are valued in one's culture.

acquired: developed only through exposure to certain environmental conditions. Speaking the English language is an acquired characteristic, for example.

acquisition phase: in stimulus-response learning, the period when the organism is first learning to give the response to the stimulus.

ACTH: the adrenocorticotropic hormone.

adrenal cortex: the outer portion of the adrenal gland, an endocrine gland at the end of the kidney.

adrenal medulla: the inner portion of the adrenal gland, an endocrine gland at the end of the kidney.

adrenocorticotropic hormone: a hormone secreted by the pituitary gland and controlling production of corticosteroids.

aerial perspective: the increased haziness of something seen at a distance.

afferent: carrying impulses toward the brain.

affiliation motive: a desire to have close interpersonal relations with others.

amnesia: a person's inability to remember a period of his life experience.

anchor point: a stimulus which is so familiar to a person that he compares other stimuli with it. For example, a person familiar with the weight of his bicycle might perceive the weight of other bicycles largely in terms of whether they are lighter or heavier than his.

androgen: a male sex hormone.

anomie: the lack of norms.

antagonistic muscles: pairs of muscles having opposite effects. The muscles which flex the elbow and those which extend it, for example, are antagonistic.

anticipatory socialization: the adoption of the apparent characteristics of a group or class one desires to join.

antidiuretic: inhibiting the production of urine. An antidiuretic hormone thus helps conserve body liquids.

anxiety: a state similar to fear except that, in anxiety, the cause of the fear is not known. A central concept in a psychoanalytic theory of personality.

artificial pupil: a hole in a surface placed in front of the eye which eliminates many depth cues.

ascription: assignment to a group on the basis of characteristics which can often be determined at birth, such as age, sex, or kinship ties.

assimilable discipline: discipline that is not highly threatening to the child.

assimilation: the perception of something as more similar than it actually is to something the perceiver expects or is familiar with.

associationist: a member of a school of philosophy which explained the succession of ideas in consciousness through their having acquired connections with one another.

assumptive context: the assumptions, based on past experience, regarding the physical source most likely to be causing stimulation of a given sense organ.

asthenic reaction: a reaction to anxiety characterized by feelings of fatigue.

attention: the selection of some of the available stimulation for special and immediate handling by brain centers.

attitude: a relatively enduring readiness to respond to an object in some way. It is composed of both beliefs about the object and sentiments toward it.

attitude scaling: the development of questionnaires composed of sets of interrelated opinion items, yielding more extensive information than opinion polling.

authoritarianism: a constellation of attitudes and personality factors related to sympathy toward fascist ideology.

authority: anyone seen as having a legitimate right to apply sanctions.

balance theory: a theory that people modify their perceptions to make them more internally consistent. Consistent perceptions are called balanced, and inconsistent ones, imbalanced.

behavior: the action of an organism from the point of view of an external observer.

behavior therapy: an approach to improving the human condition which places primary emphasis on changing the individual's responses to stimulus situations.

behaviorism: a school of psychology maintaining that psychology is the study of behavior.

belief: a cognition about the nature of the world.

binocular parallax: the difference in the retinal images of an object resulting from the two eyes being located at slightly different points in space.

bit: the amount of information needed to divide the number of equally probable alternatives in half. If someone is trying to guess the name of a certain person, telling him whether the person is a male or a female would give approximately one bit of information.

blank-slate hypothesis: the idea that no important components of human thought and behavior are innate.

Bogardus social-distance scale: a device for measuring attitudes toward members of a minority group by finding out how close a relationship to them the subject is willing to accept.

brightness constancy: seeing an object as remaining the same in brightness even though the amount of light reflected from it varies.

carpentered world: a world in which there are many straight lines and rectangular corners because it is filled with man-made structures.

caste: a rigid and endogamous social class.

catalyst: a substance which helps a chemical reaction to take place although it is itself not permanently changed in the reaction.

cathexis: a learned liking or aversion.

centrality: the relatedness of an item to a number of similar items. A central personality trait is related to many other traits, and a central member of a group has interpersonal relations with many members of the group.

central nervous system: the brain and the spinal cord.

cerebral cortex: the surface of the two large hemispheres of the brain which lie immediately under the skull. This portion of the brain is most enlarged in man as compared with other animals.

chance: factors having no relationship to those under investigation. Selecting the person who draws the highest card from a card pack is a way of leaving the selection to chance, for example.

character disorder: one of a wide variety of types of symptoms having in common that the individual does not live up to the expectations of his society.

chronological age: what is usually meant by age, the length of time since the person was born.

classical conditioning: a type of learning in which the organism comes to give an already existing response to a new stimulus.

closure: a gestalt principle of perceptual organization indicating that stimuli which form closed forms are likely to be seen as going together.

cochlear duct: a spiral tube in the inner ear. Movement of fluid in this duct stimulates the sensory receptors for hearing.

cochlear nucleus: a collection of cell bodies within the brain that process auditory stimulation.

cocktail-party effect: the filtering of stimulation so that one voice is attended to and others are ignored.

coding: changing the form in which information is transmitted or stored.

coercive power: the ability of one person to influence another by being able to punish or compel him.

cognitive: concerning ideas.

cognitive dissonance: an unpleasant state resulting from discrepancy between a person's beliefs and his behavior. The central concept in a theory by the same name first proposed by Festinger.

cognitive learning theory: a theory that not all learning is the learning of responses to stimuli, but that, instead, some learning involves associating stimuli or ideas with one another.

cognitive structure: a person's ideas about all his realities and the relationships of all these ideas to each other.

cohesion: the force(s) holding a group together, such as mutual attraction.

completion effect: the perception of an object as being continued behind something which is interposed between the observer and the object.

compulsion: a feeling that one must do something although he does not understand the underlying motives.

concept: a class of stimuli which may be described in general terms so that a person can recognize a novel example.

conditional reflex: a type of learning, first studied by Pavlov, in which a new stimulus comes to call out a response similar to a reflex response.

conditional response: a response, similar to an unconditional response, which comes to be called out by a stimulus paired with the unconditional stimulus.

conditional stimulus: a stimulus which is paired with the unconditional stimulus and which comes to call out the conditional response.

conditioned avoidance: a learning task in which the organism learns to make a response to a stimulus in order to avoid unpleasant stimulation.

conditioned reflex: conditional reflex.

conditioned response: conditional response.

conditioned stimulus: conditional stimulus.

confederate: a helper of the experimenter who poses as a subject.

conflict: opposition of the parts of something to one another.

conformity: modifying one's perceptions or behavior to achieve more similarity to the perceptions or behavior of others.

congenitally: from birth.

conscience: one's standards of what one ought or ought not to do.

consolidation hypothesis: the idea that it takes some time for memories to be permanently stored.

consonant: consistent, given the individual's assumptions about the world. Campaigning for a political candidate and having a high opinion of him are consonant, for example.

constancy phenomena: tendencies for objects to be perceived as remaining the same even though the stimuli coming from them change. See **brightness constancy, shape constancy, size constancy.**

contact comfort: Harlow's term for the motive which made baby monkeys prefer contact with a soft surrogate mother to contact with a wire surrogate mother.

content analysis: the categorization of verbal materials so that the proportion of materials falling in different categories will provide a relatively objective measure of their content.

contiguity: closeness together, in time or space.

contiguity theorist: a learning theorist believing that learning can take place without reinforcement.

contrast effect: a stimulus seeming to differ more from one with which it is compared than it actually does. An observer who noticed that one person was shorter than another might, for example, exaggerate the difference in their heights in his memory.

control group: a group similar to the experimental group in all respects except the level of the independent variable.

conversion: a radical change in a person's most important beliefs and values, usually accompanied by a reinterpretation of his past.

conversion reaction: the development of a specific physical symptom as a way of dealing with anxiety. The name stems from an earlier view that the anxiety was somehow converted into the symptom.

corpus luteum: a yellow mass which develops in the ovary at the point where an ovum was released if pregnancy has resulted. It is a source of hormones.

correlation: the extent to which things tend to go together. There is a correlation between the height of boys and the number of points they make in a basketball game, for example.

cortex: the outer layer, as of the brain or adrenal gland.

cortical: concerning the cortex.

corticosteroid hormones: numerous chemical substances produced by the outer layer (cortex) of the adrenal glands. They have diverse functions, such as control of water and salt balance, production of carbohydrate from fat and protein, and various responses to stress.

CR: conditional response.

criterion: a standard. A common criterion of learning is one errorless repetition. A person who can recite the material without error has reached the criterion and is presumed to know the material.

critical experiment: a single experiment making possible a choice among theories. It is thought seldom, if ever, to exist.

cross-pressures: influences pushing an individual to act in mutually contradictory ways, such as attempts to influence his vote in different directions.

CS: conditional stimulus.

culture: patterns of thought and behavior transmitted from generation to generation by learning, and the material products of those ways of behaving.

data: the actual observations on which theories are based.

decision tree: a series of questions the answers to which enable one to characterize concepts.

defended hostility: aggression expressed in an indirect or a disguised manner.

defense mechanism: a way of protecting the self from anxiety.

defining the situation: deciding what concepts one's culture would apply and hence what norms should be followed. One of the main functions of leaders.

dependency: a state of needing another.

dependent variable: a variable observed to see what effect the experimental conditions may have had.

depressive psychosis: a variety of severe mental illness especially characterized by self-hatred and negative emotions.

desensitization therapy: the reduction of an undesirable response to a stimulus by gradually introducing the stimulus while calling out a response incompatible with the response being eliminated. A horse which rears whenever it is saddled might have increasingly heavy weights put on his back while eating oats. As he cannot rear without taking his head out of the oats bucket, he may gradually learn to tolerate the weight without rearing.

developmental quotient: a measure, similar to an intelligence quotient, of how well a child performs for his age.

deviant: a person who is atypical of the group.

differentiation (as a way of reducing imbalance): the process of coming to see something as made up of different parts which are evaluated differently.

digit span: the number of digits a person can correctly repeat back immediately after hearing them.

diluted water: a solution of salt and water having a higher osmotic pressure than pure water.

direction: a gestalt principle of perceptual organization indicating that visual stimuli which line up with each other are likely to be seen as going together.

discrepancy principle: the idea that a person will be particularly attracted by a stimulus pattern which differs only slightly from a familiar pattern.

discriminated operant: behavior which has come to be called out by a stimulus by being reinforced only when that stimulus is present.

discrimination: the giving of different responses to slightly different stimuli.

discrimination learning: acquiring different responses to different stimuli, such as learning to approach a triangle but not a circle.

disinhibition: the reappearance of an extinguished response when an attention-demanding stimulus is presented.

displacement: the expression of a motive toward a substitute object.

dissociative reaction: a splitting off of some of a person's memories from consciousness. The most extreme cases would involve alternation of personalities.

dissonance: see **cognitive dissonance**.

dissonant: inconsistent, given the individual's assumptions about the world. Perceiving that one is campaigning for one political candidate while actually hoping that his opponent will win would generally be dissonant, for example.

division of labor: the breaking down of a task into various subtasks so that different people perform different roles.

dominance hierarchy: an ordering of organisms from the most successful fighter to the least successful fighter.

dorsal: toward the back of an organism.

drive: a motive, often one presumed to be based on a need of the organism.

ecological validity: the accuracy of perceptions because the world is such that the perceiver's assumptions about it are usually justified.

ECS: electroconvulsive shock.

EEG: electroencephalogram, a record of the electrical activity of the brain.

efferent: carrying impulses away from the brain.

ego: processes in the personality most in contact with the real world.

ego-alien: largely unconscious and unrecognized by the ego. Either impulses or moral standards may be ego-alien.

ego-defensive: serving to raise a person's opinion of himself by concealing the extent to which he is failing to live up to his moral standards or his idealized self.

ego ideal: one's long-range goals and aspirations.

eidetic imagery: what is popularly called photographic memory, though it is not truly photographic.

Electra complex: in psychoanalytic theory, the attraction of a girl to her father and its psychological consequences.

electroconvulsive shock: the causing of unconsciousness and convulsions by means of an electric current.

electroencephalograph: a device to amplify and record small changes in electrical potential spontaneously occurring in the brain.

embryology: the study of the development of an organism prior to birth or hatching.

emotional leader: an expressive leader; one who expresses emotions which other members of the group are feeling. Almost synonymous with socioemotional leader.

empathic: understanding others, presumably at least partially through identification with them.

empiricist: a member of a school of philosophy holding that all knowledge comes from experience.

endocrine gland: an organ secreting substances directly into the bloodstream.

endogamous: marrying within, rather than outside, the group.

environment: conditions external to the organism, including the intrauterine environment as well as conditions to which the individual is exposed after birth.

enzyme: an organic catalyst.

epinephrine: a hormone produced either by the adrenal medulla or artificially. Among its effects are increases in heart rate and blood pressure.

equal-appearing intervals: a method of attitude scaling developed by Thurstone and depending on judges who sort opinion statements into categories.

equivalent-stimulus technique: a method of discovering what an organism has learned by testing to see which new stimuli the organism will respond to in the same way it has responded to the previous stimulus.

ethnic group: a group of individuals sharing a common culture or subculture.

ethologist: a biologist specializing in the study of animal behavior, frequently under naturalistic conditions.

expedient: based primarily on considerations of practicality. In the study by Gross et al., a school superintendent who seldom said that a superintendent should always or never do a certain thing, but, instead, said that it depended on the circumstances.

experience: consciousness as viewed by the conscious organism.

experimental control: the elimination of alternate explanations of experimental results through the study of control groups.

experimental group: a group exposed to the conditions the effects of which are being investigated.

experimentation: a research method in which conditions are actively manipulated.

expert power: the ability of one person to influence another through having knowledge or ability which the other lacks.

externalization: the perception of one's difficulties as being due to some external cause when in reality they are caused by one's own characteristics.

extinction: the cessation of giving a learned response when the response is no longer reinforced.

facilitation of consolidation: an improvement in the efficiency of the process by which material is stored in long-term memory.

feedback: information on the state of a system used in the control of the system.

field expectancy: a learned idea about relations of different parts of the environment to one another.

figure-ground relationship: the tendency for a portion of what is perceived to stand out more clearly in consciousness than the whole.

fistula: a tube or opening, such as into the throat or stomach.

fixed action pattern: an organized motor response which is innate.

fixed-interval schedule: a pattern of reinforcing the organism for the first response after a certain period of time has elapsed since the last reinforcement.

fixed-ratio schedule: a pattern of reinforcing the organism once every time it makes a certain number of responses.

focal attention: processes making one thing occupy a person's consciousness at a given moment.

forced compliance: an approach to attitude change in which behavior is altered in the belief that attitudes will then change also in order to become consistent with the behavior.

formal organization: the structure of a social grouping as it exists on paper. Many informal groups and relationships arise within any organization which are not provided for in its table of organization and are thus not part of the formal organization.

fractional anticipatory goal response: in Hullian learning theory, a partial response, of the type made at the goal, which is made before the goal is reached, and which acts both to motivate and to reinforce behavior.

frame of reference: all those things a person considers in judging a particular stimulus.

fraternal twins: individuals born at the same time but no more similar genetically than any brothers or sisters.

frustration: failure to achieve a goal or an individual's reaction to such a failure.

functional equivalents: behaviors that serve the same motive for an individual.

functional fixity: failure to see a new use for an object because of its frequent use for a different purpose in the past.

functionalism: a school of psychology seeing the central problem of the field as discovering how mental activity helps the organism to survive.

general adaptation syndrome: a complex reaction of the whole body to stress first described by Hans Selye and often abbreviated as G.A.S. It has both adaptive and maladaptive consequences for the organism.

generalization: the transfer of previous learning to a similar situation either by stimulus generalization or by response generalization. If used without qualification, the term usually means stimulus generalization.

generativity: the property which human language has of being able to put symbols together in new combinations to create new utterances.

gestalt theory: a theoretical approach to psychology which emphasizes the extent to which things are influenced by their context.

gonadotrophin: a hormone secreted by the pituitary gland and stimulating hormone production by the gonads.

gonads: the glands secreting the most important of the sexual hormones.

group affiliation: a motive to belong to a real or imagined class of people. An attitude serves a group-affiliation function if it helps an individual to fit in with the group.

habit-family hierarchy: a learned set of alternate ways of achieving the same goal.

halo effect: the perception of a person as good in other ways when one favorable thing is known about him.

hedonism: the theory that individuals seek pleasure above all else.

higher-order conditioning: conditioning in which a previously acquired conditional reflex plays a role usually performed by the unconditional reflex.

homeostasis: the maintenance of a relatively constant internal environment.

homeostatic drive: a motive to behave in a way which will help maintain a constant internal environment.

hormone: one of several chemicals formed in specialized body tissues effecting changes in tissues in other parts of the organism.

hyperthyroidism: having an excess of the secretions of the thyroid gland.

hypertonic: having a higher osmotic pressure than blood.

hypochondriacal reaction: an anxiety reaction in which the anxiety is focused on particular physical symptoms.

hypothalamus: a structure at the base of the brain which plays important roles in motivation and emotion.

hypothyroidism: having an insufficient amount of the secretions of the thyroid gland.

hypotonic: having a lower osmotic pressure than blood.

hysteria: conversion reactions and dissociative reactions.

iconic memory: a very brief preservation of an image of sensory input. For a fraction of a second after stimulation, this image may be seen, heard, or felt.

id: the unsocialized impulses of the individual.

identical twins: two persons who have developed from the same fertilized ovum.

identification: feeling as if the self and another were one.

ideology: a powerful interpretation of reality the widespread acceptance of which is usually actively sought by those who hold it.

idiographic approach: an approach to theory construction in which generalizations are drawn which would apply only to a restricted population of individuals or to a single individual.

illusion: an inaccurate perception.

impression formation: the way in which strangers develop perceptions of one another. Includes studies of what causes individuals to act in different ways and studies of how their behavior is perceived.

imprinting: a type of one-trial learning which is highly resistant to extinction.

incentive: a goal object.

incentive effect: a change in performance brought about by altering the expectations of the organism about the rewards it may obtain for the performance.

independent variable: the element in an experiment that is manipulated so that the effects of changing it may be studied.

informal organization: groupings and relationships which are not provided for in the official structure of an organization. Compare **formal organization.**

innate: not dependent on specific experiences but, instead, developing from hereditary causes in any normal environment.

innate releasing mechanism: a perceptual system responding to certain types of stimuli without previous learning.

insight learning: learning in which the solution to a problem appears suddenly and completely rather than developing gradually on the basis of trial and error.

insight therapy: an approach to improving the human condition which places primary emphasis on helping the individual to better understand himself.

instinct: a complex, stereotyped, unlearned pattern of behavior shown by all members of a species (or of one sex of a species) under the appropriate circumstances. Used by earlier theorists in a more general way as roughly equivalent to drive.

instrumental: serving to help an individual achieve a goal.

instrumental conditioning: a type of stimulus-response learning in which the presentation of reinforcement is contingent on the response the organism makes.

intelligence quotient: see **IQ**.

interaction: mutual influence on one another.

interaction (social): the sequence of events by which two or more individuals influence one another.

interaction (statistical): the additional effect of one variable when another is at a particular level.

interaction process analysis: a technique for objectively recording social behavior.

interference theory of forgetting: the idea that learning some material causes other material to be forgotten because the memories interfere with each other in some way.

intergroup: between groups.

internalization: the adoption of the standards of another as a part of the self through identification.

interposition: the blocking of something the observer is viewing by something coming between him and what he is observing.

interrole conflict: different things being expected of someone because he simultaneously occupies more than one status.

intraception: a concern with subjective phenomena.

intracranial: within the skull.

intragroup: within the group.

intrarole conflict: different things being expected of the holder of one status.

introspection: reporting on internal experiences by trained observers.

IQ (intelligence quotient): a fallible measure of intelligence, deriving its name from being initially calculated by dividing mental age by chronological age.

just-noticeable difference: the least change in stimulation which is, on the average, noticeable to an observer.

kinesthesis: the sense which tells the individual the positions of his limbs by means of receptors in muscles, tendons, and joints.

latent learning: learning which is not apparent in performance.

lateral geniculate body: a collection of cell bodies within the brain which processes visual stimulation.

law of effect: Thorndike's principle that the tendency for a stimulus to call out a response will be increased if the response leads to a satisfying state of affairs, and decreased if the response leads to an annoying state of affairs. Later considerably modified.

law of exercise: a principle, first proposed and then later abandoned by Thorndike, indicating that learning takes place through the simple repetition of responses.

legitimate power: the ability of one person to influence another through his holding a position seen as giving him a right to make certain decisions and perform certain acts.

leveling: a failure to perceive, or a forgetting of details in the thing perceived.

level of aspiration: the performance for which an individual is striving.

limbic system: a ring of related structures surrounding the brain stem, involved in motivation and emotion.

limited central-processing capacity: the inability to deal actively with very much information at any one moment in time.

linear perspective: the apparent convergence of parallel lines receding in the distance.

long-term memory: the ability to remember events of the more distant past. Because of the great length of time that things may be remembered, long-term memories apparently may be stored by means of structural changes in the nervous system.

manic-depressive psychosis: a severe personality disturbance characterized by states of wild excitement, states of withdrawal and self-hatred, or both in alternation.

maturation: the development of innate potentials with time.

mental age: the average age of children who mentally perform at the level of the child being tested. If a five-year-old child performs as well as the average six-year-old, his mental age is six, for example.

metabolism: the chemical processes by which protoplasm is formed and food is broken down.

mnemonic device: an aid to memory.

mode: the score or property which is most frequently represented in the set of all scores or properties under consideration.

molar: organized or studied in terms of large, rather than small, units of analysis.

molecular: organized or studied in terms of small, rather than large, units of analysis.

moral anxiety: a disturbed state based on fear that one will feel guilty about one's behavior.

motion parallax: the apparent movement of the world observed when the head is moved. It may be used as a depth cue, since objects nearer the observer seem to move more than those farther from him.

motivation: the internal forces producing behavior.

motor area: a portion of the brain which, when stimulated, gives rise to a muscular response.

motor-impairment study: an experiment in which an animal is trained to give a response and then is made unable to make that response so that its substitute response may be studied.

multiple T-maze: a maze made of a number of sections, each one shaped like the letter T.

nativism: the position that much is inherited and little is learned.

natural experiment: an experiment in which the independent variable is not actively manipulated, but which uses the natural changes in its level as the basis for learning its effects.

negative reinforcer: a stimulus whose removal strengthens learned behavior.

neo-analytic: based on psychoanalytic theory, but modified to take account of findings about human nature since the time when Freud wrote.

neurosis: a mental disorder which does not involve as great disturbances of emotion, perception of reality, and behavior as does a psychosis.

neurotic anxiety: a disturbed state based on fear that one's impulses will get out of control.

neurotic depression: a disturbed state characterized by negative emotional reactions similar to those found in mourning. Characterized by more anxiety but less self-hatred than is found in depressive psychosis.

nomothetic approach: an approach to theory construction in which generalizations are drawn which would apply to all normal individuals.

nondirective therapy: an approach to psychotherapy in which the therapist tries to help his client solve his own problems rather than giving him specific advice.

nonsense syllable: two consonants separated by a vowel, not forming a word.

norepinephrine: an adrenal hormone chemically closely related to epinephrine, but apparently having rather different effects.

norm: a standard applied to members of a culture regardless of their specific positions within their society, and enforced by sanctions.

object choice: the directing of a motive toward a particular object, with resulting learning of a preference for this type of object.

observer bias: the categorization, either conscious or unconscious, of data so as either to prove or to disprove a point.

obsession: the recurrence of a thought or image, often a highly unpleasant one. A person who keeps imagining scenes of airplane crashes, for example, suffers from an obsession.

obsessive-compulsive reactions: obsessions and/or compulsions. They are classed together because they frequently occur in the same individual.

occupational mobility: the extent to which a person is moving upward to a job generally regarded as more desirable, or downward to a job regarded as less desirable.

Oedipus complex: in psychoanalytic theory, the attraction of a boy to his mother and its psychological consequences.

operant behavior: behavior for which no unconditional stimulus is known.

opinion: a quite specific idea about something. Similar to an attitude except more specific and limited in scope.

opinion polling: the asking of isolated questions, such as "Do you favor reelection of the President?" It yields less extensive information than attitude measurement, where a series of related questions is asked about each topic.

organic therapy: the treatment of a disorder by physical means.

osmotic pressure: a measure of the tendency of water to pass through a semipermeable membrane into the fluid being measured.

ovary: the organ producing female germ cells.

overactive deviant: a member of a group who initiates a great deal of interaction but who is not seen by other group members as being either productive or likable.

overlearning: continuing to study material after it is apparently learned.

paired comparisons: a highly precise method of attitude scaling devised by Thurstone, but an extremely laborious method to use.

paradoxical sleep: the stage of sleep in which dreaming generally occurs. It is characterized by great relaxation but also by a pattern of electrical activity of the brain similar to that found when the person is awake.

parallel processing: the carrying out of two mental activities at the same time.

parathyroidectomized: having had the parathyroid glands removed.

parathyroid gland: a gland controlling the level of calcium in the blood.

parsimony: utilizing the simplest explanation which can account for the specific phenomenon.

partial correlation: the extent to which two things would go together if a third thing were held constant.

partial reinforcement: a reward to an organism for only a portion of its correct responses. There are several varieties of partial reinforcement—fixed-ratio, in which the organism is reinforced for perhaps every tenth correct response; fixed-interval, in which it is reinforced for the first correct response after a given period of time; etc.

passive decay: the theory that memories deteriorate merely through the passage of time.

perception: experience based on information coming in through the sense organs. See also **sensation**.

peripheral: not central.

phobic reaction: the externalization of anxiety by fixing it on certain objects or situations. An unreasonable fear.

phoneme: the class of sounds considered identical in a particular language. In the English language, the (aspirated) "p" in pit and the (unaspirated) "p" in spit are classed as the same sound. In the Hopi language, on the other hand, these are regarded as two different sounds, or phonemes.

phylogenetic scale: an ordering of organisms in terms of their evolutionary development.

pituitary gland: a structure attached to the base of the brain and influencing many other glands.

place code: the representation of the frequency of a sound by the location on the cochlea of the receptor cells which respond to it.

placebo: a treatment which has no effect except through the suggestibility of the patient.

place learning: learning to go to the same place even though doing so requires different muscular responses.

placenta: the organ of communication between the mother and the embryo.

pleasure centers: areas of the brain in which positive reinforcement seems to be localized.

positive reinforcer: a stimulus, the presentation of which strengthens learned behavior.

preattentive mechanisms: processes by which sensory input is continuously analyzed even if the individual is not paying attention to it.

prejudice: a judgment, usually negative, made without evidence.

prestige suggestion: a suggestion that makes something more acceptable by linking it to some highly regarded thing or person.

primacy effect: the influence caused by material being presented first.

primary process thinking: irrational thinking characterizing both young children and adult fantasy and humor.

primary sensory area: the main location in the brain in which the input from a particular sensory modality is analyzed.

principle of least interest: the generalization that the person who cares least about maintaining a relationship is in the best bargaining position.

proactive inhibition: the interference with learning of later material by earlier learned material. If knowing your old telephone number made it more difficult for you to learn your new telephone number, you would be giving an example of proactive inhibition.

probability: the proportion of the times that an event will occur in a long series of trials.

process (applied to mental disorder): developing gradually without the precipitating conditions being clear.

projection: the attribution of qualities to others which are not there but which explain one's own emotional reactions.

proximity: nearness. A gestalt principle of perceptual organization indicating that stimuli which are close to one another are likely to be perceived as going together.

psychiatrist: a medical doctor specializing in the treatment of mental illness.

psychiatry: a branch of medicine specializing in the treatment of mental disorder.

psychoanalysis: a theoretical approach to the study and treatment of personality disorder initiated by Sigmund Freud.

psychopathic: violating the laws and customs of one's society without apparent guilt.

psychophysics: the study of the relationships between variations of physical energy and experience.

psychosis: a serious mental disorder involving major disturbances in the perception of reality, in speech and thought, and in mood and social relations.

psychosomatic disorders: illnesses in which physical symptoms are partially or entirely due to psychological causes.

psychotherapist: a psychologist specializing in the treatment of mental illness.

psychotherapy: the treatment of mental disorders by psychological means.

psychotic: having or characterizing a psychosis.

punishment: the presentation of a negative reinforcer or removal of a positive reinforcer following behavior.

purposive: oriented toward a goal.

RAS: see **reticular activating system**.

rationalization: the assertion of a more rational motive for an action than the actual motive for it.

reaction formation: an act based on a motive which is unacceptable to the self, although it gives the superficial impression of being based on the opposite motive.

reactive (applied to mental disorder): characterized by sudden onset, as if in reaction to a particular situation.

reality anxiety: a disturbed state in which one fears punishment from the world for behavior which is unacceptable to oneself.

recall: the reproduction of a stimulus in awareness through memory.

recency effect: the influence caused by material being presented last.

receptor cell: a cell responding to some aspect of its environment by altering the frequency with which it fires.

recognition: the identification of a stimulus with one perceived previously.

reference group: a group whose possible judgments of a person are very important to him. It may be a group, such as "literary critics a hundred years from now," to which the person does not himself belong.

reference point: see **anchor point**.

referent power: the ability of one person to influence another because the other identifies with him.

reflex: a simple, stereotyped, innate response given to a particular stimulus by any normal member of the species.

regression: a return to an earlier mode of adjustment.

reinforcement: in a broad sense, anything which alters the probability that a response will be given to a stimulus.

reinforcement theorist: a learning theorist believing that some reinforcement is necessary to all learning.

reinforcer: a stimulus which strengthens learned behavior. See **positive reinforcer** and **negative reinforcer**.

reintegration: the recall of the context in which a stimulus was previously encountered.

relearning: learning something again, generally with the expenditure of less time than was required to learn it the first time. The amount of time saved is the most sensitive measure of previous learning.

releaser: a stimulus which calls out a fixed action pattern.

reliability: the extent to which a measuring instrument gives consistent results.

replication: a repetition of a research study to establish whether the specified procedures will reliably produce the expected results.

representative sample: a number of cases selected from a population in such a way that the proportions of various characteristics in the sample and in the population will be approximately the same.

repression: the active exclusion of material from consciousness.

respondent behavior: behavior for which an unconditional stimulus is known.

response generalization: giving somewhat different responses from those that were learned.

reticular activating system (RAS): a complex formation of neurons which is involved in attention.

reticular formation: a network of neurons in the brain stem that influences the activities of the cerebral cortex.

retina: the layer of the interior of the eyeball that contains the receptor cells.

retroactive inhibition: interference with memory for things learned earlier by things learned later. If learning a new telephone number makes a person forget one he has learned before, he would be experiencing retroactive inhibition.

retrograde amnesia: loss of a considerable portion of a person's memories, usually following a blow on the head.

reversal learning: a type of discrimination-learning task in which the correct answer is arbitrarily changed from time to time. After encountering a number of tasks of this type, the subject learns to change his choices rapidly when the formerly correct choice is no longer reinforced.

revitalization movement: a deliberate effort by members of a society to produce a more satisfying culture.

reward power: the ability of one person to influence another by being able to offer him something he wants.

rigidity of behavior: the continuation of the same behavior under conditions where it is inappropriate.

role: the behavior expected of a person holding a certain position in a given society.

role playing: the adoption of the behavior of a position other than that a person actually holds in society. A boy who pretends to be an airplane pilot is role-playing, for example.

rules of correspondence: statements of what specific characteristics of the world correspond to what specific entities in a theory.

sampling bias: the comparison of groups which differ in ways other than the level of the independent variable, or the generalization from cases to a population of which they are not representative.

sanction: a reward (positive sanction) or punishment (negative sanction) administered to one who does or does not comply with social expectations.

scalogram analysis: a method of attitude scaling developed by Guttman. It has the advantage that no judges are needed to sort the items, but it also has disadvantages.

scapegoat: a substitute target for the expression of aggression.

schema: a mental representation of a series of events.

schizophrenia: a psychosis especially characterized by disturbances of language, thinking, and attention.

secondary process thinking: the realistic thinking which characterizes rational problem solving in the adult.

secondary reinforcer: a stimulus which, through association with a reinforcer, acquires the property of also acting as a reinforcer.

self-actualization: a person's active development of his personality toward goals which he sets for himself.

self-oriented needs: motives to defend the ego.

semantic generalization: the giving of a learned response to a new stimulus which is similar in meaning to the old stimulus, although different in physical properties.

sensation: awareness of energy impinging on a sense organ. Although a distinction used to be made between sensation, which was thought to involve no interpretation of the stimulation, and perception, believed to involve interpretation, it now appears that pure sensation is probably never experienced.

sense organ: a portion of the body specialized in the perception of stimuli of a given type. The eye is the sense organ of vision, for example.

sensitivity training: group experience designed to make the participants more aware of group processes and the emotional reactions of other individuals.

sensory area: a portion of the brain which, when stimulated, gives rise to a sensation, such as that of light, sound, or taste.

sensory memory: see **iconic memory**.

sentiment: a positive or negative feeling toward something.

septal area: a region of the brain near the band of nerve fibers connecting the two cerebral hemispheres.

serial-position effect: the tendency, when a series of items is to be learned, to learn the first and last items best and the middle items least well.

serial processing: the sequential analysis of sensory input.

set: the readiness either to perceive something or to respond in a certain way.

shape constancy: seeing an object as remaining the same shape even though the retinal image of it changes in shape.

shaping: getting a learner to produce a desired response by reinforcing successively closer approximations to it.

sharpening: exaggerating the differences between something perceived and other things which the perceiver expects or is familiar with.

short-term memory: the ability to remember events of the immediate past. It is so easily disrupted that it seems to depend on an ongoing process.

sign: a response used to designate the actual presence of some stimulus. Growling in a cat is a sign of anger, for example.

significant results: results which would occur by chance less than some arbitrarily set proportion of times, frequently one time in twenty.

similarity: a gestalt principle of perceptual organization indicating that stimuli which are similar to one another are likely to be perceived as going together.

situational factors: influences on behavior which are environmental rather than personal.

size constancy: seeing an object as remaining the same size even though the size of the retinal image changes.

social class: a position in a prestige hierarchy to which a person is assigned more on the basis of the roles he plays in society than on the basis of how well he plays them.

social group: used loosely to apply to any aggregation of individuals or even to a class of individuals, such as "men over the age of forty." Used strictly to apply to an enduring organization containing few enough individuals that they are responded to on the basis of their personal characteristics.

social institution: the traditional ways in which a particular culture provides for a given area of human activity. All cultures, for example, have certain institutionalized ways of rearing children.

socialization: induction into a role or

roles which a person will play in society.

social power: the ability to reward and punish others.

social reality: the nature of the world according to the views of a particular social grouping.

social role: the behavior expected of a person holding some particular status or position in a society.

socioeconomic status: social class as judged by a set of indicators, largely economic, devised for analyzing social science phenomena.

socioemotional leader: the person most effective in dealing with the emotional tensions and conflicts arising in a group.

spontaneous recovery: the reappearance of an extinguished response after a period of time when the conditional stimulus is not present.

standard stimulus: a stimulus provided so that others may be compared with it.

statistical control: the elimination of alternate explanations of experimental results by the study of the relative effects of different variables when more than one are allowed to vary at a time.

status: (1) any position in a society with which a role or set of expected behaviors is associated; (2) a position in a hierarchy of class, prestige, or power.

stereotype: a widely held idea not supportable by evidence. Frequently, a negative view of a group to which the viewer does not belong.

stimulus: anything which may be perceived and responded to.

stimulus error: in classical introspection, the reporting of perceptions rather than sensations.

stimulus generalization: response to a new stimulus in a way similar to the response the organism has learned to give to a similar stimulus in the past. Initial generalization occurs without reinforced practice with the new stimulus, and conditioned generalization occurs after positive reinforcement for generalization.

stimulus-response theory: a learning theory maintaining that what is learned is to give certain responses to specific stimuli.

structuralism: the first formal school of psychology. It saw the basic task of the field as finding the elements of experience.

subcortical: areas of the brain reached by afferent stimulation before it reaches the cortex.

subliminal: below the threshold, or limen. The limen is the amount of stimulation which will be reported on the average.

successive-comparison system: a system of learning a list by visualizing images which combine each successive pair of stimuli.

successive intervals: a method of attitude scaling more refined and accurate than equal-appearing intervals. The task of the judges is the same as in equal-appearing intervals, but the data are analyzed differently.

superego: the individual's internalized moral standards and idealized goals.

symbol: a response used to stand for a stimulus in talking about it. The stimulus need not actually be present.

synthesis: the combination of elements to form a more complex whole.

task leader: the person most effective in enabling a group to be productive.

TAT: see **Thematic Apperception Test**.

testosterone: a male sex hormone.

Thematic Apperception Test (TAT): a test of personality and motivation based on the subject's telling stories about pictures.

theory: a set of symbols and the rules for their manipulation.

thoracic ganglion (plural, ganglia): a nerve center in the chest.

thymus gland: a gland found in the chest which is involved in immune reactions of the body.

thyroid gland: a gland found in the neck regulating general metabolic rate of the body.

total institution: a social structure attempting to provide for all the needs and activities of its members.

transposition experiment: an experiment in which an organism is trained to respond to one stimulus rather than another and then tested on a different pair of stimuli. The name derives from the transposition of a melody into a different key. An example would be an experiment in which an animal is trained to go toward a bright light rather than a dim one and then goes toward a still brighter light paired with the original bright one.

traumatic anxiety: a disturbed state which is based on the present situation rather than on memories of earlier situations.

traumatic discipline: discipline which is highly anxiety-inducing for the child either because the child is unclear as to what behavior is being punished or because the punishment is harsh and unusual in nature.

UCR: see **unconditional response**.

UCS: see **unconditional stimulus**.

unconditional positive regard: the total acceptance of the patient by the therapist, thought necessary in the school of psychotherapy founded by Carl Rogers.

unconditional response (UCR): a response which is always called out by a particular stimulus, without training. See also **unconditional stimulus**.

unconditional stimulus (UCS): a stimulus which always calls out a particular response, without training. The stimulus and the response make up the unconditional reflex.

unconditioned response: unconditional response.

unconditioned stimulus: unconditional stimulus.

unconscious: not present in consciousness for any one of several reasons, including lack of appropriate sense organs and motivated unconsciousness.

unit of analysis: the size element into which the data are broken down in being studied.

value: a positive or negative view of something broad enough to help the individual evaluate many other things. Similar to an attitude but more general.

value-expressive: serving to bolster or to communicate a person's ethical or moral judgments.

ventral: toward the abdominal side of the organism.

visual cortex: the primary sensory area for seeing.

visual-deprivation experiments: studies in which organisms are kept from having normal opportunities to see.

volley code: the representation of frequency of a sound by the temporal spacing of nerve impulses.

von Restorff effect: the better learning of a stimulus which differs from accompanying stimuli.

word salad: a highly disturbed use of language characteristic of schizophrenia.

Zeigarnik effect: remembering uncompleted tasks better than completed tasks under nonthreatening conditions.

NAME INDEX

Page numbers in **boldface** indicate figures or quotations.

SUBJECT INDEX

Spontaneous recovery, 79
Stages of development (see Ego development)
Stanford case study, 295–296
Statistical significance, 26
Status, 219, 225–232, 363–366, 369–373
    (See also Roles)
Stimulus, nature of, 57–65, 74, 75, 81, 82, 93–95,
    144, 147
Stone, Frank, example of, 225–226
Stress:
    brain mechanisms in, 156–157
    defense against, 81, 155, 159, 165, 242–243
    effects on eating, 150
    as origin of schizophrenia, 252
    (See also Anxiety; Arousal; Attachment; Gen-
    eral adaptation syndrome)
Strikebreakers, use of, 321–322
Structuralism, 10–13, 15, 17
Success:
    experiences of, 209–211, 218
    level of aspiration and evaluation of, 211–212
    (See also Competence)
Successive comparison system, 121
Suicide in manic-depressive psychosis, 255
Superego:
    definition, 183, 189
    ego ideal, 189, 194, 200, 210, 230–232
    origin of, 184–189, 200, 201, 230–232
    positive bases of, 180, 181, 185, 189, 200
    (See also Conscience)
Symbols, 92, 95–99
    (See also Coding; Language; Problem solving)
Symptoms:
    of anxiety, 241
    associated with problems attaining au-
    tonomy, 179–181
    as attempts to adapt, 239–243
    autistic, 174, 177–179
    function of, 81, 155, 159, 242–243
    psychological, use of term, 239
    of psychosis, 247–258
    situational stress in developing, 189
    traumatic socialization and, 179–181,
    184–189
    (See also Defense mechanisms; Failure; Psy-
    chotherapy)

Thematic apperception test (TAT) 160–163, 217
Theoretical issues:
    contemporary, 5, 18–20, 29
    historical, 5–17, 28
    in origins of schizophrenia, 249–255
    in psychotherapy, 258–270
    sociological, 224, 231, 232
    (See also Data; Scientific method)
Theory:
    common sense, 21–23, 31, 32, 35
    idiographic, 4, 12–15
    nomothetic, 4, 12–15
    (See also Methodology; Theory construction)
Theory construction:
    consistency, 21–23
    explicitness, 21–23
    goals of, 5, 9, 10

influence of assumptions, 6, 13, 17–20
    on origins of schizophrenia, 249–250,
    253–258
    specification of relevant observations, 21–23
    subjective nature of, 18–20, 28
    (See also Data; Methodology)
Therapeutic approaches, 260–271
    (See also Psychotherapy)
Therapy (see Psychotherapy)
"There Was A Young Woman Who Swallowed
    A Lie" (song), 307
Thinking:
    coding through language, 94–96
    efficient learning and remembering, 115–124
    interpretation of emotion, 150, 154–160, 165
    parallel and serial processing, 42–45
    problem solving, 89–92, 124–132
    semantic generalization, 81, 82, 99
    (See also Attitudes; Perception)
Thirst, 138, 139, 147–149
Threat to self, 240, 251–253, 256, 324–325,
    339–344, 347
    (See also Anxiety; Identity; Traumatic sociali-
    zation)
Timing of persuasive messages, 287–289
Tip-of-the-tongue phenomenon, 104–106, 132
Transfer of learning to new situations (see Gen-
    eralization)
Transmuting pot, 323
Traumatic socialization, 179–181, 184–189, 201,
    222, 223, 226–227, 231–232
    (See also Anxiety; Battered-child syndrome;
    Identity)
Trust, basic, 173–179, 182, 187
Twin studies, 253–254

Unanimity in conformity, 216
Unconscious processes:
    motivated unconscious, 16, 20, 110, 111, 115,
    132, 160, 165, 179–181, 185, 188–195, 200,
    201
    in nonverbal communication, 92
    in perception, 43–45, 49, 50
    in problem solving, 127
    (See also Defense mechanisms; Motives; Psy-
    choanalytic theory; Symptoms)
Understanding in learning, 82, 89–90, 110,
    116–119, 132
United Mine Workers Union, 352, 354
Utilitarian authority, 220–221, 232

Values, 285–287, 309, 316–319, 344–347
    in practice of psychology, 170–173, 284
    (See also Attitude)
Variable:
    controlled, 24–25, 29
    dependent, 24–25, 29
    independent, 23–25, 29
Verification in problem solving, 130–132
    (See also Methodology)
Vicarious learning:
    conditioning, 86–87, 99
    social, 180
    trial and error, 84
    (See also Adult models; Identification)